Facing Fearful Odds

To Claris, James, Josephine and Isadora
so they should know what their grandfather did in the war
that they might live

Facing Fearful Odds

My father's story of captivity, escape and resistance 1940–1945

John Jay

Pen & Sword
MILITARY

First published in Great Britain in 2014 by
PEN & SWORD MILITARY
An imprint of
Pen & Sword Books Ltd
47 Church Street
Barnsley
South Yorkshire
S70 2AS

Copyright © John Jay, 2014

ISBN 978-1-47382-734-9

Typeset by Concept, Huddersfield, West Yorkshire, HD4 5JL.
Printed and bound in England by CPI Group (UK) Ltd, Croydon CR0 4YY.

Pen & Sword Books Ltd incorporates the imprints of Pen & Sword Archaeology, Atlas, Aviation, Battleground, Discovery, Family History, History, Maritime, Military, Naval, Politics, Railways, Select, Social History, Transport, True Crime, and Claymore Press, Frontline Books, Leo Cooper, Praetorian Press, Remember When, Seaforth Publishing and Wharncliffe.

For a complete list of Pen & Sword titles please contact
PEN & SWORD BOOKS LIMITED
47 Church Street, Barnsley, South Yorkshire, S70 2AS, England
E-mail: enquiries@pen-and-sword.co.uk
Website: www.pen-and-sword.co.uk

Contents

List of Plates

Rifleman Alec Jay, teenage 'Terrier', 1938.

Alec relaxes at Queen Victoria's Rifles' 1938 summer camp.

Alec's Queen Vics B Company platoon on exercises, 1938.

Queen Vics B Company group photograph, 1938.

Corporal Jay supervises Bren Gun cleaning at 1939 camp.

Queen Vics on exercises with new motorcycle 'chariots', 1939.

Terence Cuneo's *The Defence of Calais 1940*.

Luftwaffe reduces Calais to rubble during siege.

Zec's June 1940 cartoon showing Calais garrison's sacrifice.

Nazi photograph showing British captives marching through Calais.

Nazi photograph showing Calais captives during Long March.

Stalag VIIIB/Stalag 344 entrance at Lamsdorf, Silesia.

Alec's POW *Personalkarte* showing him 'joining' the Church of England.

Wehrmacht plan of Stalag VIIIB at Lamsdorf.

Alec's officers, John Austin-Brown and John Ellison-Macartney, as POWs.

Lamsdorf's *Strafe Kompanie* and *Straflager* punishment cells.

'Greetings from abroad': Lamsdorf POWs' 1941 Christmas card.

Russian POWs at Lamsdorf forced to live in holes in the ground.

One of 42,000 corpses of Soviet POWs exhumed at Lamsdorf.

'Ukraine Joe', the brutal guard who ran Lamdorf's *Straflager*.

The Sudeten lime works where Alec did forced labour for 2½ years.

Alec's first POW group photograph, Setzdorf, Sudetenland, spring 1942.

George Chapman, who led a Queen Vics bayonet charge at Calais.

Bill Brett, a Queen Vics POW who stopped Alec admitting he was Jewish.

Ludwig von Poschinger, a Lamsdorf commandant.

Bill McGuinness, co-leader with Alec of a POW strike in February 1944.

Funeral of Nelson Ogg, a POW the Germans let die through neglect.

Introduction & Acknowledgements

My father should have written this book. After my mother died in 2005 I discovered he had made a start. As I sifted through dusty papers in old carrier bags, I found some notes he had banged out on our ancient typewriter, summarizing the contents of twenty-five chapters. There was no title, only a few details – Chapter 1's were typical: 'Time of joining, reasons and parental reaction'. Then came another discovery: seven pages of narrative intended as the opening of a memoir of the Second World War experiences of Rifleman Alec Jay of 9 Platoon, C Company, 1st Battalion of the Queen Victoria's Rifles, service number 6896204 – and prisoner of war number 15129.

About 135,000 Britons were captured by the Germans so my father's was not a singular experience. It did, however, have an unusual texture – he was Jewish, and in the lottery of POW life this meant the odds he might die were greater than for most *Kriegsgefangene* – or 'Kriegies' as they called themselves.

After his capture at Calais in 1940, my father behaved as though such odds did not exist, with one exception: as 'an involuntary guest of the Third Reich', he hid his ethnicity. A prisoner's duty was to escape so he became a serial escaper, one of the few among thousands of 'other ranks' who sat out their captivity. Five times he escaped. Four times he was recaptured but he eluded capture the fifth time. He did not achieve a 'home run' – 1,200 or fewer than 1 per cent of POWs managed that – but he did end the war a free man, fighting as a guerrilla. Had he been recaptured then, he would have faced death or concentration camp incarceration. When not on the run or in solitary confinement for his 'crimes', he risked being exposed as Jewish by using his schoolboy German to interpret and to bait his captors. Few Englishmen spoke German in 1940 – and they were mostly Jews.

Unfortunately, he abandoned his memoir, the typescript petering out a year before shots were fired in anger. Yet as I read those seven pages, I felt my father had lost the chance to exorcize his demons, and he had left his children only fragments of the mosaic that was his wartime life.

That he enjoyed writing was clear from one fragment that sat close to his armchair – a battered exercise book into which he had transcribed thirty-six poems written in captivity. This slim volume was bought towards the war's end with *Lagergeld* – money that prisoners on *Arbeitskommandos* (working parties) received at a rate of 70 pfennig per day and was exchangeable for certain goods. On the front he wrote the book's title, *Prisoner of War Poems*;

inside the front cover, for the benefit of curious guards, he wrote in German, *Kriegsgelangenen Gedichte ab dem 26 Mai 1940* (War Poetry beginning from 26 May 1940). Below was a short poem in German:

Einmal macht' ich Gedichte
In der fernen Friedenszeit
Eine einfache Geschichte,
Wenn alles liegt bereit.

Und als Gefangenensoldat
Ich möchte weiter schreiben.
Erinnerung und Heldentat.
Das hilft mir Zeit vertreiben.

Roughly translated it reads:

Once I wrote poems
In distant peacetime,
A simple story
When everything was clear.

And as a captive soldier
I'd like to continue writing
Of memory and heroic deeds
To help me pass the time.

That the censors thought its contents innocent was evident from the official stamp, '*Geprüft*' (inspected). Buried in a haversack, it survived his final escape to sit at his side, unopened other than in moments of solitary reflection.

My original plan was to publish the poems as a volume of wartime verse. Few Second World War poems have passed into popular consciousness, in contrast to verse from the Great War as my father knew it as a child. John Pudney, a writer-turned-airman, wrote in 1941:

Do not despair
For Johnny-head-in-air;
He sleeps as sound
As Johnny underground.
Fetch out no shroud
For Johnny-in-the-cloud;
And keep your tears
For him in after years.
Better by far
For Johnny-the-bright-star,
To keep your head,
And see his children fed.

Yet writers such as W.H. Auden and Cecil Day-Lewis were poets who wrote during wartime, not war poets. Thus, today's schoolchildren study Great War poems, typically those describing the slaughter in Flanders, not Second World War poetry.

Perhaps Britain's war against Adolf Hitler did not produce much memorable verse because it seemed so clearly a just war. Perhaps, it was because it was more prosaic: a technological conflict where great machines – tanks, aircraft, battleships, submarines and, finally, atomic bombs – drove events. Most British warriors killed at a distance, unlike the men who fought in Flanders fields between 1914 and 1918. Things were different in Russia and Hitler's Reich, but few Britons had first-hand knowledge of Stalingrad or Auschwitz. When Day-Lewis wrote 'Lidice', after Hitler wiped a Czech village from the map as a reprisal for the assassination of Reinhard Heydrich, architect of 'The Final Solution', he was working from media reports, not experiencing actual fighting like Owen and Sassoon.

My father saw Hitler's Reich from the inside so his verses were testimony that, I thought, deserved to survive rather than vanish into a skip in the house-clearance that followed my mother's death. I did, however, wish to set the poems in context, so I began researching his war, aiming to write an introduction. As I researched, I became enthralled, and now, after five years' labour, that introduction has become this book.

Like a demon, survivor guilt pursued my father despite everything he contributed. As a POW, he became 'a fully paid-up member of the awkward squad', doing his bit through escapes, sabotage and other acts of defiance. In doing so, POWs such as he absorbed resources and drained their captors of that sense of impending victory that propelled them in the war's early years. Yet few of their efforts were publicized and many former POWs lived out their lives bitter that their sacrifices had gone unrecognized.

Soldiers, unlike airmen, could not be promoted in captivity whatever they did. My father was a victim of this system, though he had only himself to blame. He claimed he was the only British soldier to have served the entire war and come out with a lower rank than that with which he went in. He had been a corporal but reverted in November 1939 to rifleman, the rifle regiment equivalent of private, to avoid a court martial. His crime was to thump his company sergeant-major for insulting his girlfriend. When, therefore, he raised his hands in surrender he did so as a rifleman. Had he kept his nose clean, he would probably have become an officer. On repatriation in 1945, he was offered a commission but he decided his fighting years were over. He was officer material in intellect and bravery, yet his psychological wounds were too deep for him to be a leader.

This book is an attempt to complete the story he began, an act of filial homage. It has involved a journey – to France, Poland and the Czech Republic, following in my father's footsteps as he was force-marched into xii *Facing Fearful Odds*

captivity then shuttled from *Arbeitskommando* to *Arbeitskommando* to slave away for Hitler's Reich. It has also been a psychological voyage towards my father across that void of incomprehension between someone who has lived only in peacetime and someone for whom the defining period of his life comprised a six-year war.

I have called the book *Facing Fearful Odds* first because my father was one of 3,000 lightly-armed Britons who were attacked by two fully-mechanized Panzer divisions yet managed to hold them off for four critical days in May 1940. Years later, Airey Neave, a Calais captive who achieved a home run from Colditz, posed this question about the Queen Vics in his book, *The Flames of Calais*: 'Why was this fine Territorial battalion launched so badly equipped into the bitter street-fighting of Calais against tanks, artillery and well-armed German infantry?' His answer was that in 'the hurry and confusion of the moment', the War Office selected the Queen Vics for a role that bore no relation to the facts. They were not the only Territorial battalion destroyed in 1940 but were exceptional in being 'compelled to fight on such unequal terms'. That they kept firing to the end said 'much for their sense of duty and their pride'. My father said:

> We were three crack regiments, we were brilliantly led and we had a great esprit de corps. There were about 3,000 of us, against two and a half German divisions, 25,000 men plus the most sophisticated weaponry. How did we do so well? Truthfully I do not know. For a long time we didn't know we were beat. Until 26 May there were still rumours that we might be evacuated but at that stage if we'd been told we were to be issued with cheeses to throw at the Germans we would have believed it.

After the surrender, my father also faced fearful odds because he was imprisoned by a regime dedicated to exterminating his race; finally, he spent the war's closing weeks as a Czech partisan, once again fighting against Germans with far superior weaponry.

The phrase comes from Horatius, one of Lord Macaulay's *Lays of Ancient Rome*:

> Then out spake brave Horatius,
> The Captain of the Gate:
> 'To every man upon this earth
> Death cometh soon or late.
> And how can man die better
> Than facing fearful odds,
> For the ashes of his fathers,
> And the temples of his gods?'

While a Roman army fled to safety behind him, Horatius, with two companions, held a bridge over the Tiber against the invading Etruscans. After the bridge was demolished, he swam to safety and was carried back to Rome a hero. The Calais garrison's classically-educated members may have recalled Horatius as they stood on the Old Town's canal ramparts trying to halt Panzer tanks with Bren guns and rifles. The odds were fearful indeed. But my father had a further reason to recall Macaulay: in 1830, he used his maiden speech in the as-yet-unreformed House of Commons to demand Jewish emancipation. Not until 1858, a year before Macaulay's death, did a practising Jew become an MP – but Macaulay was something of a hero in London's East End, where my father's family had lived since Oliver Cromwell reopened the borders to Jews in 1656.

If my father had written this book it might have been a better one because it would have contained more personal memories. But its focus would have been narrower. I have been able to draw on a far wider range of sources. First, POWs who slept a few bunks from my father in various prison barracks have published first-hand accounts, while unpublished narratives have piled up in the Imperial War Museum. Secondly, broader histories about POWs have been published. Thirdly, fresh archive material has become available in Britain and in the old Eastern bloc, where openness about the war has replaced Soviet distortions. This is important because most POWs were confined in places that disappeared behind the Iron Curtain, yet I have seen documents that lay hidden in Soviet archives for decades.

Lastly, the internet has, at the click of a mouse, vastly increased the resources into which a researcher can tap. These range from the BBC's *Wartime Memories* project to personal websites and online forums. For example, my father would look up in 1944 from forced labour at a Sudeten *Arbeitskommando* to see hundreds of American bombers overhead. He knew they were our planes and, to his guards' fury, he would cheer as they crossed the sky. He did not, however, know their destinations; yet today a net surfer can discover within seconds the answers to questions he asked himself as he counted the vapour trails.

This book is not a work of academic scholarship and I have not annotated the text. Those who wish to discover more will find a bibliography at the back. I have, however, endeavoured to write material I believe to be grounded in fact. Old soldiers embellish their stories, typically not through malicious intent but because the passage of time causes rumour to harden into fact and transforms incidents reported second hand into firsthand experience. If I have doubted the veracity of an incident recalled decades later, I have left it out. But if I have made mistakes of fact and interpretation, *mea culpa*.

In mentioning place names, I have used those known to my father, not those prevailing today. As I quickly discovered, every place my father lived from his arrival at Stalag VIIIB on 21 June 1940 to his escape from a Sudeten barn in March 1945 has been renamed by the Slavs who expelled the Germans from Eastern Europe after the war. Those wishing to follow my father's travels on a modern map will find a glossary at the back.

In writing this book, I must thank many people, although for some my thanks are posthumous because they died shortly after I talked to them. Among the old soldiers who were in their nineties when we spoke, Leslie Birch, a Kent Yeoman, and John Lockyer of the Royal Sussex Regiment, worked alongside my father on working parties in the Sudetenland. Royal Engineer Bert Gurner was in my father's first *Arbeitskommando* in 1940, while Sidney Reed of the Middlesex Regiment served with him in the punishment camp they were sent to for 'making a nuisance of themselves' in the war's closing months. Within my father's regiment, the Queen Victoria's Rifles, Dennis Saaler fought alongside him at Calais in May 1940 while 'Tommy' Hummerstone trained with him before Calais. Norman Barnett, an Army medic, described the medical facilities at my father's main Stalag at Lamsdorf. The airmen who helped with my narrative included Tony Iveson, Harry Levy and Gordon Mellor.

Among historians, Christopher Andrew, Antony Beevor, Philip Chinnery, Jon Cooksey, Richard Evans, Will Fowler, Sir Michael Foot, Sir Martin Gilbert, Tomás Jakl, Sean Longden, Simon MacKenzie, Tony Rennell, Martin Sugarman and Adrian Weale provided advice. Archivists who helped me included James Collett-White of the Whitbread family archive, Ken Gray and Christine Pullen of the Royal Green Jackets (Rifles) Museum, Jessica Hogg of the BBC Written Archive, Rob McIntosh of the Army Medical Services Museum, Jane Munro of the Fitzwilliam Museum, Amanda Pattison-Wilson of the Highlanders Museum and Violetta Rezier-Wasielewska and Anna Wickiewicz of Poland's Central Museum of Prisoners-of-War, as well as numerous people at the British Library, the Imperial War Museum, the National Archives and the National Army Museum.

Slava Konkov of the Russian Embassy in London smoothed my path when I sought time-efficient access to the State Archive of the Russian Federation and the Russian State Military Archive in Moscow. Once I was in Moscow, Svetlana Chervonnaya and her son, Alexander Araksyan, and Natalia Makarova helped me negotiate the labyrinthine byways of Russian archive research, acting as interpreter-guides and translators. Petr Kollmann and his daughter, Denisa Hejlova Kollmannova, did sterling service as my interpreter-guides in the Czech Republic.

At home, my greatest helper has been Richard Frost, honorary secretary of the King's Royal Rifles Corps Association. For five years, Richard gave me free run of the Queen Vics archive, introduced me to Calais survivors, ferreted out unpublished material and straightened me out on matters military. Thank you, Richard.

At Pen & Sword, I must thank the team and in particular my publisher, Brigadier Henry Wilson, who provided avuncular advice and injected much-needed discipline into my thinking, George Chamier, who deployed keyhole-surgery-style skills as my editor, Tony Williams, the proof reader, who spotted my numerous 'howlers', Jon Wilkinson, who showed himself a magnificent jacket designer, and Matt Jones, who ably kept the show on the road.

Family members such my paternal aunt, Phoebe, and my siblings, Rebecca and David, contributed memories, while John Duffield, my senior partner at Brompton Asset Management, and other colleagues put up with me when I may have appeared more interested in prison camps than price-earnings ratios, boring for Britain about the war.

Lastly, but most importantly, my wife, Judi, and my daughter, Josephine, were tolerant and understanding when I went 'absent without leave' during weekends and on family holidays and spent hours over the dinner table, on weekend walks and on car journeys discussing my attempt to answer the question so many children of the twentieth century asked their fathers: 'What did you do in the war, Daddy?'

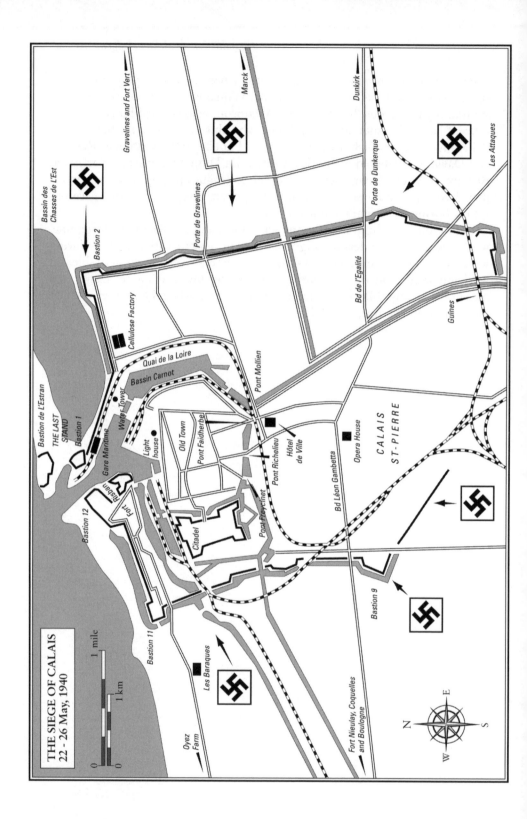

THE SIEGE OF CALAIS
22 - 26 May, 1940

1 mile

1 km

Bassin des
Chasses de L'Est

Gravelines and Fort Vert

Marck

Dunkirk

Bastion 2

Porte de Gravelines

Porte de Dunkerque

Les Attaques

Cellulose Factory

Bd de l'Egalité

Guînes

Quai de la Loire

Pont Mollien

Bassin Carnot

Bastion de L'Estran

THE LAST
STAND

Bastion 1

Water Tower

Old Town

Pont Faidherbe

Pont Richelieu

Hôtel
de Ville

Opera House

CALAIS
ST-PIERRE

Light
house

Gare Maritime

Fort
Risban

Bastion 12

Citadel

Pont Freycinet

Bd Léon Gambetta

Bastion 11

Les Baraques

Bastion 9

Oyez
Farm

Fort Nieulay, Coquelles
and Boulogne

N
E
S
W

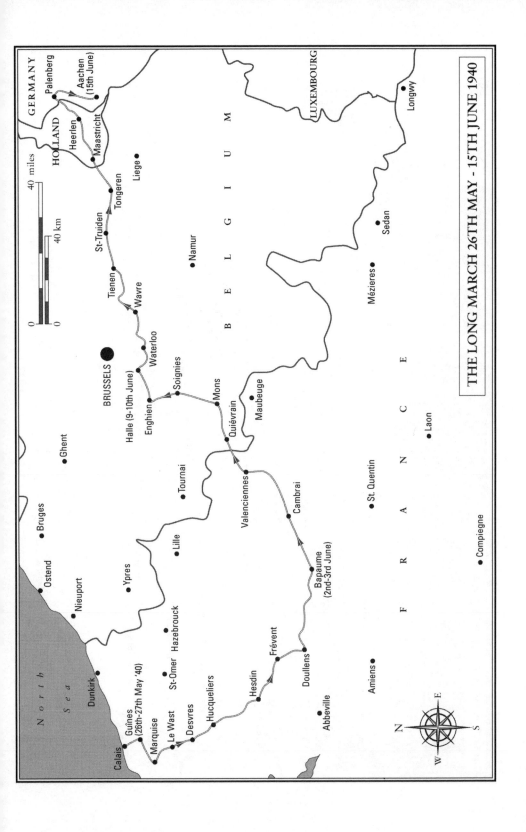

THE LONG MARCH 26TH MAY - 15TH JUNE 1940

GERMANY

Palenberg
Aachen (15th June)
Heerlen
HOLLAND
Maastricht
Tongeren
Liege
St-Truiden
Tienen
Namur
Wavre
Waterloo
BRUSSELS
Soignies
Halle (9-10th June)
Enghien
Mons
Quiévrain
Maubeuge
Ghent
Valenciennes
Cambrai
Tournai
Lille
Bapaume (2nd-3rd June)
Bruges
Ostend
Nieuport
Ypres
Hazebrouck
Frévent
Hesdin
St-Omer
Doullens
Dunkirk
Guînes (26th-27th May '40)
Marquise
Le Wast
Desvres
Hucqueliers
Calais

B E L G I U M

F R A N C E

LUXEMBOURG
Longwy
Sedan
Mézieres
Laon
St. Quentin
Compiegne
Amiens
Abbeville

North Sea

40 miles
40 km

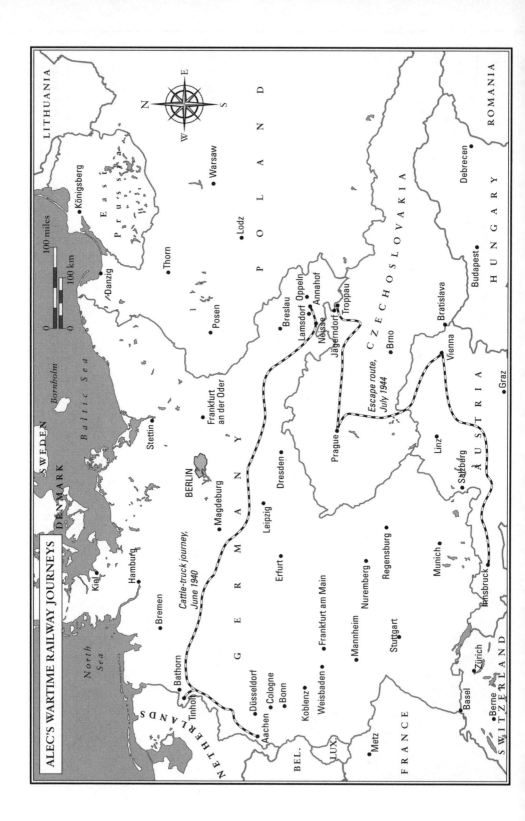

ALEC'S WARTIME RAILWAY JOURNEYS

LITHUANIA

SWEDEN

DENMARK

ROMANIA

HUNGARY

Debrecen

Budapest

Bratislava

Vienna

AUSTRIA

Graz

Linz

Salzburg

SWITZERLAND

Berne

Basel

Zürich

Innsbruck

Munich

CZECHOSLOVAKIA

Brno

Prague

Escape route,
July 1944

Jägerndorf

Troppau

Annahof

Neisse

Oppeln

Lamsdorf

Breslau

POLAND

Königsberg

East Prussia

Danzig

Thorn

Posen

Lodz

Warsaw

Frankfurt
an der Oder

Stettin

Baltic Sea

Bornholm

North Sea

Kiel

Hamburg

Bremen

Bathorn

Tinholt

NETHERLANDS

Düsseldorf

Aachen

Cologne

Bonn

Koblenz

Weisbaden

Frankfurt am Main

Mannheim

BEL.

LUX.

Metz

FRANCE

Stuttgart

Nuremberg

Regensburg

Dresden

Erfurt

Leipzig

Magdeburg

BERLIN

GERMANY

Cattle-truck journey,
June 1940

100 miles

100 km

N E
W S

Chapter 1

Beaches

The young man stood on the sand listening to the sea. It was August 1945; he was three months back from the war. His face was gaunt and his clothes hung loosely about his frame. How was he dressed that day as he strolled from his rented room on the Cornish coast? His standard attire was tweed jacket, check shirt, cords and brown brogues. When he wore a tie it would be a school or regimental one. If his shirt was open at the neck he wore a cravat. He had known this beach as a teenager, yet returning gave him no comfort.

After pausing to reflect, he began writing on a scrap of paper in an even if almost impenetrable hand, occasionally crossing out and replacing an infelicitous word. Later, he transcribed the poem into a notebook, calling it Beaches:

> Secluded, sea-bound, havens of repose;
> Sole sounds, sea's surging symphony on shore,
> And poised gulls' long drawn, doleful, keening cry,
> Perhaps the joy-filled song of distant birds,
> But nothing more.
>
> I lay there silent in the afternoons
> And looked up at the distant, winding track.
> I let the hot, dry sand run through my hands,
> And felt in harmony with all the world.
> Those days will not come back.
>
> Because, I cannot see a beach today,
> Unless I think of days not long ago
> With beaches shaken by exploding bombs,
> And stained red by the blood of countless men.
> That picture will not go.
>
> I seem to hear the guns again. The cry
> Of some man hit, another's dying groans.
> I seem to smell the awful smell of death;
> To hear the jagged splinters whistling by
> To strike against the stones.

Then, while machine guns rattled on that beach,
I thought of beaches where I'd lain before.
I wondered if I'd see them once again,
Or be uncaring in the summer sun,
When there was no more war.

And now the beaches do not seem the same,
For, as I watch the surging tide in flood,
My mind flies back five years, and I still see
My dead companions' faces in the sand,
And smell their blood.

His name was Alec Jay. He was approaching his 26th birthday and on leave from his Territorial Army regiment, the Queen Victoria's Rifles. Three months before, he had stepped down from a Lancaster at a Royal Air Force aerodrome at Wing, Buckinghamshire having spent five years incarcerated in Silesia and the Sudetenland. He returned weighing seven stone and was, that day, still two stone short of his natural weight.

The carnage described in Beaches was the British last stand on the sand-dunes near Calais' Gare Maritime on 26 May 1940. The siege was one of those debacles with which Britain typically starts her wars. It also comprised the five most important days in Alec's life. In the early hours of Tuesday 22 May, 550 Queen Vics riflemen set out from billets in Kent. By Sunday night, all were dead or captured.

Alec's battalion, an experimental motorcycle unit composed mostly of volunteers, was one of three in the hastily-constructed 30th Infantry Brigade, which under Brigadier Claude Nicholson was pushed across the Channel in the twilight days of the Allies' effort to halt Hitler's *Blitzkrieg*. The others were the 2nd battalion of the King's Royal Rifle Corps, the Queen Vics' sister battalion – known informally as the 60th Rifles, and the 1st battalion of the Rifle Brigade. To the brigade were added the forty-eight tanks of the Royal Tank Regiment's 3rd battalion, diverted from the 1st Armoured Division to join Nicholson at Calais. Their orders were incoherent, their armour in-adequate, their air cover non-existent, their French allies in disarray, and the opposition they faced overwhelming in numbers and weaponry. Unlike at Boulogne before and Dunkirk later, Winston Churchill sent no boats – little or large – to bring them home.

Yet while most of the leaderless rabble of French soldiers who fled into Calais hid in its cellars as the battle raged, the outnumbered English fought with a tenacity that stunned the Germans. They fought until their ammunition ran out, surrendering only when they realized resistance would cause loss of life to no purpose. The 3,500 survivors of Calais' garrison were marched off into captivity to spend the rest of the war in POW camps spread across German-occupied Europe. Only about sixty evaded capture and returned home.

Nicholson was handed one impossible task after another, his orders each time based on inadequate, out-of-date intelligence. Task one, to block roads into Calais, began on 22 May with the Queen Vics' arrival. Task two, spearheaded by the tank battalion, was supposedly a mopping-up exercise – destroying the 'few German tanks' the War Office thought were operating ahead of the main Wehrmacht push between Calais and Abbeville. Lieutenant Colonel Reggie Keller was told his twenty-one Vickers-Armstrongs Mk VI light tanks and twenty-seven Cruiser medium tanks faced seven light and four medium German tanks. In reality, five Panzer divisions were within twenty-five miles of Calais by 23 May; at full strength, each had 300 tanks, leaving Keller hopelessly outnumbered and outgunned.

The next task was to deliver 350,000 rations to the British Expeditionary Force as it retreated towards Dunkirk, yet 1st Panzer Division tanks were sitting on the Calais-Dunkirk road blocking Nicholson's way. The fourth task, once Calais was surrounded, was to hold the port until troops could be removed by sea. Finally, Nicholson's men were ordered to resist to the last without hope of rescue. Later, they were told their resistance delayed the German push towards Dunkirk, making Operation Dynamo possible. Revisionist historians say they were sacrificed on the altar of Anglo-French unity.

*   *   *

Alec was a 9 Platoon, C Company Bren gunner. The first he knew his war was about to shift from 'phoney' to real was on 21 May in his billet near battalion headquarters at Ashford, Kent. The battalion, with 566 soldiers, 153 motor cycles and 85 trucks, had been billeted in Ashford and surrounding villages for ten days.

From November 1939, Alec's quarters had been at Beltring Hop Farm, belonging to the Whitbread brewing family, at Paddock Wood, twenty miles inland. On 10 May, a few hours after Adolf Hitler sent his Panzers across the French border, the battalion, then part of the 1st London Division, was ordered towards the coast. No reason was given but from newspapers and the radio Alec knew action was not far away.

The next day, villagers waved farewell as the Queen Vics set out in 'Full Marching Order' with their motorbikes, trucks and scout cars. The destination for the thirty-odd men of 9 Platoon was Kennington, near Ashford, where they were billeted in three cottages and ordered to stay close to their vehicles. Alec made himself at home as best he could – there were no laundry facilities, no hot water and no inside toilets; Alec washed his clothes in a copper pan. The rations were late in arriving and the Queen Vics' Medical Officer, Lieutenant Edward Gartside, sent Alec out on a fatigue party to pick nettles for making soup. To his surprise, their spinach-like flavour was 'not too bad'.

At Ashford, the Queen Vics remained within the War Office's Home Defence Scheme, charged with watching the skies for paratroopers and post-ing alerts – green for normal conditions; blue for standby; red meant the enemy were landing. Such activities lent a new realism to Alec's soldiering. Patrols were looking for an actual, not an imagined, enemy; roadblocks were positioned for use, not as an exercise. There were scares as frightened civilians reported suspicious strangers. Mostly, life continued as normal – and there were long periods of languor. Some men were disappointed they were still not in France: 'History is being made,' complained one, 'and the QVRs aren't part of it.'

Each evening, Alec would listen to the radio. Two days after his arrival, amid news that British fascists and communists were being interned and IRA sympathizers deported, he learned of Churchill's first House of Commons speech as prime minister. This included the disturbing news that German tanks were 'in unexpected places behind our lines'.

After an exceptionally cold winter, spring brought relief. Alec's command-ing officer was Lieutenant Colonel John 'Plushy' Ellison-Macartney, an Old Etonian with decades of Territorial experience. 'Plushy' was pleased by the way his men overcame the disadvantages of a 'less concentrated billet' and with their reception by locals: 'Farming, sport and business quickly adjusted themselves to the military influx, while the start of the cricket season soon took first place for interest among the inhabitants.'

But the war was getting closer: on Saturday 18 May, Alec saw Blenheim bombers returning from a raid with holes in their wings. The following Tuesday was another sunny day, but there was a buzz in the air. 'When the big balloon went up in 1940 our small balloon went up as well,' Alec recalled. 'We had been training hard, honing our fighting abilities to a fine cutting edge, using the special equipment we had been given as one of the first three experimental motorcycle battalions and generally preparing ourselves for come what may.' After all the training, it seemed shots might finally be fired in anger.

There had been false alarms – 'shithouse griff' was the phrase for battalion gossip. The first came in February 1940, when Alec was asked if he skied because the Queen Vics might be sent to defend Finland against the Red Army. Russia's Communists and Germany's Nazis had carved up Poland and Hitler was giving Josef Stalin a free hand against the Finns. Yet 'the Winter War' ended in a Russian victory before British troops could be deployed. A few weeks later, Alec was told he might go to Egypt. Then on 24 April, the Queen Vics were allotted to Nicholson's 30th Infantry Brigade alongside the 60th Rifles and Rifle Brigade regulars. Shortly afterwards, Nicholson informed the Queen Vics they were heading for Norway. This showed they were regarded as one of the finer Territorial battalions. From his prison camp cell, Ellison-Macartney wrote later that 'no more acceptable compliment or greater pleasure could have been offered'. Nicholson's orders were to evict the Germans from Trondheim, but the situation deteriorated rapidly and British troops were withdrawn from the area before the brigade was ready to sail. Thus, the Queen Vics were returned to the 1st London Division. Now, in late May, was Alec heading for France?

Across the Channel, General Heinz Guderian's Panzer Corps had won the 'race to the sea', arriving on the Somme estuary near Abbeville. This isolated the BEF and much of the French Army in northern France and Belgium, separating them from supply ports in western France. Only ten days after the invasion began, the *Sichelschnitt* (sickle stroke) had triumphed. The War Office had not understood Guderian's coup yet knew it must secure Calais as a port through which to supply the BEF and withdraw the wounded.

In Kennington, Alec was put on twenty-four hours' notice to move. Then, at tea time, this shifted to six hours' notice. Alec was upset because 21 May was the day of the London premiere of Gone with the Wind and his parents, John and Annie, had four tickets courtesy of John's younger brother, Woolf, UK representative of a Hollywood studio. He planned to join his parents and his girlfriend, Netta Rose, at the premiere, after which he would return to Ashford. Shifted to six hours' notice, he had to cry off without explaining why. He would not see his parents again for five years.

Even had he wanted to give a hint, he could not because he did not know where or when he was going. His commanding officer knew little more at that point. Then, as the sunny day turned into a 'cool and lovely' evening, Ellison-Macartney made a routine visit to 1st London Division headquarters to be told his battalion was now directly under War Office orders and should prepare to go 'overseas' though 'probably not for two days'.

Events then moved swiftly but chaotically forward as officers struggled to get their men back to their billets. One group had gone to see Greta Garbo in Ninotchka but even before the film began there was a Tannoy announcement: 'All personnel of the Queen Victoria's Rifles are to report back to billets immediately.' The war had finally caught up with them.

At 10.30pm, with air-raid warnings sounding, D Company Second Lieutenant Tony Jabez-Smith had a strange conversation with an Eastern Command staff officer in Hounslow, West London. He was told the Queen Vics should head to Dover by train and sail for France. This appeared straightforward, yet as the conversation developed it became clear the staff officer had no idea about the battalion's location or nature. The files showed the Queen Vics still at Beltring, and the officer thought the battalion was an 800-man infantry unit, not a motorcycle reconnaissance unit of fewer than 600. Then the final blow was delivered: he said the Queen Vics should abandon their heavy equipment – troop carriers, wireless trucks, mortars and motorcycles, with which they had trained for months, even picks and shovels for digging trenches.

Abandoning the motorbikes added insult to injury. The previous Saturday, the battalion had surrendered its twenty-two scout cars – its only offensive vehicles – to Keller's tank battalion, itself short of equipment as it prepared to go overseas. A battalion that a week before had possessed 238 vehicles was first 'mutilated', in the words of one rifleman, then stripped of its remaining mobility and modern communications. Thus, it was sent into battle on foot without any training as infantry. This was disturbing evidence that chaos was reigning at the top of Britain's military machine. Ironically, the scout cars travelled with Keller's tanks to Calais, where they were left driverless on the quayside.

The battalion's diminutive adjutant, Captain Stephen Monico, a scion of the family that owned the Café Monico in London's Piccadilly Circus, felt that evening that 'the grip had gone'. Others were equally alarmed. For Rifleman Vernon 'Taffy' Mathias, an Oxford Street shop assistant, the excitement of leaving for France was tempered by the loss of his 'beloved motorbike'. His time had been wasted, and 'such irrational planning' meant the situation was far worse than the media had reported.

Yet orders were orders, and at 11.23pm, Major Theodore 'Tim' Timpson, Ellison-Macartney's second-in-command, issued instructions to his quartermaster, Lieutenant Frederick Trendall, who died at Calais four days later:

> No vehicles will be taken. Baggage will be loaded into train by [companies] concerned. Baggage will be loaded into lorries and trucks … Pouch ammo 15 [rounds] per pistol 100 [rounds] per rifle. Loading party consisting of one officer thirty other ranks should proceed on baggage vehicles when ordered.

Shortly afterwards, a bugler motorcycled through Kennington blowing the Rouse call, getting men out of bed and on parade with helmet, gas mask and rifle. For the next hour, officers destroyed documents while riflemen packed rucksacks and searched for telephones to call home. Some, including Alec's 35-year-old company commander, Major John 'Buster' Austin-Brown, a solicitor, failed to say goodbye. Only months later could Austin-Brown write to explain to his wife Paulette what had happened. He was then at Oflag (*Offizier-Lager*) VIIC in Laufen Castle.

While battalion cooks improvised a meal, hurried adjustments were made, including substituting infantry anti-gas clothing for protection used by motorcyclists. Weapons, ammunition and supplies were split into amounts a man rather than a vehicle could carry. C Company Sergeant Major 'Tex' Austin handed Alec 100 rounds of ammunition in a bandolier and thirty for his pouch. Then the trucks were loaded for the trip to Ashford Station. Once at Ashford, they faced further delays. Finally, the first train pulled out forty-five minutes late at 5.30pm, taking with it Alec's company and Headquarters Company; B and D Companies boarded a second train at 6.00am, leaving behind a station yard strewn with abandoned trucks and motorcycles. The destination was 'Port Vic', code for Dover.

The trains crawled towards the coast, taking ninety minutes to cover nineteen miles. It would have been quicker had the battalion gone by road, enabling them to load their bikes on the SS *Canterbury*, the ferry selected for the crossing. But that was not to be; the War Office thought the Queen Vics were infantry and it was as lightly-armed infantry they would confront tanks. The 550 men had only forty-three Bren guns; only two-thirds had rifles; the rest, being drivers and classed as cavalry, made do with revolvers; some officers did not even have revolvers. Their 3-inch mortars were left behind; they only had smoke bombs for their 2-inch mortars; and their twenty Boys anti-tank guns were, as they later discovered, useless. Billed as armour-piercing, the bullets bounced off tanks. 'The battalion left for Calais short of its mobility and customary means of communication,' Ellison-Macartney wrote. 'It fought a role divorced from its training and practice; it dived straight into battle.'

Years later, Airey Neave recalled the situation. Neave had an illustrious wartime career. After his successful 'home run' he joined MI9, the intelligence department dedicated to escaping and evading. Then, as a German-speaker, he read the indictments to Nazi leaders at Nuremberg. At Calais, he was a 1st Searchlight Regiment lieutenant and, having retreated from Arras on 20 May, he fought alongside Nicholson's brigade. 'On 22 May, the [Queen Vics] officers ... had not even been issued with revolvers,' he wrote. 'The Waugh-ish nature of the operation was demonstrated by their need to acquire weapons and transport abandoned on the quay ....' Neave thought the battalion's hasty dispatch to Calais was 'shameful ... farce and tragedy intimately combined'. Their orders were 'depressingly obscure and they had no idea what to expect on arrival at Calais'.

Some Queen Vics initially thought their night-time flit to Dover was just an exercise. No one told them their destination – even the officers had merely been told it was 'overseas' – and, as the train crawled through the night, they discussed what might happen. Even if he was headed for France, Alec thought he had little to fear. It seemed unreasonable to believe he would be thrust straight into action. Perhaps he might go to a reception camp and be tasked with patrolling a relatively safe rear area; dangerous duties would be left to the regulars, not Territorials. This view seemed logical given the shallowness of their preparations. At the point of departure, the majority had only fired the Bren gun annual course once. A few had fired a Boys anti-tank gun, but only five rounds, while most of the 200-odd men armed only with revolvers had not received proper pistol practice.

Reality dawned when Alec heard the 'crumps and thumps' of gunfire coming across the water as his train pulled into Dover. On arrival, he saw RAF fighters circling as embarkation staff struggled in the drizzle to load the Queen Vics' kit onto the *Canterbury* while loading Keller's tank crews onto the SS *Maid of Orleans* nearby and taking newly-arrived BEF stretcher cases off the boats and into ambulances. Keller's tanks, then still at Southampton, followed later on the *City of Christchurch*.

Having hauled his equipment up the gangway in what became driving rain, Alec headed to the canteen for a breakfast of sausage rolls, tea, biscuits and raisins. This was full of troops back from France and one transport officer said ominously, 'Most of the movement today seems to be in the opposite direction to yours.' This was the first sign a major retreat was occurring.

At that moment, Ellison-Macartney was trying to make out 'top secret' orders delivered by a motorbike courier and handed to him on the quay by Timpson, a 60th Rifles regular drafted in two months previously to 'professionalize' his weekend warriors. The orders stated that a few German tanks had broken through in the Pas de Calais. The Queen Vics should proceed to Calais while the 30th Brigade regulars would 'disembark next day at Calais or Dunkirk according to the situation'. In the meantime, Ellison-Macartney should report to the officer in charge, who *might* be Colonel Rupert Holland, or, in his absence, take 'the necessary steps to secure the town'. Holland had arrived three days previously to evacuate 'useless mouths' and strengthen Calais' anti-aircraft defences by pulling anti-aircraft guns and searchlights back from Arras. Until then, its only French defenders were one and a half companies of reservists, sailors manning ancient coastal guns, a company of *mitrailleurs* (machine-gunners) and artillerymen with two 75mm field guns. In addition, an Argyll and Sutherland Highlander platoon was guarding a nearby radar station at Marck Aerodrome.

How he could take 'necessary steps to secure' Calais, Ellison-Macartney did not know. Without wireless trucks and motorbikes he had no communications. He telephoned battalion HQ at Ashford to get bikes driven to Dover, but none arrived by the time the *Canterbury* and *Maid of Orleans* sailed at 11.00am.

Soon after, the skies cleared and the two ships headed towards Calais escorted by destroyers and RAF fighters. On the upper deck, Bren gunners scanned the sky for enemy planes as colleagues waved to dockers on the quayside. Then a corporal rigged up a signal lamp to exchange messages with signallers on Dover's cliffs. The cliff-top signal was 'Good luck and hope you come back soon'. At that point, Edward Watson, Alec's youngest colleague, asked, 'We're not going, are we?' Hearing the reply, he said, 'But I can't, I haven't told my Mum.'

Once out of the harbour, Ellison-Macartney assembled his senior officers in the first-class saloon, issued them with small-scale maps, rather inaccurate as they later discovered, and improvised his plan. He was not even sure the Queen Vics were back in 30th Infantry Brigade – he was left to surmise this from the wording of his orders and it was only confirmed the next day when the 60th Rifles and Rifle Brigade arrived. Nor had he a clue about conditions at Calais. The enemy might arrive at any time, so his men might have to fight their way ashore. Alec's company would disembark first to secure the quay-side, he decided, B Company would give covering fire, D Company would provide anti-aircraft defence initially, then unload the baggage.

The briefing over, 'Buster' Austin-Brown spoke to his second-in-command, Second Lieutenant Denis 'Emma' Hamilton, and to Second Lieutenants Bobby Allen, in charge of Alec's platoon, Timothy 'Larry' Lucas of 8 Platoon, and Basil Banbury of 10 Platoon, known as the 'John Lewis' platoon because its volunteers mostly worked at the Oxford Street store. He also briefed 'Tex' Austin, another regular added to the Queen Vics Territorials. Austin, a Gordon Boys Home orphan, had enlisted as a boy soldier and joined the Queen Vics in 1938, the year Alec volunteered.

Finally, the platoon commanders briefed their men. Allen told Alec to head for sand-dunes east of the port to cover the left flank. Such urgency conflicted with news reports before the Queen Vics' hurried departure, leading some 9 Platoon members to think Allen was over-dramatizing the situation. That morning's *Times* had contained a map showing the front line hundreds of miles away, while the ship's radio had just broadcast a communiqué saying the BEF was regaining ground. The reality was different: 'We were going to Calais, our platoon commander told us,' Alec recalled. 'We might well have to fight our way off the boat, but we were there for the defence of Calais.'

The briefings over, the men, wearing life-belts, assembled on deck in fighting platoons. The atmosphere, after the frivolity of the train journey, turned darker. Half way across, Alec saw a Navy destroyer firing off depth charges after a submarine warning, and his mood turned darker still as the gunfire grew louder. Nearby, Jabez-Smith sat beside the battalion chaplain, Richard 'Pooh' Heard, and opened his copy of Shakespeare's *Richard II* in search of an omen. The book fell open at the page describing the Duke of Norfolk's banishment. Jabez-Smith, then twenty-five and a solicitor, shut it and changed the subject.

In fact, the Germans had not yet reached Calais. Three Stuka dive-bombers appeared just before the convoy's arrival but were driven off by anti-aircraft fire, and the vessels berthed without incident to shouts of welcome from French sailors manning the harbour entrance forts. Yet the sight of heavily-bombed quays alarmed the Queen Vics' 'weekend soldiers'. Standing on deck as they steamed towards the quay, Alec saw smoke pouring from oil storage tanks to his left, while just above the waterline he saw a sunken tugboat's funnel and bridge. This was the *Calaisien*, which sank during an air-raid on the first day of Hitler's invasion. As he marched down the gangway at just after noon English time, wearing his greatcoat on orders despite the sunshine and laden with ammunition bandoliers and his Bren gun, he could see a hole in the roof of the Gare Maritime nearby and bomb craters all around. At the station's end, the front wall of a house had collapsed, exposing the rooms within; the quayside and platforms were covered with glass from the Customs House and station restaurants. The tracks were littered with overturned trucks. In the distance, fires burned in the Courgain district, home to Calais' fishermen, and around a lighthouse at the Place de Russie.

In front of Alec were scores of British wounded, some upright, some on stretchers, waiting to board ferries home. They included RAF ground crew attacked by Stukas and tanks as they fled to the coast. One rifleman asked a wounded man what the fighting was like. 'Bloody awful,' he replied. The Germans were formidable. 'They just let you carry on and you think everything's OK; then when you've gone too far to get back, they let you have it. It's just murder. I'm glad I'm out of it.'

Alongside the wounded were panic-stricken refugees – old men, women and children – who had to be restrained from charging the gangways. As the air-raid sirens sounded, the disembarkation was completed without incident. Two Spitfires circled above, but all Alec saw of the Luftwaffe that afternoon was a solitary bomber that took a hit while attempting to raid the port, burst into flames and crashed into the sea.

Once on dry land, Alec's company raced to form their protective screen around the harbour, while other riflemen hurried to bring equipment ashore before German bombers returned. It was a struggle. They had to unload the *Canterbury* by hand – bomb damage had put Calais' electric cranes out of action and the French dockworkers had fled – at the same time as wounded men were lifted aboard for the return journey. They also had to control the weeping, pleading refugees struggling to board the ship. Tank commander Second Lieutenant Quentin Carpendale thought it 'a most extraordinary way to go to war'.

With the unloading complete, the men assembled on some sand-dunes where Ellison-Macartney established his initial headquarters beside an old railway truck. He then set out for Holland's headquarters on the Boulevard Léon Gambetta, the main east-west road through Calais-St Pierre, the new town south of the port. Holland said German tanks had reached St Omer and La Forêt de Guînes, less than ten miles from Calais. Stunned that the Queen Vics had abandoned their transport in Kent, he told Ellison-Macartney to block the six main roads into Calais, guard the submarine telephone cable at Sangatte and reconnoitre the beaches.

At 5.00pm, Ellison-Macartney issued orders. While B Company and D Company were sent south and west, Alec's company was to block roads into Calais from Dunkirk, Marck and Gravelines and Fort Vert, half a mile beyond Calais' eastern ramparts, relieving the Argylls. Alec's platoon was told to march in 'extended order' ready for conflict, to patrol the shoreline up to three miles outside Calais, to engage enemy infantry advancing along the dunes and 'prevent German aircraft landing at low tide'.

It was hardly a textbook deployment. Until reinforcements arrived the next day, the 550-odd Queen Vics troops had to defend a twenty-mile perimeter without transport or communications. Keller's tank guns, meanwhile, were still packed in mineral jelly when they arrived at 4.00pm on the *City of Christchurch*, so could not be ready for a day.

Troop movements had to be limited to the distance exhausted, sleep-deprived men who had done four loadings and unloadings in eighteen hours could march, carrying weapons and ammunition. Officers improvised rudimentary communications by commandeering lorries, cars and motorcycles, yet progress was hampered by truckloads of French troops moving in both directions. Some hoped to be evacuated from Calais; others were fleeing towards Dunkirk. That evening, thousands of disorganized French and Belgian troops poured past the Queen Vics, most unarmed and all in a panic, shouting, *'Les Boches! Les Boches!'* The front had collapsed, they said; German tanks were roaming the countryside; and roads not blocked by Luftwaffe bombing and abandoned French military hardware were choked with fleeing soldiers and civilians.

Alec felt bewildered as he moved slowly forward, weighed down by ammunition and equipment and looking, in the words of one of his officers, like a Christmas tree. In D Company, Sam Kydd, then a budding actor, reflected on the situation:

We ... were a motorized battalion ... trained as a mechanised reconnaissance unit with scout cars and motorcycle and sidecar combinations upon which a machine gun was to be mounted to search out and account for the enemy – in theory that was – and in practice in England that was. But not in France – all of a sudden we were now infantry and as infantry we marched. This was for real. You can imagine the grumbling that went on.

By nightfall, D Company's platoons were closest to the enemy. As they established a roadblock on the road to Guînes, five miles south, some army lorries passed through. Their unarmed convoy had been attacked by German tanks ten miles down the road and most vehicles had been destroyed.

To the east, Austin-Brown selected a barn just north of the Marck Canal as C Company headquarters and set out to review his men. His platoons had built roadblocks using tree trunks, oil drums and other detritus, but their lack of equipment meant they would not pose much of a problem to mechanized opposition. Austin-Brown was also conscious his platoons had not chosen the best sites for anti-tank defence, making a reshuffle necessary the next morning.

Alec's platoon set off at 7.00pm listening to distant gunfire and air-raid sirens. At dusk, the guns went quiet and Allen, a 25-year-old stockbroker, selected a position for the platoon to bivouac on dunes overlooking the shore-line. As he looked back, Alec marvelled at how quiet and beautiful Calais looked in the setting sun. Was it possible this could become a battle zone?

That evening, Alec munched on army biscuits and listened to the long grass rustling in breeze, the waves lapping on the shore and the trills of a nightingale in woods nearby. He was transfixed by the bird's song; for a moment nothing else seemed real. The feeling was so powerful he tried to recapture it in The Nightingale, a poem he wrote three years after the Calais garrison surrendered as he lay on his bunk in a POW billet in the snow-covered Sudeten hills.

In the dark green depths of a quiet wood,
Where seldom a sound is heard;
Only the rustle of breeze stirred leaves,
And the sleepy notes of some little bird.

As the evening approaches, and darkness drops down,
When the air is sweet and cool,
Then the wild animals timidly come
To drink at a solitary pool.

Two rabbits, some mallard, a doe with her child,
A squirrel, a fox, and a stoat,
And lastly, a little bird drinking, before
He pours out his soul through his throat.

The whole wood is silent, no murmur is heard.
Through the trees the pale moon shines,
Her face in the water reflected.
Twigs and leaves form a million designs.

Suddenly, one voice in the wood is in song,
Note upon note, trill upon trill.
A cascading torrent of melody.
And the whole of the world stands still,

And listens enchanted, unable to stir,
Oblivious, inarticulate.
I too stand there spellbound, unconscious of all,
Save the nightingale's song to his mate.

Soon, however, other thoughts intruded. Alec was the only Jew in his platoon. What might happen if he were killed? His religion was in his Army Book along with his service record, pay, Army number, surname, first name, date of birth and trade on enlistment; the word 'Jew' was stamped on the identity disc around his neck. Both were there to ensure he would receive an appropriate burial.

Yet would Nazis give a Jew a decent burial? Should he 'convert' to Christianity? His Army Book stated: 'You are held personally responsible for the safe custody of this book … You will always carry this book on your person.' There were times, however, when rules might be broken. Quietly, without attracting attention, he dug a hole in the sand, removed the identity disc from his neck and the pay book from his battledress pocket, placed them in the hole and covered them up. From then on, he would be 'a fully-paid member of the Church of England'.

'It never entered my mind I'd be a prisoner-of-war,' he recalled. 'I was virtually certain I would be killed and if I was killed I would rather be buried as a Christian than left for the dogs to eat. There had been photographs in the *Jewish Chronicle* of the sort of thing the Germans did in Dachau.'

Chapter 2

The Greenjackets Arrive

Claude Nicholson, from an aristocratic family, was at forty-one, one of Britain's youngest brigadiers. He arrived to take charge of Calais' garrison at lunchtime on 23 May on the SS *Archangel* with his brigade staff and the Rifle Brigade. The conditions at the Gare Maritime were grim – one of Nicholson's first sights was a line of corpses on the platform.

He had sailed from Southampton the previous evening, arriving at Dover in the morning to receive final orders from Lieutenant General Sir Douglas Brownrigg, the BEF's adjutant-general. The day before, Brownrigg had been evacuated through Calais, where he had told Reggie Keller to support the Welsh Guards twenty miles away in Boulogne. Keller's tanks, however, were not ready, which was fortunate because superior numbers of German tanks had already arrived outside Boulogne and were preparing an attack. Airey Neave wrote of these instructions: 'Few commanders, since the days of Balaclava, have issued such suicidal orders.' But Brownrigg was still unaware of Guderian's triumphs when he briefed Nicholson, so the message was similar: his brigade, despite lacking artillery, should relieve Boulogne.

That this was impossible was clear from Nicholson's first conversation with Holland, who said Germans were attacking Searchlight Territorials at Les Attaques, three miles south-east of Calais. His next shock came when he made contact with Keller. The tank battalion did not yet know it was part of the 30th Brigade and had received fresh orders from the BEF to secure bridges over the Aa Canal at St Omer twenty-five miles to the south-east. Keller was, however, only four miles outside Calais when his men spotted some stationary tanks. At first they thought they were French and the two lines got within twenty yards of each other before a German officer opened fire at Lieutenant Carpendale as he peered from his tank turret. It was an uneven fight: Keller's cruiser and light tanks were no match for the 1st Panzer Division's Assault Group Krüger and he lost twelve machines, a quarter of his total, before withdrawing. As he directed the retreat, Keller's battlefield communications were interrupted by a radio message that Brigadier Nicholson – at that point unknown to him – wished to meet him. 'Get off the air,' he replied. 'I am trying to fight a bloody battle.'

With Keller's tank battle before Guînes audible in Calais, Nicholson decided defending Calais took priority whatever Brownrigg's orders and he needed to deploy his men accordingly. At the time, Calais, with its population of 60,000, was divided in two. The Old Town with its medieval winding streets was best known to the British. Beau Brummell, the Regency dandy, had lived here in exile having fled his creditors, while Nelson's mistress, Emma Hamilton, had died nearby. To the south-west of the harbour stood the Vauban-designed Citadel, surrounded by a moat. Further defence of this inner area was provided by the Bassin Carnot and the Bassin de Batellerie. Calais-St Pierre's newer industrial and residential districts, divided by the north-south Canal de Calais, lay to the south and south-east. Their most significant feature was the Hôtel de Ville's clock tower.

The town, a rough square two miles across, was virtually surrounded by twenty-foot earth ramparts with steep grassy slopes and flat tops ten to fifteen feet wide. These were strengthened at points by bastions while beyond the ramparts was a thirty-foot moat. In the north, linked to the Old Town by two swing bridges, the Gare Maritime stood on a tongue of land, and beyond it a further defensive feature, the Bassin des Chasses de l'Est. West of the harbour stood Fort Risban and Calais' beaches, while a few hundred yards beyond the western ramparts stood Fort Nieulay, another Vauban creation left to rot after Napoleon's defeat. To the harbour's east lay the Bastion de l'Estran, a second abandoned fort.

The ramparts provided a defensive barrier, yet there were weaknesses: to the south-west, a mile of ramparts and two bastions had been levelled to make way for railway lines; elsewhere they were overlooked by factories from which snipers could operate. The canals and *bassins* might protect Calais against tanks but only if the bridges over them were blown.

The countryside beyond was mostly flat and criss-crossed by canals and ditches, restricting tanks to the roads, but there was high ground to the west from which artillery could operate. If the 30th Brigade was to make its stand on the ramparts to keep the port in operation it would have to defend a line six miles long. If it could not hold this perimeter, it could withdraw to an inner perimeter of canals and *bassins* sealing off the Old Town, Citadel and harbour, through which it could be resupplied, reinforced and, if necessary, evacuated.

This situation was not ideal. During the Great War, Churchill told his Cabinet colleagues Calais was 'simply an enceinte' protected by 'a few well-executed field works'. It could not, however, 'be counted on to hold out for more than a few days against a determined attack'.

Nicholson divided responsibilities between his regular battalions geographically, with the 60th Rifles defending Calais west of the Canal de Calais and the Rifle Brigade defending the east. The Queen Vics he split company by company depending on where Ellison-Macartney had placed them – B Company and D Company would support the 60th Rifles while C Company and Headquarters Company would support the Rifle Brigade. They should remain outside Calais as long as possible, but if their positions became untenable they should retreat and dig in alongside the regulars on the ramparts.

Lastly, he deployed the 229th Anti-Tank Battery's eight guns on the main roads out of town.

The regulars' arrival cheered the Territorials – here were professional soldiers to fight alongside them. Gordon Instone was a Searchlight Territorial captured at Calais, becoming a serial escaper like Alec but, unlike Alec, making a 'home run', reaching England via Spain in 1941. In his memoir, *Freedom the Spur*, he wrote that the Territorials, like 'so many uniformed but appreciative spectators', watched the regulars' 'quiet confidence and smooth efficiency' as they 'did quickly and automatically what was necessary'. Instone realized 'only too clearly and alarmingly' the inadequacy of his training.

Both regiments, with proud histories dating back centuries, were known for innovation. Both were early adopters of green uniforms as opposed to traditional red and thus became known as Greenjacket battalions; such uniforms, with black buttons and belts, helped them blend in with the countryside as they operated ahead of traditional troops. The origins of the 60th Rifles were in eighteenth century colonial America, where in 1756 George III created the 62nd (Royal American) Regiment to fight the French and their native allies. Armed with new-fangled rifles, which were more accurate and had a longer range than traditional muskets, they became the 60th after two older regiments disgraced themselves by surrendering.

The Rifle Brigade was formed in 1800 as a unit of 'sharpshooters, scouts and skirmishers' and, like the 60th, was armed with rifles not muskets. The rifles were fitted with 21-inch sword-bayonets to give them the same reach as muskets in a bayonet charge – hence rifle regiments fix 'swords' not 'bayonets'. In the Napoleonic War, the Rifle Brigade specialized in moving at speed over difficult terrain to protect the main army. The attributes required in the troops were quickness and independence of thought and mobility.

Both regiments were recast after their 1914–18 experiences. The Great War's later battles had shown the impact tanks could make, and specially-trained infantry were needed to work alongside them. Such units would need mobility to keep up with tanks in open terrain and step in to maintain momentum if tanks got bogged down. Thus, these two regiments became motorized units.

Whatever Brownrigg's orders, Nicholson was right. Three hours after the young brigadier's boat docked, Guderian, nicknamed 'Hurrying Heinz', gave Lieutenant General Ferdinand Schaal, the 10th Panzer Division's commanding officer, his orders: 'Capture Calais. Details of the enemy there not known.'

The Germans had encountered only ineffectual resistance after their Ardennes breakthrough but feared that a heavily-defended Calais could be used to land reinforcements to halt the Panzers as they attacked the BEF outside Dunkirk. 'Assault Group Krüger', according to the 1st Panzers' war diary for 23 May, 'stood at the gates of Calais when darkness fell. It was reported that the town was strongly held by the enemy and that a surprise attack was out of the question. The siege of Calais was, therefore, handed to 10th Panzers while 1st Panzers were ordered to push towards Gravelines and Dunkirk.'

At fifty-one, the 10th Panzer commander led seasoned troops. The division contained 300 tanks, supported by two rifle regiments, an artillery regiment and a motorcycle battalion, plus reconnaissance, anti-tank, engineering and logistics personnel. As part of Guderian's XIX Panzer Corps, Schaal's men were the first to encounter the enemy, routing the 2nd French Cavalry. Held up for a while by artillery fire, they crossed the Meuse on 13 May near Sedan and surged forward. As he advanced, Schaal's great problem was not the French in front but the clogged roads behind, hampering efforts to resupply his tanks.

One reason for their success was that German soldiers were better warriors than the French; basic training was tougher, the officer selection process more rigorous. In 1940, they were ideologically on the offensive, lending a fanaticism to their fighting. They were the Master Race's shock troops; their Führer had reversed the Versailles Treaty and had cleansed Germany of Jews. They were now creating a Greater Germany at the expense of decadent colonialists and effete democrats.

Schaal's advance was a critical early triumph in the Battle of France. Just eight days later, after sweeping towards the coast, he developed his plan to capture a key Channel port. He decided his tanks, artillery and his 86th Panzer Grenadier infantry should advance up the Boulogne road to high ground near Coquelles, south-west of Calais, while to the east his 69th Panzer Grenadiers would advance from Guînes.

As Nicholson steamed up the Channel to Dover, Alec's platoon caught a few hours' sleep, interrupted by unfounded rumours about enemy parachutists landing on the dunes. The platoon spent the early morning patrolling the dunes as the sounds of gunfire came closer. Soon after dawn, Bobby Allen visited the Queen Vics' new battalion headquarters at the Dunkirk Gate at Calais' south-east corner. There he received fresh orders: his men were to move from the dunes to a roadblock previously manned by 10 Platoon on the Gravelines road.

This roadblock comprised two handcarts drawn across the road and could not have been defended against tanks. Anti-aircraft gunners with three 3.7-inch QF guns and some Searchlight Territorials were nearby; Allen said all should withdraw at the first sign of the enemy. In the meantime, Alec and his colleagues had to deal with refugees and stragglers clogging up the road.

This was part of the largest mass flight in European history as eight million French people took to the roads, and it forms the core of Irène Némirovsky's *Suite Française*. Némirovsky, who was gassed at Auschwitz, described it thus:

> Silently, with no lights on, cars kept coming, one after another, full to
> bursting with baggage and furniture, prams and birdcages, packing cases

and baskets of clothes, each with a mattress tied firmly to the roof . . . They looked like mountains of fragile scaffolding and they seemed to move without aid of a motor, propelled by their own weight.

Jim Roberts, a member of Alec's company, recalled 'the constantly increasing stream of refugees pushing carts and old perambulators laden with as many of their worldly possessions that they could cram on to them . . . occasionally there were animals tied to the handles – not only dogs but cows and goats.' Then there were the soldiers. Most 'had vacant expressions on their faces and blank looks in their eyes'. They stared straight ahead, 'blindly following the back of the one in front', failing to acknowledge the British and giving 'the terrible and overwhelming impression of total defeat and despair'.

This was alarming because Germans in disguise might infiltrate the refugees, reach Calais as 'Fifth Columnists' and undermine the defence from within. At one point, the Queen Vics' headquarters came under sniper attack and suspected Fifth Columnists were arrested. One claimed to be a Belgian officer, who, according to Monico 'appeared to be too interested in what was going on'. He asked Stephen Houthakker, the Queen Vics' South African-born intelligence sergeant, to approach the 'Belgian' from behind and call, '*Achtung!*' The man flinched so he was led away and imprisoned.

Allen told his platoon to turn back civilian refugees from the roadblock, along with Allied soldiers who lacked weapons and ID papers. Yet the order could not be fully implemented as queues built up. On the Dunkirk road, at the next roadblock south, 8 Platoon's Lieutenant Lucas faced similar problems. Lucas, who was one of few Queen Vics to return from Calais and who gave families a first-hand account of the debacle, wrote that it was 'impossible to check up on the many different nationalities who were swilling to and fro and though they all swore that they were allies it would have been easy for enemy agents to pass through on forged identity cards'.

In a letter to his wife from POW camp, Alec's company commander summed up his first full day in France: 'Calais was full of evacuating troops, transport and refugees. There was some heavy shelling during the day. There were many Fifth Columnists and nobody could be trusted. The French and Belgian troops were like a herd of lost sheep. Two hours' sleep.'

On the Gravelines road, Alec's platoon took it in turns to man the barricade while Allen established his base in a farmhouse nearby. There Alec discovered warfare had its picturesque moments. In the farmyard, he was greeted by a French veteran who, bedecked in medals and with scars to show his bravery, volunteered to fight alongside *les Anglais* against *les Boches*. In the meantime, he produced some cognac and drank various toasts with his guests – to Germany's downfall, to France, to England and to Germany's downfall again – until the bottle was empty.

Then it was back to roadblock duty and endlessly repeating, '*Vous ne pouvez pas passer!*' to refugees. One woman begged on her knees to join relatives in

Calais until two men dragged her to her feet. Finally at dusk she gave up and turned back.

While Alec spent 23 May on checkpoint duty, other Queen Vics were experiencing a softening-up exercise as the 10th Panzers probed Calais' defences. HQ Company came under mortar attack in the evening, and German heavy artillery began pounding the harbour and oil storage tanks nearby. That night, as Chaplain 'Pooh' Heard wandered among them dispensing tea, the Queen Vics could see a ring of bonfires in front. These had been lit by Germans to show Luftwaffe pilots their front line and protect them from friendly fire.

Fearing that aerial bombardment would demoralise his Territorials, Nicholson toured their positions at dusk. Wearing a soft hat while everyone else wore helmets, he stopped to ask individual riflemen if they were 'all right'. When one confessed to being frightened by the explosions, he offered comfort: 'You mustn't worry about those because if you hear them you're safe. It's when you don't hear them that you've got trouble, so you needn't worry. If you are going to get hurt you're not going to hear it anyway.' The message seemed to do the trick.

That afternoon, Nicholson had been given his second impossible task – a rations truck convoy sitting on the dockside should be escorted to Dunkirk as a priority 'overriding all other considerations' because BEF soldiers were already on half-rations as they retreated. How his brigade might fulfil this mission while defending a town already under shellfire was left to him to decide.

Even assembling vehicles for the rations convoy was difficult; the lack of cranes, exhaustion among British dockers who had worked for thirty-six hours virtually without rest and the build-up of German shellfire had slowed the unloading of Rifle Brigade equipment from the *Canterbury*. Much of it was still in the hold that evening so Lieutenant Colonel Sir Chandos Hoskyns, the Rifle Brigade's commanding officer, had to throw together an improvised unit comprising a few Bren gun carriers and troop carriers to escort the ration trucks.

By the time the convoy and escort, by then including some of Keller's tanks, was ready to set off, it was too late – Calais was encircled. The first officer to grasp this was Second Lieutenant Tony Rolt, a racing driver who won the British Empire Trophy in 1939 and, therefore, a romantic hero to his men. Alec watched as Rolt led his Bren gun carriers through the Gravelines Road checkpoint at 9.00pm on 23 May. When Rolt reached Fort Vert, 4km east of Calais, villagers warned him about Germans in the area. Rolt told his men to take up 'all-round defence' positions to await the ration column. It never arrived. As darkness fell, Rolt saw fires surrounding his little scout platoon – these were the 1st Panzers' warning signals to the Luftwaffe– but he did manage to withdraw to Calais in the early hours without incident.

The second patrol to move through the Queen Vics' roadblocks comprised four tanks under Major Bill Reeves, who wanted to check the main road to Dunkirk. If it was blocked by Germans, he would return; if it was clear, he would ask BEF troops to meet the Calais convoy halfway to provide protection. Reeves set off in the dark and after a few miles saw German tank silhouettes in the moonlight by the road. Through a stroke of luck, the sentries thought his tanks were German and did not challenge them. Thus, they reached Gravelines at 2.00am on 24 May and subsequently fought on the Dunkirk perimeter.

Finally, at dawn, the main convoy set off from the Porte de Dunkerque led by 'Boy' Hamilton-Russell of the Rifle Brigade and consisting of five tanks, three Bren carriers and three platoons of riflemen in trucks in front and two platoons in the rear. They did not get far before coming under fire. As casualties mounted, Hamilton-Russell decided to retreat, mission not accomplished.

Chapter 3

The Siege Begins

While Nicholson attempted to send his rations convoy to Dunkirk, the War Office dithered over whether to reinforce Calais or abandon it. As the Queen Vics had discovered two days previously when their motorbikes were left behind, poor intelligence was causing havoc in Whitehall.

Before Nicholson landed at Calais, Major General Andrew McNaughton of the 1st Canadian Division was told by General Sir Edmund Ironside, Chief of the Imperial General Staff, to take a brigade to Calais to re-establish road and rail links with Hazebrouk, a key defensive position thirty miles inland on the BEF's original left flank. But by the time McNaughton arrived in Dover, the picture was so uncertain that he received two alternative sets of orders: if Calais was still viable as a supply port he should take command, but if not he should send his men to Dunkirk.

McNaughton landed at Calais at 11.30pm on 23 May. Nicholson was away organizing the rations convoy but other officers on the quay persuaded him of the seriousness of the situation. Thus, as he sailed on to Dunkirk, he signalled Dover: 'Most present garrison can be expected to do is to hold perimeter in face of attack. Troops in good heart.' Arriving at Dunkirk, he sent a second signal emphasising Calais' importance and saying his brigade should be dispatched there.

In the meantime, the view in London changed again and at 3.00am, before McNaughton had reported from Dunkirk, Nicholson received a message from Major General Dick Dewing, War Office Director of Military Operations: 'Evacuation decided in principle. When you have finished unloading your two M.T. [motor transport] ships commence evacuation of all personnel except fighting personnel who will remain to cover final evacuation.' Three hours later, Dewing phoned Nicholson to say evacuation would not take place for at least twenty-four hours.

At dawn, Hoskyns told Ellison-Macartney about the planned evacuation but added that 'everything must be done to prevent the enemy becoming aware of this'. To prevent the Germans from concentrating for an attack, the RAF would begin bombing, said Hoskyns, on an arc around the town supported by a barrage from Navy destroyers. The Queen Vics, on being told to withdraw, would head for the Gare Maritime and embark first.

This decision to abandon Calais a day after the regular battalions had arrived was reversed a day later after protests by General Fagalde, newly-appointed French commander at Dunkirk and overall commander of the Channel ports. Yet although it was only in force a day it had dire consequences for the garrison. This was because two trainloads of wounded BEF troops had arrived at the port on 23 May, and transport officers decided they should be repatriated immediately, acting on what they thought were Nicholson's orders. Thus, they said the *Canterbury* should take the wounded home even though Rifle Brigade equipment was still on board. Their actions were unsurprising. German shelling had intensified so they thought they were saving lives. Stephen Sykes, a Royal Engineers officer, described emerging from a stuffy cellar at dawn to be met by 'a new and very unpleasant smell'. This was the stench of 'scorched flesh, coming from the corpses of men who had received direct hits on the quayside'. Taking the last boat out that morning, Sykes looked back at a quayside covered by corpses and equipment. His relief as the ship sailed 'was overwhelming – but clouded by a sense of the great disaster in which I had been involved'.

The Rifle Brigade's officers were horrified. Major Alex Allan, second-in-command and acting commander after Hoskyns was mortally wounded the next day, was on the quayside trying to hasten the unloading of supplies as fires blazed. He protested, yet the *Canterbury* sailed with half his battalion's weapons, transport and equipment in its holds. Confusion had again trumped planning, and the Rifle Brigade was left to defend its half of Calais with Bren carriers for only two scout platoons, its communications enfeebled, its trench diggers without tools and its doctor without supplies. Scrounging abandoned equipment addressed some shortages, but the *Canterbury*'s premature departure would rankle with survivors for decades. Had a Fifth Columnist infiltrated the quayside officers and given the order to sail, they asked. Why else were they sent into battle so ill-equipped?

As the *Canterbury*, her decks strewn with stretcher cases, steamed away, the third phase of the battle began – the 30th Brigade's struggle to defend Calais while the authorities back home were supposedly preparing to evacuate it. The outlook was not propitious. Nicholson had few troops and insufficient matériel. Of the few French guns, some were put out of action to prevent them falling into German hands. Just twenty-one of Keller's tanks had survived, the regular battalions had few 3-inch mortars and Nicholson's artillerymen had only eight 2-pounder anti-tank guns. Thus the Greenjackets would mainly be defending Calais with Bren guns, Boys anti-tank guns and rifles. Even with limited supplies, Nicholson's men might have held out longer had they had sufficient gelignite to demolish the bridges over the canals and *bassins*; but, once again, chaos prevailed and only one bridge was blown during the battle.

The defence of Calais' outer perimeter began at dawn on 24 May when the 69th Panzer Grenadiers, comprising about 1,600 men, began a mortar barrage. It was another fine day, perfect conditions for an assault. The Queen

Vics of D Company bore the brunt at Les Fontinettes to the south-west, the weakest point in the perimeter, where the ramparts made way for railway tracks. After the mortar barrage, a few Germans advanced but went to ground when fired upon.

The next Queen Vics to face the advance comprised Captain Tim Munby's scout platoon and 6 Platoon under Second Lieutenant Freddie Nelson, seventy-five men in total. They had been told to block the Calais-Boulogne road, and the derelict Fort Nieulay in front of the western ramparts offered good cover. This was occupied by 150 Frenchmen under the command of a Captain Herreman, who said, ominously, that Munby could enter only after he submitted to French command and agreed not to retreat.

The battle for Fort Nieulay began at dawn the next morning, when the 1,600-strong 86th Panzer Grenadiers advanced from Coquelles, aiming to take the strongpoint 'by a surprise raid'. Munby told his men to hold fire until the Germans came within 500 yards, but French machine-gunners opened up when they were still a mile away, to little effect yet showing the enemy the derelict fort would be defended. With the phone line to Calais cut by bombardment, Nieulay's occupants were left alone to face the assault.

The first attack was beaten off but casualties mounted as tank shelling joined the mortar fire and the Grenadiers moved in for a second assault. Just after 4.00pm, Munby visited Herreman in his underground shelter to ask for orders, but Herreman said he was in the process of surrendering because the fort was surrounded. As he spoke, the French raised a white flag and Munby found himself 'at the wrong end of a tommy gun'. Feeling 'more humiliated' than ever before, he collected survivors and marched out. Only then did he see the strength of the opposition, 'heavy tanks, artillery and numerous infantry'. He did, however, take consolation from counting the German dead and wounded. 'Perhaps,' he wrote, 'the defence of Fort Nieulay had not been quite such a futile affair as it appeared to those inside.'

Having taken Fort Nieulay, the Panzers advanced towards Calais' western ramparts. The German numerical advantage was enormous. Lieutenant Gris Davies-Scourfield of the 60th Rifles was standing at Bastion Nine behind Fort Nieulay watching a long line of German tanks on a ridge overlooking his position. Three British tanks stood nearby to provide support, so Davies-Scourfield asked a tank officer whether the ramparts might block tanks and whether his Boys anti-tank rifles would be effective. The reply was, 'None whatsoever. They'll laugh at this bank and your Boys rifles wouldn't blow a track off at point blank range. Our only hope is to bluff them ... make them think we have a big force here.' For a while, the bluff worked – the 60th Rifles' response to probing attacks persuaded the Germans to withdraw.

There were other reasons for German caution. Although the garrison's heavy artillery was virtually non-existent, two British destroyers, HMSs *Wessex* and *Vimiera*, and the Polish destroyer, ORP *Burza*, did support the defence, though not without cost. *Wessex* was sunk in an air-raid while *Vimiera* and *Burza* were damaged and could only limp back to Dover. Yet the sound of the Navy in action raised Alec's morale, as did the sight of Blenheims staging air-raids from Sangatte to Gravelines. Unfortunately, when the Blenheims turned for home, their pilots mistook Queen Vics withdrawing west of Calais for enemy and bombed them. Only two men were wounded, but it was an unwelcome introduction to 'friendly fire'.

At the 10th Panzers' headquarters, Schaal complained of British 'air superiority', and at 5.00pm, with the assault on the western ramparts in progress, Guderian ordered a rethink. 'If there are heavy losses during the attack on Calais,' he said, 'it should only be continued with support from dive-bombers and when heavy artillery can be brought up . . . There must be no unnecessary losses.'

A few British fighters also appeared above Calais on 24 May. Peter Cazenove crash-landed his Spitfire on the beach near Alec's platoon that morning after losing out in a duel but he emerged unscathed and walked into Calais to join the defence. After Cazenove's squadron withdrew, the Germans controlled the skies over Calais as Fighter Command pulled back its Spitfires from France in response to accidents caused by pilot unfamiliarity with the new planes. This would rankle with Queen Vic survivors for decades.

When Alec resumed his roadblock duties in the morning, the refugee problem became overwhelming as more exhausted, panic-stricken French soldiers joined the tide of civilians. Later in the day, a Belgian officer and his female companion drove up in a car. 'The Germans are very near,' she said. 'Do you know that?' Before she could say anything more, she was interrupted by explosions as shells landed nearby. It was time to withdraw.

Alec jogged back towards Calais before flopping down to rest beside a quiet gravel road just outside the town. He could see Calais had become a battle zone. Above, he saw a Hurricane downed by two Messerschmitts, leaving a cloud of smoke as it disappeared from view. The noise built up as the whine of mortar fire nearby mingled with the distant thunder of heavy artillery. To the south, smoke from Boulogne drifted closer. There, the French garrison was still holding the citadel against the 2nd Panzers. To their chagrin, most British soldiers had been lifted off by the Navy the previous day, although many Welsh Guardsmen were left behind, marching into captivity beside Alec when Calais fell two days later.

As dusk fell on 24 May, with the 60th Rifles and Queen Vics having held their positions on the western and southern ramparts, the German assault died down. A few Germans were lodged in buildings in Calais-St Pierre, but this was not the easy ride the 10th Panzer officers had expected after their rapid victories over the French since 10 May. Resistance from 'scarcely perceptible positions was so strong it was possible only to achieve quite local successes', wrote the 10th Panzer diarist, and 'a good half' of its tanks were out of action as were a third of its equipment, vehicles and personnel.

Yet Nicholson knew Calais-St Pierre could not be held. At that time he believed his brigade would be evacuated, so his priority was to hold the area around the port. He, therefore, established a new inner perimeter behind the Canal de Marck and the other canals and *bassins* surrounding the Old Town. Three bridges spanning the waterways, Pont Freycinet, Pont Richelieu and Pont Faidherbe, were his weak points and, in the absence of dynamite, these were barricaded with vehicles. As the battle developed, they were the locations of some of the fiercest fighting.

At the Queen Vics' Dunkirk Gate headquarters, Ellison-Macartney received Nicholson's orders to withdraw to the northern ramparts, which lay south of the Bassin de Chasses, at 6.00pm. Alec's company was to withdraw through the Rifle Brigade's eastern rampart positions and head north in two columns, one on the Canal de Calais' east bank, the other along the ramparts; next, D Company would retreat from the southern ramparts, initially to the Boulevard de l'Egalité, the continuation of the Dunkirk road within Calais; HQ Company would bring up the rear.

The Germans did not press home their advantage as the Queen Vics withdrew, but retreating was painful. 'Fifth Column' sniper activity increased, with Alec's platoon coming under fire from an apparent civilian in a deserted building. Later, the men took refuge for an hour beneath abandoned French troop carriers as mortar bombs exploded around them; finally, as he reached the edge of the Bassin des Chasses, Alec had his first experience of being dive-bombed by a Stuka.

With their trademark inverted gull-wings, each carrying two bombs, Stukas would terrify targets before they had even attacked, swooping down with 'Jericho Trumpet' sirens wailing. Alec's platoon ran for cover, rolling down the banks of the ramparts and diving beneath vehicles. The nerve-shattering whine, the thud of bombs dropping and the splatter of machine-gun fire mingled in a cacophony of sound that made one of Alec's platoon 'scrabble at the shuddering ground in what was a purely reflex action' to dig himself deeper in. The raid only lasted a few minutes but it seemed an awfully long time to Alec. 'Never look a dive-bomber in the face,' said a colleague. 'Pray hard and run, run like hell for the nearest ditch and dive in.'

That evening, Alec learned what had happened elsewhere in Calais during the day. After hours of sweating in sunshine with not a breath of wind, his colleagues were in a sorry state – food, water and ammunition were scarce and Germans in civilian clothes were sniping from houses and shops. One German sniper even dressed as a priest and stood on a church roof, until a bullet dispatched him.

In an atmosphere of increasing paranoia, the Greenjackets came to regard any man not in khaki as a potential enemy. It was a tragic situation. Some

Frenchmen did fight at Calais but the British often felt they were let down despite the exhortation from General Weygand, France's supreme commander, that his men should 'fight like dogs'. The worst incident occurred that morning. At dawn, French sailors manning the coastal forts agreed to turn their guns inland to target advancing Germans, but by noon all but one gun had been spiked, with the gunners sent to the docks to be evacuated by tugboats. Yet they did not all vanish. As the tugs prepared to leave, Captain Carlos de Lambertye called for volunteers to reoccupy the coastal batteries. These 'Volunteers of Calais' marched back to occupy Bastion 11 on the perimeter's north-west corner and Bastion 12 west of the port entrance. In all, 800 men attempted to retrieve the honour of France rather than flee or hide in Calais' cellars waiting for the surrender; tragically, a few Frenchmen who did fight were shot as spies as British suspicions grew.

'Taffy' Mathias, a member of Alec's company, saw a French deserter with a 'beautiful weapon', a short rifle with a long slender bayonet. Mathias thought it would be useful to one of his officers, then armed only with revolvers, so he asked the deserter to hand it over. The Frenchman did so and vanished. Later, a French officer spotted the rifle and asked the British officer carrying it why he was using a French weapon. He did not like the answer. After a few seconds' silence, he said, 'Sir, would you kindly give me the rifle number in order that I can bring this soldier who has dishonoured France to justice.' After noting the number, he saluted, saying, 'Thank you, Sir. I am sure you will bring honour to this weapon.'

Bill Harding, an artilleryman who later marched into captivity with Alec, watched Frenchmen fleeing through the British lines. 'Look at them, sir,' he said to an officer. 'It's their country and they are running away. Why are we here?'

Apart from tales of French cowardice, gossip included rumours that Canadian troops were coming and that HMS *Verity*, then at the quayside, would take the Queen Vics home that night. But the brutal truth was broken to Alec by a sergeant: 'No one's going on board. The ship has brought us more ammunition to keep us going, that's all.'

The destroyer had not only brought ammunition. Vice Admiral Sir James Somerville came ashore to confirm to Nicholson, then resting in a Gare Maritime cellar, that Ironside had accepted the French demand that there be no pull-out:

> In spite of the policy of evacuation given you this morning, fact that British forces in your area now under Fagalde who has ordered no repeat no evacuation means you must comply for the sake of Allied solidarity. Your role is therefore to hold on, harbour being for present of no importance to BEF. Brigade Group 48th Div started marching to your assistance this morning. No reinforcements but ammunition being sent by

sea. Should this fail RAF will drop ammunition. You will select best position and fight on.

Nicholson accepted this news 'with Spartan unconcern', saying he expected as much. 'Given more guns, which were urgently needed, he was confident he could hold on for a time.' By that time he had only two anti-tank guns and two anti-aircraft guns left. He agreed that *Verity* and *Wolfhound*, which could have taken his men home, should leave the port before daylight for their safety. As for the supposed 48th Division relief column, it was a Whitehall fantasy.

'Spartan unconcern' was a Nicholson trait. One uncle fought in the Boer War; another was a Great War 60th Rifles major, a third a Royal Scots Greys lieutenant. Nicholson's younger brother Godfrey was a Royal Fusiliers captain, while his wife's father died in 1915 of wounds sustained on the Western Front. Yet once again, Britain's generals showed their lack of grip, now adding callousness to incompetence. In *The Fight for the Channel Ports, Calais to Brest 1940: A Study in Confusion*, Michael Glover wrote: 'Seldom can men have been asked to sacrifice themselves in words less inspiring.' Men such as Alec were being asked to defend a port the War Office thought 'of no importance', in the interests of maintaining solidarity with Frenchmen unwilling to defend their town, preferring instead to hide in its cellars or flee.

Churchill thought this 'no way to encourage men to fight to the end', axing Ironside two days later. Meanwhile, Anthony Eden, the War Secretary, sent something more inspiring to Nicholson:

> Defence of Calais to the utmost is of highest importance to our country as symbolizing our continued cooperation with France. The eyes of the Empire [24 May was Empire Day] are upon the defence of Calais and HM Government are confident you and your gallant regiments will perform an exploit worthy of the British name.

Churchill and Eden hated what they were doing. Churchill wrote later of the Greenjackets: 'These were the splendid trained troops of which we had so few.' For Eden, a 60th Rifleman himself, it was like sacrificing his family. Why Churchill chose to lift the Welsh Guards from Boulogne but sacrifice the Greenjackets at Calais remains obscure. Perhaps, in ignorance of the scale of the Continental debacle, he expected the BEF to rescue them; perhaps he believed a sacrifice would symbolize Britain's 'continued cooperation with France'. Three weeks later, he even suggested the two countries merge.

Grand diplomacy was a long way from Alec's mind as he marched from the quayside to grab some sleep on waste ground near the northern ramparts. But German shelling continued until 1.00am, and the rest did not last long because Nicholson wanted two Queen Vics companies to march to the Pont Mollien on the Canal de Calais to act in reserve for the Rifle Brigade. To fulfil this order, Tim Timpson took charge of C Company and D Company, but it took some time to get the men moving. Ellison-Macartney recalled, 'The men had to be roused individually owing to their exhaustion although when roused they accepted the new task cheerfully.' Then Alec's company was diverted into the Citadel to reinforce the 60th Rifles, only to be told it was not needed and consequently marched back to the ramparts. Finally, at 2.30am on Friday, they snatched a little sleep. Timpson, meanwhile, reported to Nicholson in his Gare Maritime cellar and was told the Greenjackets would not be evacuated.

A few yards south of the Gare Maritime, Alex Allan weighed up the day's events at Rifle Brigade headquarters. It had been 'a day of great tension', he wrote after the war. 'Not a great deal of fighting had been done by the Rifle Brigade nor were many casualties incurred, but the noise of bombs, artillery, automatic weapons and sniping; the fantastic stories put about by enemy agents; the abandonment by the French of the forts and above all the fact that no commander ever had a moment to look around him and think and plan for more than the immediate future, all tended to intensify fatigue.'

Chapter 4

No Surrender

Schaal achieved little during the first day of his assault. His men, apart from a few snipers disguised as civilians, were held outside Calais and did not impede the British as they retreated into the Old Town during the evening. He needed more men and matériel. This garrison would not melt away as had happened elsewhere; he would have to take Calais street by street, house by house. His first move, before commencing attacks on Saturday, was to send tanks through Guînes to meet the 1st Panzers east of Calais and cut off all escape routes to Dunkirk.

In London, Churchill felt the weight of his order that the Greenjackets stand and fight. In 1948, he told Robert Boothby:

> I did Calais myself. I personally gave the order to stand and fight it out to the end. I agreed to the evacuation of Boulogne with reluctance; and I think now that I ought to have ordered them to fight it out there too. But the order to [defend] Calais meant certain death or capture for almost the entire garrison.

In sacrificing 4,000 troops in sight of Dover's cliffs while Navy ships were standing offshore, was Churchill simply trying to impress the French? Later, he would say the stand at Calais was intended to hinder the German advance, contributing to Operation Dynamo, during which the bulk of the BEF was brought home from Dunkirk, the critical precondition of Britain staying in the war. This motive was, however, unclear at the time, and Nicholson still thought his men might be evacuated.

That morning, behind the new and shorter British line of waterways and ramparts, Alec greeted the dawn in an exhausted state. Once again, it was a fine morning, the weather seemingly in league with the enemy. The sun beat down and there was not a breath of wind as Alec and the men around him lay stiff and sweating on their stomachs, their battledress clinging to them, dust in their throats and their 'eyes red and sore', recalled Gordon Instone, through 'ceaseless watching in the sun-glare'.

Yet the Greenjackets fought on. In the absence of dynamite to blow the bridges, they strengthened their roadblocks and erected barricades across streets leading back from the canals and *bassins*; in houses facing the water riflemen crouched at the windows ready to fire on besiegers.

It was soon clear, however, just how precarious was the British foothold. Once the Germans realized Nicholson had abandoned Calais-St Pierre, they pushed forward, and soon after dawn a Swastika flag was flying above the Hôtel de Ville 200 yards from the new front line. Now, reconnaissance men peering from its Flemish Renaissance tower could observe troop movements inside Nicholson's shrunken perimeter, enhancing the accuracy of heavy artillery fire from outside Calais and mortar fire within. Next to them, snipers could fire on 60th Rifles officers and NCOs as they moved round their front line relaying orders to their men.

On the east of Nicholson's shrunken perimeter, Austin-Brown roused his men from their brief slumbers and, after a quick breakfast, they dug trenches on the northern rampart. These were designed for defence against attack from outside Calais, but Austin-Brown also had to reduce his men's vulnerability to sniper fire from within. At the east end was Bastion Two, abandoned by the French and now a Queen Vic strongpoint; at the west end was a water tower; to the north was the Bassin des Chasses and the start of a canal snaking round the ramparts to meet the Canal de Marck further south. In front of the Queen Vics was open space; to their right, 200 yards south, were the bombed ruins of a four-storey cellulose factory.

Entrenching tools abandoned in Kent, Alec dug with his helmet, interrupted by occasional sniper fire, and waited for the onslaught. It began at 7.00am when 69th Panzer Grenadiers opened fire from the east. Standing close by, Andy Vincent, a platoon colleague, watched as 'the Germans settled down in earnest to the task of destroying Calais and everyone in it'. Soon after dawn, artillery and mortar fire poured into the town. Fortunately, 9 Platoon was now dug in along its section of the northern rampart. Then the first Stukas appeared above. Alec tried to make himself as small as possible in his foxhole as the bombs dropped, sending plumes of earth into the air. As each wave came over, he counted the thuds as the bombs exploded and cursed the absent RAF.

In a moment of respite, a sergeant ran past dropping packets of Woodbines into the foxholes. Later, a dog joined some Queen Vics in a shell-hole and, despite the noise of battle, curled up and went to sleep. This strange little incident seemed to calm nerves. Peter Monico noted the lack of panic. After training that mostly involved 'a lot of running around with rattles and red flags' his men had gone straight into battle. He was amazed at their coolness under fire.

At 9.00am, after some sniper fire from the cellulose factory, Alec was ordered from his foxhole to help rid it of unwelcome visitors. The snipers had gone by the time he arrived, but it was a tense moment as he slipped through the gates and raced with colleagues towards the building, which had scores of windows from which snipers could fire. A sergeant was telling the men to retrace their steps when the scream of a mortar bomb in flight interrupted him. As Alec ran for the gates, one mortar landed in the yard, then another hit the factory wall, creating a cloud of dust and smoke. A thirty-minute artillery barrage followed, although casualties were light: most shells went over Alec's head into the canal behind or the narrow causeway south of the Bassin des Chasses; even those that landed nearby did little damage: typically they would sink into the soft rampart banks, throwing up plumes of sand but not exploding.

In taking the Hôtel de Ville, the Germans captured Calais' mayor, a Jewish shopkeeper called André Gerschel, and in the late morning Schaal decided to make use of this prize. His men were exhausted and RAF and Navy attacks the previous day had reduced his firepower. Might the garrison surrender without further bloodshed, he asked himself. At 11.00am, Gerschel was thrust into an armoured car displaying a white flag and driven to the Pont Richelieu. By this time, Nicholson had moved to the Citadel, where he could maintain contact with Commandant Raymond Le Tellier, the senior French officer. There, a few moments later, Gerschel was led, blindfolded, to deliver Schaal's ultimatum: Calais would be reduced to rubble unless Nicholson surrendered. Nicholson responded by placing Gerschel under guard and sending his German escort back with an unequivocal reply: 'Surrender? No, I shall not surrender. Tell [your commanders] that if they want Calais they will have to fight for it.'

Shortly afterwards, Schaal launched his full-scale attack. His artillery, reinforced by guns sent by Guderian after Boulogne fell, fired on the Citadel and Fort Risban with improved accuracy. This was because the RAF's absence left the Luftwaffe's Fieseler Storch planes free to fly over Calais marking out defenders' positions with smoke trails. Mortar bombers and machine-gunners attacked the front line; Stukas swooped down to bomb and machine-gun the defenders behind. Above them, Dornier twin-engine bombers flew in search of strategic targets.

Gerschel, meanwhile, survived the siege but died at Auschwitz. He was 'respected and courageous,' wrote Airey Neave. His dilemma 'was that of many a civic functionary in war'. If the British held out, the Old Town would be destroyed, yet as a Jew he had every reason to hate the Germans. While others fled, he had 'most bravely remained at his post'.

At this point, Nicholson made an error. Radio operators intercepted a German signal instructing infantry to attack the south-western perimeter. Nicholson decided to send two tanks and eleven Bren carriers supported by motorized infantry east along the dunes, from where they would circle round and attack the besiegers from behind. Hoskyns protested that the tanks and Bren carriers were vital to maintaining the Rifle Brigade's positions, so Nicholson cancelled the column – but not before the leading vehicles had set off and got stuck in the sand. By the time they returned, the Germans had broken through the Rifle Brigade's lines in two places and were pushing through the streets to its rear and attacking front-line platoons on three sides. This, wrote Allan, led to 'desperate close fighting' involving hand grenades and bayonet charges.

In his book, *Dunkirk: Fight to the Last Man*, Hugh Sebag-Montefiore highlighted Nicholson's mistake. Whereas previously the British had sat behind a continuous line of waterways and ramparts, now 'each company was reduced to conducting its own guerrilla war, withdrawing from street to street, from building to building, as it retreated towards the harbour often without knowing where neighbouring units were holding'.

Holding individual positions, at whatever cost, now became the prime objective. Airey Neave thought lack of sleep had dulled the Greenjackets' senses to everything except fighting Germans: 'They thought only of killing Germans and by the end of the battle took suicidal risks in hand-to-hand fighting. Their tenacity and boldness was to stagger General Schaal.'

Bill Harding described this 'desperate close fighting' in his book, *A Cockney Soldier*. As mortar bombs exploded all around, he saw a Greenjacket dragging himself along on his elbows leaving two trails of blood behind. Both feet were missing. Then, he saw riflemen with fixed bayonets run across in front of him. When the last one was hit by a mortar bomb, he 'completely disintegrated, with his head resting on his neck, his arms and legs close by'.

Most French troops wanted to surrender. On Saturday afternoon, Peter Peel's Rifle Brigade company came under fire from in front and behind on the eastern ramparts. French machine-gunners nearby raised a white flag, but a British officer took it from them. Hundreds of Frenchmen streamed into Bastion Two on the northern rampart of whom only twenty said they would fight; so the Queen Vics evicted the rest at gunpoint and blocked the entrance with cars to prevent their return.

At 3.00pm, there was another lull as Schaal issued a second ultimatum, sending a 69th Panzer Grenadier called Hoffman, accompanied by two prisoners, a French captain and a Belgian private, to the Pont Richelieu to deliver his message: the Old Town would be flattened unless Nicholson surrendered. Nicholson had just received Eden's 'eyes of the Empire' rallying call and it may have been in his mind when he wrote his response. It was later recorded in the 10th Panzers' war diary:

> 1. The answer is no as it is the British Army's duty to fight as well as it is the German's.
> 2. The French captain and the Belgian soldier having not been blindfolded cannot be sent back. The Allied commander gives his word they will be put under guard and will not be allowed to fight against the Germans.

When the blindfolded Hoffman was returned across the bridge at 4.35pm with his message, Schaal resumed his attack. As Greenjackets on the east came under renewed mortar assault, they looked behind to see the Citadel resembling 'a vast sheet of flame' according to Alex Allan, now the Rifle Brigade commander. At 6.00pm, Navy destroyers shelled German artillery outside the town and fired at Stukas coming in to attack. This, once again, lifted morale. During one raid, Alec climbed out of his foxhole to watch. As he saw the anti-aircraft shells streak across the sky, he forgot for a moment the bombs dropping around him, cheering as a Stuka plunged in flames towards the sea.

Yet the naval barrage provided only temporary respite. Towards the end of the afternoon, Schaal's tanks attacked the three bridges into the Old Town. The 60th Rifles pushed them back at two, but some Germans got across the third and occupied houses on the north bank of the water. Then, for the third and last time, Schaal demanded surrender. This time, Fieseler Storches showered the defenders with leaflets. The planes flew sufficiently low to come within Bren gun range and one was shot down by Lieutenant Jerry Duncanson, who was killed the following afternoon in the dying moments of the battle.

Schaal's leaflet demanded immediate surrender. The garrison should leave town by the Coquelles road without weapons and with their arms raised within one hour. Further resistance would be met with fresh air-raids and artillery shelling. Boulogne had capitulated at 11.30 that morning and the Greenjackets should follow suit.

But the British were not beaten. To Davies-Scourfield, the idea that he throw down his weapon and walk arms aloft down the Coquelles road seemed 'hilariously ridiculous'. Instead, he used the hour's grace to improve his platoon's positions and distribute food and ammunition. The 60th Rifles scout platoon roared with laughter. Though they were outnumbered and outgunned, their commander, Lieutenant Philip Pardoe, was confident that, at best, a reinforced 30th Brigade would break through the Germans; at worst, it would be evacuated.

At this point in the siege, after three days of sunshine and amid the destruction of battle, even getting a drink became problematic. Calais' mains had been wrecked and water had to be carried long distances. Yet the British kept their sense of humour. 'It was very hot weather, they got very hot and tired and thirsty,' wrote Davies-Scourfield. 'But their morale was cheerful. I mean they were Cockney soldiers and it takes a lot, as you know, to get a Cockney down. They were mostly Cockneys, jokes all the way through.' At one point, when 'things were really very bad and a lot of people were being killed', he entered a street so narrow that mortar bombs went over, not into it. There he found the 60th Rifles officers' mess sergeant 'with a table and a white tablecloth cooking scrambled eggs for any officer or soldier that happened to come past'.

Looking towards the sea, Alec's platoon saw a dozen prostitutes in tight satin skirts and fur jackets walking along the dunes shepherded by their madame, apparently oblivious to the explosions around them as they headed east. But the incident provoking the biggest laughs occurred at Bastion Two, where anti-aircraft artillerymen tried to repair a gun spiked by the French. The plan was to turn it inland to fire on German tanks. The gun was fired at the first tank that appeared, yet all it produced was an enormous bang, after which the barrel rolled down the bank towards French deserters, suitcases at their sides, shouting '*Guerre fini!*' They were, thought Jim Roberts of Alec's company, 'strolling along as if they were going on their summer holidays'. There were hundreds, yet none 'carried any weapons nor did they appear to have taken part in any fighting'.

This sole attempt at a heavy artillery barrage generated a roar of laughter on the ramparts, but a Headquarters Company sergeant was not amused. 'It is all right for you to laugh,' he yelled. 'What about the poor lads inside Bastion Two?' There was a hush, but later he returned from the bastion looking as black as thunder, saying, 'They're laughing their heads off like you silly buggers.'

After the one-hour delay, Schaal ordered fresh shelling then sent his tanks forward to attack the bridges into the Old Town. The 60th Rifles had to hold these bridges as long as possible, which they succeeded broadly in doing. The Rifle Brigade and the Queen Vics, under pressure from German infantry advancing along the eastern ramparts and through the woods outside, could shorten their lines even further to form a screen across the southern access to the Gare Maritime. At this point, some Queen Vics still thought they were going home. As Alec headed towards the station, he heard fresh rumours of evacuation: supposedly they would withdraw to the beach, then Navy boats would come in sufficiently close to take them off.

The Queen Vics built a barricade between the rampart and some woodpiles in the cellulose factory grounds to hold up Germans advancing from the east. Then, with Alec's company leading the way, followed by Headquarters Company then D Company, most Queen Vics on Calais' east side pulled back north east of the cellulose factory on the spit of land separating the Bassin des Chasses from the harbour; on the sand-dunes, the Rifle Brigade established trench positions east of the Bastion de l'Estran.

With only half an hour of daylight remaining, Alec and another Bren gunner were selected as the rearguard:

> Major Timpson told us, 'D Company are going to withdraw through us. We've got to sit here and wait until they all get through and Jerry is not far behind them.' So that is what we did until Vic Jessop, the D Company commander, said, 'Right, I'm the last', after which Timpson said, 'Come on, blokes, let's go.' All the time we were getting concentrated in an ever smaller space in the centre of Calais, which was burning merrily.

Austin-Brown ordered Alec's platoon and other Queen Vics, about 150 men in total, to hold a line between a Rifle Brigade roadblock at the north end of the Quai de la Loire and the water tower at the end of the Bassin des Chasses, and as night fell the riflemen selected positions among abandoned vehicles. By this time, Ellison-Macartney's men were fairly mixed up and he could do little that night to reorganize them back into platoons and companies.

As railway wagons burned in goods yards south of the station, Austin-Brown toured the line jerking his men awake. From his POW camp, he described 25 May in a letter to his wife:

> During the morning there was heavy enemy shelling and our position was twice dive-bombed and machine-gunned from the air. This was repeated in the afternoon. We had no aeroplanes, nor artillery. Some battleships bombarded the enemy positions from the sea. At dusk we again withdrew. That night there was intermittent machine-gun fire and some bombing. No sleep.

Unfortunately, not every Queen Vic moved back behind the new line. At 9.00pm, the Stukas swept over the Bassin des Chasses to attack Bastion Two. The attack caused no casualties but did create confusion and in the dark Tony Jabez-Smith led his men east not west so they dug in near a blockhouse east of the Bassin des Chasses. At first light, he discovered they were in a dangerously forward position.

That evening, Guderian's Panzer Corps diarist summed up his frustration: 'No visible result is achieved; the fighting continues and the English defend themselves tenaciously.' The 10th Panzer report was similar: 'The attack on the Old Town has been held back. The enemy fights in a most tough and ferocious manner . . . The Enemy fights with a hitherto unheard-of obstinacy. They are English, extremely brave and tenacious. They have at least one reinforced infantry regiment, armour supporting them and naval guns firing from ships in the Channel.' Schaal called a halt at 9.45pm, admitting that, 'Today's attack has shown that the enemy will fight to the last man and holds strong and up to now unshaken positions. The attack itself is at present at a standstill.'

Nicholson told his brigade staff of the latest War Office order that Calais be held 'to the last man and the last round', and during the night this message was relayed to battalion commanders. Meanwhile, Schaal grew increasingly fearful that reinforcements were crossing the Channel to support the garrison. His officers said their men had been 'finished' by the fighting, arguing the onslaught should be postponed for two days. He was, however, determined to press ahead.

Schaal was right. His colleagues' pessimism belied the extent of their gains. Their tanks had been halted on the bridges but some infantry had pushed past the British. Thus, when battle resumed the following morning, the 30th Brigade fought as isolated units. Alex Allan, having lost contact with Nicholson, summed up the position in his last signal to Dover. Timed at 7.55pm, it was an anguished plea for help:

> From Rifle Brigade Calais. Citadel a shambles. Brigadier's fate unknown. Rifle Brigade casualties may be 60 per cent. Being heavily shelled and flanked but attempting counter-attack. Am attempting contact with 60th fighting in the town. Are you sending ships? Quay is intact in spite of very severe bombardment.

Allan's signal sparked a Cabinet debate on whether an eleventh-hour rescue should be mounted. The minutes record:

> Those who believed that it was permissible to sacrifice the soldiers for the greater good held sway ... It was essential to hold on to Calais for as long as possible. If we attempted to withdraw our garrison from Calais, the German troops in Calais would immediately march on Dunkirk. A message should be sent to our troops in Calais telling them that every hour that they could hold out would be of immeasurable value to the British Army.

During the evening, therefore, the War Office signalled Nicholson:

> Every hour you continue to exist is of greatest help to the B.E.F. Government has therefore decided you must continue to fight. Have greatest admiration for your splendid stand. Evacuation will not (repeat not) take place, and craft required for above purpose are to return to Dover.

When Nicholson re-established contact with Allan, he relayed the news. Visiting Rifle Brigade HQ in a bomb crater on the northern rampart at 11.30pm, he congratulated the battalion on its efforts, declaring himself 'highly pleased and satisfied' the Germans had been held. Once again, he said Calais had to be held to the last; there would be no evacuation. With the guns silent but with Calais in flames behind them, the Greenjackets absorbed Nicholson's words. Until that evening, they still believed they would be evacuated. The latest rumour had been that ships would arrive on Sunday morning. Now it was clear they faced death or capture.

Nicholson suggested Keller's surviving tanks, the Rifle Brigade and the Queen Vics could join the 60th Rifles in a final stand at the Citadel. Allan, however, thought it would be 'most difficult' because the troops were too dispersed and contact had been lost with various units. Nicholson conceded the strength of his argument. He, therefore, wished Allan luck, said good night and returned through the Old Town's ruins to the Citadel. It was the last Allan heard from him before the surrender.

From his isolated position east of the Bassin des Chasses, Tony Jabez-Smith could make out the dark forms of Navy warships, behind which the sky was 'crossed and re-crossed with the beams of hundreds of searchlights from the English coast and from the ships'. All Calais seemed on fire, with 'red, orange and yellow flames' leaping up. Watching the flames reflected in the Bassin des Chasses, he felt he was 'witnessing the sacking of some medieval walled city'.

Chapter 5

The Last Stand and the Road to Guînes

In July 1938, the Queen Vics had held their summer camp at Lympne, near Folkestone. To mark the occasion, B Company posed for a photograph. Rifleman Alec Jay, a raw recruit of four months' service, stood fifth from the right while close by stood another recent recruit, Reg Dowell. They had different backgrounds – Alec, a Hampstead public schoolboy stockbroker, Reg, a Willesden labourer – but they became friends.

In the last stand at Calais, Reg, by then a lance corporal, was one of the battalion heroes in that darkest of dark hours – but not a lucky one. 'He was very courageous by going out on patrols and bringing back information,' wrote a colleague in a letter from POW camp eleven months later, when Dowell was still listed as 'missing'. 'He played the game of his life.' It was his last game: in the siege's final hours, he died a death so violent his body could not be recovered and buried. Thus, when he was posthumously mentioned in dispatches after the war, he was described as 'presumed died of wounds', not 'killed in action'.

Reg was Alec's closest friend to die during the siege. In February 1942, while working in a Sudeten lime quarry *Arbeitskommando*, Alec distilled his sadness into a four-line Epitaph for Rifleman Reginald Dowell:

He was an average English working man,
Who turns his hand to anything he can.
He sacrificed his life at country's call.
He had not much to give, he gave it all.

For many survivors, 26 May was the most significant day of their lives. Allan's reckoning the previous evening of 60 per cent casualties was an underestimate. His battalion began that Sunday with fewer than 300 fit men; the unwounded Queen Vics and anti-aircraft and Searchlight troops on his front totalled about 200.

The arrival of eighty-five Royal Marines led by Captain George 'Darby' Courtice on HMS *Verity* in the early hours of Saturday morning had stoked rumours that the Canadian 1st Division would soon land. This had been a last-minute decision – some of them were still in service dress when they joined the exhausted Greenjackets. Yet it soon became clear their arrival did not herald more significant reinforcements, leaving Jim Roberts to conclude their contribution to the defence was 'as useful as trying to empty the English Channel with a teaspoon'.

Some Queen Vics still hoped the Navy would rescue them. They could see Dover's white cliffs bathed in sunshine twenty-one miles across the calm blue-grey Channel. Small boats had taken off the wounded – but only the wounded. The appearance of three destroyers offshore the previous night had produced a cheer. Could their arrival, Alec asked himself, herald a full-scale evacuation after all. For an hour they bombarded German positions, but they had vanished by dawn.

It was time for desperate measures. For two days, stragglers had gathered around the harbour hoping to catch a boat home. Some were drunk, having plundered the station hotel wine cellar. Now, Greenjacket officers thrust rifles into their hands and ordered them to head for the ramparts.

The ammunition shortage was as acute as the lack of men. The previous day, the Rifle Brigade and Queen Vics had exhausted their supplies, including 20,000 rounds landed by the Navy. Their few Bren guns and their rifles became easily clogged with sand, with the result, said Allan, that 'many excellent targets must have been inadequately dealt with' during Sunday's fighting. His battalion's few 3-inch mortar shells were quickly exhausted.

With a few hundred weary, hungry and thirsty men at his command, without artillery or air cover, Allan prepared for Schaal's final assault. His men were utterly exhausted but he thought they could resist for a few more hours. Standing at a signal box in the middle of his front line running from the Bassin des Chasses to the Bassin Carnot, Allan gave orders for the day at 4.30am: 'All troops stay in these positions to the last. There will be no further withdrawals.' He then repeated Eden's message that 'the eyes of the whole Empire' were on the Greenjackets. Shortly afterwards, shells began crashing on to the Gare Maritime, shattering windows and setting cattle-trucks alight in the marshalling yard. It was the start of Schaal's heaviest barrage. Guderian had given him all the XIX Panzer Corps' artillery, double the guns of the previous day. Ellison-Macartney recalled that the explosions 'hardly roused the exhausted troops'.

In the early hours of the morning, thirty-five Royal Marines equipped with a Vickers machine gun were placed under Allan's command, enabling him to reshuffle the Queen Vics. Initially, Alec's platoon pulled back to the Gare Maritime. This inspired fresh optimism that they were going home, intensified when an embarkation officer began rounding up riflemen. Austin-Brown wrote later to his wife: 'At dawn we moved to the quay. We had hoped that we would be evacuated but there were no ships to be seen and the prospects appeared very gloomy.'

At 8.00am, the Stukas arrived for their first assault, coming over in squadrons of three; their second began at 11.00am. At any one time, Alec could see three squadrons, one making its run in V formation, the second circling, waiting to attack, the third returning to base to reload. As the squadrons came in, each pilot would peel off, dive almost vertically towards his target, release his bombs then flatten out and climb. Sometimes, it seemed as if the pilots were locking eyes with him and heading straight for his foxhole. Soon, fresh fires were burning throughout the Old Town and harbour, with smoke and dust making visibility a problem for both sides.

The Queen Vics had ringside seats for the early-morning attack. Turning their weapons to the sky, Bren gunners tried to bring the Stukas down. Despite the punishment they were taking, the men 'behaved splendidly and, although tired and dazed, did not seem to be the least perturbed,' wrote 'Tim' Timpson in his POW memoir; Alex Allan thought the Greenjackets attacked the Stukas from their exposed positions 'as coolly as participants in a pheasant shoot'. At one point ammunition ran low, but Second Lieutenant Tom 'Fi-Fi' Field-Fisher, the Queen Vics' transport officer, rounded up men to distribute bullets discovered in an abandoned truck at the station. Like most Queen Vics, 'Fi-Fi' was captured but was called to the Bar in his absence in 1942. At Nuremberg, he prosecuted Germans who committed POW atrocities in 1940.

Guderian was perplexed. The German XIX Corps 26 May diary entry stated:

> 0900 hrs. The combined bombing attack and artillery bombardment on Calais Citadel and on the suburb of Les Baraques are carried out between 0900 and 1000 hrs. No visible result is achieved; the fighting continues and the English defend themselves tenaciously.

Overnight, the 10th Schützen Brigade, comprising Schaal's infantry, established a new command post in the Calais Theatre on the Boulevard Léon Gambetta in Calais-St Pierre. Colonel Wolfgang von Fischer, the commanding officer, described the attack in a Nazi-era book:

> At about 09.00 hours [German time], the first Stukas roar in. With deafening crashes, bomb after bomb does destructive work. Red flames flicker in various places, thick smoke and sand clouds rise skywards and large chunks of masonry spin through the air. The effect is overwhelming. The preparation for the attack is rounded off by the artillery with its usual superbly directed bombardment, so that the instant the last shell falls, our men charge forward into the attack, confident of victory.

Of this final assault, Alec recalled, 'Sunday came and we still fought on, having to withdraw yard by yard, house by house, being Stuka'ed unmercifully, being mortared and being shelled by German heavy tanks.' He witnessed many individual acts of heroism. One corporal from a first-floor flat 'dropped a grenade through the turret of a German tank and put it out of action'. But he knew the Greenjackets 'were really fighting a losing battle'. From his position nearby, Bill Harding heard shouts of 'rapid fire' and watched the Greenjackets send forward 'a wall of steel, deterring any German attempt to overrun us'. There was 'a grim defiance about it all'.

For Cockney 60th Rifleman Edward Doe, the lack of bullets was desperate: 'There were chaps pleading for ammunition and being told "I'm sorry, you can't have any of mine; I might need what I've got".' The bullets that were available could not stop German tanks, as Doe discovered when, for the first time, he fired a Boys anti-tank gun, 'a terrifying weapon' that had to be gripped 'like grim death because it would dislocate your shoulder if you didn't'. Doe fired from his bridge barricade at a tank fifty yards away, scored a direct hit but merely scraped its paintwork: 'That's all it done, it never penetrated, it just bounced off; it made a noise like a ping-pong ball – "ping" and that was it.' An officer nearby said, 'Leave the blasted thing there, Doe, get the hell out of it.' He did so just in time: the tank blew half the bridge wall away when it returned fire.

This was street fighting at its most basic, combat for which the Queen Vics had no training. Corporal Nick Day described how he would identify houses occupied by German snipers by watching windows and doors for any movement, while keeping himself concealed: 'It was mostly self-preservation, I should think, the way we were fighting. Nobody wanted to be a hero.' The instructions were: 'Get him if you can and the least you expose yourself the better.'

After the war, a 10th Panzer officer told Davies-Scourfield the Germans thought they faced 'a very strong force in front of them' and had been 'absolutely astounded at the heavy casualties they suffered from small arms'. Yet Davies-Scourfield regretted the Greenjackets' passivity. They were 'a bit bewildered' by street fighting and, if they had been trained, they might have acquitted themselves better 'by getting into alternative positions and changing round a bit more'. Instead, amid the smoke and dust, riflemen would get in position, sit behind their weapons and wait to be killed or forced out. 'We had our backs to the sea, literally.' In retrospect, he was amazed he did not think about surrender until the end.

The Germans knew more about street fighting. As they advanced, they would seize crossroads, establishing mortar and machine-gun positions to support further advances. Davies-Scourfield was astonished by the speed and accuracy of German mortaring: 'If you'd gone out of your cellar or your building and stood talking to a chap in the street almost anywhere a mortar shell would land very close to you ... within five or six, seven or eight seconds ... It wasn't worth standing anywhere in the open.'

As the morning developed, the German tank commanders realized the British anti-tank guns were useless and became bolder, shooting down narrow streets to open them up for infantry. At one point, Schaal was so confident the battle was won he withdrew his tanks to coastal positions to forestall the rumoured arrival of British reinforcements. Fischer was less sanguine. In his wartime account, he wrote:

> From our observation post we hear increasing machine-gun and rifle fire; the enemy has come back to life and is fighting for his very existence. Individual groups of shock troops have penetrated the citadel but are pushed back by a British counter-attack almost to their starting point. On the southern edge of the old town, almost all the enemy's machine guns are back in operation, preventing us from crossing the canal, exactly as before.

In response, Schaal ordered further artillery attacks on Fort Risban and the Citadel and sent his tanks back into the Old Town to support Fischer's infantry. Guderian visited his headquarters at lunchtime to discuss halting the attack and having 'the town destroyed by the Luftwaffe' instead. But Schaal insisted Calais would fall that afternoon. He was right. After 1.00pm, the garrison's position worsened, with the Germans taking ground and holding it. In the west, Bastion 11 fell while the 60th Riflemen defending the Old Town's southern bridges were forced back to a new line stretching from the harbour to the Place Norvège in the south-east. At 2.30pm, Fischer told Schaal the British would crumble within an hour or two.

House by house, the Germans mopped up pockets of resistance as they advanced towards the Citadel and the harbour. Without a unified command, some Greenjackets surrendered as their bullets ran out, some hid in cellars until rooted out, others fought into the afternoon.

The Germans suspected foul play. 'The British now seek to attain their objective by trickery,' wrote Fischer. 'They hoist white flags, only to receive the unsuspecting approach of our brave assault troops with machine-gun fire from various quarters. A new crisis has developed at the very moment that victory seems within our grasp.' He was wrong. As on the previous day, the only white flags raised in surrender that morning were French; the Green-jackets maintained discipline. The first sign the French were weakening came at 8.00am when troops near Fort Risban raised a white flag. Alex Allan per-suaded Captain Lambertye to order the flag be taken down, but it was soon flying again as Fort Risban came under Stuka attack. In another incident, a French civilian ran in front of a 60th Rifleman waving a white flag. In response, the soldier shot him dead, behaviour that Philip Pardoe thought typical of his men: surrender was 'simply unthinkable and it was absolutely natural to kill anybody waving a white flag'.

Organized resistance was, however, becoming impossible as the Germans moved through the streets and turned to attack the 60th Rifles from the rear.

As commanding officer, Lieutenant Colonel Euan Miller reluctantly accepted that further resistance could not be coordinated. Having lost contact with the Gare Maritime defenders, it was 'every man for himself' – his men should break up into twos and threes, hide until dark, then try to slip out of Calais and head for Dunkirk.

Once the 69th Panzer Grenadiers had taken Fort Risban, they concentrated for their final assault on the Citadel. By 3.00pm, it was surrounded by tanks. Then German infantry fought their way across the canal to the south, forced open the gate and mounted the ramparts. Once again, the French caved in first, as Nicholson discovered when a French sailor ran towards him shouting, 'Gentlemen, the French commander has surrendered.' This produced a cheer from French soldiers nearby. This shocked Nicholson, who now faced being captured, although he could not surrender on behalf of his brigade because communications had broken down the previous evening. There was, therefore, no formal garrison surrender. Having split into small groups, the Green-jackets were hunted down, killed or captured piecemeal.

Pardoe's agonising moment of surrender came as he hid with three men on the first floor of a house. Peering through the curtains, he saw Germans going from door to door down the street, finally arriving next door. It was the biggest dilemma of his life. He could kill the leading German as he entered the house but others would follow. 'The inspiring yet daunting thing' was he knew his men would accept his orders. He had no one from whom to take advice yet nothing in his training prepared him for this moment. Eventually, he told his men to lay down their weapons and, when the Germans entered the house shouting 'Come out, Tommies!' he went downstairs with his hands up.

The Germans were also closing in on the Gare Maritime. Units advancing from the east took Bastion Two then linked up with men advancing from the south to hold the southern and eastern sides of the Bassin des Chasses. By this time the ramparts near the Gare Maritime offered little protection – the eastern slope was open to German fire from the east and Queen Vics on the western slope were vulnerable to fire from the town. By lunchtime, German mortars were landing on them from the cellulose factory, from railway tracks south of the station and from the recently-captured Fort Risban across the harbour.

Under cover of this mortar barrage, German infantry advanced, bringing the defenders within range of machine-gun fire. On the sand-dunes separating the *bassin* from the sea the Germans captured the blockhouse at its eastern end and by 1.30pm they were 400 yards short of the Rifle Brigade trenches in front of the Bastion de l'Estran. These advances compressed the area of Calais still occupied by the Rifle Brigade and Queen Vics down to little more than a school sports ground.

And yet, the Greenjackets fought on, their spirits high even as their fortunes waned. 'The hour before the end should have been the worst part of it,' thought one rifleman, 'but surprisingly it wasn't.' Shells were falling around the station and along the Bassin des Chasses banks and the area was littered with corpses. There could be no more illusions about rescue, and the Queen Vics decided 'the only thing to do was to make the best of it and an almost ebullient gaiety had begun to enliven the proceedings'. Everyone seemed in good spirits, cracking jokes and swearing, with one Great War veteran reducing Alec's platoon to giggles when he said, 'You know, it's too bad. This is the second bloody war I've been in and I haven't advanced yet.' At this point of maximum danger, the comradeship was intense. Dennis Saaler of B Company, the Army's youngest sergeant, recalled the situation shortly before he died seven decades later: 'The QVRs were a close family. We fought for each other.'

The Germans overran the Queen Vics nearest the cellulose factory at about 2.30pm, forced the Marines back from positions across the railway tracks and dislodged the Greenjackets from ramparts west of the Bassin des Chasses.

Alex Allan tried to hold the Gare Maritime to provide a refuge for 60th Riflemen fleeing the Old Town. Two platoons, therefore, established new positions there while the Marines brought their Vickers gun back to Bastion One to provide covering fire for scattered groups of infantrymen running towards the station and beyond. From 2.30pm, however, the Germans opened up a creeping barrage of mortar fire that moved northwards up the quays and platforms. In response, Allan gave the order to evacuate, prompting a stream of frightened unarmed soldiers to emerge from the cellars, further complicating the defenders' task.

As the stragglers ran towards the sand-dunes, a Very light fired from the cellulose factory gave the 69th Panzer Grenadiers the signal to advance. Pushing through the station, they sprayed machine gun bullets around, producing a sound like a swarm of bees as they ricocheted off train undercarriages. By 3.00pm they were only 200 yards from Bastion One and the tunnel beneath it, where many Greenjackets had retreated, taking casualties from machine-gunners firing from Fort Risban. There at Bastion One and on the sand-dunes nearby the Rifle Brigade and Queen Vic remnants made their last stand. In the final minutes of the battle just a few score were left to defend an area about 300 yards square between the harbour entrance and the sea.

Having abandoned the station, Allan rounded up Alec and other Queen Vics including 'Taffy' Mathias and George Chapman to reinforce Rifle Brigade troops led by Major Peter Brush and Peter Peel trying to halt the German advance from trenches in front of the Bastion de l'Estran. Facing mortar fire, they had to make do with rifles, one Lewis machine gun and one Bren gun. Now, reinforced, they could counter-attack.

If Calais was the hinge on which Alec's life turned, this was the moment of movement. Years later, he would tell the story of the few minutes that transformed his world view, his psychological wounds as open and bloody as on the day they were sustained:

> We had been taking an almighty pasting particularly from a machine gun somewhere out on the sand dunes. Brush called for volunteers to attack the machine gun nest, which was on high ground with a commanding view over the dunes. Chapman turned to the Queen Vics and said, 'Come on you lot – fixed swords.' The tradition in the rifle regiments is that you never fix swords, which everyone else calls bayonets, unless you are going to use them, and we went out to try and deal with this machine gun nest and deal with it we did.

This was warfare at its most basic. Making their way through the undergrowth, the mixed group of a dozen Greenjackets came to a clearing from which they could see five or six Germans. Taffy Mathias, like Alec, had vivid memories of the incident:

> They had not seen us and so when we broke out of our shelter they were completely surprised. The clearing was about 100 yards across and we raced across as fast as we could. Time seemed to stop and I was aware that we were all shouting and yelling. There was a young, blond German in front of me and then he was not there and it was all over ... I had often wondered how I would react to such a situation. I found that it was all a sort of make-believe and a jumbled dream at the time.

'In ten minutes I must have gone back 2,000 years,' Alec recalled. 'We were complete savages. Every bit of civilisation had gone from me. I was running like a dervish, running as fast as I could towards this machine-gun nest. We suffered a lot of casualties but we did put the machine-gun nest out of action.' Thus Alec crossed a line to which few people come close, as they contemplate military morality from the comfort of their homes. This was war undiluted by distance. This was not killing with a rifle from hundreds of yards away, where the target is identified only by uniform and helmet. This was war as a desperate life-or-death struggle with a single opponent whom one has to kill to avoid being killed. 'The minute it was all over something suddenly hit me. I realized what we'd been doing, which was killing people – not from a distance of 20,000 feet like a bomber crew or a distance of 600 yards like a sniper but from a few inches away. And I was quietly but very comprehensively sick. War is not a civilising influence.'

Despite such counter-attacks, the Germans pressed forward and shortly after 3.00pm broke through between the fort and the sea. With the fort surrounded, the British inside surrendered. Its thick walls provided a shield against ground fire but there was nothing inside to protect defenders against mortars. Some troops fought on in the trenches beyond but they too were soon surrounded.

The end came at about 3.30pm. Having captured the Bastion de l'Estran, the Germans mounted a machine gun at its gates facing Bastion One and aimed it at the tunnel beneath. At this point, they were already spraying bullets into the other end from Fort Risban. The tunnel was the Queen Vics' regimental aid post and its side chambers housed wounded men being tended by British medics and French nurses. The conditions were gruesome. As the battle raged, the Queen Vics' medical officer improvised with a knife to carry out amputations. Then he found a hacksaw, sterilised it and put it into service.

Alongside the wounded, the tunnel became crowded with stragglers. Meanwhile, on the mound above, Queen Vics led by Captain John 'Tarzan' Palmer continued to fight, and Captain Monico organized reinforcements in the final minutes from men in the tunnel. 'The adjutant called for all QVRs to come outside, which they all did at once,' recalled Timpson. 'They were sent to reinforce the firing line on top. The adjutant assembled the sergeants of other units and got them to collect small parties of their own men who were still in possession of firearms and in a fit state to fight and to take them up also into the firing-line.'

'At the end we were very short,' recalled Monico. 'We could not have gone on – there was nothing left to fight with.' He had scrounged ammo in the town but had the Queen Vics faced an infantry assault it would have been quickly exhausted. Now he asked himself whether the only alternative to being killed for the sake of being killed was surrender. In the tunnel below, Austin-Brown thought the troops 'were in a peculiar state owing to lack of sleep and food and continual bombing and enemy fire'.

There was no final frontal charge, just intensive mortar and machine-gun fire. 'The Germans decided to pound the troops to pieces. There was no point in trying to storm us,' said Monico. Shells were landing on troops defending the bastion and at the tunnel entrances below. 'The wounded were getting killed in the tunnels – the Germans did not know it was a makeshift hospital … the position was hopeless.' Meanwhile, the men of Alec's platoon whispered words of reassurance to the dying and tried to smile encouragingly.

From the Bastion de l'Estran a few hundred yards away, a captured officer, Second Lieutenant Richard Wood, appeared under escort at the tunnel with a white flag tied to his rifle to parlay with the defenders. Speaking first to Austin-Brown, he said the Bastion de l'Estran had surrendered and the Bastion One troops must cease firing too or face being shelled until no one was left standing. Austin-Brown said Bastion de l'Estran's surrender did not necessarily involve the surrender of Bastion One, but Ellison-Macartney, by then with a bullet wound in his hand and quite groggy, overruled him, telling the Greenjackets remnants to lay down their arms. From his prison camp cell, he wrote, 'The Germans held the fort which dominated the tunnel and could at any moment reopen fire and annihilate the defence. Nothing but useless slaughter was to be gained by further resistance.' Austin-Brown told his wife: 'As we were surrounded and there was no hope of escape, in order to avoid further bloodshed the CO surrendered.'

Alec described the denouement as bullets thudded into the earth around him:

> Gradually, yard by yard, cricket pitch by cricket pitch, we were pushed back into the area around the last fort and at around 3.30 in the afternoon when I had run out of Bren gun ammunition and all I had was six rounds in my revolver, the word was passed through that further resistance was useless and that the white flag was being run up. We were told to lay down our arms and the next thing I knew was there was a very large, very aggressive German soldier ripping away at my revolver, which was still on a lanyard round my neck, putting the muzzle within an inch of my nose and yelling, '*Soll ich? Soll ich?*' which I jolly well knew was German for 'Shall I? Shall I?' Fortunately, he didn't.

A few yards away, a D Company officer took out his white handkerchief, waved it and turned to his men saying, 'Sorry fellows, it's bloody hopeless.' Not everyone stopped firing. On the top of the bastion, Sergeant Major Freddie Walter and Dennis Saaler saw unarmed British soldiers with their hands aloft being marched from the Bastion de l'Estran towards them and were told arrangements were being made to surrender Bastion One; but they refused to believe this until Ellison-Macartney arrived to deliver his bitter message. The position, he said, was that, as the last group holding out, they were surrounded, adding that if there was further resistance the enemy would open fire on the wounded in the tunnel below. He told Walter the enemy 'could concentrate all his tanks, mortars and infantry on us, and already had them in position, and his Stukas would again be brought into action, against which we, on the top of the tunnel, had absolutely no protection'. Surrender terms had been concluded so the men had to drop their weapons. 'This we reluctantly proceeded to do,' said Walter, 'breaking our arms until a German officer brandishing a pistol and looking exceedingly angry ordered us to desist.'

Even after Walter's surrender, there was more shooting when twenty riflemen unaware of Bastion One's surrender tried to establish a line of defence at a road junction nearby. The Germans had reached the junction, but troops led by Tony Rolt, the rally driver, charged forward, killing some and driving the others back. In this last act of defiance, Rolt used up the bullets in his two revolvers and only surrendered after he learned the Greenjackets in the Bastion had been overwhelmed.

At this point, Airey Neave lay wounded in the tunnel. Of the fighting spirit he witnessed, he wrote:

> Few ordinary soldiers in the streets and sand-dunes had time to ponder the strategic importance of the battle. They were in a hand-to-hand fight – bayonets were used more than once – to prevent the capture of the town … They were fighting for their lives and never more boldly than after 1.00pm on the 26th … Many of the younger men of the Rifle Brigade and their officers, although tired, were still fighting as if this were the last stages of a football match. Shouts of encouragement, even laughter, came from the trenches in the sand-dunes.

For some Queen Vics, surrender felt inglorious. For others, it felt honourable – they fought hard; men who a few months previously had been civilians had confronted their fears. They had faced an onslaught from an overwhelmingly stronger enemy and had surrendered when encircled and having exhausted their ammunition. To Alec, it seemed like a modern-day replay of the Battle of Thermopylae in which a tiny Greek force held off a Persian army for seven days. Though the Persians triumphed at Thermopylae, the Greeks defeated their invasion after a year. For soldiers captured at Calais in 1940 victory would be five years in coming.

In London that day, Churchill's War Cabinet began a three-day debate over whether to accede to France's request that Benito Mussolini mediate an armistice that would have led to Britain disarming and abandoning parts of the Empire to the Axis Powers. Yet part of his mind was focussed on Calais: 'It was the only time during the war that I couldn't eat', he told Boothby. General 'Pug' Ismay, who was with him at the time, wrote:

> This decision affected us all very deeply, especially perhaps Churchill. He was unusually silent during dinner that evening, and he ate and drank with evident distaste. As we rose from the table, he said, 'I feel physically sick.' He has quoted these words in his memoirs, but he does not mention how sad he looked as he uttered them.

* * *

Once resistance had ceased, the Germans herded the remnants of Bastion One's defenders still standing – about 150 men – into the rubble-strewn area in front of the fort. With their faces pale and covered with stubble, their eyes bloodshot from lack of sleep, their throats sore through breathing smoke and their tattered uniforms covered in mud, grease and dried blood, they learned the meaning of surrender. As they walked between two rows of Panzer Grenadiers sporting hand-held machine guns – a weapon Alec had not seen before – the humiliation sank in. Friends of years' standing would not make eye contact for fear of seeing the hopelessness each one felt.

Having been assembled, they were ordered to sit bunched against each other while a Panzer Grenadier colonel, whose smile revealed a mouth full of gold teeth, called for the senior British officer. As a regular, Alex Allan led the defence, but John Ellison-Macartney outranked him and thus stepped forward, his hand bandaged.

'Our colonel called for anybody who could speak German,' recalled Alec, also on his feet despite shrapnel wounds showing through torn battledress trousers. Armed with his Higher School Certificate in German, he stepped forward. 'The Colonel then said to me: "Can you translate what this officer is saying to me?" And this German colonel looked at our colonel and then he looked at this sorry little band of those of us that were left behind and said: "Is this all there are of you?" And that's the nearest thing to a compliment I ever got from a German.'

The two colonels shook hands and Ellison-Macartney turned to address the captives. They had, he said, fought a gallant fight against overwhelming forces; the surrender had been the only course left open but it was honourable. He then passed on Alec's translation: the German commanding officer congratulated the British on their fierce resistance, expressed his surprise at their small numbers and lack of arms and assured them they would be well treated.

After this speech, a Wehrmacht *Dolmetscher* (interpreter) stepped forward and warned the captives they would be shot if they tried to escape and would be punished if they concealed weapons. They were then grouped by regiment and told to wait for ambulances to collect the wounded. German soldiers, meanwhile, amused themselves riding captured motorcycles round Bastion One. Andy Vincent thought the ceremony ridiculous, as if the Queen Vics were members of a defeated cricket team, hearing cries of 'Bad luck, sir!' before going in for tea and crumpets.

The Germans were genuinely surprised by the resistance. At the Citadel, a German officer asked a British captain where the heavy guns were. When the captain replied there were none, he said, 'I cannot believe that men with only rifles held up my army.' As Nicholson was led away to Fischer's headquarters, his officer escort said in French, 'You have fought very courageously.'

Why did Alec fight to his last Bren-gun bullet when the situation appeared hopeless? The ethics of surrender were not part of his training. During the Great War, soldiers surrendering without serious wounds were stigmatized. Mass surrenders, such as those of the 80,000 men who capitulated in Singapore, were yet to happen. Most soldiers still thought only of victory or death. Ellison-Macartney went to war 'magnificently unprepared for anything'. He thought he might be killed or maimed but had never considered imprisonment until he was told on Calais' sand-dunes he was to have 'the honour of being a guest of the great German Reich'.

Yet officers such as Ellison-Macartney and riflemen such as Alec decided individually there came a time when surrender was correct. Alec thought it right to continue killing Germans as long as possible – as he did in the siege's dying moments – but there was a point when killing one last German and sacrificing one's own life achieved nothing. Instead he would survive to fight another day.

As the dispirited Greenjackets were corralled at bayonet point, Navy guns sprang into action. The prisoners broke out in ironic cheers; the Germans were furious – but victors and vanquished hit the deck as some shells fell short, crashing into the dunes. One German officer demanded the British contact the ship's captain to tell him to stop firing. They refused. Then the shelling stopped and an eerie silence descended over Calais' burning ruins. The Navy appeared to have vanished, although HMS *Gulzar*, a wireless station motorboat, did return to port after midnight searching for survivors. Despite coming under attack, *Gulzar* hovered close to a pier long enough for forty-seven men hiding beneath it to leap on board.

Of the moment of victory, Fischer declared: 'We hold the Old Town, the Citadel and the entrance to the port. A jubilant mood prevails in the command posts in the Opera House.' The War Office might have dismissed Calais as a port 'of no importance' but the future 10th Panzer commanding officer was convinced of its value: 'A stubborn and ferocious struggle was needed to wrest this fortress, Britain's gateway to France, from the enemy. It was precisely the unexpectedly obstinate British defence that proved to us how much store they set by the irreplaceable port city and thus how painfully they must be feeling its final loss.' In his wartime narrative, Fischer failed to identify Nicholson's brigade accurately. Years later, however, Queen Vic veterans smiled wryly on learning he had said his opponents belonged to 'the Queen Victoria Brigade, a formation well known in English military and colonial history'. Greenjacket regulars were not so amused.

Prisoners who could walk were now marched, hands on their helmets, from the surrender points to a concentration area. Their captors' behaviour varied. A Queen Vics officer who asked if the British might smoke was told officers might smoke but not their men. 'In that case I won't smoke,' he replied. The respect German officers showed to their opposite numbers surprised some brought up on Great War stories of Hun bestialities and were well aware of atrocities in Poland the previous autumn. The 10th Panzer officers seemed keen to make a good impression as they offered their captives chocolate and cigarettes. 'For you there will be no prison, only honourable captivity,' one said. 'That is what our Leader has said.'

'The war is over for you, my gallant friends,' declared a *Feldwebel* (sergeant). 'The victorious German Army will be in Paris in two weeks and a fortnight later the Wehrmacht will be marching through the streets of your famous London. Meanwhile you are all going to Germany. But do not worry, in a couple of months, maybe three, the war will be over and you will be sent back to England. We are not barbarians.'

Yet the other ranks were treated very differently, being called '*Schweine-hunden*' (pig dogs). The first humiliation Alec faced was being stripped of possessions. First, he was told to place the contents of his pockets on the ground alongside his helmet; then he was sent to a line of guards who searched each man – if something significant was found the consequence was a punch in the face. In addition to concealed weapons and potential escape materials, the Germans were looking for Army paybooks, useful documents should they wish to impersonate British soldiers in future battles. Some wanted victory mementoes. Many captives lost their helmets to souvenir hunters, along with wedding rings, watches and family photographs. They were wryly amused to be told jewellery would be returned after Britain surrendered. Photographs that served no purpose as souvenirs were torn up and discarded.

Germany had signed the Geneva Convention, which stated that prisoners on capture 'must not be threatened, insulted, or exposed to unpleasantness or disadvantages of any kind whatsoever'. Nor should they be tortured to gain intelligence. Having put up such resistance, however, some Queen Vics feared they would be slaughtered. Edward Watson, just eighteen when captured, said his captors 'didn't sort of wallop you straight away but they were very rough, they were very frightening'. Watson feared he would be 'taken back and shot'. Norman 'Ruby' Rubenstein, a Searchlight Territorial who lived in Frognal Lane, Hampstead, near Alec's old school, heard rumours 'that we were going to be shot, that the Germans were cut off and did not know what to do with us'.

Such fears were not entirely fanciful. For Waffen SS troops, France was a dress rehearsal for their later butchery in Russia. On the two days after Calais surrendered, SS men executed ninety-seven Royal Norfolk prisoners near Le Paradis and eighty Royal Warwickshire prisoners at Wormhout. Colonial French troops had most to fear. At Chartres, 180 Senegalese were massacred after surrendering. A battlefield massacre was not, however, the Greenjackets' fate. The 10th Panzer officers might humiliate their captives, but killing them was not yet on the agenda in 1940.

An hour before dusk, the Queen Vics were told to form up in rows of three. Not everyone obeyed immediately. While some sat and stared at the cliffs of Dover turning pink in the early evening sun, others had fallen asleep in their exhaustion, and the Germans spent the next few minutes running around kicking them, shouting '*Raus, raus! Alle Mann raus!*' ('Out, out! All men out!'). Then to the cry of '*Los*' ('Move off'), they headed south. All had barely slept for five nights; they were hungry, most having not had a cooked meal during the siege, and thirsty.

Stumbling along, dishevelled and grimy, they were pushed, to a chorus of shouting by German infantrymen, through what had been their lines of defence on the northern ramparts. This had been the location of the Queen Vics' battalion headquarters and most of the military transport commandeered during the siege was still there. It was a pitiful sight – dead colleagues lying mutilated across their weapons, the seriously wounded, unable to stand, pleading for water. 'Get me help, boys, get me help. They've shot me in the goolies,' one Greenjacket cried as Alec shuffled by. There was nothing he could do. When Queen Vics stooped to tend wounded men they were shunted forward with rifle butts to continue their nightmare journey. Alec recognized the body of a friend he had last seen wounded but croaking the regimental marching song to cheer up colleagues. To the tune of Green Grow the Rushes, O! the last verse went:

I'll give you ten, Sir. Way! Way! For the Black Brigade.
What are your ten, Sir?
Ten for the Ten Commandments,
Nine for the Cooks of the Army Shield,
And Eight for the eight bold Captains;
Seven for the seven pals in my tent,
And Six for the Cook-house Door, Boys;
Five for the rest of the Black Brigade,
And Four for the Sergeant-Major;
Three, three for the Colonel;
Two, two for Myself and You, and Here's a jolly good Health, Oh!
One for the Queen Victoria's, the best of the whole Brigade, Sir.

The words ran through Alec's head as he stumbled forward. Nearby he could see RSM Chapman, wounded in the leg and limping, and beside him, his company sergeant major, 'Tex' Austin.

From Bastion Two, the Queen Vics were pushed south parallel to the eastern ramparts and around Calais-St Pierre. As the POWs clambered over the rubble past burning tanks and the remains of an RAF plane, the town's citizens emerged from their cellars to watch. At one point, a tank thundered towards the prisoners, causing them to jump sideways to avoid being run over. As it swept by, its commander looked back and laughed.

Being marched through the scenes of defeat was bad enough, but there was worse to come. As the British moved through the town, they were swamped by thousands of French soldiers – the Germans said later they captured 20,000 French, Belgians and Dutch at Calais. Alec was dumbfounded. Some Frenchmen had fought, but not these men. They looked fresh, clean-shaven and in good spirits. Most had bulging suitcases and large rucksacks, off which hung cooking utensils and water bottles. They had not fought in the siege, but had simply prepared themselves for capture. Unlike the British, they had not been robbed of possessions. 'Well, where the hell were they?' asked Edward

Doe as he watched the parade. 'We never saw them; they weren't with us when we were fighting.' Doe later discovered, 'They'd simply downed tools early ... and hid in the cellars.'

At dusk, the Greenjackets moved into open country on the St Omer road. Behind them, the flames from burning oil tanks resembled a beacon. Beyond, they could just make out anti-aircraft searchlights in the sky above Dover – so near but so far. The Germans provided no water, and for hours the defeated British stumbled on, the walking wounded supported by the fit. Some fainted, and after a kick to ensure they were not faking they were left lying where they fell. Later they were hauled on to lorries and reunited with the rest.

Finally, the column arrived at Guînes, the scene, as Alec knew from his history lessons, of the extravagant Field of Cloth of Gold meeting between Henry VIII and François I. The atmosphere on the evening of 26 May 1940 was rather different. As the British trudged along, the townsfolk watched in silence. Some women brought out buckets of water but German guards, screaming obscenities, kicked them over and pushed the women away with rifle butts. During subsequent days, similar incidents took place time and again.

Eventually they arrived at a church on a hill, and a German officer with aquiline features made an ominous announcement: 'Tomorrow you will march much further than today. We will rest here now. Any attempt to escape at any time will mean instant execution. New guards will take over tomorrow.' Frenchmen were allowed first into the church, leaving room for few Britons. The rest bedded down in the graveyard, perhaps, thought Alec, a German idea of a joke. Shoehorned in, the wounded and the fit had to sleep on grave-stones or on bare earth. No food or water was issued. The church had a tap but few could reach it, while the single lavatory soon became blocked, leaving most men to empty their bowels outside. One soldier tripped over a wounded colleague and bent down to help, but the man died in his arms. The French, meanwhile, resting comfortably among the pews, were soon tucking into the bread, cheese and wine they had carried into captivity.

Stephen Houthakker collapsed into 'the sleep of one who was completely oblivious to his surroundings. What pleasure was that sleep! Dreams of pleasant days that seemed centuries ago.' For others, the night was less peaceful. Tony Jabez-Smith, concussed by a bullet that dented his helmet, had nightmares during which he rose to his feet, shouting unintelligibly.

And what of Alec, the British Jew who had considered death or victory but not capture by a regime dedicated to extinguishing his race? 'I stumbled into that churchyard at Guînes downcast, dispirited, dejected and disillusioned, to pass my first night as a prisoner-of-war. I had come to Calais on a one-way ticket; there was no passage home.' A few officers and NCOs were already contemplating escape, but Alec's first response to a surrender so shocking and so sudden was apathy. In four days of battle he had had perhaps a dozen hours' sleep and now, with the adrenalin rush gone, all he could contemplate were the consequences of defeat.

Graham Palmer, a Territorial held in captivity alongside Alec, wrote in his book, *Prisoner of Death*, that he felt like a boxer thrust into the ring with one hand tied behind his back, facing inevitable slaughter. Cheated of a fair fight, he now 'faced a diabolical future', a reward for War Office ineptitude. Nothing would ever make up for his humiliation and the inhuman treatment he was now to receive from his 'swaggering conquerors'.

Chapter 6

The Longer Road to Guînes: Childhood

A people tormented
Crushed by oppression
And our tragic faces
Have a wild expression.
We talk, but as well we listen
As though someone was near
Who was hearing each syllable
With a spy's ear.
Our one hope is that soon
Will arise a Maccabeus
Who will lead us from our persecution
And once more free us.

On 7 November 1938, a Polish Jew assassinated a German diplomat in Paris, an event Hitler used as a pretext to launch a pogrom against Germany's Jews, adding new levels of violence to the discrimination they already suffered. His propaganda minister, Joseph Goebbels, said it would not be surprising if people were so outraged by the murder that they ransacked Jewish businesses, synagogues and community centres; the Nazis should not openly organize 'spontaneous outbursts' but neither should they oppose them. Within hours, they had launched *Kristallnacht* – the Night of Broken Glass, the starting gun for Hitler's Final Solution. More than 90 Jews were killed and 30,000 sent to concentration camps, where 1,000 died, while 200 synagogues and thousands of Jewish homes, shops and offices were destroyed.

In Golders Green, North London, Alec Jay, just nineteen, trainee stockbroker, weekend anti-Fascist demonstrator and Territorial Army volunteer of eight months' standing, wrote The Jews, the poem above. Initially, he used the third person plural: 'their tragic faces' ... 'their one hope' and so on.

Alec's nationality and ethnicity reinforced his anti-Fascist sentiments as Europe polarized between democracies and dictatorships, Britain divided over appeasement and British Fascists preached Continental-style totalitarianism. Yet, in using the third person, Alec showed his ambivalence about German Jews. Between 1933 and 1938 refugees poured into London, many settling in and around his teenage haunts in Hampstead. Might the influx fuel anti-Semitism, he asked himself. Might these immigrants threaten his self-image as a thoroughly assimilated ex-public schoolboy more interested in sport than prayer?

For Alec, however, it was a time to be counted. He might shudder at the refugees' guttural accents and strange manners, but in the struggle between Nazi and Jew they were members of his tribe. Shortly after finishing the poem, he took up his pen again and, line by line, crossed through each 'they', 'their' and 'them', substituting 'we', 'our' and 'us'.

Kristallnacht confirmed two things for Alec: Jews could not appease Hitler but must fight like Judas Maccabeus, whose victory is celebrated in the festival of Chanukah; and his place in the struggle was as a British Jewish volunteer soldier.

*   *   *

Alec was born on 30 October 1919 in a Clapham Common mansion block, the middle child and only son of John and Annie Jay. John was born John Jacobs, the eldest of the four sons of Alexander Jacobs, a Hackney fishmonger, and his wife, Phoebe. Annie was the younger daughter of Noah Cohen, an East End wholesaler, and his wife, Rebecca. John's brothers were Woolf, a film executive, Lou, who joined his father's business, and Harry, the baby of the family. At the time of the wedding on 2 June 1915, the Jacobs and Cohen families lived two streets away from each other in Stoke Newington.

John Jay unofficially changed his name during the Great War, formalizing the matter by deed poll the week before Alec's birth. John had been a dentists' supplier but after his marriage he became 'chief traveller' for his father-in-law, whose speciality was 'ladies' and gents' undergarments'. One family myth was he changed his name because he was called Mr 'J' in the business. A more likely reason was that he wished to assimilate – Jacobs sounded German even though the family had lived in London's East End for centuries. Name changes among Jews were common during that period. Noah Cohen's Warsaw-born father-in-law, Moses Reisfeld, changed his surname to Rice-field, while his mother-in-law, originally Krusse, became Caroline.

John Jay moved from Stoke Newington to Clapham before Alec's birth, and subsequently to Golders Green, then the northern terminus of one branch of the Northern Line. There the Jays lived in a semi-detached house large enough to accommodate Alec, his older sister, Phoebe, younger sister, Bobbie, a nanny and a cook. Noah had bought the land as a wedding gift, but the war halted construction on the sloping fields of Hodford Farm so they had to wait until peacetime to move in.

The Jays were not particularly religious. They gave their children classical not biblical names, they did not attend synagogue regularly or abstain from travel on the Sabbath, while Annie's signature dish was boiled gammon.

When John was not working as Noah Cohen's 'chief traveller', he would be a bookmaker at weekend race meetings at Brooklands Motor Course, trading as 'Jack Linton', with Phoebe as his assistant. With his salesman's charm, he was one of the characters of England's grandest motor-racing circuit. Phoebe thought he could 'sell snow to the Eskimos'. The Jays did, however, wish their children to have a grounding in Judaism and they became early members of the Golders Green Synagogue, which opened in 1922 close to their home and was the location ten years later of Alec's Bar Mitzvah service, in which he read the story of Noah's Ark.

John's profits share from the Noah Cohen business enabled him to send his children to fee-paying schools. The girls attended South Hampstead High School for Girls while Alec went to University College School, Hampstead, an offshoot of University College, London, the 'godless college' founded by the nineteenth century Utilitarian philosopher and atheist, Jeremy Bentham. Other North London public schools operated Jewish quotas, but UCS was a genuine meritocracy.

Alec arrived in September 1932 just short of his thirteenth birthday and stayed until the 1936 summer term, when he was approaching seventeen. He was considered Oxbridge material. 'He seems well capable of taking responsibility on his shoulders and carrying it conscientiously,' wrote his housemaster in his leaving report. 'He did well in the General Schools Examination, in which he matriculated with "credit" in English and Mathematics, "distinction" in German, and "good" in Latin, French and Arithmetic.' Yet the housemaster's report also contained evidence of Alec's other side – a passion for sport: 'I formed a very favourable impression of his general ability and keenness – and in particular had a remarkably satisfactory account of his efforts in helping to organize the school athletics stats last spring.'

Even at sixteen, two years younger than the oldest boys, Alec was playing 2nd XI cricket as batsman and wicket-keeper and 2nd XV rugby as full-back and earning his athletics colours for cross-country running. His hero was Harold Abrahams, who lived locally. Abrahams, whose achievements featured in the film *Chariots of Fire*, had been a star Cambridge athlete before winning a gold medal at the 1924 Paris Olympics.

John Jay did not approve of Alec's desire to follow in Abrahams' footsteps. If he funded his son through sixth form and university, Alec would, he feared, spend more time on the playing fields than in lectures. This was too frivolous a prospect for a man who had so recently escaped the confines of East End ghetto life. Instead, Alec was removed from school and apprenticed to a City stockbroker via an introduction from Uncle Woolf. The firm was A.R. Barton & Company, with offices close to the Stock Exchange at 20 Copthall Avenue. Its founder and senior partner, Alfred Barton, presided over twenty staff.

Although Alec regretted not going to university, he liked the Stock Exchange's collegial atmosphere, its code of honour expressed in the motto,

'My word is my bond'. He was a keen participator in Exchange sporting activities, winning a silver medal in the junior 440 yards race in 1938. But it was at Bartons that Alec 'first tasted the sour fruit of racial prejudice'. On his first day, he was presented with an enormous kettle and an equally gargantuan tea pot and told to make tea. A little nervous, he misjudged the quantity of tea, the result being 'a pale beige liquid that tasted as vile as it looked'. Most of his colleagues forgave Alec this first-day mistake but one clerk looked up from his cup and bellowed, 'What's this then, Ikey, kosher tea?' Alec buttoned his lip and made sure his tea duties were later performed to perfection, but decided he must stand up and be counted in the struggle against anti-Semitism.

Street anti-Semitism was gaining ground where Alec lived. His last years in school coincided with the rise of Sir Oswald Mosley's paramilitary Black-shirts. In Hampstead, Fascists congregated at the King of Bohemia pub and held outdoor meetings near Whitestone Pond on the Heath. Alexander Raven Thomson, Mosley's chief ideologue, made speeches and the Blackshirts would chant, 'We've got to get rid of the rats!' 'The rats were the Jews and the socialists,' recalled Alec. 'At the time, I qualified under both headings.'

Fascists, he decided, should be driven from his neighbourhood, and he would not be squeamish about methods. In 1935, photographs smuggled out of Dachau and published in the *Jewish Chronicle* showed SS-sponsored criminals torturing Jews. Alec believed Fascists had to be prevented from gaining a foothold in Britain to stop something similar happening here.

Opposition at Fascist meetings would start with heckling; typically, some reference by Alec or a friend to Mosley's wife, Diana, would light a fuse, spark-ing a brawl. Diana was one of Lord Redesdale's daughters. Another, Unity, fell in love with Hitler, and the Führer was guest of honour at Diana's wedding. One anti-Fascist taunt was that Diana had Jewish blood; for Blackshirts, this was a red rag to a bull. Fights erupted and only ceased when police whistles and sirens caused both sides to run for it. 'The danger of being arrested was not very great,' said Alec. 'The real danger was to be knocked down. It was easier to kick effectively than punch effectively and what the Blackshirts lacked in skill they made up for in vigour. It was not just fists and feet that they used. Knuckle-dusters, heavy metal rings, coshes and even knives were used.'

These skirmishes were trivial compared to Mosley's marches and meetings. On Sunday, 4 October 1936, soon after Alec joined Bartons, Mosley tried to march through the East End. In 'the Battle of Cable Street', Alec and other North Londoners joined with East End Jews, trade unionists and other anti-Fascists to stop him. About 100,000 anti-Fascists gathered to oppose 3,000 British Union of Fascists members. Soon fighting broke out and the police ordered Mosley to retreat. Alec was in the thick of the scuffling but 'was lucky enough to come away with nothing worse than a few bruises to show as battle scars'. For the government, however, the Battle of Cable Street was so dis-turbing that it banned paramilitary uniforms. Three years later, in July 1939,

Alec joined protesters when Mosley made his swansong speech in front of thousands of Fascists at Earls Court.

While fighting Fascists at home, Alec became fascinated by the Spanish Civil War, in which General Francisco Franco's Nationalist rebels were supported by Fascist Italy and Nazi Germany. In response, 30,000–40,000 Communists, Socialists and Anarchists, including 2,000 Britons, joined International Brigades to fight for the Loyalist Republicans. Alec was 'irresistibly drawn to the Loyalist side' and made inquiries 'as to the best method of signing up and going to fight in Spain'. He was not the only Jew having such thoughts. A quarter of International Brigade members were Jews. Of the 2,000 Britons, 300–400 were Jews and they fought alongside 500 Palestinian Jews. Unsurprisingly, casualty lists included men from London suburbs such as Cricklewood, Hendon, Highbury, Maida Vale and Muswell Hill. It seemed natural to move from brawling with Blackshirts to fighting against Fascism in Spain.

Alec did not, in the end, go to Spain. Instead he joined Britain's Territorial Army, becoming, in pre-war argot, a 'Terrier'. His decision came in early 1938 during a lunch break as he strolled past the Mansion House, where Territorial units were holding a recruitment fair. By chance, Alec chatted to a Queen Vics officer who said B Company had a drill hall near his old school. Alec read the recruitment brochure. Britain, it began, had the smallest 'standing army of any first class power' and a large proportion served as an 'Imperial Fire Brigade' to put down 'tribal insurrection' and guard the frontiers. Behind this tiny force stood the Terriers, 'the sole second line of defence'.

A volunteer Queen Vic would learn to shoot, drive and use Morse code, while belonging to a gentleman's club without the snobbery. The Davies Street headquarters – open six days a week for a 10-shilling annual subscription – contained a canteen 'where refreshments of all kinds, both food and drink, may be obtained at low cost', a 'well-stocked lending library', indoor sports facilities and a miniature shooting range. Regimental dances, dinners and concerts were organized each winter.

If Alec volunteered to 'defend Britain and all that Britain stands for', he had to commit for four years. To become eligible for the £3 10s 'proficiency grant', he would need to do forty hours' training and fifteen days at the annual summer camp; extra training could earn the £5 'full bounty'. Service dress, battle dress, boots, cap, greatcoat, webbing, rifle and 'housewife' – a sewing kit – came free, and Alec would receive full Army pay, starting at 2s per day for riflemen, and free food while attending training camps.

The brochure ended with a flourish, using bold type and capital letters: '**WILL YOU DO YOUR BIT?** If so, come forward NOW and help in your country's defence'.

The seed was sown in Alec's mind: 'I didn't do anything on the spur of the moment but I did begin to think about what might be in store for all of us.' At school, he had seen Hitler remilitarize the Rhineland in breach of the Versailles Treaty. Two years later, as he studied the Queen Vics brochure, came the *Anschluss*, Hitler's annexation of Austria. Alec concluded Europe was headed for war: 'The war in Spain was only a curtain-raiser for a much more serious conflict in which this country would inevitably be involved. If Britain was going to be at war I might as well learn something about it.'

A few days later, he returned to the recruiting fair and put his name down for the Queen Vics' B Company, taking the first step on a journey that would lead to him being one of 60,000 British Jews who served in the forces during the Second World War, a fifth of the community.

B Company was struggling to reach full strength, and Alec was ahead of his time when he reported to its Lymington Road drill hall at 6.30pm on Tuesday, 22 March 1938. Half an hour later, the company commander, Captain Charles Howkins, a civil engineer, had signed him up as a 'Saturday Night Soldier'. In his 'attestation' papers, he was declared fit, while various identification points were noted – complexion sallow, eyes brown, hair dark, religion Jew. The papers showed he was virtually a boy soldier: his height was 5ft 8½ins, 1½ins below his full adult height, his weight 11st 6lbs and chest size 37½ inches.

An early duty was to study the Queen Vics' history. It was a grand old volunteer regiment whose most famous achievement came during the Great War, when Second Lieutenant Geoffrey Woolley, an Oxford cleric, became the first Territorial to win a Victoria Cross. The regiment was originally raised by John Barber Beaumont in 1803 to defend Britain against Napoleon's threatened invasion and called the Duke of Cumberland's Sharpshooters after its honorary colonel. The unit disbanded after Waterloo but veterans reconstituted themselves in 1835 as the Royal Victoria Rifle Club, with the then Princess Victoria as patron. In 1851, amid fresh fears of French invasion, the Rifle Club was renamed the Victoria Rifles.

In the 1890s, the regiment adopted the 60th Rifles' black buttons and rifle-green uniform and became a King's Royal Rifle Corps volunteer battalion. The cap badge was a black Maltese Cross with red cloth behind to show the Queen Vics were once redcoats. When the Territorial Force was created in 1908, the regiment merged with another unit and incorporated St George and the dragon in its crest. Six years later, following the outbreak of the Great War, the Queen Vics expanded into three battalions and were placed within the London Regiment.

Geoffrey Woolley's story fascinated Alec. On 20 April 1915 near Ypres, Woolley led his company forward to take ammunition to defenders trying to resist a German counter-attack. Most were killed but Woolley disobeyed orders to withdraw, saying his company would remain until relieved. Numerous attacks were repelled during the night, and when the Queen Vics were relieved at dawn only 14 of Woolley's 150 men were alive.

Yet while the battalion had an illustrious past and a motto expressing the comradeship of its volunteer origins, *Vis Unita Fortior* (Strength in Unity), it was also at the forefront of army modernization as Britain began to respond to the threat from Hitler. In 1937 the Queen Vics were brought back under the umbrella of the King's Royal Rifle Corps, whose regular battalion, the 60th Rifles, were one of the first infantry units equipped with armoured personnel carriers. Then, a few months after Alec joined up, his battalion converted into an experimental motorcycle reconnaissance unit. At the time, his commanding officer was Colonel Hugh Combe, later George VI's aide-de-camp. The second-in-command was Major John Ellison-Macartney, bursar of Queen Mary College, which had been established by the Queen Vics' founder.

Alec was proud of his new status when he sat down to dinner the evening after his attestation and told his family he had joined up. John Jay exploded: 'Well, you can bloody well un-join yourself.' Father and son then squared up to each other verbally, while Annie and her daughters sat silently staring at their plates. Eventually, Annie protested that the food was getting ruined, and the meal was eaten amid baleful glares between father and son. As soon as he thought decent, Alec retired to his bedroom. After a few moments, Annie tapped on the door. She was, thought Alec, 'the most peaceful and gentle person' one could hope to meet but what she said was as unexpected as it was soothing: 'Don't worry about it and leave it to me. I'll talk to your father and persuade him you are doing the right thing.' And so it turned out. Alec never learned what she said, but it did the trick and 'parental opposition subsided to be replaced in the fullness of time by parental pride'.

Chapter 7

The Longer Road to Guînes: Terrier Training

Alec loved the inclusiveness of a battalion that 'embraced, metaphorically, everyone from dukes to dustmen'. Sam Kydd described the Queen Vics as 'a mixed bag of Stock Exchange types and Cockneys from in and around Paddington and even further afield'. What the Cockneys lacked in intellect 'they made up for with their natural wit, craft and friendly approach'.

Four months after *Kristallnacht*, Alec made plain his feelings in a poem called The Queen Victorias:

Back in South Africa in nineteen nought one
England was fighting with horse and man and gun
And who was it that really got old Kruger on the run?
The Queen Victorias in all their glory.

Then in nineteen fourteen there happened the Great War
Ypres, Cambrai, Hill 60, and some more
And who was it that really put the Kaiser on the floor?
The Queen Victorias in all their glory.

What will happen if war breaks again?
War with its horrors of blood and death and pain
Who'll be in the trenches swearing at the rain?
The Queen Victorias in all their glory.

B Company parades at Lymington Road were strictly conducted by Company Sergeant Major Harry 'Queenie' Worsfold, a gas fitter. When drill and the lectures were finished, however, the men would mix in the Company bar; Sergeant Neal became Ernie and Corporal Langley, Bill.

Alec respected his company commander. Young subalterns with questionable qualities were posted to Lymington Road so 'Charles Howkins could make or break them'. Through his lectures, Alec absorbed knowledge painlessly: 'The terrors of map-reading and the use of a compass ceased to exist for me after a couple of his talks.' Alec had less respect for 'Queenie', who felt more at home at Davies Street, where there was a separate sergeants' mess: 'The CSM thought so much of himself that it was beneath his dignity to mix with the common herd of riflemen and, frankly, nobody missed him.'

Training took place on Tuesday and Thursday evenings, beginning with naming the parts of a rifle, how it worked and how to hold it. Then came rifle drill and marching, with B Company using Alec's old school in Frognal as a parade ground. The drill involved rapid movements and minimum noise, while marching was at a 'quick step' – 160 paces to the minute, not the ordinary infantry speed of 120. There was also instruction in gas warfare, which Fascist Italy had practised in Abyssinia. Then, once Alec had learned 'the theory of musketry', he put theory into practice at weekend sessions at Purfleet in the Essex marshes. His weapon was the Lee-Enfield Rifle No. 1 Mk III, whose fast-operating bolt action and large magazine capacity allowed a skilled rifleman to perform 'the mad minute', during which he could fire as many as thirty .303 rounds.

The trips to Purfleet were a toughening-up exercise for a teenager brought up in a house where servants cooked and cleaned: 'It always seemed to rain and one would fire the course lying on a groundsheet and trying to wind as much of it as one could over one's shoulders to avoid being completely soaked.' The men would cram into 15cwt trucks for the journey with haversack rations – 'dry sandwiches that inevitably became soggy, greasy sausage rolls that disintegrated in one's fingers and apples that were sometimes wizened and wrinkled on the outside and like cotton wool when one tried to eat them'. Company cooks would provide tea that was 'strong, sweet and stewed beyond all recognition'.

Once the course had been fired and tea dispensed, the battalion field kitchen would provide hot water for 'boiling out'. Intended to prevent a rifle barrel rusting, this involved pouring hot water down the muzzle to flush out corrosive salts left behind by cartridge primers. When Alec finished this, he would clean his barrel with gauze patches measuring four by two inches, hence known as 'four-by-twos'. These were attached to a loop at one end of a 'pull-through', a cord with a weight at the other end. Alec would drop the weighted end down the barrel to the rifle's opened breech, then pull on the cord, and the gauze would remove dirt and grease as it passed through. Finally, he would oil the outside.

Alec was one of B Company's best shots. This meant he could fire the course and clean his rifle before the area around the field kitchen became a mud bath. He could also qualify for proficiency pay – an extra sixpence a day during training camps.

The journeys back to Hampstead in trucks smelling of damp uniforms, cigarettes and beer were noisy, with much good-humoured ribbing of the less successful shooters and boasts from the better marksmen of what they would achieve if called on to shoot in anger. When that time did come, however, there was no time on Calais' ramparts for boiling – a quick pull-through was all the rifles got.

In March, Alec attended the battalion's four-day Easter camp at Tidworth Barracks on the edge of Salisbury Plain. Here he discovered army life proper – barrack room rituals, the 'wet canteen' serving beer, and the NAAFI serving tea, coffee and snacks. The induction's more informal aspects were carried out by 'barrack-rats' wearing good conduct stripes on their sleeves and 'rooti gongs' on their breasts. 'Rooti gong' was army slang for the Long Service and Good Conduct Medal, awarded for eighteen years' service or, as one 'barrack-rat' explained, 'eighteen years of undetected crime'. 'We smooth-cheeked young Territorials were a never-ending source of amusement to them and they were a never-ending source of wonderment to us,' Alec recalled. 'They must have blessed those four days because not one of the "barrack-rats" ever had to put his hand in his tunic pocket for the price of a pint of beer.' The beer was cheap but known as 'Arms and Legs' because it had no body.

On camp, Alec acquired skills that could not be gained in a drill hall. He learned about cover and advancing in extended order in a frontal assault – with intervals of two to three paces between each man – and was introduced to bayonet drill, which he hated. Instructors would tell him to scream as he charged the target and plunged his weapon in. Unsurprisingly, his early attempts were condemned as insufficiently fierce.

Alec also put into practice his theoretical knowledge of navigation, earning plaudits for the accuracy of his navigation across Salisbury Plain with the aid of compass and linen-backed waterproof ½inch-to-the-mile map. The most important thing he learned was how to bond with others regardless of background: 'We learned to live together and to realize that respect for or from our fellow men was not automatic but had to be earned. In the barrack-room it didn't matter whether one was an articled clerk or in the family business or whether one was a dustman or delivery boy. It was how you shaped up and mucked in that counted. It was there I first learned that all riflemen are brothers.' It was a lesson he would recall during his five years of captivity.

While the Easter camp was in barracks, the fortnight's summer camp was under canvas at Otterpool Lane, close to Lympne Aerodrome in Kent, later a Battle of Britain fighter base. The weather was glorious and Alec trained in 'shirt sleeve order', but the seriousness of the activities was not in doubt. The notice summoning him said he could only duck out for 'the most urgent reasons' and would be prosecuted if he went absent without permission.

Each day began with a march – fifty minutes per hour followed by ten minutes' rest. Typically, the men would sing the Queen Vics' unofficial regimental song in praise of the 'Black Brigade'. This referred to their status as riflemen with black buttons, not shiny ones. Then there were the Great War songs such as 'Bobbing Up and Down Like This' and 'If You Want to Find the Sergeant Major', whose words were not designed to appeal to 'Queenie' Worsfold. Some were clean, others, such as 'An Engineer Told me before he

Died', were so rude Howkins would entreat his men to 'sing a decent song' to avoid upsetting the locals.

Company exercises occupied week one. Initially, Alec trained under his platoon commander, Second Lieutenant Humphrey 'Whumps' Whitbread. The men began with trekking through woods and streams to get into a final assault position, progressed to mock battles between platoons, then 'fought' company against company. The second week's training involved manoeuvres to weld the battalion together as a unit, with other London Territorials cast as opposition. One exercise on the second Wednesday involved the Queen Vics acting as an advance guard to a brigade opposing the Rangers, who were based at Tottenham Court Road and known as 'The Gas Light and Coke Company'. The climax was 'Brigade Day' on the second Thursday, when the Queen Vics joined the Rangers as 'Southland's' army to 'capture' Brabourne, a village held by 'Northland', comprising the Tower Hamlets Rifles, the London Irish Rifles and a Royal Fusiliers battalion nicknamed the 'Hackney Gurkhas'. With the sound of blank ammunition giving the mock battle a pretty authentic feel, regular Army officers acting as umpires would test the recruits' training by suddenly popping up during a manoeuvre and placing them in imaginary perilous situations.

Between exercises, Alec attended lectures. Soldiers from the Small Arms School at Netheravon, Wiltshire, demonstrated the new Bren gun and Boys anti-tank gun, Royal Engineers showed how to dig a trench and Royal Berkshire regulars demonstrated how to use new equipment in a mock attack on a farm. Alec also got more informal tips from experienced Terriers. 'Don't fire any blank cartridges unless you are absolutely forced to,' said one. 'They mess up your rifle something rotten.' It was not, however, all hard work – at one point pilots from the aerodrome offered some Queen Vics a ride, giving them 'an unofficial demonstration of low-flying aircraft' as they seemingly tried to knock the knobs off the Officers' Mess tent.

There was much reorganization in 1938. Having been taught to march four across, the Queen Vics learned to march in threes, spaced further apart. Gone was the Support Company armed with Great War-vintage Vickers machine guns, which needed six men to operate them, while Bren guns theoretically replaced Lewis light machine guns. With the support company gone, the battalion consisted of three fighting companies and a headquarters company. Each fighting company consisted of three platoons and a company headquarters, and each platoon consisted of three sections and a platoon headquarters. Yet little new equipment reached the 'weekend soldiers'. In theory, each platoon had three Bren guns and three Boys rifles. In practice, B Company had only one Bren gun and not a single Boys. Instead, the men would tie a blue cloth round a rifle to designate it a Boys.

As one of B Company's better shots, Alec trained as a Bren gunner. The Bren was designed by Czech military engineers in Brno, hence the first two letters of its name. The second two letters came from Enfield, home of Britain's Small Arms Factory, which built the gun under licence. Brought into production in 1938, it became the workhorse of British automatic weaponry, partly because of its combination with Vickers' Bren-gun carrier, of which 100,000 were made, a record figure for an armoured vehicle. Alec soon recognized its virtues. It was robust and easy to fix if jammed. It was also relatively accurate and, as he discovered at Calais, would function in dusty and muddy conditions. Older colleagues said it was not a patch on the Lewis, but eventually they got to like it.

As for the Boys, a limited supply eventually reached the battalion. Originally called the Stanchion, it was renamed in honour of its inventor, Captain Herbert Boys, who died just before it came into service. Unlike the Bren, it was deeply unpopular. The recoil caused neck strains and bruised shoulders. Typically, a soldier would fire not more than a dozen shots before being relieved. Even worse, it was obsolete by 1940 because of changes in tank armour, as Alec discovered at Calais.

On Sunday, 7 August, the summer camp ended and Alec resumed life as a stockbroker. The urgency of his training, however, became clear soon after, when the Sudetenland crisis erupted. Under the Munich Agreement Czechoslovakia was dismembered, the Reich gained three million more Germans and Neville Chamberlain returned from Munich promising 'peace in our time'. But before the crisis was resolved Britain went on war alert, with bomb shelters dug in parks near Alec's home.

Alec saw the country's mood change as men queued to join the Queen Vics. Two months later, the battalion had sufficient officers and a total strength of more than 500. Its conversion into a motorcycle unit meant that, in effect, the Queen Vics became a modern version of light cavalry – a move heralded by advertisements for volunteers in *Motor Cycle* magazine. The idea came from Germany, where tacticians constrained by Versailles Treaty restrictions covering tanks sought other means of creating mobility, in the shape of motorcyclists and armoured cars. These would locate and pin down defensive positions, then spread out past the flanks of strongpoints, infiltrating and turning the defenders. The British motorcycle battalion had similar aims but was more defensive in character.

The Queen Vics were assigned to the 1st London Motor Division and reorganized in theory as a unit of 25 officers and 550 men. This was to comprise a headquarters company, three motorcycle companies with a hundred 600cc Norton motorcycle combinations between them, each carrying three men – a driver, a pillion passenger with a Bren gun and a third man in the sidecar with a rifle, a scout platoon with eight armoured cars and an anti-tank platoon with Boys rifles; the other equipment comprised twenty 30cwt Bedford 'Guy' trucks, 500cc Norton bikes for dispatch riders and Austin Seven cars for senior officers. In addition to the Bren and Boys guns, the Queen Vics were to have nine 2-inch mortars, mostly firing smoke bombs for defence, not explosives; but 30 per cent of the men (a comparatively high proportion) were to be equipped with Webley pistols alone.

Having arrived ahead of the rush, Alec, though only nineteen in early 1939, was one of B Company's more experienced riflemen. After attending Rifle Cadre, he gained his rifle qualification on 23 March, a year and a day after enlisting, thus receiving a 30s annual 'bounty'. On 1 April, he was promoted to lance corporal and in July, having passed tactics and map-reading exams, he became one of B Company's eight corporals.

Training during the final months of peacetime was intensive – about four fifths of B Company had less than a year's experience, and Alec would initiate recruits into the mysteries of the Lee Enfield rifle and the Bren gun. Motorbike training took place at UCS and manoeuvres were conducted on Hounslow Heath and near Whipsnade Zoo. Easter camp was again held at Tidworth, where four days of activity included driving and vehicle maintenance, scouting, signalling, weapons training, camouflage and fieldcraft. The annual weapons training course took place in June at the Army Training Centre in Pirbright, Surrey. Equipment, however, remained a problem. By mid-1939, B Company had only one 'rather temperamental' bike but no sidecar, and men used their own bikes for training sessions. Shortages were to bedevil the Queen Vics even after the outbreak of war: during the 1939/40 winter, they had to hire civilian trucks.

B Company's 100-plus men did, however, have cause to celebrate when they met on 3 June for their annual Supper and Prize Distribution, hosted by Howkins, with Hampstead's mayor, Sidney Boyd, presenting prizes. B Company had won the intra-battalion Centenary Cup for the first time since 1928, and Alec's friend, Bill Brett, picked up the QVR Association Prize for General Efficiency. Entertainment was provided by Iris Day, a New Zealand soprano, and Robert Harbin, later the first British magician to appear on television.

When not training, Alec led the life of a typical ex-public schoolboy. On Saturdays, he played cricket and rugby. If his team were at home, Saturday nights were spent drinking and singing rude songs in the pavilion bar, interspersed with horseplay. On Saturday, 5 November 1938 a friend set off some fireworks. 'In the space of half a minute the whole bar was filled with thick smoke,' recalled Alec, 'and the noise and flashes of the exploding fireworks was a deafening foretaste of what many of us were to experience a few years later.'

Wives and girlfriends were banned from such sessions, though 'the ladies', including Alec's girlfriend, Netta Rose, might cook for their men and be rewarded with cocktails. By mid-1939, Alec had known Netta for two years and they were contemplating marriage. Netta was the only child of Manny and May Rose, who lived in a Victorian villa in Holland Park. A moody brunette with an earthy laugh, who resembled Merle Oberon, star of The Scarlet Pimpernel, she liked to stand out from the crowd by dressing in green.

The pair would play a parlour game called Confessions, in which participants revealed their likes and dislikes and other intimacies. Netta's favourite cinema was the Empire, Leicester Square and her Hollywood heart-throb was Robert Taylor, star of A Yank at Oxford. Her favourite theatre was the Golders Green Hippodrome; her preferred musician was Harry Roy, a Jewish band leader best known for the song, My Girl's Pussy. She liked all cigarettes as long as they were 'other people's' and her first action if made prime minister for the day would be to resign. She loved Shakespeare but her favourite books were, appropriately given her resemblance to Merle Oberon, Baroness Orczy's Scarlet Pimpernel novels.

Alec shared Netta's fondness for the Hippodrome, but he preferred the Tivoli cinema in the Strand and Joe Loss, whose family like Alec's came from London's East End, as band leader. His favourite actress was Jean Forbes-Robertson, who played Peter in Peter Pan. Like Netta, he would oscillate between seriousness and frivolity – if made prime minister he would 'get drunk at the expense of the government', yet he was critical of 'the modern generation' because 'they don't think'. His pet aversion was 'shaving after a bath'; his favourite cigarette was Teofani, made from Macedonian tobacco. Running was his preferred sport, while UCS's school colour, maroon, was his favourite. When asked to pick a poet, he cited Stephen Spender, an Old Boy who described UCS as 'that gentlest of schools'. Alec's favourite novelist, meanwhile, was D.H. Lawrence, despite Lawrence's contempt for socialism and liberal democracy.

Summer 1939 was miserable, with the rain almost constant as Alec trained near Burley in the New Forest from 23 July to 6 August. The battalion did, however, have a full complement of Norton, Triumph and BSA bikes, mostly with sidecars – known then as chariots – as well as some Bedford 30cwt trucks. Delivered a few days before the battalion left London, the 200 bikes were on display when a *Times* reporter and photographer arrived to record the exercises.

B Company were waved off by family and friends, to rendezvous with other companies at the Hog's Back near Farnham, Surrey. The send-off was late and chaotic; many B Company members were still novices with their machines, and the column soon broke up as stragglers were delayed by jams. Thus, it was not until after dark that B Company pulled off the road to join the other units. Then, after five hours' sleep, the Queen Vics set off towards their destination, a field two miles beyond Burley. The Queen Vics camped on one side of a lane opposite the London Scottish and London Irish Rifles. Both used bagpipes for their calls – as Alec discovered at dawn the next day.

With sufficient bikes available, the Queen Vics could now train as a motorcycle reconnaissance unit. Fieldcraft was a critical component – learning to operate stealthily, 'to see without being seen' using the terrain to mask move-ment, to select fire and observation positions, to infiltrate and plan retreat routes. Their duties were outlined in *Training and Tactical Handling of a Motor Cycle Battalion*, a manual printed the previous month. It was a makeshift affair, with some paragraphs lifted straight from German manuals as British strategists hurried to catch up with the Wehrmacht. It also failed to explain how motorcycle battalions would link with other motorized units. The text did, however, make clear the Queen Vics might be widely dispersed, acting 'entirely independently, and on their own initiative' in groups as small as ten men, or even the three-man crew of a motorcycle combination, communi-cating by wireless, Morse code and dispatch rider. For defensive observation, platoons might operate 10–15 miles ahead of battalion headquarters, with forward observation points even further forward.

The camp's other focus was learning how to use Dannert barbed wire to build roadblocks at speed. The theory was that if an enemy tank attempted to break through the roadblock, the coils would catch in its tracks, bringing it to a halt. The tank would then be vulnerable to Boys rifle fire, while enemy infantry would be picked off by Bren gunners.

During the first week, the Queen Vics marched from camp each morning en bloc, then dispersed into companies, communicating by wireless and dispatch rider. Such training led up to the centrepiece exercise, a three-day, two-nights-in-the-open mock battle. In this, Burley's battalions were ordered to defend territory against units advancing from Beaulieu, ten miles away. During the proceedings, regular Army umpires would declare men 'wounded', requiring them to lie down and await medical attention, or 'killed', in which case they would be removed from the 'battle'. Alec's platoon drove around during attacks and counter-attacks, filling gaps in the line as 'casualties' grew.

Off-duty, Alec would dry out in the NAAFI tent, enjoy a pint or three in the Queen's Head in Burley or explore the quaint New Forest villages. On the penultimate day, Colonel Combe told the men how well they had done, adding that he hoped to see them in a few weeks' time. Then Alec had one last session at the Queen's Head before staggering to his bell tent for a final truncated sleep. Reveille was at 5.00am so B Company could return to Hampstead in a single day.

In retrospect, Combe's parting message had more meaning than anyone anticipated. On 23 August, Hitler agreed the Molotov-Ribbentrop Pact to carve up Poland with Stalin. On 27 August, Poland and Britain signed a mutual assistance treaty. Four days later the Germans faked a Polish attack on Gleiwitz's radio station, giving Hitler his pretext to invade at dawn on Friday, 1 September.

For Alec, Friday had begun as a normal working day. Then a radio announcement said Territorials should report to their drill halls. Those who did not hear this returned from work to find call-up papers. The document that arrived at the Jays' home was headed 'Reserve and Auxiliary Forces Act, 1939, Territorial Army Calling Out Notice' and addressed to 'Corporal Alec Jay, Army number 6896204'. The text read: 'In pursuance of directions given by the Secretary of State for War … you are hereby notified that you are called out for military service commencing from 1 Sept 1939 and for this purpose you are required to join the 1st Bn. Queen Victoria's Rifles, the King's Royal Rifles Corps.' Signed by Ellison-Macartney, newly promoted as lieutenant colonel having replaced Combe, it finished by saying that if Alec did not report for duty he would be prosecuted. That evening, with a 'black-out' in operation, he presented himself at Lymington Road, where Captain Peter Tufton, younger son of Lord Hothfield and B Company's new commander, supervised his 'embodiment'.

With their vehicles outside, the 126 men of B Company – 5 officers, 17 NCOs and 104 riflemen – spent their first night as embodied soldiers sleeping on the drill hall floor. The next morning, they left for hotels around Bayswater's Leinster Gardens, with company headquarters located in the Queens Hotel in Inverness Terrace. Vehicles were drawn up outside, while the communal gardens nearby were turned into a fuel dump and surrounded by trip wires, with tin cans suspended at intervals to alert sentries to thieves or worse – the Irish Republican Army had recently launched its S-Plan sabotage campaign.

D Company's billets were further north, some of them in grand Nash terraces surrounding Regent's Park. One Cumberland Terrace billet, next door to Wallis Simpson's former home, had a ballroom. Ellison-Macartney, Howkins and 'Whumps' Whitbread shared a house Whitbread described as 'v comfy' in a letter to his mother, Madeline. The host was away but had provided food and drink 'on a lavish scale'. Other billets were not so 'comfy'. HQ Company commandeered the Stanhope Street School off Hampstead Road, while C Company's 'John Lewis' platoon took over a Wimpole Street shop. All were told to keep their locations secret; any family correspondence had to be sent to Davies Street.

The next day, Chamberlain demanded that Hitler order the withdrawal from Poland before 11.00am the following morning. Sunday, 3 September dawned – after August's miserable weather it was a fine late summer morning – but there was no response. Thus, at 11.15am, Chamberlain broadcast his declaration of war.

Alec was on parade receiving his pay, but parade was cut short when someone leaned out of a window and shouted, 'We are at war with Germany.' A few minutes later, air-raid sirens sounded and the Queen Vics hurried to their billets, donned helmets, armed themselves with buckets of sand to dowse incendiary bombs and watched the sky amid fears the Luftwaffe would immediately bomb the capital. Alec's first orders were to clear Baker Street station of travellers; then he was told to build sandbag barriers outside his billet. No bombs fell that day or in the early hours of the following morning, yet the Queen Vics were woken up by sirens at 2.45am. Dressing quickly, 'Whumps' Whitbread led Alec's platoon to their post at a nearby police station, where they sat for thirty minutes before the 'all-clear' sounded.

People's reactions were mixed. Some struggled to believe Britain was at war. 'No one in the streets seemed at all alarmed, only rather intrigued and slightly bored at having to wake up and be ready to be frightened,' 'Whumps' told his mother.

For people of Alec's parents' generation, who had lived through the Great War, it seemed incredible that conflict had come again so soon. The Great War had been 'the war to end all wars', so how could Hitler reject peace? It seemed he had not believed the Allies' ultimatum. He regularly reneged on agreements and thought Chamberlain would do the same. Some Greenjackets thought Chamberlain might do just that, finding some excuse to postpone yet again the act of declaring war. When Britain honoured its obligation to the Poles, Philip Pardoe felt 'the most unutterable relief'.

Edward Watson was standing in the Cock saloon bar behind St Pancras Station when Chamberlain spoke. He was seventeen, having lied about his age to become a Queen Vic at fourteen. He found the call-up and declaration of war 'a bit amusing ... very much a game'. He later confessed he had no idea about what it really meant, thinking at the time that it was like going on summer camp, but instead of 'coming home after two weeks you were going to be there for a long time'.

Yet, the air-raid sirens began to condition people for what might lie ahead. 'I think perhaps the very fact that in this war one may be as near to death in this country as at "the front" gives one a curious feeling of stepping straight into at least a part of war-atmosphere,' Whitbread told his mother. 'It is a solemn thought which will I think always keep in one's mind from start to finish the cause for which one is working.'

Chapter 8

The Longer Road to Guînes: 'The Bore War'

The winter of 1939/40 was exceptionally cold and the Queen Vics billeted in draughty oast-houses on the Beltring Hop Farm from November 1939 had little protection. Fuel ran short and Alec slept fully clothed, having spent the moments before lights out sitting in his greatcoat and writing poems about Netta. He called one Night Song:

> In the cool of an evening, an evening in March,
> When the moon was as big as a woman with child,
> As I walked in the shadows, the still black shadows,
> My heart awoke with a passion wild.

> The night breeze kissed the bare willow branches,
> Branches not touched by the first flush of spring.
> As the twigs rustled there in the shadows
> My heart rose up and started to sing.

> A dog broke the silence excitedly barking.
> The silence I'd hoped, would last for so long.
> For you were the one, I was thinking of, darling
> You were the words to my heart's sad song.

Netta and Alec had not parted immediately war was declared. For two months, the Queen Vics stayed in London to help the police in case of panic, looting or rioting, and to assist the Fire Brigade should the Luftwaffe pay a visit.

For B Company, a typical day began with Reveille at 6.30am and pre-breakfast exercise in Hyde Park. Breakfast, usually porridge, bacon and baked beans on a tin plate and a tin mug of tea reeking of chlorine, would be at 7.45. New recruits then had weapons training at Davies Street. The best Bren gunners, so the fumbling Terriers were told, could strip and reassemble their weapons in 45 seconds, or 65 seconds when blindfolded, and fill their Bren magazines in 30 seconds. Typically, the morning would end with 'square-bashing' in the park, followed by lunch: meat, two veg and potatoes, often followed by jam tart with coconut shavings, nicknamed 'toenail tart', and more chlorinated tea.

Lunch would be followed by lectures on discipline and map reading then 'physical recreation', usually soccer in the park, and finally tea at 4.00pm – bread and jam, biscuits and cake. Alec was free between tea and supper at 7.00pm unless on sentry duty. This involved one platoon per company being ready at five minutes' notice armed and equipped. Off-duty men had to remain nearby unless acting on orders. Men often slipped off, however, to cinemas and pubs – or even to their families or girlfriends if they were not too far away. After supper there was more free time, but Alec had to be back in his billet by the Tattoo bugle call announcing evening roll call at 9.30pm, or lose a day's pay.

Once a week, the battalion had 'bathing parade' – a march to public baths nearby. Alec also had free access to the YMCA's showers, swimming pool and gymnasium at Great Russell Street and Queens Ice Rink in Queensway, a few hundred yards from B Company's billets. Soon after the call-up, he had a health check and dental inspection at the Wellington Barracks in Birdcage Walk.

For spiritual health, the Christians held church parades while Alec visited the Revd Louis Rabinowitz, the Army's Senior Jewish Chaplain, at the Kings Court Hotel in Queen's Gardens, Paddington. 'Rab', as Alec called him, believed in muscular Judaism – towards the war's end, he celebrated the Palestinian Jews' contribution to Bernard Montgomery's campaigns in *Soldiers from Judea – Palestinian Jewish Units in the Middle East, 1941–1943*. In the book's introduction James Parkes, a Christian cleric, wrote, 'If I were a Jewish soldier in the present war, there is nothing better that I could ask for than to have Rab, with his deep religious inspiration, his unfailing cheerfulness and his inexhaustible resourcefulness, as my chaplain.'

In the war's early days, discipline was a problem. Ellison-Macartney nagged his men about 'the importance of smart appearance and soldierly bearing'. The dress code for 'walking out' was trousers, tunic, boots and stiff cap. Jackets and caps had to be worn over sports clothes when travelling to and from PE exercises, and side hats for parades. Identity tags had to be worn and gas masks, eye shields and anti-gas ointment carried, on and off duty. Ellison-Macartney issued instructions covering everything from the cleaning of webbing – to be scrubbed with 'plain water' without chemicals – to the care of sword-bayonets and Bren guns. Bayonets, having been browned and sand-blasted to prevent reflection in the field, had to be dry cleaned and covered with oil to prevent rust; Bren guns had to be placed in storage chests in a particular way to avoid damaging their foresights and bi-pod legs.

A few days after war was declared, gossips were warned of 'the dangers of discussing military matters, connected with the present emergency, in messes, barrack rooms, their homes or in public places'. Troop movements were 'an operation of war', so travel plans were secret. Anyone using a phone had to 'remember at all time that conversations are liable to be overheard'. Nothing that might be of value to the enemy should be discussed over an open line because the result of 'such indiscretion may be the loss of many lives'. The troops were also admonished for 'dangerous driving' as they tore around London on their motorbikes. In the war's first six weeks Queen Vics were involved in twenty-five crashes, of which thirteen involved Alec's company. Drivers were told they would be disciplined for speeding and ignoring rights of way. During marches after dark, look-out men in front and behind had to carry shielded lanterns to alert motorists, white for the front, red for the rear.

In the second week of September, Alec's platoon drove to Purfleet to complete their annual weapons training. In the third week, they marched in battledress around Hyde Park, then returned to Purfleet for air-raid training. In the event of a warning, Alec was told to put on his gas mask and eye shield then continue his tasks, taking cover only if he heard anti-aircraft fire or exploding bombs. At shooting practice, he had to take cover in the butts and unload his weapon; he was never to shoot at enemy aircraft.

After six weeks in London, the Queen Vics were asked to name their next-of-kin – Alec listed his mother – and told they were moving to Beltring for training as 1st London Division cavalry, tasked with defending Britain against invasion. The officers decided to mark the departure with a party, asking Sam Kydd to produce the entertainment. Kydd was unknown in the West End – he had only toured the provinces in comedy shows – yet his cheeky request to Bud Flanagan, then in residence with his Crazy Gang at the Palladium performing The Little Dog Laughed, paid off.

Thus, the cream of West End entertainers gathered at a Marylebone hall to perform a send-off concert for the Queen Vics. Alec knew the cast's reasons for standing up and being counted. The son of Polish Jewish émigrés who fled a pogrom on their wedding day, Flanagan was born Chaim Weintrop in Whitechapel, close to Alec's family business. The man with the baton was Oscar Rabin, a Latvian Jewish child émigré to England before the Great War, while the comic Vic Oliver had two reasons to fear Nazis: born Victor Oliver von Samek, he was both an Austrian-Jewish émigré and husband to Churchill's daughter, Sarah. Songs in the show included We're Going to Hang out the Washing on the Siegfried Line.

On Wednesday, 1 November, the Queen Vics posed for press photographs before driving down to 'the Wood', as the men described Paddock Wood in letters home. On arrival, the officers discovered 'Whumps' Whitbread, in his last duty before joining the General Staff, had organized comfortable accommodation for them. Ellison-Macartney was installed in the white clapboard Beltring House while his officers were billeted in hotels, pubs and homes nearby. For their men, however, Beltring was a comedown, because they had to sleep in oast-houses. When Alec arrived, the floors were covered with hop dust, but even when the men had got them clean the buildings were uncomfortable, particularly as winter set in. The men, with their possessions and equipment spread around, slept on straw mattresses in the designedly draughty drying rooms. Heating was rationed, with no fires lit before 4.00pm. There were no indoor toilets and the men were limited to one bath per week at Maidstone baths until showers were installed in March 1940. An improvised kitchen and mess hall were located on the ground floor of a storage building near the oast-houses, with the NAAFI and bar above.

In February, the battalion received an intake of conscripts. Once again, recruits had to be inducted into battalion routine – weekday reveille 6.30, breakfast 7.15, sick parade 8.45, dinner 1300hrs, tea, 16.30, guard duty and retreat, 1900hrs, last post 2200hrs, lights out 22.15 – and trained, as new members of a mobile reconnaissance unit, to become proficient motorcyclists or truck drivers. Motorcycle training took place at the Brands Hatch racing circuit; shooting was practised at a miniature range behind Paddock Wood's Foresters Arms pub and at Lydd army range thirty-five miles away.

Before leaving London, the battalion was stripped of half its motorcycles. Thus Ellison-Macartney had to rent civilian motorcycles and tradesmen's vans. When, two weeks after arriving at Beltring, C Company's Major Austin-Brown organized a platoon parade with the full official War Office equipment range, he had to scrounge from other companies. Gradually, however, the flow of equipment improved. New Norton motorcycles arrived to replace those on hire, followed by Daimler scout cars and Bedford trucks and finally, in May, some Humber Snipe radio trucks, taking the battalion up to its full complement of 238 vehicles. Thus equipped, the Queen Vics would travel along rural lanes in search of enemy paratroopers, the fear being that Kent's flat expanses would make ideal paratrooper landing grounds. The lack of live ammunition, however, remained a problem; Alec fired only one Boys rifle round throughout his time at Beltring.

Training focused on defence, not attack. In a November lecture, Alec learned that if he had to hold an area he should 'defend it to the end without thought of withdrawal', chillingly foreshadowing the Calais siege. The mobility introduced by armoured vehicles meant strength had to be in depth, while positions needed to offer robust defence against tanks.

Alec was taught to avoid wasteful heroics and only counter-attack in pursuit of 'a definite and useful object'. In an indication that Britain's generals were considering using gas, he was told, 'Gas may be of considerable value' in defence.

Discipline problems were exacerbated by the conscript influx. Britain had not had conscription since 1918 and few junior officers knew how to lead conscripts. Initially, there was bad blood between 'Terriers' and 'Militiamen'. The Terriers were proud members of what they thought was 'a big family'; the Militiamen had no particular feelings for a battalion about which they knew little or nothing.

Edward Watson disliked mixing with men forced into service. As a bugler, he would blow the Defaulters call but until the conscripts arrived he could not recall having played it. Now there were 'big strings of them every day'. Watson thought most conscripts were 'a shower'. They were 'slack and they didn't want to be soldiers and they used to be late back from leave'. They were 'cheeky, real bolshie types ... suddenly you got fellows in who were sharp boys, who were wide boys'. Many conscripts, meanwhile, avoided the Terriers, who they disdained as 'civilians in uniform'. Denis Hoy, a conscript who fought in Alec's company, thought the volunteers were 'better motorcyclists than they were soldiers', were 'less disciplined' than conscripts yet 'probably keener than we were'. The Territorial ethos seemed strange: 'You didn't get the corporals barking orders at you; they would, more or less, tell you to do things and expect you were enough of a gentleman to do them.'

Ellison-Macartney responded with edicts against pilfering, going absent without leave, being late back to billets after pub sessions, walking on the wrong side of lanes in the dark, leaving billets untidy, littering, vandalism, failing to shave, smoking on guard duty, not wearing identity tags, driving badly or too fast, wasting petrol, gossiping to civilians and failing to salute officers. He would admonish troops for having long hair, for wearing their side hats incorrectly, for saluting incorrectly, for not wearing gas masks for thirty minutes each morning, for being wrongly dressed on parade, and for singing and walking more than two abreast while returning from the pub.

The conscripts were not alone in struggling with the Army's hierarchy. Alec's relationship with CSM Worsfold had never been good, and their enmity came to a head shortly after he returned from a week's leave on Friday, 24 November. At some point when both men were off duty, Alec overheard 'Queenie' saying something offensive about Netta and knocked him to the ground. This was insubordination, and Ellison-Macartney convened a Monday morning hearing in the battalion orderly room.

'Plushy' had a dilemma. Alec had progressed rapidly and was considered officer material, yet under pressure he had lost his temper. Five months previously, the War Office had issued fresh discipline guidelines to Territorial officers, giving them discretion in interpreting the rules and contrasting 'Prussianism' (something 'abhorrent to a free people' and 'beneath the dignity of intelligent men') with British discipline. To function efficiently, the Army demanded 'unhesitating obedience', yet success depended on officers being fair and addressing the personal problems of their men. The War Office thought some misconduct resulted from provocation by 'impatient or self-assertive' NCOs. This was certainly relevant in Alec's case.

'Queenie' Worsfold had behaved unfairly, yet Alec had struck a superior. A narrow interpretation of the rules would dictate that Alec be court-martialled. Should Alec, however, make a formal complaint about Worsfold, this would lead to a full investigation. Ellison-Macartney offered Alec a choice: he could submit to formal proceedings or accept a solution that removed him from Worsfold's authority – moving to C Company and being stripped of his corporal's stripes, though this would not be mentioned in his military record. Alec accepted the offer. Thus battalion Part Two orders for 29 November 1939 stated:

> Cpl A. Jay of B Company reverts to rifleman at own request WEF [with effect from] 27.11.39 authorised by CO 1/QVR. Inter-company transfers: Rfn A Jay moves from B to C Company WEF 28.11.39.

The immediate consequences were clear: Alec left his Lymington Road friends and shifted his kit, including his new steel helmet, into C Company's oast-house. What he did not know then was that his reduced status would profoundly affect his POW experiences. Had he been captured as an NCO or junior officer he would not have endured the hard labour the Germans imposed on low-ranking POWs. Capture was, however, six months off, and the more immediate challenge was coping with wintry weather as Christmas approached.

The cold contributed to Alec's yearning for Netta, the subject of a poem he called Beauty:

> There are four beautiful things in the world
> Which thrill my being through
> A ship, a tree, a flying bird,
> And you, my darling, you.
>
> A great four-masted sailing ship
> With her yards almost bare of sail
> Battening home from the southern seas
> In the teeth of a northerly gale.
>
> A tall and lovely poplar tree,
> As it sways in the summer breeze;
> And sings and signs when it bows its head
> And gently rustles its leaves.
>
> With the rising sun on its long white neck,
> A swan traversing the sky at dawn;
> And all the while whooping its strange sad cry
> Like a soul forlorn.
>
> The sailing ship is a stinking barge,
> And the poplar is rotted through.
> Even the swan is a moth-eaten hawk
> If one tries to compare them with you.

There are four beautiful things in the world
Which thrill my being through
A ship, a tree, a flying bird,
And you, my darling, you.

One way to stay healthy was sport, and Alec donned his regimental red and green shirt to play rugby against the Royal Engineers, Guy's Hospital and two old boys' clubs, the Juddians and the Tonbridgians. Other battalion sports included soccer, boxing and inter-company tugs-of-war. On Sundays, the battalion would march along frosty country roads to church parade at St Mary's, two miles away in East Peckham.

Some entertainment was provided to keep the men occupied. The Salvation Army led communal singing, while the canteen became a cinema once a week, with screenings including *The Man in the Mirror*, in which a man's reflection comes to life and lives out his fantasies. Then there were concert and theatre trips to Tonbridge, plus lectures at Paddock Wood – speakers included land-speed record breaker Sir Malcolm Campbell.

With Kydd in the battalion, there were prospects for a decent home-made show. In December, the QuaVeRs concert party, a Great War institution, was reconstituted to stage a pantomime. Kydd came up with Babes in the (Paddock) Wood. It began with the chorus:

We are the Babes of the Paddock Wood,
You'll like this show 'cause it's good, good, good.
We came here to sample Whitbread's beer
And tear up his roads through the mud, mud, mud.
Now we're lost near the coast, coast, coast,
So we'll stay the night in his oast, oast, oast.
It's a lousy rhyme but a damn good pantomime so
On with the show and the fun, fun, fun.

After the show, which poked fun at the Gestapo and Stalin's secret police, both then engaged in terrorizing the Poles, there were carols, a quiz with Ellison-Macartney as quizmaster and finally the regimental song. The officers served refreshments, as was traditional on such occasions, while Whitbread supplied free beer.

The Queen Vics' commander was happy to encourage amateur dramatics but knew he had to act fast to weld his experimental battalion into a cohesive unit capable of waging war. He had gained recruits with nothing more than basic training and had lost skilled men to arms factories and officer cadet training units. The War Office feared for the Terriers' readiness. On 29 November, 'Whumps' Whitbread's new boss, Lieutenant General Guy Williams, paid a visit to see a motorcycle platoon in action. This was followed by visits from General Sir Walter Kirke, the Home Forces commander-in-chief, and Major General Sir John Davidson, the King's Royal Rifle Corps' commander.

To function as divisional cavalry, riflemen needed to drive a motorcycle or truck, so they were put through a series of tests in early 1940. Alec passed his motorcycle combination test on 2 February. Later that month, he learned how to behave if captured. Having taken a few sailors and airmen during the war's early weeks, the Germans were broadly playing by Geneva Convention rules, but they were encouraging POWs to broadcast on German radio, claiming this would let relatives know they were alive. Austin-Brown told Alec he should 'refuse to comply with any order, request or invitation to speak over the wireless on any subject or for any purposes', revealing only his name, rank and service number; but he said little about evasion and escape.

After the winter's false alarms, it was clear in the spring that action was imminent. The men received fresh uniforms and were placed 'on active service', meaning they had to carry revolvers at all times. Alec met Netta in early March, after which leave was curtailed except for recent conscripts. In April, he received typhoid and tetanus jabs, was told to learn about the French Army and had his gas mask tested. Then, on 1 May, he did some last-minute rifle practice at Lydd.

On 10 May, when Alec returned from a battalion-wide exercise, he discovered 'the Bore War' was over: Hitler had invaded France, and the Queen Vics were moving closer to the coast on invasion alert. Some colleagues were disappointed they were not heading straight for France, convinced Hitler would be quickly defeated. They had been told Britain's industrial, naval, financial, technical and scientific resources were superior, while the French Army had impregnable defence forts along the Maginot Line. Anglo-French tank production was almost three times Germany's in early 1940 and their iron ore output was four times Germany's. The newspapers were full of positive stories, and Ministry of Information newsreels showed weapons rolling off production lines. The footage of Germany, by contrast, showed tanks with wooden sides and troops marching to battle accompanied by horse-drawn wagons.

By 10 May Ellison-Macartney thought his men ready to fight as cavalry despite their weaknesses. He had a full complement of weapons and vehicles; nine tenths of his men could drive motorbikes or trucks; they had received rifle and Bren gun training; they could protect themselves from gas and could perform duties wearing gas masks. No ammunition, however, had been provided for pistol or grenade training. The disastrous Norwegian campaign showed he needed 3-inch not 2-inch mortars, and he scrounged a few from other units but could not obtain live ammunition. Thus, he discarded his 3-inch mortars before the move to Ashford.

Had the Queen Vics been used as cavalry, they might have shown their strengths. That was not their fate. 'Full effect from training is only gained when the type of fighting follows the type of training given. If this does not occur the enemy gains the advantages of surprise,' wrote 'Plushy' months later from Laufen. So it proved. The Queen Vics were thrown across the Channel to fight a battle for which they had no training. What was forced on them was 'a complete reorientation of thought and method within the hours which elapsed between the receipt of orders to move at 10.00pm on Tuesday, 21 May and arrival at Calais at 1.00pm on the following day'.

Four nights later, surrounded by barbed wire and machine guns, Alec bedded down on a Guînes churchyard gravestone as a prisoner of war.

Chapter 9

The Long March

Unprepared for mass surrenders, the Wehrmacht improvised to cope with feeding and transporting prisoners. They needed to be moved rapidly away from possible counter-attacks and then be propelled across the German border into prison camps. Yet the Wehrmacht had to keep France's roads and railways open for troops to pursue Allied armies retreating towards Paris and the Seine; trucks and trains were needed to take German soldiers west and south, not Allied prisoners east.

The solution was to force-march exhausted, bewildered POWs by meandering routes into Germany. The men taken at Calais described their journey as 'The Long March' or just 'The March'. Decades later, they would recall the humiliation of being shoved forward by rifle-butts, subsisting on starvation rations and breathing the exhaust fumes of German tanks moving the other way; Alec thought it the worst experience of his life, describing it in an anniversary poem written in prison camp at Lamsdorf called May – June 1940:

How can I face tomorrow,
And another awful march,
When my soul is sick and weary,
And my muscles are stiff as starch?

Thirty kilos we've walked today
Under a blazing sun,
And I thought I'd choke with Diesel smoke
Before the day was done.

Thirty-seven the day before,
On a road with never a bend.
The miles drag by, and I'm parched and dry
Oh God! Will this never end?

I've walked before for pleasure
Through country cool and green,
But I never knew, as now I do,
Just what a march could mean.

Plod. Plod. Plod, while your feet
Are swollen and sore,
And if you're good, you'll get some food
After eighteen kilos more.

Step. Step. Step as you fight
With the dust for breath,
And when you stop, you sleep where you drop,
With a sleep as deep as death.

Weary, and long drawn out,
With faces white as chalk;
We stumble and slip in agony's grip
On that never ending walk.

Alec's Long March began at dawn on 27 May 1940, when he was woken by
shouts of '*Aufstehen, raus, raus, los, los*' ('Get up, get out, get going'), the brutal
wake-up call he was to hear for the next five years. Rubbing his eyes and
stretching weary limbs, he realized the shouts came not from the 10th Panzer
troops who had marched him into Guînes the previous evening but from military policemen, distinguished by their silver collar-plates on chains showing an
eagle perched on a swastika and the word *Feldgendarmerie*. These chains, and
their methods, earned them the nickname *Kettenhunde* (chained dogs).

The *Feldgendarmerie* lacked *Frontkameradenschaft* – the comradeship shared
by frontline troops – and wanted instantly to assert their authority. They
repeated the warning that escapers would be shot; then, without distributing
food or water, they prodded the prisoners out of the churchyard and on to a
road heading south-west. When Alec used his German to say how hungry the
men were, the answer was always the same – a finger pointed down the road
ahead. Initially, he was fooled, but after a while he realized it was a sick joke.

Another sick joke came as the captives were marched in a big curve, first
south, then east, then north-east through Belgium and Holland into Hitler's
Reich. Time after time, Alec would ask when they would be put on trains.
Each day, guards would kid him a train was nearby, but always at the next
town. In the meantime, the metronomic command was: 'Keep marching. You
have nothing to worry about. For you the war is over.'

As the column headed south-west, the *Feldgendarmerie*, armed with rifles,
machine guns and truncheons, marched alongside, supported by colleagues
on motorbikes riding up and down the line. The Queen Vics quickly learned
more of what the change of guards meant, with the chivalry previously shown
by German officers now gone. The *Feldgendarmerie* seemed 'hulking great
fellows, very impressive in their jackboots', thought one 9 Platoon member,
personifying Hitler's *Herrenvolk* (master race). If a captive wandered slightly
out of the column or stumbled, a guard would belt him over the head with his

truncheon. Guards in the rear would create panics as they pushed stragglers forward with rifle butts; in response, the stragglers would try to push through the men in front, who would in turn starting running. In the end, the whole column would be stumbling forward 'as fast as our legs could carry us'. At this point other guards would join in the sport, 'joyfully helping us along with their truncheons'.

The guards were 'badly turned out, slack and undisciplined', thought Rifle Brigade Second Lieutenant Terence Prittie. They would shoot without warning and shout insults at the nearest prisoner, hitting him 'very much as the cattle-drover twists the tail of an offending bullock in order to encourage the rest of the herd'. Once the sun was up, the weather turned hot. To quench their thirst, prisoners scooped water from ditches and grabbed dandelions and dock leaves to eat. For some, the hunger pangs were so extreme they risked being shot as they darted into fields to scrounge potatoes or swedes. Guards would run after them, firing warning shots over their heads and using rifle butts to push them back into line.

By midday, the column had travelled 15km, and the guards halted for their lunch. Once again, Alec was herded into a churchyard, this time at Marquise, and reunited with men taken at Fort Nieulay two days before the surrender. The guards distributed no food despite Ellison-Macartney's protests, but there was help for the wounded from three Red Cross nurses. The *Feld-gendarmerie* might keep their captives in a state of semi-starvation but wished to keep most alive as pathetic trophies, human spoils of war.

After the guards' lunch was over, the prisoners were ordered back on the road. Having spent the morning marching south-west in blistering heat, they were pushed south-east. The search for food intensified. The men were so hungry they 'cleaned a hedge of all leaves just like a herd of goats', according to Bill Balmer, a marine who fought alongside Alec. Nature then took its course, but the guards were unforgiving, and 'the constant "breaking column" to relieve yourself resulted in a bashing with rifle butts, sticks or batons'.

In the evening, the column passed through Le Wast, then up a hill to Alincthun, 12km from Marquise. There, at 9.00pm, Alec was led into a field next to a church for his second night in captivity. He was given a drink that was described as coffee, but nothing more, leaving him to survive on what food he had scrounged.

That evening 'a most touching incident took place', according to Stephen Houthakker. 'Plushy' had 'managed to obtain an egg and although in just as pitiable a condition as we were offered it to numerous of his troops. All realized the tremendous spirit behind this offering and, hungry as we were, we would have murdered the man who accepted it, knowing that the colonel himself deserved the titbit if anybody did.'

While such camaraderie persisted, any residual solidarity with the French evaporated. From the point of surrender, the Germans gave them preferential treatment. If rations were available, the French were fed first; if there was nothing left for the British 'infiltrators', that was that. At Alincthun, the French lit fires to cook food they had carried into captivity, while British POWs attempting the same thing were set upon with rifle butts. Soon fights broke out between the British and French over scraps of food.

At dusk, the guards said anyone standing up in the night would be assumed to be trying to escape and would be shot. This order could not have been worse timed: after the previous days' heat, it began to rain, and by the morning, Alec was soaked. In such conditions, his exhaustion was a blessing because he could sleep even in the rain, yet it was awful to be woken up soaked to the skin by guards bellowing '*Raus, raus, aufstehen!*'

Germany had signed the 1929 Geneva Convention but the Nazis, hiding behind the fact that the Weimar Republic had been the signatory, ignored many of its 91 articles. Thus, *Feldgendarmerie*, knowing their cruelty had *Oberkommando der Wehrmacht* (High Command) sanction, quickly showed they would not honour the Convention's letter or spirit. POW rations were supposed to equate to garrison rations, yet little food was available for most of the March. Making the prisoners walk from Guînes to Alincthun in a day breached the Convention's limit on marches of 20km per day. And the march to Alincthun was just the start. Day after day, the Germans exceeded the maximum, then night after night they forced prisoners to sleep in the open, another breach. When rumours of such ill-treatment reached London, the government protested, but Berlin said it 'had no information regarding charges of bad transport conditions'.

The Calais captives were roused at dawn on 28 May with kicks and shouts and pushed on to the road at 6.00am, heading south-east. For the first time, lorries were provided for officers, but their men had to walk. Before they left, the POWs were given a hot drink but no food, leaving them again to forage for what they could find. Even stopping to urinate was punished.

After being herded along for two hours, his sodden clothes steaming in the sun, Alec was shunted to the roadside to allow an artillery convoy to pass by. As the trucks roared past, spewing diesel fumes and covering him in dust, the artillerymen yelled obscenities. Once the convoy was through, the march resumed until the Queen Vics reached Desvres, a pottery town, towards noon. There, they were led into a football stadium, where the Germans were assembling POWs from various columns, counting them and segregating them by nationality and rank. The defeated Queen Vics had marched from Calais' ruins as a unit; now they were split up.

The officers had access to water in the pavilion, but their men had to remain outside and wait for officers to bring water. Finally, they were given food, their first official rations since capture – horse meat plus watery soup and biscuits. Without a cup, Alec drank from an upturned helmet. After the horrors of the previous few days, the Greenjackets might have been excused for lacking discipline; but Basil Embry, a captured pilot, was 'most impressed with the bearing of the ... Rifle Brigade, 60th Rifles and the Queen Victoria's Rifles' among 'a motley collection' of French, Dutch and Belgian prisoners 'in a pitiable state'.

Embry and his new comrades were herded south from Desvres in the afternoon, amid heightened security, with machine-gunners sitting at the back of German half-tracks and captured Bedford trucks ready to shoot prisoners trying to escape. Officers and men were separated. The Germans could claim Geneva Convention sanction in segregating their captives, yet it was also convenient – officers might provide leadership in escape attempts.

Once out in the countryside, the Germans invented a new torture. At seemingly random moments, a guard in the front vehicle would fire over the POWs' heads. As they dived to the ground, the truck behind would accelerate, forcing the POWs to jump up and sprint forward to avoid being run over. The guards thought this was funny and repeated it frequently. Mostly, the joke ended harmlessly, but not always. At one point, Alec turned round after hearing a burst of machine-gun fire to see the corpse of a straggler being kicked aside by a guard.

The enhanced security did not, however, deter Embry, in a better state than the soldiers and determined to escape. That afternoon, after seeing a road sign to 'Embry' and taking that as a good omen, he ran from the column, rolled down a roadside bank and fled into the fields. Evading recapture as he headed south, he reached Britain after two months via Spain.

Embry's boldness was untypical, but a few officers with language skills also attempted escape. Martin Gilliat, a 60th Rifleman, slipped away near Marquise, bought some civilian clothes from a farmer and headed south. He was eventually recaptured but later escaped twice from POW camps before being sent to Colditz. Two days after Gilliat's break, Jack Poole, another 60th Rifleman, leapt over a bridge parapet and disappeared below. Poole was a Great War escaper so knew what he was doing; but a few younger colleagues also had a go shortly afterwards, darting into roadside woods when their guards were distracted.

About 15km south of Desvres, the prisoners halted at a church in Hucqueliers for their third night in captivity. The *Feldgendarmerie* instructed the priest and local women to feed the British officers but give nothing to their men. The villagers, however, took pity, distributing sugar, chocolate and cigarettes all round. 'The Frenchwomen were very kind and gave us such little things as they could find,' Austin-Brown wrote to his wife. 'Many of them were in tears. We certainly looked a deplorable sight.'

At dawn the next morning, the priest served soup to the officers, but there was nothing for the men before the shouts of '*Raus! Raus!*' announced the start of another day of forced marching – this time 40km, destination Hesdin, halfway between Calais and Amiens. Beginning at 4.00am and lasting until

5.00pm, it was the worst day Alec had so far experienced, the weather hotter and the guards more hostile.

By now a pattern had been established. Alec spent most nights in dung-splattered fields huddled together with friends for warmth, although one evening the Germans forced the Queen Vics into a ditch that had been used as a latrine by a previous column. On most days, covered in dew and shivering, he would be roused at dawn and given twenty or thirty minutes to prepare for departure. Sometimes he would be fed acorn coffee, but usually there was nothing to eat before he saw again the dusty grey road stretching to the horizon. Along this he would march, typically in silence, absorbed in his misery. Some colleagues were so disturbed they could not speak. 'No one who has not been a prisoner will ever know what they felt,' wrote Prittie. 'It was headache and stomach-ache and the death of everybody and everything they loved bound up in a complete moral concussion of every thinking faculty, a dull, meaningless despair.'

As the March proceeded, the Greenjackets accumulated an assortment of drinking vessels to hang from their tattered uniforms – tin cans, broken jugs and cups, even chamber pots scrounged from rubbish heaps. Women would often take pity, standing at the roadside with buckets, bowls and saucepans of water and even milk. Bread or meat might be available for sale to officers whose French currency had survived the initial search.

The prisoners were mostly not allowed to halt to quench their thirst, but the *Feldgendarmerie* would allow the French to scoop water into their cans as they marched. When the British arrived, the guards would kick the buckets over, screaming '*Engländer nicht!*' In one village, a tiny old lady proffered bread from her outstretched apron but a guard responded by knocking her to the ground and kicking her. The POWs booed and shouted, 'Dirty square-headed bastard!' but they were driven away with rifle butts. 'Let the English swine go without,' one officer shouted. 'They can die of thirst and hunger for all I care!'

Each evening as he ate his meagre rations, Alec discussed the Germans' cruelty and the French POWs' supine behaviour with his comrades. Nick Day suggested the cruelty was to keep the British 'too fed up to try and get away'. Another man said the French, being marched through their own terri-tory, might be more tempted to escape if they were abused, especially in front of their women. Perhaps it was divide and rule, as humble riflemen were segregated at the back of the dust-choked columns and left last in line for food. Believing the French a defeated nation, the German conquerors seemed anxious to win them over to Hitler's New Order. The British, on the other hand, the guards would say, had caused the war.

Occasionally, ugly scenes occurred among prisoners rendered savage by ill-treatment. In one village, a woman appeared with a handcart of baguettes but was knocked to the ground as prisoners fought for the bread; peace was only restored when guards fired into the crowd.

Denied water from buckets placed on the roadside by villagers, the British would quench their thirsts in any way available, drinking from stagnant ponds and horse troughs covered with algae. Despite warnings from a nearby medic, one man even drank from the running overflow of a toilet cistern.

Forced to drink unclean water and eat raw vegetables, the men were soon suffering from diarrhoea and dysentery. Denied the chance to wash, they also became infested with fleas and lice. Yet a stricken rifleman dropping his trousers by the roadside might have a rifle butt dug into his kidneys to encourage him back in line; stragglers were even killed for stopping to tie their bootlaces.

As he stumbled along, Alec saw the impact of *Blitzkrieg*: the flat country was scarred by wrecked tanks, abandoned transport and flattened villages. By contrast, the Wehrmacht's power was clear, as long convoys of tanks and half-track personnel-carriers headed west.

Occasionally, a cigar-chomping tank commander would lean over his turret and tap the side, calling out, 'Cardboard tanks, eh Tommy?' in reference to Allied propaganda. Soldiers on half-tracks photographed the POWs' misery. The more humiliating the situation the better – one favourite was to snap POWs begging for water. Then there would be lots of banter about 'Chawcheel-WC', accompanied by an obscene gesture. One private bellowed, 'Give us a message for your girlfriends. We'll soon be there to take care of them.' Another shouted, 'Your kink in Canada, Adolf Hitler soon in Buckingham Palace.' Occasionally, Germans robbed the prisoners, stripping the Greenjackets of any mackintoshes, helmets and watches that had survived the 10th Panzers' souvenir-hunting at Calais. So much, thought Alec, for 'honourable captivity'.

There were moments of relief, but not many. During the march to Hesdin, a German bomber flew overhead pursued by a Hurricane. Seconds later, the bomber crashed, generating cheers from the POWs, and the pilot then flew low and executed a victory role salute. The guards responded by firing over the prisoners' heads.

Alec would later claim he never lost hope. The British situation, the Germans insisted, was hopeless because Channel ports held throughout the Great War had fallen. Yet, Queen Vics consoled themselves with fantastical rumours and predictions: the BEF would retake Calais and advance; their guards belonged to units that had broken through but were now cut off and trying to get back to their lines; Allied forces were surging north to liberate them; the French would recover their poise and evict the Germans.

On arriving at Hesdin, the POWs were herded past an impressive bell tower and directed towards the stable block of an abandoned chateau. For the first time, officers had straw for bedding and running water. Yet their men had nothing, sleeping once again in a manure-covered meadow. For supper, the Germans provided captured British ration biscuits and sauerkraut.

After a breakfast of horse fat and army biscuits, Alec was herded onto the road the following day at 5.30am. They were now heading east, taking them further from Allied troops rumoured still to be fighting south of the Somme, and further from the coast. Escape would therefore become more difficult, but they were also moving into wooded country that offered chances for some to slip away unseen. Terence Prittie and Charles Clay of the Rifle Brigade and Stephen Houthakker of the Queen Vics were soon recaptured, but 60th Rifleman Alick Williams made it home.

Most riflemen were not, however, ready to escape. Lack of food was one factor, another was the psychological shock of defeat. A few days previously they had fought under orders in organized units; now they felt like cattle, stripped of their capacity to do anything other than place one foot in front of the other. Denis Hoy from Alec's company talked about making a break but no one seemed enthusiastic so he gave up. After the battle's excitement came 'lassitude and boredom, and the near-coma of sullen despair,' wrote Prittie. 'As with a route march or a game of football, nobody is aware of the nervous strain until that strain has been removed. To physical exhaustion was added, in our cases, everything that defeat implied.' Men would talk of escape, but apathy typically prevailed.

Alec's French and German were potential assets. An escape in France, where the population was sympathetic, would be easier than in Germany. So he participated in such debates but in the end, paralysed by exhaustion, kept his head down. He had no food, no map and no compass, and the guards had said escapers would be shot. They could be bluffing, yet to risk his life unarmed was different from taking his chances in battle armed with his Bren gun.

The French seemed content to march through their own country without escaping, believing that France would shortly surrender and they would be sent home. Even if they were wrong, and British troops were counter-attacking, why not sit tight? In fact, all around, Alec saw evidence of Allied defeat as German tanks, artillery and supply trucks pushed west. Yet optimists persisted in claiming help was nearby: 'These fellows have absolutely no idea where they're marching us to,' said one officer. 'Why, you've only got to look at their faces to see they're desperate.'

The prisoners' resting place on Thursday, 30 May was a flax factory at Frévent, where they caught up with POWs taken at Boulogne, some of whom appeared to have been treated better, perhaps because they had put up less of a fight. The reception committee included a perfectly-dressed, clean-shaven Welsh Guards sergeant holding a cup of tea, a strange sight to men denied a proper meal or drink for four days.

That evening, a British padre presented prisoners with postcards for sending home via the Red Cross's International Committee in Geneva. He also offered to post any letters the POWs had drafted. One that did reach England a few weeks later stamped '*Kriegsgefangenenpost*' had been scribbled the previous evening by Ken Wynn, an insurance broker who joined the Queen Vics the same day as Alec in 1938. Beneath the heading, 'Somewhere in France 29/5/1940', Wynn wrote:

My dear Mum and Dad,
Just a line to let you know that I am safe and well but a prisoner. I haven't been able to write before but I'll explain everything when I see you again. Please tell Tony [his girlfriend] that I'll write to her as soon as I am settled again. I've only got the one envelope so if you don't mind just spreading the news to her I'll be very pleased. I feel pretty awful at the moment as I've no money, no cigarettes, in fact no nothing. I lost my pack and all my clothes before I was captured but will get you to send me a shirt and some trousers as soon as I've got an address ... Now that there is no immediate prospect of seeing you I am missing you terribly. I wish I'd been a better son to you both but all being well will turn over a new leaf after the war.
All my love to you both, Gran and Tony.'

This was a painful moment for Alec. If a postcard reached home, his parents would gain short-term comfort, yet it might be risky. If Hitler invaded Britain, the Nazis might seize Queen Vics records showing his religion; thus an innocent postcard home could expose his family's ethnicity. As men around him filled in their details, Alec threw his postcard away.

The next morning, the POWs were woken at 3.00am, given dry biscuits but no water and ordered out onto a road signposted to Doullens. The journey was shorter than on previous days at 16km, but 31 May would be a day never forgotten. That Friday, Alec learned what the phrase 'smell of defeat' could mean – and smells stuck in his mind long after visual memories faded. He had already contended with stomach-churning stenches. Earlier in the march, he was one of a dozen men given shovels and ordered to bury a putrefying horse. Nothing, however, could have prepared him for Doullens.

The day was hot and the road particularly dusty. Three decades later, Alec retraced the March by car and wrote an article for the Queen Vics' newsletter. Its centrepiece was a description of the journey to Doullens:

Who after 34 years cannot still smell the diesel exhaust from the continuous stream of German convoys, which time and again forced our weary little column to the extreme right of the road? And after all this time, I need only to close my eyes to recall the pathetic rivulets of refugees wandering who knows where in their efforts to get away from the German invaders. Some of them like snails had all their worldly possessions on their backs. Some were wheeling prams, handcarts and even wheelbarrows heaped with the pitiful remains of their household goods. Here and there one saw a farm cart drawn by a horse so scrawny and dilapidated that even the Germans had not thought it worth their while to commandeer it.

'Almost all of us were unable to see beyond the end of a day's march when we might or might not get a meagre ration of food and a place where we could stretch out on hard ground,' he recalled. Footsore and weary, Alec asked where the POWs would spend the night. The guard's response seemed promising – Alec would have a roof over his head that evening.

The Queen Vics were herded through Doullens' bombed streets to a citadel on high ground, surrounded by a dry moat. The building had once guarded France's medieval northern frontier but had later been turned into a prison. During the Great War, it was a military hospital and thereafter, as Alec discovered from the sign outside, it housed *L'école pour la preservation des jeunes filles* – a reform school for prostitutes. The Germans had turned it into a *Durchgangslager* (*Dulag* for short), a transit camp. Later, it housed political prisoners and Jews.

By the time Alec arrived, the citadel, with one tap and one trench latrine, was crowded with prisoners. After the afternoon's heat and dust, water was a priority, and a long queue formed at the tap. Sustenance came next, and prisoners pushed against the fortress railings with arms outstretched, pleading with townswomen beyond for food. Unsurprisingly, the women fed the French, and the Queen Vics had to wait – and then only got biscuits and watery soup in dixie cans the Germans said should afterwards be used for urinating in.

The French included African troops, 'whose ideas of sanitation and hygiene were,' Alec thought, 'primitive, to say the least'. As he was pushed towards the building, he was assailed 'from the nostrils down to the very pit of the stomach by a stench so powerful that, in retrospect, I should be obliged to search through the whole of Dante's *Inferno* to find words adequate to describe it'. The source became clear when he climbed a staircase looking for space in a cell. Those parts of the floor not covered by resting bodies were 'almost ankle-deep in excrement'. The colonials had dysentery and 'had found the facilities were so inadequate and their needs so pressing they had been forced to relieve themselves wherever they happened to be at a time when nature called with a voice so strident as to brook no delay'.

Some Queen Vics squatted in the citadel but Alec retreated outside: the moat was not much better – men were squatting around emptying their bowels – 'but at least some of the malodorous emanations were carried away on the warm night air'. By this time, he had learned to sleep with his boots on

– not to avoid the excrement but because his blistered feet would swell if he slept in his socks, making it harder to get into his boots in the morning.

At dawn on Saturday, 1 June, the Greenjackets found they had new guards, who seemed even more nervous and aggressive; they distributed mildewed bread from farm carts and led prisoners past the one water tap. Those with containers filled them, others made do with sips from cupped hands. To Vincent, the bread and water tasted 'like manna from heaven' but only served to intensify his hunger pangs. Painful cramps set in, but he had to grit his teeth and walk stiff-legged until they passed.

The column soon came to a junction in the dusty road. With half the prisoners across, some Wehrmacht trucks sped by, cutting the group in two. Two men hesitated in the middle of the road as others dashed to avoid the oncoming lorries. A guard decided this was insubordination and fired at the pair, killing both. Such casual murder was made easier by a further Geneva Convention breach. Article 7 stated: 'Belligerents are required to notify each other of all captures of prisoners as soon as possible.' Yet the *Feldgendarmerie* made no attempt to log their captives. This gave trigger-happy guards confidence that insubordinate prisoners could be killed without consequence – they would merely be 'shot while trying to escape'.

The guards were nervous partly because of fresh aerial activity. Alec heard explosions as RAF planes bombed a convoy on a road nearby and, as the column passed through one deserted village, he heard a roar of engines and looked up to see an RAF fighter pursued by a Messerschmitt. Once again, the prisoners cheered, and the next time planes came near the guards forced them to lie down until the raid was over.

In the late afternoon, the POWs reached Foncquevillers and were corralled in a field. Gommecourt Wood nearby had seen fighting during the Battle of the Somme in 1916. Now the Germans were the victors, a fact rubbed home as Alec trudged past the military cemetery the next morning. Later that day, he had another painful lesson about the fortunes of war when the column passed Pozieres' Great War memorial comprising a tank and a marble column. Some men broke ranks to read the inscription describing the first use of tanks – but now Hitler's Panzers were vanquishing the Allies. Nearby, a cross commemorating the 60th Rifles' participation in the Battle of the Somme was surrounded by white headstones, gleaming in the sunshine and stretching to the horizon, interspersed with manicured lawns and flowers.

Thus the March continued, day after day. Had Alec been free he might have enjoyed the scenery – rolling hills studded with villages, picturesque farmhouses, orchards and meandering streams. Shady trees and flower-filled hedges lined the roads, beyond which were meadows and fields of ripening corn. Prittie thought the countryside had 'all the life, diversity and ripe charm of Sussex', with the land stretching to the horizon 'in a cheerful pattern of mellow colours'. Yet it was also 'a nightmare land', its beauty 'a vague, improbable background to the grey, endless miles of road and the packed, grimy, hopeless columns of men trudging listlessly along in a silence broken only by the occasional high-pitched shout of a guard or by the plaintive cries of some indignant Frenchman who had fallen out by the side of the road and was being hustled back into the stumbling ranks'.

The food situation deteriorated further after Doullens, so the only option was to live off the land like locusts. At one point, a prisoner darted into a field of potatoes and began pulling them up. Within seconds, hundreds had joined him, grabbing their prizes, rubbing off the dirt and eating them raw.

After a 22½km march, the destination on Sunday, 2 June, the end of Alec's first week in captivity, was a barbed-wire enclosed field outside Bapaume on the Somme-Artois border. The Germans had made use of Bapaume's road and rail links to establish it as an assembly point for POWs, and by the time Alec's column arrived, the field contained thousands of Allied soldiers. Some officers found refuge in a barn but Alec slept in the open. It was his parents' 25th wedding anniversary; his celebratory supper comprised mildewed rye bread and ersatz coffee.

The following morning, the Germans conducted another search. A few possessions – razors, pens, cigarette lighters and matches, walking sticks, helmets, gas masks and money – had survived the initial search at Calais; now the Greenjackets faced being deprived of these before being ordered to march 30km to Cambrai. The dusty journey was along a Roman road, whose straightness intensified Alec's misery. Overhead, there was more aerial combat, causing people to flee their homes and leaving most villages deserted. Once again, there were Great War reminders as Alec trudged past cemeteries at Beaumetz-lès-Cambrai and Louverval. Occasionally, he also saw wooden crosses marking the roadside burials of refugees killed during the Wehrmacht's advance in May.

At Cambrai, the prisoners were held inside military barracks. Cambrai had been Wellington's headquarters after Waterloo and was also the location of two battles during the Great War. The townswomen here seemed less afraid than in other places. As Alec stumbled along, he heard shouts of '*Bravo, Tommy!*', '*Vive l'Angleterre*' and '*A bas les Allemands!*' and taunting of the French soldiers for giving up. Though in a dire state, the Queen Vics formed themselves up into straighter ranks and smiled back.

The women's behaviour encouraged talk that the war was turning. Initially, there were rumours that the Allies were counter-attacking; next, they had made big gains; finally, tanks were nearby and rescue imminent. Some men convinced themselves they had heard British artillery the previous night. Inside Cambrai's barracks, however, the atmosphere changed; the French were invited in whereas the British were ordered to remain outside on a parade ground littered with abandoned military documents and pockmarked by trench latrines. The only water source was a cistern on a cart. One Queen

Vic called it 'a living hell'; another thought it 'a stinking, overcrowded, rat-infested sewer of a place'. As at Calais, the French seemed prepared for capture, carrying stoves for cooking. Fights broke out because rations were limited to stale bread, army biscuits and thin soup. A Briton would ask a Frenchman to share his food. Met with refusal, the Briton would kick over the Frenchman's stove. Soon they would be wrestling on the ground, after which the Germans would fire shots to restore order.

Alec was shocked men could sink so far, and he and other Queen Vics tried to maintain order as the fat fell from them and their battledress and boots disintegrated. They had fought at Calais as 'a close family' and would stick together as prisoners. Thus, as they marched, they organized themselves into support groups of three or four men, which later evolved into the basic units of POW society. These substitute families, called syndicates or combines, were made up of 'muckers', who 'mucked in', sharing food and cigarettes. Alec's Long March muckers included Bill Brett and Dennis McLaughlin from B Company. Bill and Dennis had trained with Alec from his first evening at B Company's drill hall. They were older and felt avuncular towards him – and the bond never broke. When Bill died thirty-six years later, Alec wrote his Queen Vics magazine obituary:

> I was with him during part of the time that we were being marched towards Germany and even the extreme misery of our physical and mental condition at the time could not entirely repress Bill's natural cheerfulness. He also supported practically the entire weight of a member of the battalion who had been taken ill on the march until the end of the day's stage was reached.

Two years later, as a result of poor diet and overwork, Alec lay in the Lamsdorf *Revier* (sick bay) waiting for his ulcerated legs to heal and reflecting on the selfishness of POWs on the March. This was the theme of Help the Other Man a Little Too:

> When life is pretty hard,
> And it's got you off your guard
> And things are getting difficult to do,
> When you've done your rotten task;
> Before he's time to ask,
> Help the other man a little too.
>
> When, at the first quick glance,
> You don't seem to have a chance
> And you're really in a pretty awful stew,
> If you think you're going mad,
> Things won't be half so bad,
> If you help the other man a little too.

Back in England, when in doubt,
You would help a fellow out
And another would do just as much for you.
Well, here it's just the same.
You've been taught to play the game,
So help the other man a little too.

It's the same, throughout life's race.
Someone has to set the pace,
And someone has to cox a flagging crew,
But when the distance has been run,
You needn't care whose lost or won
If you've helped the other man a little too.

Chapter 10

'40 hommes, 8 chevaux'

On the marchers plodded, growing weaker as near-starvation, lice and dysentery took their toll. On Tuesday, 4 June, rumours of British advances still rife, the Queen Vics left Cambrai at 11.00am on the road north-east to Valenciennes. Some walked along looking back over their shoulders, as if expecting to see British troops. Was this simple-mindedness, Alec asked himself, or did they perhaps need to believe in something, however fantastical, to get them through the day?

As Alec marched along, he saw evidence that near Cambrai, unlike at Calais, the French had resisted '*les Boches*'. In the fields he could see wooden crosses with German helmets on top between the charred remains of tanks, staff cars and dead horses. In many villages, the Wehrmacht had seized homes as billets and Germans would come out to jeer as the column passed, sometimes barging in to grab a watch or helmet as a trophy. The taunting was constant but the POWs responded in kind even if this resulted in a kick or punch. A favourite jibe was that the British would soon be sent down coal mines to work sixteen hours a day. At one point, two officers pulled up in a staff car near an elderly prisoner with Great War medal ribbons on his battledress. 'Englishman, you were in the 1914 war,' said one officer in stilted English, to which the prisoner replied in a Scots accent, 'Aye, and I'll fight ye in the next.'

In villages not occupied by Germans, POWs broke ranks and dashed into shops and cottages, stealing what they could find and causing pandemonium. Villagers yelled abuse, French and British soldiers fought over their spoils, and guards attacked the miscreants with their bayonets or fired at their legs. One scrounger purloined a rabbit and killed it but was caught by a guard, who grabbed the animal from his hand, then chased him down the road beating him over the head with it.

Some POWs dropped to their knees, unable to carry on, apparently indifferent to the guards' kicks. What became of such men was initially unclear – only later did Alec discover these 'pitiful specimens of humanity' were scooped into trucks and taken to field hospitals. In the meantime, the beatings were sufficient reason to keep going. In the crowd, helped by his muckers, Alec might be relatively safe. Alone, and still not registered by the Red Cross, anything could happen to him.

The journey to Valenciennes was one of the longest of the March and only in the early hours of 5 June did Alec walk through its streets. The townsfolk had fled west the day the invasion began, abandoning it to looters. A fire then spread, and when the Germans arrived on 27 May the town was in ruins. Dawn broke as the Queen Vics were herded into a park to bed down. All around were the sleeping figures of POWs who had arrived the previous evening.

After a couple of hours' sleep, cries of '*Raus! Raus!*' had Alec on his feet again and the column headed into Belgium at Quiévrain. As he marched along the straight Roman road he caught glimpses on his left of railway tracks, along which he still hoped to be carried. There was, however, some relief at Quiévrain. By this point, older guards had taken over the column, and when the Honnelle river came into view, they took pity on the prisoners, allowing them, for the first time since Calais, to wash. As Alec stripped and dashed into the stream it seemed the whole village turned out to watch and offer food. Some men waded in barefoot and cut their feet on the riverbed rocks; others kept their boots on. After a while, the guards ordered them back on to the road. Alec's uniform dried rapidly in the sun, and it felt good to be rid of nine days' dust. After a 39km march that lasted until 10.00pm, the prisoners were herded into a muddy field for their next overnight stop and fed sauerkraut, one loaf between five and dripping. This was outside Mons, site of Britain's first Great War battle.

Over the next four days, the prisoners were shunted in a meandering fashion, turning north-east, then north, then east again through Soignies, Enghien and Halle, south of Brussels. Alec slept in fields at Soignies and Enghien, where he was allowed his first rest day, while in Halle he slept in a jute factory. Some men thought they were marching in circles or that their guards were lost; others believed they were being used as human shields protecting German lines of communication from air-raids; yet another view was that they were being paraded as human trophies to convince the Belgians the Allies were defeated.

The ill-treatment of POWs continued. On the road to Soignies, the Germans seemed particularly edgy. Reg Beattie was an artilleryman who joined Alec's column at Doullens. In his 6 June diary entry, he wrote: 'The guards kept hustling us and one swine struck one good chap with the butt of his rifle. The squaddy ... turned round and saw red. He hit Jerry on the chin, knocking him down. As he lay on the ground he drew his revolver and shot the Tommy in the stomach and again in the chest.' The ill-treatment of friendly locals also continued. In one town, a woman who stepped forward with some bread was pushed at rifle point into the column and force-marched down the road.

Near the border, Alec saw some roadside buildings surrounded by barbed wire. It was a convent, and, as the POWs passed by, nuns offered bread and water through the wire. They also offered to take prisoners' names and addresses and send letters to their families. Bill Balmer gave his details and eventually his family received a letter via Switzerland. For a second time, Alec faced a dilemma – should he give his details? Again, he chose silence.

On 10 June, Alec breakfasted on potatoes before marching 37km from Halle via Waterloo to Wavre, where he bedded down after midnight in a field next to a ruined Catholic seminary; once again, the French were allowed inside. The *Feldgendarmerie* enjoyed the visit to Waterloo, the site of Britain's greatest victory; they laughed as they prodded their prisoners past the artificial hill topped by a statue of a lion commemorating the battle.

Waterloo's inhabitants that Monday morning were, however, determined to show solidarity, giving Alec his first full-scale show of sympathy since capture. As the column entered the main street, people on trams threw cigarettes, grocers ran forward with food and a baker tossed bread rolls from his doorway. Soon, the street was full of prisoners fighting over food and cigarettes, screaming guards rifle-butting prisoners and civilians, and stationary tram drivers ringing their bells to add to the cacophony.

Over the next two days, the Calais prisoners were herded, first 34km to military stables at Tienen, where they entertained the locals by singing Teddy Bears' Picnic, and then 20km to Sint-Truiden, later the home of NGJ1, the Luftwaffe's best night-fighter squadron. After many nights in the open, Alec camped in a factory, where he was fed bread and sausages. The conditions were, however, so dreadful some riflemen thought they would have been better off outside, despite overnight rain. Then it was on a further 21km to a cinder football pitch in Tongeren, the last Belgian town before the border.

The next day, Alec was roused at 3.00am and marched 20km, crossing into Holland at Maastricht. As at Waterloo, the townsfolk were supportive, serving bread and cakes, eggs, cooked meat and tea, coffee, milk and even wine from roadside trestle tables. Alec thought their generosity was the March's 'most striking'. It did not go down well with the guards, as a civilian couple discovered when an officer leapt from his staff car and attacked them with his baton. At one point a teenage girl cycled past Alec distributing Droste chocolate cat's tongues and calling out encouragement. One guard went 'absolutely mad ... he kicked her off her bicycle and stuck the butt of his rifle into her back and made her fall in with the column of prisoners of war until we reached the barbed wire-surrounded field where we were going to spend the night.'

The pen into which the POWs were crammed was outside Heerlen. There, a tent was erected to house a German medical officer. Despite the presence of many walking wounded, this was the first time a German medic had offered treatment, and a long queue built up.

The next day, Saturday, 15 June after twenty days on the road, having covered nearly 500km averaging almost 25km per day, Alec was prodded awake at 3.00am and marched into Germany at Palenberg, a coal-mining village near Aachen. As he approached the border, Alec could see a red and white pole across the track guarded by soldiers. To the right were a slag heap and a pithead. To the left were shabby houses, with Swastika flags festooning the walls. Lining the street, villagers jeered and threw household rubbish. Teenagers marched along in Hitler Youth uniforms waving Swastikas, shouting, '*England ist kaput!*' and, pointing at prisoners, '*Scheiss aus England!*' ('shit from England'). They had much to celebrate: German troops had taken Paris the day before.

How were the exhausted, half-starved POWs to respond? They were unshaven, their uniforms were in tatters and their boots were disintegrating. Yet they were not going to show they were defeated, and a message spread down the column: 'Get in step and march to attention.' Bowed shoulders were pushed back and weary heads raised. Initially, the prisoners responded to the taunts with insults – '*Deutschland kaput! Hitler nicht gut!*' A Greenjacket corporal yelled, 'You can shout and cheer now; your tears will come later.' Then the column began to whistle There'll Always Be an England. This did not please the villagers. As Alec passed, 'a young and quite good-looking girl' welcomed him into Germany 'by spitting full in my face'.

Thus ended the March for Alec. Having been spat at, he was taken past Palenberg's slagheaps towards Aachen, where the POWs were marshalled on a football pitch beside a railway line. Separated for good from their officers, they were issued with a third of a loaf of bread each and some sausage and told to wait. Initially, Alec was thrilled, hoping decent transport would be provided to take them to a proper prison camp. He hoped, meanwhile, to rest and recover his strength.

The Germans had other plans. The train that finally arrived had no passenger carriages. Instead, it comprised a line of French cattle-trucks, on the sides of which were stencilled the words '*40 hommes/8 chevaux*' ('40 men/8 horses'). The Germans later used such trucks to transport Jews to death camps, and the POWs taken in 1940 were subjected to similar treatment as they travelled east.

Putting forty men in each cattle-truck would have left room for them to stretch out and sleep even though conditions were rudimentary – there was straw on the floor but the only ventilation came from slits in the sides of each truck. When the train appeared, the Queen Vics cheered as they moved towards the tracks. When guards began opening the doors, those who could broke into a run, hoping their marching days were over.

But the Germans, desperately short of transport, now split their captives into groups of as many as seventy-five men, not forty, to each truck. Unsurprisingly, bedlam ensued as prisoners fought for spots to sit and rest against the sides of the trucks. It quickly became clear there was not room for seventy-five men to sit, and many POWs had to stand, with no means of supporting themselves other than leaning on their neighbours. After using rifle butts and boots to cram men in, the guards bolted the doors.

The train pulled out at 7.00pm. In their exhaustion, many POWs fell asleep on their feet, held upright by the crush around them. This was merely the start of the torture. Few trucks had bucket-toilets and, once the doors were bolted, the slits in the walls doubled up as gaps through which POWs emptied their urine. Men without cans used their boots. As the train halted in one station, a POW fought his way towards a vent clutching soiled under-pants in his hand. When the train moved off, he flung them at a German on the platform, yelling, 'Take that, you square-headed bastard!' It landed on the man's head and as the train gathered speed the POW turned to his friends and shouted, 'Bull's-eye, blokes!' After this incident, prisoners were warned they would be shot if they followed suit.

Little could be done to ease the misery of POWs with dysentery. The stronger men would hold up sufferers near the vents, hoping the wind would carry their excreta off into the night. Often, however, when the stomach-wrenching call of nature came, the only thing they could do was defecate in their trousers. Those with time to prepare would defecate into their side hats or pockets torn from their battledress before tipping the contents through the vents. Then they would use pages from books as toilet paper, with even bibles sacrificed. Soon, the stench resembled Doullens, and men would take it in turns to stand near the vents gasping for air.

As the train headed east, it would regularly be shunted into sidings while military trains came through. Each time this happened the doors would open and prisoners' hopes would rise. Each time, however, such hopes would be dashed as they discovered the doors had been opened merely to give them a '*Pinkelpause*' – a chance to urinate on the ground – and give the guards oppor-tunities to humiliate them further. '*Saustalle*' ('pigsty') they would yell, as if the prisoners could help their conditions.

The cool of the night offered some respite, yet later on as the train moved slowly through vast fields of corn, the sun heated the metal-roofed trucks until they felt like ovens. At one point, a POW leapt to his feat, screaming, 'I want to live, I don't want to die!' before collapsing in a heap. Others tried to comfort him but there was little they could do as he lay whimpering like a child. In Bill Balmer's truck, one man died during the first night, the first of five to die during the journey.

After hours of painfully slow travel – the distance covered was only 270km – the train halted at 8.00am on 16 June at Tinholt, a rural station. This time the prisoners were told to get down and form a column. After marching 5kms, they reached *Mannschaften Stammlager VI-C*, Stalag VI-C for short, at Bathorn. It consisted of four vast marquees surrounded by barbed wire.

The commandant was a distinguished-looking Great War veteran. When Alec's column marched past with as much dignity as they could muster, he wrinkled his nose and called them 'filthy English swine'. They soon discovered how primitive the conditions were. The POWs were protected from the elements, yet there were no beds, tables or seats, leaving them to sleep on bare earth or straw-covered cobbles. There were no medical facilities, and the stench from the few toilets that served the camp's 1,500 inmates was almost as bad as in the cattle-trucks. No food was provided that first day; nor was there any lighting, so there was nothing to do after dark but sleep and attempt to recover.

In the morning, the commandant returned with another officer and an Alsatian dog and called for the senior British officer. Regimental Sergeant Major 'Paddy' Martin of the Royal Lincolns stepped forward, asking Alec to interpret. The commandant then delivered a lecture on POW behaviour, ending with a warning: anyone placing a finger on the wire would be shot. Alec asked about food but the reply was brusque: 'Your navy has been blockading Germany. You will wait until we are ready to feed you.'

Food arrived in the afternoon, but not much: potato soup, one loaf of bread between nine and cheese. This became the daily ration at Bathorn. On the second day, the commandant, his deputy and the Alsatian returned, along with a private, and called for Martin. Alec accompanied him but was dismissed with the words: 'It's all right. We have our own interpreter. We don't need you.' Alec chose, however, to stay within earshot, 'because I knew everybody else standing around would want to know what was going on'.

After the commandant issued instructions, translated flawlessly by the private, he and his deputy strolled round the perimeter. At this point, the private glanced around to check no one was within earshot, walked towards Alec and said: 'You are a Jew, aren't you?' Alec's stomach 'did a quick turnover' as images of Dachau flashed through his mind. Was the hole he had dug for his identity tags and paybook in Calais' dunes insufficient? Could his ethnicity be buried so easily? Or would he be vulnerable to Jew-hunters as long as he was a POW? Were all Germans anti-Semites? Or did 'good Germans' exist and was this private 'a good German'?

As he stood rigid, desperately seeking a response that might not incriminate him, he found he was, indeed, staring at a good German. 'It's all right; you don't have to say anything. I know,' the guard said quietly. He paused before continuing: 'Let me give you a piece of advice. As long as you are in Germany or in German hands never let on that you speak German because it's going to cause you trouble. The British never speak foreign languages. Sooner or later somebody will put two and two together and they'll say: "He speaks German; it's like Yiddish – he's a Jew".' With that, the guard turned on his heels and joined his colleagues.

Decades later, Alec would recall the conversation – it was good advice from a good German, but he ignored it. He could not hide his ability to speak the language. 'Rows would break out between guards and prisoners and I would then see a British soldier and a German yelling at one another, each in his own language, neither understanding a word of what the other was saying. Then I'd see the guard shift his rifle from his shoulder and then I knew I had to step in – if I didn't intervene there would have been bloodshed.' As interpreter, Alec often had to absorb the guard's wrath: 'It wasn't funny because the heat almost inevitably got turned on to the person who spoke German.' Some POWs would also be suspicious: 'In the end I got a reputation for either sucking up to the Germans or standing up to them.'

Later, the commandant called a parade, and Alec was surrounded by POWs who distrusted the German interpreter's translation. The news was grim. The rumours of Allied counter-attacks were false. On 2 June, the last British troops had abandoned Norway. The following night, the last soldiers were lifted from Dunkirk. On 10 June Italy joined the Axis; the next day, France's government fled to Tours and on 13 June German troops marched into Paris. The day before, 8,000 51st Highland Division soldiers had surrendered at Saint-Valéry-en-Caux on the Normandy coast, the largest British surrender of 1940. This news added despair to hunger and boredom. During the March, Alec concentrated on surviving, leaving little mental space for anything else. At Bathorn, he had time to think and the more he thought the more depressed he became.

On the evening of 19 June, he was issued with mouldy bread and foul-smelling cheese for the next leg of the journey, which, he was told, would end with permanent incarceration. The following morning, the POWs were woken at 3.00am and marched back to Tinholt. Once again, the guards used rifle butts to cram as many as seventy-five men into each cattle-truck. Once more, prisoners took it in turns to squat or stand, swaying about as the train jerked forwards. As before, there was no water, while any sanitary facilities were limited to a bucket that could only infrequently be emptied; with many men still suffering from diarrhoea or worse, the air within each windowless truck rapidly turned fetid.

In the early hours of 21 June the train reached Silesia. The prisoners were now in a province known for fanatical anti-Semitism. At its heart was Breslau, home to the *Wehrkreis VIII* headquarters, administrative centre of Hitler's most extensive network of concentration camps and POW camps including *Stalag* VIIIB, to which Alec was heading, and *Stalag Luft* III at Sagan, where the Great Escape took place.

Finally, at 3.30pm on Friday, 21 June, after a 900km journey, the train with its cargo, in Alec's words, of 'extremely hungry, extremely dirty and very dispirited' prisoners, pulled into a rural halt comprising three sidings, a passenger shelter at the centre of the one low platform and a ticket office at the end. The station was on the edge of a hamlet identified by the station signs as Annahof. The guards threw the doors open and yelled '*Raus Engländer! Raus! Schnell! Ihre Fahrt ist fertig!*' Alec realized his journey was over.

Chapter 11

'The Zoo in Silesia'

Stalag VIIIB at Lamsdorf was Germany's largest prison camp, housing 13,000 men at its peak. Camps such as Colditz and *Stalag Luft* III became famous for escapes, but Lamsdorf was known simply for its conditions. It was, wrote Frederick Forsyth in *The Fourth Protocol*, 'the worst *Stalag* of them all'.

Nicknamed 'the Zoo in Silesia' by one POW, 'the home of sacrificed souls' by another, the camp, half a mile long and a quarter of a mile wide, began as a barracks for an artillery range. Its huts were first used for prisoners during the Franco-Prussian War. During the Great War, Russians and Britons were held there, dying in their thousands from disease and neglect. Thus, one of Alec's first views of Lamsdorf was its cemetery.

As the cattle-truck doors opened, the POWs were dazzled by the sunlight. Most were so weak and stiff they could not jump down. Instead, they rolled onto their bellies and lowered their feet onto the platform below. 'We didn't as much as get out of the trucks, we fell out,' said one Greenjacket. All around, men's legs buckled beneath them. They would get up, stagger round in circles then fall again as they tried to recover the use of their limbs. Some POWs were lifted down. Whether they were dead or alive, Alec did not know. The guards were impatient, but further cries of '*Raus! Raus!*' and rifle-butt prods were required before the ragged column was organized into lines of five to be counted and recounted. Then the prisoners were herded from the station down a sandy lane flanked by deep drains.

The march to Lamsdorf passed through flat farmland before entering a pine forest. After 3km the forest gave way to a sandy plain, and the prisoners were led towards a single-bar barrier marking the entrance to *Stalag* VIIIB's *Vorlager*. To the left was a guardhouse, to the right a stone eagle perched on a swastika. The *Vorlager* housed two companies of guards and a back-up company of regular soldiers equipped with armoured cars for emergencies, as well as the *Kommandantur*, housing the commandant, the *Kartei* (records and mail office), delousing block, search, security-check and court-martial room. A chestnut tree-lined road led through the *Vorlager* towards two five-bar wooden gates eight feet high, laced with barbed wire and manned by two guards in crumpled grey-green uniforms. These gates, a flagpole from which flew the Third Reich's battle flag – two black and white crosses on a red background with a Swastika in the middle – and an inner set of gates six feet behind and manned by two more guards marked the entrance to the prison camp proper.

The camp itself was surrounded by two parallel barbed-wire fences nine feet high. The barbed wire, as thick as a pencil with long spikes, was strung on pine posts driven into the ground at six-foot intervals. At the top, the wire sloped inwards to deter climbers, while the space between the fences was filled with barbed-wire coils from which hung tin cans that jangled if disturbed. Every 100 yards and at each corner stood twenty-five-foot watchtowers, housing two sentries equipped with machine guns, rifles, a searchlight and binoculars. About eight feet inside the inner fence was a single tripwire fifteen inches high. Anyone stepping over that wire on to 'the death strip' beyond would be ordered three times to halt; those who did not would be shot. This was no empty threat: eighteen months after Alec's arrival, Jeffrey Reid, an airman, was killed while scrounging wood the wrong side of the wire. The guards thought he was trying to escape. One fired a warning shot at which Reid froze. A second guard fired the fatal shot, claiming Reid had moved.

At night, sentries with Alsatians and Doberman Pinschers would patrol the perimeter, which was floodlit. To the east, a strip of sand seven yards wide separated the fence from the pine forest; to the south-west, moorland stretched towards distant hills.

As Alec's column arrived, one guard opened the gates while the second ordered the prisoners to walk slowly forward so he could count them. Ahead of him, Alec saw a road running north-west through a complex laid out as a grid. The road was lined on each side by compounds individually fenced off with barbed wire. To his right lay further compounds, through the middle of which ran a parallel road. In each compound there were long concrete and wooden single-storey huts, many of them dilapidated, plus parade grounds and exercise areas. There was no glass in the windows – only shutters that could be bolted from the outside at night. There were no trees or grass to break up the brown earth packed hard by marching feet.

By the time Alec was counted in, 21 June had turned boiling hot, and he was sweating heavily when the prisoners were given permission to sit or crouch to listen to a speech from the commandant, Colonel Bornemann, an immaculately dressed Great War veteran. With Lamsdorf already crowded with POWs, mostly Poles, Bornemann had his introductory speech well rehearsed. The equally immaculately dressed interpreter alongside him, tall, thin and sporting a toothbrush moustache, also knew his lines well. This was *Sonderführer* Oskar Lange, nicknamed 'Yankee Joe' because he spoke English with an American accent. He had been a New York docker, then a waiter, but had returned to Germany impressed by Hitler's 'New Order'. Later in the war, he recruited POW traitors for the British Free Corps, a Waffen-SS unit.

Bornemann began with the standard line, 'For you the war is over.' Germany's enemies, he said, would soon sue for peace – indeed, Marshal

Philippe Pétain, France's new leader, had commenced negotiations that day near Compiègne in the same railway carriage in which the Germans capitulated in 1918; the armistice was signed the next day, the formal surrender on 25 June. Meanwhile, prisoners should be patient pending being sent home – possibly as early as Christmas. During this period, they would be well treated. The Wehrmacht would honour the Geneva Convention provided the other ranks toiled diligently on *Arbeitskommandos*, to which they would soon be sent.

As was, however, made clear many times later, abiding by the Convention was a concession, not a right – and prisoners tempted to quote its articles in disputes were given short shrift. The Germans would simply do what they thought they could get away with. Thus, some guards became more diligent about their treatment of POWs later in the war, after German prisoners were taken in large numbers – for fear that their colleagues might face reprisals.

In June 1940, the idea they might be home by Christmas generated cheering from some men stripped of patriotism and honour by the privations of the March. Others protested, but one defeatist conscript was defiant: 'What the hell do I care who's won the war? All I want is to get home.' Alec shuddered.

After the cheering died down, 'Yankee Joe' continued: *Appell* (roll-call) would be at 6.00am, evening roll-call at 6.00pm and lights out at 10.00pm. Smoking was forbidden in the huts and on camp roads. All German officers should be saluted on sight; refusal would lead to four weeks' solitary confinement. The POWs were, however, forbidden to use the greeting *'Heil Hitler'*, for fear they would ridicule their captors. Once a prisoner had been allotted a compound, he needed permission to move to another. Food would be provided after prisoners had settled into their billets – although nothing came that first night. Sexual relationships with German women were forbidden, the maximum penalty being death.

Towards the end of his speech, Bornemann moved to the subject of escape. His message was ominous: 'Any attempt to escape will be punishable by death.' Finally, with an air of casual nonchalance, 'Yankee Joe' translated his final sentence: 'If there are any Jews among you, come forward.' For Alec, it was another gut-wrenching moment. Having buried his identity tags at Calais and been cautioned by the 'good German' at Bathorn, should he come forward? If he owned up, what might happen? If he did not own up and was unmasked later, might his fate be worse?

No one moved, so 'Yankee Joe' repeated his command: 'Come, come, England is full of Jews.' After a moment, a man stood up and stepped forward. Alec agonized. Finally, he decided he would 'confess' and he uncrossed his legs, preparing to stand. At this point, Bill Brett and Dennis McLaughlin, sitting either side of him, came to his rescue. As he sat 'like a rabbit hypnotised by a snake', they did his thinking for him, grabbing his elbows and holding him down until he recovered his composure.

Similar displays of solidarity occurred in other camps where Germans sought to segregate Jews. Black Watch lieutenant Clifford Cohen was captured at Saint-Valéry-en-Caux and taken to an Oflag. On arrival, the prisoners were ordered out on parade and Jews were told to take two paces forward. Cohen stepped forward – but then all the other officers also moved forward two paces. As a result, the Germans took no action.

What became of the Lamsdorf Jew who stood forward alone? Royal Welch Fusiliers Regimental Sergeant Major Sidney Sherriff tried to find out, having been nominated as *Hauptvertrauensmann* (Chief Man of Confidence) by the Germans. It is possible he was placed in ethnic quarantine alongside Polish and French Jews, his British uniform giving him some protection from the Holocaust. It seemed the Wehrmacht wished to abide by some of the Geneva Convention when dealing with their Western enemies. The regime, as Alec discovered, was different for Russians: 'When the Russians arrived at Lamsdorf they were sent for baths and the German guards singled out every circumcised man.' Only after the Soviets liberated the Russian camp at Lamsdorf in March 1945 were the consequences of that selection process revealed.

After Bornemann finished his speech, the new arrivals were counted again and prodded forward past Polish POWs, British soldiers captured in Norway, some merchant seamen and a few airmen. By June 1940, many Poles had spent nine months in captivity but were still sufficiently defiant to cheer the British and shower them with cigarettes and bread. The cigarettes, made from Makhorka tobacco, were a mixed blessing. Supercharged with nicotine, they were too powerful for the enfeebled British. After one puff, Alec's head was spinning. Later, he was led towards stables, where he slept in conditions as bad as Bathorn. The Poles, however, were determined to lift the new arrivals' spirits, treating them to a concert of folk songs and patriotic ballads. One song 'was at once a salute and a lament', recalled Doug Collins, later a serial escaper, 'something magnificent that caught at the throat even if you didn't know what it was, and the visors of the cavalry caps flashed as the survivors of the first *Blitzkrieg* sang their hymn to the lost land and greeted the remnants of the second one as though the Battle of France had been won rather than lost'.

Alec spent the weekend and Monday morning queuing for food – a half litre of soup, a ninth of a loaf of bread and a ladle of ersatz coffee made from burnt barley was the ration – before joining a batch of fifty men to take a cold shower and have his uniform disinfected. Before his shower, he was shaved all over and deloused. Virtually all his body hair – from head, chest, armpits and groin – was removed, although Alec told the British barber to leave his moustache. The process was humiliating but worth it. By the time Alec reached Lamsdorf, body lice – eighth-of-an-inch bloodsuckers that punctured the skin with stiletto-shaped mouth parts – had multiplied in the warmest parts of his body, wherever there was hair, driving him wild with irritation.

When Alec's clothes had been disinfected, he dressed and marched to his allotted hut. The single-storey huts, four in each compound, dated from the Great War and were crumbling. Each was 200 feet long and housed 400 prisoners. The sleeping area comprised three-tier bunks standing on concrete and split into two sections, each with an entrance. Each bunk had eight six-inch-wide boards on which POWs initially slept. Only later were they issued with mattresses made of hessian sacking and filled at best with *Holzwolle* (wood wool) or straw but mostly with bits of paper. Each man received just one badly-worn blanket but no sheets or pillow. The lowest bunk was six inches off concrete across which rats would scurry, while the top one was seven feet in the air.

To the right of each entrance stood trestle tables and benches, where POWs ate their meals in shifts. At the end of each barrack was a tiled stove eight feet high and four feet wide, yet inadequate to heat the room. The washing facilities between the two sections consisted of a concrete basin like a horse trough with a dozen cold water taps that flowed only briefly each morning, forcing everyone to wash in the same water. There was no soap. A bucket stood near the trough for POWs needing to urinate after they were locked in at night. By the morning, the air would be heavy with the smell of stale urine mixed with the body odour of 400 unwashed men, of whom some had open wounds.

On the far side of each compound stood a toilet block. There was no privacy: POWs emptied their bowels alongside each other in four rows, each with ten crudely-cut holes in them, earning such blocks the nickname 'forty-holers'. They were also dubbed 'reading rooms' or 'houses of parliament', because they were the locations for circulating rumours. There was no toilet paper, and once Red Cross supplies of books arrived these were torn up and used instead. Initially, the holes were covered with lids, but these were soon burned as firewood.

Below the holes was a cesspit from which rose a vile stench. Those with the stomach to peer inside could see the surface was alive with white slugs, which would crawl up the pit walls and out through the holes. When the cesspit level rose above a certain point, Poles – and later Russians – came to empty it, pumping out the sewage through a pipe into a 200-gallon barrel on a cart drawn by an old mare. This was nicknamed the 'honey wagon' because of the stench as it trundled through the camp. The sewage would be sold to farmers and spread on fields as fertiliser. If the wind blew in the wrong direction the stench would float back into the camp – as would soiled toilet paper, which would catch on the perimeter wire. Besides the slugs, the 'forty-holers' were infested with rats that would run along concrete ledges below the seats. It was not long before rumours spread of testicles being bitten off.

Having been shown his accommodation, Alec was marched back to the *Vorlager* to be searched again and registered officially as a POW, with the number 15129. This was stamped twice on an oblong zinc disc, which Alec had to wear permanently around his neck and keep polished for inspection. If a POW died, the disc would be broken in half; one half would be buried with him, the other would be sent to his family via the Red Cross.

The next step was the creation of a *Personalkarte*. This covered personal details and the locations of *Arbeitskommandos* to which POWs were later sent. It was thus the source of information sent to America initially and then Switzerland as the Protecting Power, the prisoners' legal guardian under the Geneva Convention, and to the International Committee of the Red Cross, responsible for their health and hygiene. It contained a reminder, lest POWs doubt the commandant's words, that sex with German women was illegal – the master race's purity was not to be sullied by enemy combatants.

This *Personalkarte* was Alec's next hurdle. Taking out his fountain pen, a birthday gift from Netta, he filled it in. Most questions were simple and he completed the boxes in a mixture of English and German. Name: Jay; first name: Alec; date and place of birth: 30.10.19, Wandsworth, Surrey; father's name: John; nationality: British English; rank: rifleman; regiment and company: 1st battalion, Queen Victoria's Rifles, C Company; Army number: 6896204; date and place of capture: 26.5.40, Calais; health: fit; height: 1.75m; hair colour: *braun* (brown); special distinguishing marks: *keine* (none); name, address and relation of next of kin: *Vater* (father), John Jay, 38 Hodford Rd, Golders Green, London NW11.

Then he turned to trickier questions. The Germans wanted to know his profession. Writing 'stockbroker' would mark him out from the working class privates and NCOs around him. Instead he opted for 'clerk', something close to the truth and an easy story to sustain. Then came religion: he wrote 'CofE,' – initials that confused the camp clerk, who inserted the word 'protestant' alongside while translating 'clerk' as *Bankangestellter* (bank employee). Finally, he reached the line where he had to write his mother's maiden name. Cohen would give the game away. If he invented a name such as Smith or Jones he might forget it. Instead, he needed something that sounded like Cohen but betrayed no hint of Jewishness. He settled on 'Cone', the surname of a London dance school owner. Even if under torture he blurted out he was the son of 'Annie Cohen' he could claim he had been misheard.

The day after registration, the POWs were collected from their compounds, handed cards with their POW numbers in chalk to pin on their tunics and photographed in groups of twenty, like criminals in a rogues' gallery. Each man put a thumbprint on the front of his *Personalkarte*; then the photographs were cut into individual passport-style shots and placed by the thumbprints.

The following day, the prisoners were issued with 'capture cards', pre-printed postcards written in German with *Stalag* VIIIB at the top saying the sender was a POW and recording his health, fit or injured. These were then sent home via Geneva, so within a few months most families of prisoners taken in 1940 knew their loved ones were alive and in a *Stalag*. Alec hesitated. This was his third opportunity to tell his mother he had survived. Should he fill in the card and put her mind at rest? Or was his – and possibly her – safety more important, whatever the anguish he caused by maintaining his subterfuge? What if they wrote to him and some throwaway remark exposed the family's ethnicity?

For one Jew, this question was more than theoretical. Captain Julius Green, a Glaswegian 51st Highland Division dentist who ended up in Colditz, also ditched his identity tags and became a Presbyterian. This 'harmless little deception' lasted until a relative wrote to him with gossip about Glasgow's Jewish community. The Colditz guards demanded to inspect his penis. Fortunately, the Colditz surgeon accepted the assertion of the British medical officer, Captain Hugh Dickie, that Green had been circumcised for medical reasons and was Christian, whatever the letter might imply.

As Alec watched friends fill in their cards, he toyed with Netta's pen but then crumpled his card. There might come a time when it would be safe to contact his family, but now was not that time.

The early weeks at Lamsdorf were the worst. In the chaotic summer of 1940, the Red Cross parcels that later ameliorated Alec's lot had not yet arrived. Instead, he subsisted on German rations. The Geneva Convention said POW rations should 'be equivalent in quantity and quality to that of depot troops', but prisoners were provided with little more than half the calories needed to sustain a sedentary man.

Each day began with *Appell*. At 6.00am, guards would kick the hut doors open, yell '*Raus! Raus! Aufstehen! Aufstehen!*' and shake the prisoners awake, prodding them with rifle butts and dragging them from their bunks. With such cries ringing in their ears, men would shuffle out to stand in lines of five on the *Appellplatz* to be counted – '*Fünf, zehn, fünfzehn, zwanzig*'. The guard's count would be checked by another, and if the numbers differed there would be a recount.

After roll-call, Alec would wash in cold water before drifting back to his bunk. A morning drink would be distributed at about 9.00am from iron cauldrons known as 'keebles'. This was ersatz black coffee or tea made from linden leaves or mint. Both tastes were unfamiliar to the British, and once razor blades became available some would simply use the yellowy-green tea as shaving water.

Lunch was at noon, when there would be a scramble as prisoners equipped with tin spoons and rusty dixie cans raced to be first in line for 'soup' – greasy water containing traces of meat, bones and vegetable matter such as cabbage or swedes – and unwashed potatoes boiled in their jackets, typically past their best and discoloured. Brought from a central kitchen, the soup would be served by orderlies armed with wooden sticks on which were fixed tin cans to measure out rations. Alec learned that however hungry he felt, it was better to hang back in the chance of catching some solid matter such as pork rind or vegetables from the keeble bottoms.

Bread, with dripping or margarine made from coal and foul-smelling cheese or jam, would be distributed at 4.00pm. Initially, one loaf of bitter-tasting bread the size of a small Hovis was shared between five. Unsurprisingly, a lot of attention was devoted to the division of loaves. Alec discovered the width of his POW tag was about the length of a fifth of the loaf so he used it as a measuring tool. Achieving identical slices was difficult, and rituals developed to ensure fairness. Some 'combines' drew lots; some took it in turns to pick the first slice; others selected a different man each day to cut the bread, with that man having the last slice.

After the bread Alec went without food from teatime until noon the next day. He first experienced real hunger on the March but this was worse. It would begin with an empty feeling in the stomach, then nausea, then wind; finally he would feel weak and dizzy. Even getting a drink was a trial because each 400-man hut had only two standing pipes for drinking water and these would only be turned on in the evenings. Thus, Alec would join others standing on equally shaky legs in long queues. Dinners only came later when Red Cross parcels arrived. In the meantime, Alec would squirrel away a corner of bread so he had something to chew during the evening.

Between each roll-call and meal, there was nothing to relieve the boredom – no books, no writing materials or any other means of passing the time, another contravention of the Geneva Convention, whose article 17 said belligerents should encourage prisoners' 'intellectual and sporting pursuits'.

Prisoners strong enough to walk and start contemplating escape – whatever 'Yankee Joe' had said – would peer through the wire. To the east was pine forest, to the north and west a plain, to the south distant hills, the *Eulengebirge* (Owl Hills) near the old Czech border. Occasionally, guards would toss cigarette ends over the wire and laugh as prisoners scrambled for them. '*Schweine, verdammte schweine!*' ('Pigs, fucking pigs!') was their standard insult as they watched the losers stand around the victor in the hope of a puff.

For 'entertainment', 'Yankee Joe', as propagandist-in-chief, would use the loudspeakers on telegraph poles around the camp. These would blast out German military music including Fürst's Badenweiler March, a Hitler favourite that featured in pre-war Nuremberg Rally newsreels. News about Luftwaffe air-raids on Britain and tonnages of British ships sunk by U-boats were followed by commentary from William Joyce, the Irish-American Fascist collaborator known, because of his drawl, as 'Lord Haw-Haw'.

Alec would denounce such news as 'propaganda' but he feared some items were true. He would say the same – and fear the same – when guards distributed the first issue of *The Camp* magazine. Printed in Berlin, this contained POW contributions about how well they were being treated, plus news reports and photos showing Luftwaffe raids on Britain.

As morale sank lower, prisoners played the blame game, hunting for scapegoats. Some blamed Britain's allies; some blamed their generals for sending them to France poorly equipped. Others blamed the RAF for being absent as Stukas dive-bombed them; the standard insult was 'RAF – Rare As Fucking Fairies'. They knew nothing of the Spitfire and Hurricane pilots' heroism during the Battle of Britain. One Queen Vic ran a sweepstake for the likely month of surrender – January and June 1941 were popular, as were February and October 1942.

Already undernourished after the March, Alec continued to lose weight– eventually falling to seven stone. He also suffered unbearable itching from lice. Shamed by their lack of hygiene, men initially fought secret battles with lice beneath their blankets. Later, they became less sensitive, and delousing would be done in the 'forty-holers', where men would sit absorbed in plucking white lice eggs from their battledress seams and squashing them between their nails. Some would run lighted matches down the seams to burn the eggs. If a prisoner caught an adult louse, he might hold it up for inspection before crushing its blood-swollen body, sometimes black, sometimes red, between his thumbnails and sending the juice spurting in the air. The scratching caused sores that were slow to heal. When they did, they left red-blue scars resembling shrapnel wounds, which some POWs claimed they were.

Some Queen Vics began to lose teeth; some with dark hair turned grey; some were reduced to sifting through the contents of the camp bins looking for rubbish that might be edible. Unsurprisingly, many came down with dysentery – including Alec. Soon, the huts were full of feverish men lying on straw-covered concrete with their trousers down and their knees tucked beneath their chins; some would pass blood and mucus thirty times a day. Eventually, the Germans issued charcoal tablets, but until then British medics could do nothing except keep the men hydrated and clean them with bundles of straw. Finally, Alec stopped passing blood but his stomach remained weak; the watery soup passed straight through him, necessitating a dash to the 'forty-holer'. The humiliation compounded the pain. 'You would be queuing for your grub, sugar beet soup or something like that, and it just used to run down your leg,' recalled Norman Bartlett, a Lamsdorf medic. 'You just could not do anything about it.'

Camp life descended into a Hobbesian state of nature. The bayonet charges at Calais had taught Alec how thin a veneer of civilisation separated men from barbarism. Now he learned that lesson a second time as he watched the men around him and contemplated his own actions.

Sidney Sherriff and other NCOs tried to preserve discipline. Sherriff, a stern but modestly-spoken Welshman from Rhyl, Flintshire, knew its importance for morale. Soon after Alec's arrival and in the face of the guards' ridicule, Greenjacket NCOs organized 15-minute drills each morning to show their men remained unbroken. The sergeants would also attempt to maintain order within the huts, stressing the need for personal hygiene.

Trust, however, broke down between NCOs and privates. With food an obsessive conversation topic, replacing sex, the division of rations became a source of conflict, and many privates became convinced their superiors were abusing their privileged positions to increase their rations or those of their favourites. With the guards largely absent from the compounds between roll calls, the result, despite the NCOs' efforts, was social chaos. Starving men became thieves, and Alec learned to keep his meagre possessions with him at all times, even when visiting the toilet.

Stealing from the Germans seemed legitimate. Potato storage silos lay between the kitchens and the compounds. Sometimes a prisoner could slip away from his escort and fill his pockets, but it was dangerous work – one thief was spotted by a watchtower guard and was lucky to survive the bullet that passed through his greatcoat an inch from his stomach.

Stealing from fellow POWs was not acceptable, and the punishment was to be dropped in a latrine pit or beaten. Such was the fate of a lance corporal from the Gloucestershire Regiment – nicknamed 'the Glorious Glosters' because of their illustrious past – who was temporarily blinded during a rearguard action outside Dunkirk. Caught stealing bread, he was beaten, then dragged round his compound with a card bearing the words 'I STEAL' round his neck. The beating left him almost unrecognisable: he had lost his vision again, his front teeth were knocked out and his nose resembled a jelly.

The worst thieves comprised 'razor gangs' of conscripted former criminals, but violence spread throughout the camp population, with fights regularly breaking out in soup and potato queues as men reduced by starvation to physical wrecks still summoned up vestiges of strength to fight their neighbours for scraps.

With their uniforms in tatters and their boots disintegrating, the POWs needed fresh clothing, which, the Geneva Convention stated, the Germans should supply. The Lamsdorf authorities did not have replacement British uniforms but they did have captured uniforms from Europe's defeated nations. Thus the POWs wore trousers, overcoats and tunics from France, Belgium and Poland. Some uniforms, blood-stained and with bullet holes, appeared to have come straight from the battlefield.

There were no cobblers, so Alec exchanged his boots for clogs and his threadbare socks for *Fusslappen*, cloths wrapped around one's feet and secured with boot laces. For the Germans, the clogs had benefits, for a prisoner would struggle to escape in them. It was agony even to walk fast and, as Alec discovered, the only way to progress was to scrunch up his toes and shuffle along, hoping his *Fusslappen* would stay on. On parade, once-proud Queen Vics felt humiliated. In the scramble for fresh clothing, some had to take French cavalry breeches, leaving their bare calves exposed.

The days passed slowly – 'dead days of despair' according to one Greenjacket. In the second week of July, however, change was afoot, heralded by 'Yankee Joe' making a circuit of the compounds. As senior German interpreter, he would lecture POWs on the virtues of obedience. He even tried to recruit captured military policemen to bring order to the camp, issuing riot sticks and armbands bearing a swastika and the words 'Camp Police'; but this initiative dissolved as other POWs made clear what might happen to Red Caps collaborating with 'the Huns'.

This time, his announcement had substance: 'volunteers' passed as fit by a Wehrmacht doctor would go out on *Arbeitskommandos*. The Geneva Convention permitted belligerents to make physically fit POWs work, other than 'officers or persons of equivalent status', and Germany's hunger for labour was growing as its swelling armed forces sucked manpower from factories, mines, construction sites, transport enterprises and farms. Employers, therefore, clamoured for permits to exploit Lamsdorf's captive workforce.

'Volunteers' seemed a strange word because any soldier not an NCO, defined by the Germans as lance corporal and below, had to work provided the work was safe and did not contribute to Germany's war effort. Anything that might sustain Germany's economy would indirectly aid Nazi aggression, yet, for Alec, the chance to leave Lamsdorf's suffocating boredom behind had attractions even if manual labour would require an adjustment for a stockbroker who had until a year before been looked after by servants. 'Yankee Joe' said food and shelter would be provided by civilian employers. These, Alec hoped, would be better than Lamsdorf's near-starvation rations and dilapidated, overcrowded huts. *Arbeitskommando* soup, he was told, was so thick you could stand your spoon in it.

Alec might also look forward to a change of scene and the conviviality of a smaller group, as opposed to being cooped up among thousands in Lamsdorf's dusty compounds. He would even be paid – though the rate was 70 pfennigs per day, less than two thirds of the unskilled German labour rate after deductions for food and lodging. It would be paid in *Lagergeld*, prison 'Monopoly' money that could only be spent in designated shops on a restricted range of goods such as soft drinks and toiletries. The notes, measuring 3 inches by 1 inch, had a red triangle in the centre, the German sign for a POW. Alec soon learned how artificial the system was, with essentials sold at inflated prices; a pack of razor blades would cost him a month's pay. The aim was to prevent prisoners accumulating escape materials.

For now the prospect of leaving Lamsdorf and having extra food lifted his spirits. On the morning of 18 July 1940, he lined up with scores of other POWs in preparation for the 3½km march back to Annahof. From there, a train took the POWs 30km to Oppeln's main station, from which another track led to their new quarters. Alec's *Arbeitskommando* was designated E34 – E stood for *Engländer*, 34 indicated it was *Stalag* VIIIB's 34th working party. Its location was Groschowitz, an industrial suburb of Oppeln.

Most prisoners set off with little more than the clothes they wore and their makeshift cutlery. Alec also had some scraps of paper, and these survived the guards' exit search. On one, five days previously, he had written his first POW poem. To My Mother was an epistle of filial love to Annie Cohen, whose maiden name he had twisted into Cone for the purposes of his *Personalkarte*:

Out of the boom of the guns, and the whine of the bullets;
Born from the whispering whistle of jagged steel;
Weaned in the tedious hours of the prison camp's boredom;
There rose a vision wonderful and real.

When chance of life seemed small, and death loomed huge as a monster;
When the man next to me fell back with a ghastly grimace;
When the ground shook from the blast of an aerial bombardment;
I was not frightened, if only I thought of your face.

Later, when captured, and marching through France and through
   Belgium;
The hot dusty roads and a sense of impending doom,
When each day followed the last, like an awful nightmare;
Merely to think of you meant a release from my gloom.

And, when this war ends, and we are sent back to our country;
When the journey is finished down to the last long mile;
I shall not care what agony I have suffered,
When, once again, I see that face and that smile.

Chapter 12

'A Living Hell'

Groschowitz was on a bend of the Oder 7km south-east of Oppeln. Its main industry was cement. Unemployment had soared during the Depression, and Groschowitz's politics had polarized between Nazis and Communists. Then Hitler's civil engineering projects revived demand for cement and by 1940 new infrastructure was needed. Thus E34's POWs were ordered to build a dam to capture water flowing into the Oder from a tributary.

Their billet was a barn filled with two-tier bunks. At one end was a 'tortoise' stove on which Alec would cook any potatoes he managed to scrounge. The men slept on straw beneath one blanket and used buckets as toilets. Soup was cooked by two local women in coppers more typically used for washing clothes. One was known to the POWs as Frau Muller; her young assistant was called Trudy. Bert Gurner, a Royal Engineers sapper captured outside Dunkirk, recalled how Frau Muller and Trudy would teach the POWs folk songs as they cooked and served up. Frau Muller was the more generous with her portions, he recalled, 'so everyone liked to get on to that copper'.

Building the dam was Alec's introduction to manual labour. On his first day, as he shovelled earth beneath the gaze of guards never backward in prodding POWs with rifle butts should they show insubordination, he asked himself how could he get through the days ahead. He was not ready to escape but he might find internal refuge by focusing on childhood memories. This was the subject of Reminiscence, his second POW poem:

Each day dawning brings forth nothing:
Empty as a chrysalis shell
Monotony's incessant hammer,
Existence in a living hell.

Every minute is an hour,
Every hour another day,
Past one sees, but never future,
As the seconds drag away.

Sole relief from mental torpor,
Are the pictures of the past;
When each scene of reminiscence,
Seems more precious than the last.

As Alec worked, the Groschowitz guards would trumpet the latest Luftwaffe triumphs over London, Bristol, Birmingham and Portsmouth and predict an imminent invasion of Britain. Their message was: while you work for us we are bombing your womenfolk into oblivion – and those who survive will be ours following our victory march down Whitehall.

As Alec marched to the construction site, he saw anti-Semitic posters festooning the town. One depicted a villainous-looking Jew in a dinner suit and top hat with large hooked nose and protruding eyes putting his arms around an Aryan girl. The message was clear: Jews must not defile the Aryan race. Another – for the anti-Semitic film, *Der Ewige Jude* (*The Eternal Jew*) – showed a similarly-caricatured bearded Jew with money in one hand and a whip in the other, alongside a hammer-and-sickle superimposed on a map of Germany. The film depicted Jews as decadent, cruel, money-grabbing capitalists in league with communists to destroy hard-working and morally superior Aryans. A third poster, addressed to Poles, declared, '*Żydzi, wszy, tyfus plamisty*' ('Jews, lice, typhus').

Confrontations between POWs and guards happened constantly. The guards would menacingly aim rifles and Alec, as interpreter, would intervene to restore calm. Such confrontations did not, however, always end peacefully, and information sent to London via Switzerland contained regular reports that prisoners on *Arbeitskommandos* had been killed for no reason.

Come the evening, the Groschowitz POWs would conduct their bread-cutting rituals. Then came the *Appell*, when the near-starving men, wobbly on their legs and longing to lie down, would stand while counted. After that, the guards would tell their commandant about prisoners guilty of misdemeanours – fainting from hunger was classed as refusing to work. A typical punishment involved the prisoner having to run in circles until he collapsed – this, thanks to lack of food, did not take long.

Sabotage was a way to fight back. Alec might bite his lip and submit to Nazi boasting but he would not behave like a slave. In his lecture at Beltring, Alec's company commander had described the POW's legal position as a kind of limbo. If captured, Alec would have to obey orders yet would have non-belligerent status – a chess piece removed from the board, in the words of one historian, intact but out of the game. Yet Alec itched to be back in the game. He might be imprisoned but he could still pursue his own personal war – passively awaiting the end was not an option. Sabotage was a way forward, contributing in some small way to Britain's war effort by undermining Germany's economy and morale.

How might one sabotage a dam? This question was discussed in hushed tones in the Groschowitz billet at night. Supervision was not that close, so the answer was to toil as slowly as possible without incurring the overseer's wrath and to do shoddy work whenever one could, making sure to cover one's tracks. Every task was examined for how it might be done badly and when work resumed such ideas were put into practice. The Germans might think the dam a construction site – the E34 POWs would render it a site of destruction.

All over Greater Germany, POWs engaged in similar subterfuge – in factories, down mines, in quarries, on the railways and on building sites. They would set fire to the factories in which they worked or adulterate aviation fuel with sugar. Saboteurs who were caught faced reprisals ranging from beatings to long prison sentences. Sometimes, like the men of E34, they got away with it. Alec and his fellow POWs employed 'good old British workmanship' in building the Groschowitz dam 'so beautifully that the floods washed it away the next winter'.

Sabotage helped maintain self-respect. So did 'goon-baiting' – playing mind games to confuse or enrage a guard to the point when he would lose his composure. The trick was to achieve maximum impact without endangering oneself. Alice the Goon was a Popeye character, and from the mid-1930s people used the term to describe intellectually-challenged professional bullies. Thus it seemed apt for guards too weak or stupid to be frontline troops. They had the weapons, but the prisoners had superior wits.

'Goon-baiting' would begin with *Appell*. Some men might stay in their bunks and have to be 'encouraged' outside with a kick; others on the parade ground and already counted would then run behind the lines to be counted again, inflating the numbers. If these did not tally with the official figure, the 'goons' would recount amid much shouting and waving of revolvers, delaying the start of the working day.

Once roll-call was finished, baiting would proceed in various ways. Some were primitive. POWs would sing banned songs such as 'The National Anthem', 'Land of Hope and Glory' or 'Hitler Has Only Got One Ball'. Cockneys would mock the German language. Guards ended roll-call with the announcement, '*Alles ist in Ordnung*' ('Everything is in order') but this would be parroted back as 'Alice is in horse dung'; while *Feldwebel* became 'febble wobble'. Officers would indulge in exaggerated salutes to demonstrate disdain, although this could lead to punishment, as Captain Norman Altham, a Gordon Highlanders medic, discovered in July 1941 when he was sentenced to five days in Lamsdorf's *Straflager* (punishment block) for an 'improper salute to the commandant'. Even padres would crack jokes at the guards' expense. Alec heard one begin his Sunday sermon with 'If any of you chaps are thinking of taking a walk ...'

The crimson-faced Major Richard 'Jumbo' Sampson, formerly HQ Company's commanding officer but too unfit to go to Calais, learnt in a letter from Sam Kydd about mischief making: 'I agree with you on your remarks about trying to be funny in this life, especially here! They [the guards] certainly don't appreciate it. Still we get a kick out of doing it – that's the main thing!' Kydd published a camp newsletter called *Prisoners Pie*, replete with jibes at his captors – his jokes column was headed 'Haw-Haw'.

Alec's officers at Oflag VIIC did not have to work, leaving more time for plotting escapes and goon-baiting. Ellison-Macartney thought a *Stalag* resembled boarding school. It involved 'a pretty tough form of disciplined living' in which inhabitants learned self-protective techniques to defend themselves against their neighbours and wage psychological war against their 'masters'. 'The masters really carried all the guns – and yet, how often did they lose out?' he wrote. 'Whether the price was high or low, some of us certainly found a use to which these extramural accomplishments could be put when we found ourselves involuntary guests of Hitler and the Great German Reich in the years 1940 onwards. And they were applied with consummate skill to the discomfiture of our hosts.'

Ellison-Macartney thought arriving at Laufen like 'the first day at prep school all over again … the living conditions were a trifle worse – the food not so good or so plentiful and the beds, triple-tier bunks, far from ideal'. The commandant and guards, however, 'occupied much the same position as the headmaster and his assistant masters, and indeed, behaved not unlike the more unimaginative specimens of that breed … They were so humourless in their attempts to enforce discipline. The rules were drawn up on the assumption that the Germans knew everything and that we stupid English knew nothing.'

One bait involved teaching guards English, causing an enraged sergeant on one occasion to call out, 'You English think I know fuck nothing about your escape plans! Indeed, I know fuck all!' Another was to subvert guard dogs by feeding them. This did not go down well with the commandant, and during a morning roll-call the interpreter made the following announcement: 'It has been observed that the British officer prisoners-of-war have been feeding the German guard dogs. The British officer prisoners-of-war are strongly forbidden to feed the German guard dogs. The German guard dogs for their parts have been strongly forbidden to accept food offered to them by the British officer prisoners-of-war.' The 'laughter from 1,200 throats rang around the countryside', recalled Ellison-Macartney. The Germans looked bewildered, but 'but it made our day'.

Some of the finest goon-baiting occurred at *Oflag* IVC, the *Sonderlager* (special camp) at Colditz into which the Germans gathered the most persistent escapers and mischief-makers, earning it the nickname 'the Bad Boys Camp'. A disproportionate number of the Bad Boys were Calais veterans who, like Alec, wanted to stay in the game. Davies-Scourfield described a 1942 incident in his memoir, *In Presence of My Foes*. Colditz's French inmates were asked to volunteer their skills to benefit Hitler's New Order. In response, one said he wished to offer his 'services and professional skill' to the German people – and the more work he was given, he added, the more pleased he would be. What, a guard asked, was his profession. 'I am an undertaker,' he replied to cheers, before being led away into solitary confinement.

Douglas Bader, the legless Spitfire pilot whose exploits featured in *Reach for the Sky*, was also an accomplished goon-baiter. Bader ended up in Colditz after being held in Lamsdorf's RAF compound, an overflow facility housing 1,000 men who could not be accommodated in specialist camps such as *Stalag Luft* III. Goon-baiting as Bader played it resembled the children's game, Last Across, in which the winner is the last child to race across a street in front of an oncoming car. In Lamsdorf, the winner was the POW who baited a guard to the point where the enraged victim pulled his revolver from his holster or took his rifle from his shoulder. At this point, the POW would become suitably compliant. Steady nerves and judgement were required – to goad too far could be fatal. Another airman in Lamsdorf would walk from his hut, look around furtively, pretend to take something from his pocket, dig a hole in the earth, bury his non-existent object, then walk away, whistling nonchalantly. As often as not, guards, with sniffer dogs at their sides, would waste hours on fruitless searches of his compound.

At Lamsdorf, loudspeakers would broadcast propaganda every Monday at 2.00pm. The broadcast might begin with the song Engeland-Lied, whose chorus included the line, '*Denn wir fahren gegen Engelland*' ('We sail against England'), after which the announcer would say, '*Hier ist ein Sondermeldung*' ('Here is a special message'). Lord Haw-Haw would then detail the Wehrmacht's progress in Russia and North Africa and the tonnages of British shipping sunk by U-boats. To close, there would be more patriotic songs and military marches. The response of the airmen – 'mad British' in their guards' eyes – was to goose-step around their compound, shouting 'Heil Hitler!' and flinging out Nazi salutes in time to the music.

Canadian infantry captured at Dieppe in August 1942 and held in a compound next to the RAF were masters of the art of ironic subservience. This was on display when a German interpreter, 'Yankee Joe' or Sonderführer Max Meyer, whose moniker was 'South American Joe', ran through the camp rules: prisoners who hit guards would be shot; prisoners who failed to salute German officers would face solitary confinement; prisoners who had sex with German women would be shot. There was only one problem for the two 'Joes': as each rule was read, the Canadians cheered.

Goon-baiting could backfire, however, as Alec discovered at Groschowitz in October 1940. One night, three men escaped from the billet and 'all hell was let loose' at morning *Appell*. As interpreter, Alec had to answer the guards' questions: 'How did they get out? And where have they gone?' Alec's insolent reply was designed to enrage the *Unteroffizier* (NCO): 'Number one, I don't know, and number two, if I did know I wouldn't tell you.' The guard responded by laying into Alec with his rifle butt, then shouting, dangerously, 'You speak good German. You must be a Jew. Admit you are a Jew.'

When Alec returned home after the war and filled in his POW repatriation report for MI9's intelligence staff, he described the incident laconically:

'Attempts were made by the Under Officer in charge of my first working party to find out if I was a Jew (Groschowitz '40). A rifle butt was used as a "persuader".' The assault was a war crime – the Geneva Convention's Article 46 banned corporal punishment – yet it went unpunished. The guard learnt nothing about the escape or Alec's ethnicity. Alec did, however, take a blow in the mouth and the POWs nearby winced as they heard the sickening sound of teeth being smashed. After a medical orderly staunched the blood and cleaned him up, he discovered he had lost thirteen teeth.

The assault convinced Alec that, like the trio who escaped from E34, he had to move beyond sabotage and goon-baiting and become a more active player in the fight. Indeed, escaping was the only way to get away from the guard he had enraged. How many more beatings would he take as a POW and a clandestine Jew in Hitler's Reich? Even before the beating, the poor diet, poor sanitary conditions, punishing work routine and nervous strain had taken their toll on his health, with ulcers developing on his legs. 'After I had been kissed in the mush with the rifle butt, thereby having a lot of front teeth smashed, I decided there was absolutely no point in staying there,' he recalled. 'I was a marked man.'

First, he needed an opportunity – and one did not emerge for seven months. With the dam completed in October, the men of E34 were shifted to road-building at Neudorf and Gumpertsdorf, two villages 6km west on the railway line between Oppeln and Lamsdorf and close to a Luftwaffe airfield. The Germans wanted to improve the roads to the base and were willing to bend Geneva Convention rules by using POW labour. Neudorf had opened in 1936 disguised as a sports airfield to subvert Versailles Treaty restrictions. Three years later, Heinkels and Stukas took off from Neudorf on the first day of the invasion of Poland, a few minutes' flying time away. Hitler was so pleased with their achievements that he visited the base. The Stukas of 77 Squadron were then sent west and deployed above Calais, while Neudorf became a flying school, preparing pilots for Hitler's Russian invasion. Greenjackets such as Alec, who had faced 77 Squadron Stuka attacks the previous May, were ordered to start work on 2 November 1940, breaking stones with 14lb hammers. Was this slave labour? 'We were given a bowl of soup and some bread made from sawdust,' wrote Les Allan, later founder of the National Ex-Prisoners of War Association. 'If you didn't do as you were told you were shot. Therefore it was slavery.'

At Neudorf, Alec learned how harsh a Silesian winter could be. The first snowflakes had fallen at Groschowitz on 26 October and, for the next few weeks, the snow was almost constant; the POWs struggled to keep warm in the cold east winds. There was, however, a major improvement while Alec was building roads around Neudorf: the arrival of the first Red Cross and cigarette parcels. Red Cross parcels, delivered from Switzerland throughout most of the war, were lifesavers for Allied prisoners subsisting on bread and watery soup. Hitler's officials flouted Geneva Convention rules that POWs should be properly fed but they found reasons to follow Article 78 stating that Red Cross representatives be allowed 'to distribute relief in the camps and at halting places'. Thus, eighteen months into the war, Berlin used the existence of Red Cross parcels to cut *Stalag* rations by a third. German civilians had suffered reduced rations so Hitler decided the Allies should subsidize his war machine.

The typical parcel resembled an oversized cardboard shoebox, containing about 11lbs of canned and dry food. The contents provided nutrients missing from Nazi rations; dried milk, margarine and cheese were particularly important. The savoury ingredients ranged from vegetables to sausages, bacon, tinned meat and fish and stock cubes. Sweeter items included biscuits, syrup, jam, rice pudding, raisins, custard, sugar and chocolate, while beverages included tea, coffee and cocoa. Soap might also be included. After their contents were consumed, the boxes were recycled as playing cards and toilet paper while the crates in which they came became makeshift armchairs or even partition walls for NCOs' private quarters.

In Britain, parcels were packed by the Joint War Organization of the Red Cross and the Order of St John of Jerusalem, operating from offices in St James' Palace. Canadian boxes, which at one point were arriving in Geneva at a rate of 22,500 per week, were particularly popular: they contained Klim (milk spelt backwards) powder and pure meat rolls – rationing meant British parcels' meat was adulterated with fillers.

In theory, Alec was entitled to one parcel a week, but there were long periods when he went without. Germans would steal parcels from trains or pilfer their choicest contents. The worst 'shrinkage' occurred as parcels were transported from Lamsdorf to its *Arbeitskommandos*. The first Red Cross parcels and cigarette issues reached Lamsdorf on 6 December. There were so few, however, that POWs were only given a quarter of a parcel and twelve cigarettes, and parcels did not reach some *Arbeitskommandos* until February, when the men had to make do with an eighth. Only months later did issues become regular.

For the near-starving men at Neudorf, the first Red Cross parcels and cigarette issues, even divided between eight, were manna from heaven. Alec's first cigarette puff overpowered him: 'My head spun around and I felt so dizzy I thought I was going to faint.' The food, meanwhile, was too rich for the POWs' weakened stomachs, producing, according to Doug Collins, 'a retching and a spewing unknown since the manorial feasts of the Middle Ages'.

Unfortunately for Alec, the Red Cross parcels came too late to restore his health. By Christmas, his ulcerated legs had made manual labour virtually impossible, while the stress of not knowing his fate should Hitler win the war was overwhelming. Sitting in his hut on the last evening of 1940, he described his feelings in a poem entitled New Year's Eve 1940–1:

The snow falls softly to the ground,
As the old year draws to a close,
And 1941 draws nigh
What will it bring? Who knows?

The old year brought disaster;
And many a mother and wife,
Still cries when she thinks of her loved one,
Who, for England, laid down his life.

The war still follows its weary course,
Right to the bitter end,
But who knows what 1941,
And the bright new year will send?

We, the prisoners of war
Are tired of waiting here;
But who knows what lies in store for us
In the bright new year.

Two days later, showing symptoms of pneumonia, Alec was returned to Lamsdorf and admitted to the camp *Revier*. The conditions were primitive but he could, at last, receive treatment from Royal Army Medical Corps doctors.

Chapter 13

Early Escapes and Clink

Alec spent early 1941 recovering from pneumonia and leg ulcers. The Germans who ran the *Revier* were an *Oberstarzt* (colonel doctor) called Rudolf, and his deputy, Dr Krauchner. Rudolf was a stout, chubby-faced man in his late twenties with duelling scars on his cheeks and rings on his fingers. POWs thought him 'a dandy' but they soon learned that he would force men suffering from diphtheria to work, and some died as a result. Krauchner, a tall grey-haired Silesian in his forties with slim build, sallow complexion and sharp features, would also haul sick POWs from their beds.

The British medics, led by Major 'Tiny' Weston, an imposing RAMC regular, tried to ameliorate matters. Weston's second-in-command was 'Whistle' Horncastle, a Territorial radiologist, and the anaesthetist was Barry Barker. Duncan Macrae, a Seaforth Highlander and Scottish rugby international, and Charles Donald dealt with infectious diseases, while Alf Slater and John Sherman did the surgery; Arthur Wilkinson led the dentistry team. The *Revier* also contained a familiar face for Alec – Edward Gartside. The Queen Vic medic's pre-war career as a Folkestone family doctor hardly prepared him for his work in patching up the wounded at Calais, yet survivors were full of praise for him, and he carried on earning their thanks in the years that followed. Gartside also addressed POWs' cultural needs, playing violin in the Lamsdorf Lazarett Theatre Orchestra.

Revier conditions were better than Alec experienced on *Arbeitskommandos*. On admission, patients were given a hot bath by Paddy Ashby, an Irish physiotherapist, and were then supplied with pyjamas and blankets. After that, they had one hot bath per week. For meals, German rations and Red Cross food were combined by POW cooks under the supervision of a lugubrious guard nicknamed 'Happy'. Breakfast consisted of porridge, potato meal bread and mint tea; lunch might be meat roll, potatoes and pudding; for tea, Alec would have bread and jam or beans on toast; supper was Red Cross cheese and hot drinks.

The medical care suffered from wartime constraints, although the *Revier* and the larger 450-bed *Neue Lazarett* (new hospital), built by POWs and opened on 13 October 1941, were among the best in the *Stalag*s. The Allied blockade left the Germans short of medicines, so Alec's medics had to rely on supplies sent from Britain via Geneva. Though some did get through, the doctors fought a constant battle against shortages of drugs, bandages and equipment; beds were reserved for the worst cases, and operations that would have been deemed necessary in peacetime were delayed. Diseases such as pleurisy, bronchitis and asthma went untreated, as did frostbite, while shortages of sulfa drugs meant infections were slow to heal if at all, and dentistry was limited to extractions. 'The bed linen in the *Lazarett* is neither changed nor washed sufficiently often,' wrote Red Cross inspectors. 'There are not nearly enough medical supplies.'

Germans did not mind POWs dying from wounds or non-infectious diseases, but typhus petrified them. It had been rife on the eastern front during the Great War, and their fear, which proved warranted when Russian prisoners reached the Reich after Operation Barbarossa, was that captives would infect the German *Übermenschen* (supermen). The Poles had developed the first typhus inoculation, and although not totally effective it provided some protection. Alec received his first injection in Groschowitz on 19 September 1940, an event recorded in his *Personalkarte*, and his second in the *Revier* on 7 May 1941.

Alec's convalescence was slow, but he was sufficiently improved by February 1941 to return to writing, and his first poem was to the girl he had left behind. By early 1941, most POWs were in contact with loved ones, yet Alec decided to leave her in ignorance for fear of a German invasion. He called the poem To Netta:

> Though you are so far away
> Your features haunt me,
> And, when I think of bygone days
> The memories taunt me.
>
> Accurate in every detail
> The past-pictures are crystal clear,
> And your face, your voice, your laughter
> Though now remote, are yet so near.
>
> Until I see you once again,
> And that day will come at last,
> I can remain content and happy
> With my pictures from the past.

A month later, with snow still thick on the ground, the theme of internal escape – that he might find freedom in contemplating happier times – resurfaced in Pictures from the Past:

> While I lay here as a prisoner
> Miserable in every pore,
> I can travel greater distance,
> Than I ever went before.

All I do is close my eyelids.
In a second I can go
From the snowy wastes of Lamsdorf
To a village that I know.

In the south of sunny Cornwall,
And once more its harbour see,
Once more hear the seagulls crying,
As I walk along the quay.

Instead of guttural German voices,
Discordant harshness on my ear,
Comes the soft smooth burr of Cornish,
A tonic in these days so drear;

Or, I can go to busy London,
Mingle with the laughing throng.
New Year's Eve in Piccadilly,
Listen to the voices strong.

Raised in carefree happy singing,
As the New Year's ushered in.
In one second, I can be
Singing with them once again.

But alas, a time must come.
My eyes I cannot always close,
And once more I'm back in Lamsdorf,
Prisoner amongst the snows.

By the late spring, Alec was sufficiently recovered to contemplate the future. Mostly, the news broadcast through Lamsdorf's loudspeakers was grim, as Erwin Rommel's *Afrika Korps* pushed the British back to Egypt and his colleagues swept through the Balkans and Greece in a rerun of their 1940 French campaign. Yet, there was some good news. On 10 May, Rudolph Hess, Hitler's deputy, cracked under the strain of war, fled Germany in a Messerschmitt and parachuted out over Scotland, aiming to persuade Britain to make peace. Then, on 27 May, Navy battleships and torpedo bombers sank the *Bismarck*, one of Hitler's largest battleships. Such items helped to sustain Alec's hopes that the Allies would triumph and he would return home for victory celebrations. With Netta uppermost in his mind, he wrote When I Go Back:

How strange the outside world will seem
When I go back.
When the dividing wall is crossed,
I'll meet those friends I thought half-lost,

And have the things I've wanted most,
When I go back.

I'll be a wanderer no more,
When I go back.
I shall have no more urge to roam,
I shall not want to cross the foam.
I'll be content to stay at home,
When I go back.

I'll be a wiser man, I hope
When I go back.
I've had the leisure to reflect,
The time, the right part to select,
And I shall hold my head erect,
When I go back.

And yet, somehow, I shan't forget,
When I go back.
The miseries, that I've been through,
Unpleasant things I've had to do
Were nothing when I thought of you,
When I go back.

Discharged from the *Revier*, Alec discovered conditions were improving. Personal parcels from home, permitted under the Geneva Convention's Article 38, now provided POWs with essentials such as underwear and blankets – although the commandant responded by withdrawing issued blankets to maintain the ration at two, even in winter. The Red Cross began sending books, while the War Office dispatched replacement uniforms and boots. But Red Cross reports from 1942 also made references to 'a recrudescence of ill-treatment', to trigger-happy guards and to failures to honour 'numerous promises' made to rectify injustices.

Alec did not have much time to enjoy the improvements. For him, getting well meant returning to work. Soon after being declared fit, he was marched to Block 26, Lamsdorf's Working Compound, which housed POWs scheduled to go to *Arbeitskommandos*. A German *Unteroffizier* was nominally in charge but the real work was done by Sergeant Major Reg Charters, a Grenadier Guardsman attached to the Territorials of the Worcester Regiment and taken prisoner outside Dunkirk on 7 June, three days after the last British boats departed. Once in Lamsdorf, he took charge of allocating POWs to the hundreds of *Arbeitskommandos* in the *Wehrkreis VIII* military district. Charters seemed taciturn, but his discretion was vital because he was a critical cog in Lamsdorf's escape machine, as Alec discovered later.

Alec's new *Arbeitskommando*, E130, was in Heuerstein, a village dominated by a Schloss and an onion-domed church 30km south east of Oppeln. His journey there began at 7.00am on 25 May (one day short of the first anniversary of his surrender), when he was marched into the *Vorlager* for his 'exit search'. From there he was escorted to Annahof to catch a train to Oppeln, where he and his escort changed to the line leading south-east towards the Silesian coalfields. Snow had fallen as late as 16 May, but spring finally arrived in Silesia a few days later and the weather was mostly warm and sunny. The journey was a novel experience. Instead of being crammed into a cattle-truck, he sat on a wooden bench, a comparative luxury, although he found the curious stares from fellow passengers uncomfortable.

Heuerstein, where seventy POWs toiled away crushing stone, introduced Alec to lime quarrying. First, top soil would be removed; then the limestone would be blasted with explosives – a civilian task, with POWs kept well away – and broken up. The crushed stone would then be burned in a kiln to create chemicals for use in whitewash, mortar, plaster, fertilizer and other industrial processes, including steel production and sugar refining.

Conditions were notoriously bad. As late as 1944, Swiss inspectors reported to London about a regime that involved ten-hour days breaking stone and demanded that the commandant submit the POWs to health checks. What was worse, Alec found himself back under the authority of guards who had been at Groschowitz the previous autumn. He remained a 'marked man' and felt he had to get away. The first opportunity, on 3 June, came nine days after his arrival.

Alec's escape from Heuerstein was primitive. His decision to flee came during a rainstorm, when the guards had taken refuge in a hut and were paying little attention. Alec, wearing work overalls over his uniform, put a shovel over his shoulder and slipped into woods nearby, 'the idea being just to get as far away from the working party as possible'. If recaptured and asked where he was from he would say, 'Lamsdorf, Lamsdorf, Lamsdorf', in the hope that he would be sent to the main camp 'to be disciplined in the normal way' then sent to another *Arbeitskommando*.

Putting distance between himself and Heuerstein was vital, because POWs who escaped from *Arbeitskommandos* and were returned would be beaten in front of colleagues, or worse. Alec would later tell his children about John Collings, a Royal Northumberland Fusilier who escaped from an *Arbeits-kommando* but was later taken back. As a guard marched Collings into the barbed-wire enclosure, he took the rifle from his shoulder and shot him dead.

That was not Alec's fate. Not long after his break, he was challenged and immediately raised his hands, saying, 'I am an English prisoner of war' and showing his uniform beneath his overalls, and his identity tag. He was then marched to a police station to be interrogated. As he had planned, he insisted he had escaped from the main *Stalag* VIIIB camp but refused to reveal more than his name, rank and Army service number. Fortunately, the story worked and he was dispatched to Lamsdorf for his first brush with the camp's punishment regime – the POW slang was 'clink' or 'the cooler'.

The process of returning a recaptured POW began in the *Vorlager*, where the offender would greeted by a reception committee. This was headed by 'Yankee Joe' and included a guard nicknamed 'Fat Boy' – 'an almost perfect sphere' according to Cyril Rofé, a Jewish airman downed in June 1941 during a raid on Düsseldorf, 'and a source of unceasing wonderment to all those of us who wanted to know where he drew his rations'. The POW would be searched for escape tools, although prisoners soon learned which guards could be bribed into cutting short their investigations. Then, the POW's identity would be checked against his *Personalkarte*. In Alec's case, this showed his story about escaping from Lamsdorf was fiction.

The next stage involved Alec being marched in his underwear past giggling women working in the *Kartei* to the delousing unit. First, he was issued with a canvas bag into which went everything he possessed except his boots. His clothes were then fumigated with cyanide gas while he was shaved from head to toe. Alec feared his circumcised penis would label him as Jewish. Fortunately, circumcision was sufficiently widespread among English gentiles for this not to be a problem. When one guard noticed his circumcision and queried his 'dark and swarthy looks', Alec invented a Spanish grandmother. There was a fragment of truth in this – his father's ancestors were Sephardi Jews expelled from Spain at the end of the fifteenth century.

After being shaved, Alec washed in cold water with carbolic soap. Hot showers did not arrive until 1942, when a bathhouse was built to service 600–800 men a day out of Lamsdorf's population of up to 13,000. Having dried off, Alec collected his clean and louse-free uniform.

Finally, he was marched to a hearing conducted by Lamsdorf's *Gerichts-offizier* (court officer), Oberleutnant Wilhelm Jelen, a white-haired Sudeten, and Captain Jentz, the discipline officer, nicknamed 'Bull's Piss' after he said the POWs' *Appell* lines were 'as straight as a bull pisses'.

'Why did you escape?' Jelen asked Alec, to which he replied, 'Because it is a soldier's duty'. This remark and others were noted down by a female clerk and typed up for the record.

The standard tariff for a first escape was, depending on its sophistication, seven or fourteen days' solitary confinement in Lamsdorf's *Straflager*, although this might be reduced if the POW had spent time in a civilian jail. Shorter sentences were handed out for minor offences such as stealing potatoes. Persistent escapers might face the maximum thirty days prescribed by the Geneva Convention, but serious offences might lead to transfer to a punishment camp.

In the war's early years, Lamsdorf's prison within a prison was a hut in its own barbed-wire compound near the *Vorlager*, with dedicated guards and machine-gun tower. The forty 6ft square concrete cells were separated by a central passage. The only furniture was a 2ft wide wooden platform bed along one wall. Blankets were provided but no mattress, along with a Red Cross bible fastened to the bed end, a dixie of drinking water and a latrine bucket. The cell windows were high and barred, but inmates fit enough to jump up and cling to the bars could see into the next compound. It was not a pleasant sight: this was where guards trained dogs to hunt escapers by dressing a dummy in British battledress and tying meat to its throat. The steel doors to the internal corridor had a peep-hole to check for suicide attempts and a notice stating the prisoner's name, crime and dates of arrival and departure.

The man in charge was *Unteroffizier* Joseph Kissel, a bovine, menacing figure with a broad face and snub nose who would march around barking orders and waving a steel rod. The POWs nicknamed Kissel 'Ukraine Joe' for his Slav appearance. Such was his harsh reputation he was later promoted to run the RAF compound, home to some of Lamsdorf's most insubordinate inmates.

Each morning, Alec would be roused, told to empty his bucket and given water to wash but not shave – razorblades were banned. Having washed, he would be ordered to fetch a bucket of water and scrub his cell and the corridor outside, before being locked in again.

Watery soup and bread would arrive at midday but Alec was denied Red Cross parcels. Twice a day, at 10.00am and 3.00pm, a guard would shout: 'Exercise! Walking for sport!' and Alec would file out with other inmates into a walled circle behind the hut for twenty minutes' exercise. Typically, this involved walking in single file around the sandy ground, staying four feet from the next man. Conversation was banned and inmates who spoke would be threatened with being shot. Sometimes, guards would force prisoners to run round the circle, fling themselves to the ground on command, then jump to their feet and run on at the order '*Raus!*' Those slow in rising would find Ukraine Joe's boot on their backs pressing them into the dust.

Occasionally, Alec could exchange a word with a fellow inmate while washing or emptying his bucket, but the only official communication with other POWs was during the twice-weekly medical check-up. If POWs were lucky, they might persuade the medic to prescribe something 'medicinal' to supplement their punishment rations – a favourite was malt syrup. Sometimes, guards could be bribed to produce extra food, while the POW cooks occasionally slipped inmates some stew from the guards' rations.

For some inmates, the time spent inside was a test of their sanity; for others, the silence and enforced idleness was a luxury. For Alec, it was a chance to read – a limited supply of books was allowed – and commit poetry to memory. It was also a chance for the first time since September 1939 to enjoy privacy – to be alone with his thoughts, free from the crowded huts, the stench of unwashed bodies, the dirt, the bedbugs that would crawl over him at night and give off an appalling smell if crushed, the lice – and the distortions of character caused by imprisonment and deprivation.

On the March, Alec discovered that shared hardship did not always bring out the best in men. At Lamsdorf and on his early *Arbeitskommandos* he felt his own instincts harden as scarce food was divided. This process was described by Robert Kee, a bomber pilot shot down over Holland: 'Though the differences were minute they were capable of calling forth the highest passions: great content if you did well, or jealousy and despair if you did badly. You loathed it when you saw other people behaving like this and yet you could no more control it in yourself than you could any other automatic physical reflex.'

In his cell, Alec would read and play patience with cards he had been permitted to bring into 'clink' – the harder the game the better. One, taught him by his Auntie Lillie, was so difficult it remained undefeated throughout the war. Never had he had such a sustained period to think and to reflect on everything that had happened since boarding the SS *Canterbury* – heroism, selfishness in the struggle for survival, defeatism and German brutality. He decided he would respond by becoming a committed escaper – and if he could not escape he would make a nuisance of himself in other ways. If he could get home he might be of further use to his country; and if not, unlike men who accepted captivity and were content merely to survive, Alec would keep fighting, even if it was from behind barbed wire.

At the end of his sentence, Alec strolled from his cell rested but hungry and sprouting a beard, and, having given the thumbs-up to the POW about to replace him, was escorted back to the main camp. Denied Red Cross parcels in 'clink', he made an early trip to Lamsdorf's parcel store to collect his overdue issue. There, he was looked after by a sergeant major whose standard greeting to former clink residents was a grin, then a bark to a colleague in classic NCO-style: 'Take that man's name and number, corporal, he needs a haircut and a shave!'

Alec was then returned to the working party compound, where Reg Charters told him his next *Arbeitskommando* would be in Hindenburg, in Upper Silesia's coalfield. The town's previous name, Zabrze, was Polish but it was renamed to honour Field Marshal Paul von Hindenburg, victor in 1914 against the Russians at Tannenberg and nineteen years later the President who appointed Hitler as Chancellor. In the post-Versailles plebiscite, 59 per cent of Hindenburg's townspeople voted to stay with Germany and they had been overwhelmingly pro-Nazi during Hitler's rise to power. During *Kristallnacht*, they destroyed a synagogue that had stood since 1872. Alongside coal, Hindenburg was a centre for steel, glassware, chemicals and brewing. POWs were put to work in various *Arbeitskommandos*. Some mined coal, others maintained the local railways.

Alec did not stay long. Within days he staged a second escape but was again picked up and sent to Lamsdorf for another spell in clink. This time, he had to wait to serve his punishment. Summer was Lamsdorf's escaping season and there were insufficient cells to accommodate all recaptured POWs. Instead, he was led into a special compound called the *Strafe Kompanie* to wait his turn. There he was greeted by a block sergeant major who told him it was 'a great honour' to be held in a Nazi military prison.

This segregation might have suited the guards, but it had unintended consequences, because the *Strafe* hut and exercise yard became a university of escaping – and the 'lecturers' and 'undergraduates' included some of Lamsdorf's brightest and boldest captives, men who had recovered their self-respect by doing everything possible to keep their captors busy. Some were waiting to serve sentences for insubordination or damaging property. Others were in for escapes that were, like Alec's first break, not serious home-run attempts. Alec could, however, benefit from 'lectures' by men genuinely trying to get home and back in the war.

Escape routes were a core part of the curriculum. Alec was brought up on tales of Great War escapes from camps located close to neutral Holland or Switzerland. Silesia, however, was a long way from Switzerland, while routes to other neutral countries went through occupied territories. Some men headed for the Baltic port of Stettin, where they hoped to stow away on boats bound for neutral Sweden. From there, England was a plane journey away, and home-runners taking this route sent innocent-looking postcards to Lamsdorf referring obliquely to their adventures. Some escapers headed for the Balkans; others tried to reach Vichy France via Belgium and then hike though the Pyrenees into neutral Spain. The word was Belgian police were so anti-Nazi they would put escapers in touch with underground networks that ran escape lines to Spain.

Before June 1941 no POW could be sure of a safe reception in Russia, as James Allan, a Calais captive, discovered. After getting there, Allan was accused of spying, tortured and incarcerated in Moscow's Lubyanka prison. Only in October 1941, four months after Hitler invaded Russia, was he returned home. His reward was a Distinguished Conduct Medal, but the citation remained secret for fear of embarrassing Stalin.

From routes, the discussion would move to whether it was better to travel on foot or take trains. Escapers on foot made slow progress and endured hours of nerve-wracking inactivity. Some stuck to moving only at night but, because of German-imposed curfews, they were easily picked up. Goods trains were extensively searched, while freight yards were difficult to leave unobserved. Express train passengers faced intrusive questioning by railway police but less curiosity from other travellers than those on commuter trains. To travel successfully by express train involved posing as a foreign worker and having robust forged documents.

Some escapers were lone wolves; others travelled in pairs. Some avoided contact with people in occupied countries; others sought out Poles and

Czechs because of the kindness they showed when they encountered POWs on *Arbeitskommandos*. Sam Kydd witnessed Poles taking 'their lives into their hands by helping and making life more bearable'. He saw a Pole beaten for giving a POW tobacco; he saw another thrown into the Vistula for talking to POWs. 'For guts, courage and unselfishness and a great love for anything British the Poles stand alone,' he wrote. 'They believed to the bitter end that the British would come and rescue them from the German yoke.' Typically, women proved more willing, perhaps because men were under greater suspicion. Czechs tended to take more risks than Poles, but POWs had to be careful in the Sudetenland, where most Sudeten Germans were Nazis. Having thought themselves underdogs in post-Versailles Czechoslovakia, they now revelled in their *Übermensch* status.

What factors led to recapture? Gordon Woodroofe, a New Zealand airman downed during a raid on Turin in September 1941, attended the Lamsdorf escapers' university after an abortive break-out. There he learned that tiredness, hunger and dissent could lead escapers to take unnecessary risks and behave in ways that provoked suspicion. Luck, however, would so often be the deciding factor. This, Alec later discovered, was wisdom indeed.

With the theory part of his escape curriculum complete, Alec did his stretch in clink and returned to the main camp. There he encountered victims of the Wehrmacht's sweep through the Balkans and Greece in spring 1941. These included Serbs, who like the Poles before and the Russians later, were treated by the Lamsdorf guards as *Untermenschen*. Thus, they faced machine-gun fire for offering cigarettes on the day they arrived to British POWs.

Then Alec encountered Palestinian Jews captured in Greece and on Crete. Of the 1,500 taken, two thirds were sent to Lamsdorf, arriving in August. These were mostly European Jews who had emigrated to Mandate Palestine before the war; a few came from Silesia and were familiar with the area around Lamsdorf. Alec was fascinated by their stories.

While Palestinian Arabs sought Hitler's support, Palestinian Jews rallied to the British Empire despite the fact that Britain had reneged on its Balfour Declaration promise of a Jewish homeland by restricting emigration in the 1930s. In their enthusiasm for the cause, virtually every able-bodied man and woman volunteered. Nowhere else in the Empire witnessed such high levels of volunteering. These were the latter-day Maccabees Alec had invoked in his *Kristallnacht* poem. Like the Jews who fought against Franco, these men fought for democracy, embodying the spirit of Jewish resistance and dispelling the myth that Jews were incapable of taking up arms against anti-Semitism. A number survived Lamsdorf to become leading lights in the young Zionist state and the Israel Defence Forces. Sergeant Josef Karlenboim, a Russian who became Yosef Almogi, was one of David Ben-Gurion's ministers. Gecel Perski, a Royal Engineer, was the father of Shimon Peres, Israel's President from July 2007.

Most Palestinian Jews spoke German but unlike Alec they could not melt into the crowd of gentile POWs. At the point of capture, some Palestinians were so fearful of what might happen they contemplated a Masada-style mass suicide. About 150 Viennese Jews had committed suicide after Hitler absorbed Austria in the *Anschluss*, but among the Palestinians calmer voices prevailed. Wehrmacht officers were divided over how to treat these men, of whom some had been their classmates in Weimar Germany. One Wehrmacht lawyer considered branding them 'fugitives from justice', thus denying them POW status. After much debate, however, they merely separated them from gentiles on the journey to Germany. Similarly, when they arrived at Lamsdorf they were segregated, and SS officers were invited to interrogate them.

The Germans also tried to enforce segregation at *Stalag Luft* VI at Heydekrug but the senior British officer, Sergeant James 'Dixie' Deans, responded by saying Jews were members of 'the King's Service', whose rules said all faiths should be respected, 'even bloody tree-worshippers' – adding that tree worship and other pagan rites were promoted by Goebbels. When the commandant distributed anti-Semitic pamphlets, the prisoners set fire to them on the parade ground in front of their guards.

At Lamsdorf, the new camp commandant, Alfred Minsinger, persuaded Swiss inspectors he was 'efficient though perhaps rather strict'; he was, in reality, a vicious anti-Semite who hoped British gentile POWs would shun Jews as *Untermenschen*, as French anti-Semites had done. Minsinger began by proposing that the Palestinians wear the yellow stars worn by civilians in the Reich's Jewish ghettos. The Wehrmacht vetoed the idea, but he was permitted to deny them Red Cross parcels, send their NCOs out on *Arbeitskommandos*, limit their access to entertainment and ban communication with gentiles.

Sidney Sherriff said gentiles would refuse their parcels if the parcel ban continued and protested to Swiss inspectors about the issue of NCOs and working parties. Eventually, Minsinger compromised – NCOs would be segregated in Lamsdorf while privates would be sent to special *Arbeitskommandos*. Yet anti-Semitic treatment continued under Colonel Lüger, who replaced Minsinger in 1942. Tall and heavily built with dark lank hair, Lüger walked with a stoop. In evidence to war crimes investigators after the war, one POW described him as 'a typical German criminal type' who would command his guards to beat Palestinians with rifle butts for no cause. Sentries were told, meanwhile, to shoot Palestinians if they were near the trip wire even if standing still.

Conditions in Palestinian *Arbeitskommandos* were worse than average. Jewish POWs were more likely to be sent down coal mines and their guards tended to be more brutal. This led to hunger strikes and complaints to the Swiss. One of the finest negotiators was Yosef Krelenbon, a Pioneer Corps sergeant who led the POWs at a forestry *Arbeitskommando*. Krelenbon struck a deal with the commandant – his men would deliver their quotas of logs plus bribes of Red Cross soap, tea, chocolate and cigarettes, but only if the guards left them in peace to continue their bartering with local civilians.

Jewish POWs in Lamsdorf and its segregated *Arbeitskommandos* fought back in other ways, particularly those who came into contact with Jewish civilians. They would smuggle food, clothing, cigarettes and medicine to Jews in ghettos and write coded hints in letters and postcards to their families about the Holocaust. One group at a coal-mining *Arbeitskommando* in Jawozno, 20km north of Auschwitz, learned of its gas chambers from a civilian. Others came across Polish underground newsletters, one of which carried on its front page a photo of a naked corpse hanging by the neck.

Culturally, these latter-day Maccabees, nicknamed the Jordan Highlanders by gentiles, differed from the assimilated Jews Alec grew up with in Golders Green and encountered in the City of London. Though clad in British uniforms, they seemed alien to Alec's gentile colleagues and they were sometimes envied for their facility with German, which enabled them to barter aggressively for food and other items. The Palestinians, wrote Cyril Rofé, spent their time 'refusing to work, going on hunger strike over bad food, committing sabotage, escaping, black marketing, spreading pro-British propaganda – never mind whether it was true or not so long as it was anti-German – and generally causing the Hun far more trouble than they could possibly have done as a mere fighting unit'.

Yet Jewish POWs could be harshly punished for trivial offences. In one incident, the commandant of an *Arbeitskommando* at Ehrenforst complained to superiors that the ten-day standard penalty for fraternization with civilians was insufficient for David Baum and Abram Elberg, two Polish-born Palestinians, who had given chocolate to German children while picking blueberries under armed escort. In another incident, an *Arbeitskommando* guard opened fire without warning on Private Naphtali Strassler, who had left his line to pick up potatoes on the edge of a field. Jews were also more likely to be sent to Colditz and 'shot while trying to escape'. A classic example occurred on 17 May 1944. Eliahu Krauze from Bnei Brak, near Tel Aviv, had been recaptured after escaping with another Palestinian from their coal-mining *Arbeitskommando* at Beuthen Schonberg. The commandant and *Unteroffizier* led the pair into some fields, ostensibly to look for a third escaper. While there, the Germans turned their guns on them, killing Krauze. His partner was initially denied treatment for his wounds and died soon afterwards of pneumonia.

Sherriff besieged the authorities with complaints about 'most unsatisfactory' Palestinian *Arbeitskommando* conditions and protested when commandants' responses were 'evasive'. Factory police, he said, 'mete out corporal punishment', sick Palestinians were refused medicine and some died from 'criminal neglect'. The discrimination even extended to the dead. The

Wehrmacht allowed military funerals for POWs, with honour guards, six-gun salutes and a prisoner escort of thirty men. When a Palestinian sergeant died of pneumonia, however, the commandant initially denied him a proper funeral. He was due to be buried the same day as a gentile airman shot dead for stepping into 'no-man's-land'. When pallbearers arrived at the cemetery, they realized the airman would be buried with military honours, but not the Jew. The Palestinians protested, followed by the airmen, who downed their coffin and halted their service. Sherriff then led a deputation to the commandant, who eventually reversed his decision. Thus, the guards were, recalled Rofé, 'obliged to fire not only a volley in honour of the airman they had murdered but also another in honour of the Palestinian Jew'.

During summer 1941, Alec discovered how Germans treated Russians. Barbarossa, the largest operation in military history and the war's defining event, began on 22 June. Alec saw one newspaper headline reading: 'Settlement with the red rabble'. It was 'the showdown with Bolshevism', offering the chance to create *Lebensraum* (living space) and colonize the conquered regions. Victory would give Germany control over the Ukraine's 'bread basket', provide millions of slave labourers and offer unimpeded access to Baku's oilfields.

Within six weeks, the Wehrmacht captured almost 800,000 Russians; yet their fate bore no resemblance to that of British POWs. The Wehrmacht had already practised systematic mistreatment of Polish POWs, with Jews suffering particularly badly. Some 50,000 were segregated on the basis of their names and whether they were circumcised, then used as slave labour. Six months later, half were dead. Yet this was merely a dress rehearsal for what happened to Russians, of whom three million died in captivity.

Russians not massacred at the point of capture were stripped of useful clothing and force-marched to camps in conditions worse than anything experienced by Alec in 1940. One of these camps was *Stalag* VIIIF, which was visible from *Stalag* VIIIB's perimeter fence. Initially, it was just a field surrounded by barbed wire, so the Russians had to build their own shelters but were given no materials. Thus, they dug holes in the ground and covered them with blankets. Then the numbers were thinned out by SS men given two priorities: killing Red Army political officers and, in the words of Field Marshal Walter von Reichenau's 'Severity Order', the 'subhuman species of Jewry'. Some were used for target practice; others had dogs set on them while SS men gambled on which dog would inflict the worst injuries. Only 68 of the 60–80,000 Jews taken in Operation Barbarossa were still alive by April 1942.

At Lamsdorf, the British had some contact with Russians temporarily housed alongside them in *Stalag* VIIIB. The contrast was appalling. On one side of the barbed-wire separating the two compounds, the British would stand, relatively well fed and clothed thanks to Red Cross and personal parcels. On the other stood 'Russkies', emaciated, unshaven and dressed in rags but still able to summon up vestiges of energy to sing songs to keep their spirits up. British POWs tossed cigarettes over the wire but watched, appalled, as the Russians fought for them like animals then ate the tobacco for its marginal nutritional value.

The Russians died like animals too, and British POWs were ordered to dig burial pits in woods nearby. These would eventually contain 42,000 corpses. Alec was part of this working party and thus had to perform the most grue-some task he had ever undertaken. Decades later, he found it impossible to discuss, leaving only an oblique reference in some notes that read 'digging pits for Russian camp'.

In desperate situations, desperate men do desperate things. In *Stalag* VIIIF, guard dogs would disappear, leaving only a few bones. Men fought to strip tattered uniforms off corpses. Dead men were hauled out on parade and propped up to be counted so their rations could go to survivors. Russians fought for morsels of cabbage each time soup was distributed from vast con-tainers. In one incident, starving men fought so desperately the container tipped over into the snow. The Russians dropped onto their stomachs and lapped up the liquid from the ground, clawing and biting each other to get their share. The guards opened fire, but those captives still alive continued to drink the now bloodstained blend of melting snow and soup. With all vestiges of civilization gone, 'desperate things' even included cannibalism – as British POWs discovered when they sifted through corpses whose legs no longer had thigh muscles.

Richard Pape, a *Yorkshire Post* journalist and airman, described being detailed to bury Russian corpses in his book, *Boldness Be My Friend*: 'I never realized that human life could be so debased. I never imagined that the smell from human beings could be so horrible.' Barracks had become morgues 'full of emaciated and presumably dead Russians, their faces like white, dried, fatty bacon, limbs like sticks and the mockery of flesh which covered them riddled with big blue scabs'.

He was told to load bodies on to wagons to be taken to the pits. One Russian was still alive, but when Pape protested a guard told him to mind his own business and sling the bodies down in layers prior to tossing them into the pit. Once this was completed, a civilian, unconcerned as if 'icing a cake', pumped lime foam over the corpses to accelerate decomposition. Pape real-ized more than one Russian was still alive: 'White-covered corpses bucked, jerked, twisted and trembled, but the noise which the lime burned out of them was most terrifying of all. It was a concerted hissing throat-grating.' If Pape resisted he might join the Russians in the pit. Instead, he followed the guards' orders to cover the pit with earth, which was then flattened by a steam-roller.

The horror of what Alec saw digging Russian burial pits reinforced his determination to escape again. Breaking out of Lamsdorf itself seemed diffi-cult. Later in the war, Lamsdorf POWs dug escape tunnels, but there was no tunnelling in 1941. Security, however, was not always perfect when prisoners were marched out on working parties. Thus, once again acting as a lone wolf, he slipped away from a column when the guards' backs were turned. Once again, however, he was quickly recaptured and sent back to the *Straflager*, for the third time.

Alec thought himself unlucky because he was then sent to a supposedly escape-proof *Arbeitskommando*. He was, however, lucky in one respect, because he left Stalag VIIIB just before typhus arrived. As the Germans feared, lice-ridden Russian prisoners brought 'gaol fever' to Lamsdorf. They were happy to see the epidemic do their job of racial extermination for them within Stalag VIIIF, as the Russian camp filled up with coughing, shivering men suffering nosebleeds, nausea, vomiting and rashes. But Minsinger needed to stop 'gaol fever' spreading outside, so he ordered Soviet slave labourers to be put through Lamsdorf's delouser. Unfortunately, British orderlies who processed their lice-laden clothes caught the disease, so Minsinger placed the camp under quarantine on Thursday, 20 November 1941. British medics then imposed a curfew, segregated men in their compounds, cancelled religious, educational and entertainment gatherings and compelled every man to be disinfected and shaved of every strand of hair on his body.

The epidemic was brought under control, although the medics found they could do little beyond nursing to alleviate victims' symptoms, as Donald and Barker reported in a paper submitted to the *British Medical Journal*. Entitled 'Louse-borne Typhus Fever', it appeared the following September beneath the sub-heading, 'From a Prison Camp in Germany'. In the absence of drugs, doctors sponged down patients with tepid water and kept their fluid intake up, with glucose sometimes introduced rectally or intravenously. Gradually, after two or three weeks, most sufferers, including Donald himself, recovered, but three Britons died, including one doctor, 27-year old Captain Altham of the Gordon Highlanders.

Chapter 14

Life in a Limestone Quarry

Arbeitskommando E173, to which Alec was sent, was in Setzdorf, a village 50km south-west of Lamsdorf just across Germany's old border in the Sudetenland. German speakers, living isolated from their Slav neighbours in small towns and villages, comprised 45 per cent of the Sudeten population; the rest were Polish and Czech Christians and a few Jews. The Wehrmacht thought the Sudetenland a good place to locate *Arbeitskommandos* – and they thought E173 escape-proof. In the Sudeten mountains winter conditions were severe, with snow on the ground for months. If the weather was the enemy in the winter, summertime escapers had to contend with human obstacles: most Sudeten Germans were fanatical Nazis. Sudeten factories helped sustain Germany's blockaded economy, yet Operation Barbarossa had stripped them of workers. Now they could use POW labour, and soon the Sudeten hills were peppered with parties of press-ganged POWs.

Alec's journey to Setzdorf began at sunrise on 18 August 1941, when he was marched into the *Vorlager* for his 'exit search' for escape materials. Like snails, travelling POWs would carry their houses on their backs – blankets, underwear, utensils made from old tins, Red Cross boxes containing scraps of food, photographs, postcards and letters, cigarettes and books. Alec's meagre possessions included his sheets of poetry and Netta's fountain pen. He had contemplated trading it for food but continued to resist the temptation; it came home with him in 1945.

The search completed, the escort demonstrated their rifles were loaded, then marched the prisoners to Annahof, where they prodded them towards the rear carriages of the 7.19am train, occupied by locals who stared, some with hostility, some with compassion, at the *Engländer*. After a few minutes the train entered a town with fine gothic and baroque civic buildings and onion-domed church towers. This was Neisse, where travellers changed trains for the Sudetenland 22km away. After the dust of Lamsdorf's compounds, the scenery was a treat for the POWs. Monday, 18 August was a fine day, and Alec looked out at the lush and varied countryside as the train made its way slowly through the hilly border country. As he listened to the chugging of the engine and the regular rhythm of the wheels, it seemed for a while as if the titanic struggles in Russia and North Africa were a world away, irrelevant to his circumscribed existence. On the walls of the villages through which the train passed there were, however, regular reminders of the regime holding him prisoner. One poster had the slogan '*In den Staub mit allen Feinden Gross-Deutschlands!*' ('Into the dust with all enemies of Greater Germany') surrounding an image of a giant Teutonic fist smashing cartoon figures of Charles de Gaulle, Churchill and a top-hatted Jewish financier into the ground.

Finally, after a ten-hour journey, the train pulled into a station in the Reichensteiner hills. This was the halt for Setzdorf, home to the Anton Latzel Kalkwerke (limestone works) and Alec's home for the next two and a half years. Latzel, who became a *Reichsrat* deputy after the Habsburgs embraced constitutional reform in 1861, had introduced modern limestone processing into the Austro-Hungarian Empire, and by the 1920s, eleven kilns operated in Setzdorf, but the business suffered during the Depression. When Communist workers staged a hunger march in 1931, police opened fire, killing ten. These shootings marked the peak of Communist agitation, and from then on Hitler's German Sudeten Party allies took control.

The arrival of British POWs, exotic beasts in a remote Sudeten village, was an event. The reception committee not only included *Unteroffizier* Schittenhelm, the commandant, and his guards but also the village policeman and numerous inhabitants. To one side of the tracks stood the village and the hills beyond; to the other, Alec could see a quarry and some kilns below.

From the station, Alec was marched up a path to his new billet, a two-storey stone building with an exercise yard enclosed by the now familiar barbed-wire fence. On the ground floor, two-tier bunks for forty men were arranged along three sides of the main room, with a tiled stove, benches and tables in the middle. The kitchen, where two POWs would cook soup, lay to one side, along with a camp office and store rooms. A staircase on the north side led to the first floor, where Alec found the same arrangement of bunks, benches and tables. There were toilets on both floors, while the washroom was in a lean-to shed. There was no hot water, but Alec was told the Latzel works provided hot showers. The building's windows were barred but he had good views on all sides – up the narrowing Weidenauer river valley on one side, down to more open country on the opposite side, across to the quarry at the back and down to the kilns and the village from the front. A separate hut contained a workshop for mending clothes and a Red Cross parcel store. A Wehrmacht doctor in Freiwaldau would deal with serious illnesses, but dental treatment was limited to extractions.

The following morning after roll-call, Alec learned what the director, Arnold Latzel, had in mind for him. Latzel was a Great War veteran who dressed traditionally in tweed knickerbockers and a Tyrolean hat with goat's tail 'brush'. He had modernized the family business, and the more knowledgeable POWs were impressed by his British equipment such as a Ruston & Hornsby engine. Yet he had not aged well and at forty-seven was badly overweight; Alec thought he resembled Sidney Greenstreet, the Hollywood villain.

Latzel's introductory message was that most of the POWs would work in the quarry, breaking boulders into smaller slabs and loading them into skips on a narrow-gauge track sloping down to the kilns. The skips were linked together, typically in fives, and connected by cable to a revolving drum in a hut at the top. A brakeman controlled the drum with a wooden *Bremse* (brake) resembling a railway sleeper. Other POWs would load stone into the kilns to be fired, then shift the burnt stone into skips. This would be ground into powder in the mill, bagged and transported on rails to a ramp, down which the bags would slide into open-topped railway wagons.

Did this involve indirectly serving Germany's war effort? Lime went into fertilizers and building materials, yet it was also used in Hitler's industrial-scale extermination machine, as Alec had discovered while digging burial pits for Russian corpses in Lamsdorf. After the war, POWs returned home to discover Sudeten lime had been sent to the ghettos of Hitler's *Generalgouvernement*. There it was sprayed over Jewish corpses to speed up the decaying process in pits the Jews themselves were forced to dig. Alec had, unwittingly, been making Holocaust chemicals.

At Setzdorf, Alec again became the interpreter, this time for Suffolk Regiment sergeant 'Dilly' Saunders, the camp *Vertrauensmann*, taking complaints to the guards and overseers. His working week was from Monday to midday Saturday, mostly in the Latzel works, although sometimes he had other duties such as snow-clearing in Freiwaldau, to which he would be transported in a truck driven by a Sudeten who had been a Great War POW in Britain. In Alec's first winter, the snow arrived on 12 October 1941, and there were heavy falls in November and from January 1942 through to March. The consolation was he was classed as a 'heavy worker' alongside coalminers. This meant he had 'heavy worker' rations – larger portions of potatoes, bread and vegetables, alongside his Red Cross parcels. The typical issue was one parcel per man per week through Alec's first year at Setzdorf, although there were periods when his ration was halved.

Alec's parcels were powerful negotiating assets. Through bartering with his *Rotenkreuz Pakete*, he could obtain eggs, vegetables and even meat from civilians. Rabbit was a particular treat, and he learned to cook rabbit stew with pre-soaked barley, a dish he would make for his family after the war. Meanwhile, some of his guards, rationed to five cigarettes a day and dependent on Latzel for food, would take parcel contents in return for more illicit items. 'It was a game of cat and mouse,' according to one of Alec's Setzdorf muckers, Leslie Birch.

Prisoners would spend Saturday afternoons cleaning their billet. When someone reported bedbugs, the bunks would be dismantled, scrubbed with antiseptic and reassembled. Alec initially slept on the top floor near the stairs, but the guards tired of shouting up to him with orders to interpret, so he moved to a top bunk on the ground floor. On Sundays, prisoners were left to their own devices – it was typically a day for postcard and letter writing – and occasionally on Sunday afternoons they would be led to a disused part of the quarry to play football.

Their trivial pay was distributed once a month. Alec, or Alex, as the Germans called him, would then tow a cart under escort into the village to exchange *Lagergeld* for goods. His haul seldom varied – ersatz honey, French mustard and blancmange powder, which, mixed with hot water, created a drink that made a change from coffee and tea. The march was an exercise in humiliation – POWs were banned from Germany's pavements so he had to walk in the road. The trips would, however, enable Alec to see newspapers such as the *Völkischer Beobachter*, the official Nazi daily, and bring copies back to translate to unlock their sometimes hidden meanings. 'Plenty about the Final Solution in there,' was his verdict years later. Once read, the *Völkischer Beobachter* served a piquant purpose as lavatory paper.

Humour was one way to lighten the load, and the POWs quickly awarded nicknames to their hosts. The brakeman became Slim Summerville, the movie comedian cast as a foil for Fatty Arbuckle. Unteroffizier Schittenhelm, who, Alec thought, 'could be an absolute pig and mostly was', became 'shit-head', an insult POWs muttered as he strutted about with one hand tucked into his tunic and a sardonic smile on his lips. The Schittenhelms were prominent Nazis, one family member, Rudolf, being *Kreisleiter* (district leader) for Aussig and regional representative in the Reichstag. Four days after the war ended, he murdered his wife and two children before shooting himself.

Schittenhelm's bow-legged second-in-command became 'the Sheriff' to some, because he wore his pistol and bayonet slung low on each hip. To others, he was 'Sneaky Rat Face', a reference to his facial contortions as he walked among POWs 'yelling and shouting' and full of 'viciousness' and 'crudity'. Joseph Gabriel, a kiln worker who wore thick spectacles, became 'Speckie'. 'Black-Arse', the kiln overseer, had black patches on his trousers; the yard-master became 'Judge Hardy', the Lionel Barrymore character in *A Family Affair*; the yard-master's assistant, with his nervous itch, was christened 'Scratch-Arse'.

Then there were the Hauke clan: Albine Hauke worked alongside 'Speckie' in the kiln. Dietrich, the kiln bricklayer, was a charming man and not afraid to show his anti-Nazi sentiments, while the mercurial pipe-smoker who stoked the fire from the kiln's roof was dubbed 'Doctor Syn', the eponymous anti-hero of a 1937 film.

Goon-baiting remained a source of satisfaction. One of the best practitioners was Jim Nixon, a Kensington Regiment lorry driver from London's

East End attached to the 51st Highland Division and taken at St Valéry. Nixon arrived with some other St Valéry captives at Setzdorf a month before Alec and was put to work grinding burnt limestone into powder. The details of the 51st Highlanders' defeat were new to Alec but the themes were familiar – French cowardice, British Territorial inexperience and poor coordination between infantry, sailors and airmen. Positioned initially on the Maginot Line, the troops avoided encirclement in the Dunkirk pocket and were pulled back to the Somme as the Germans advanced. There, they tried to evict the Germans from their Abbeville bridgehead, but the counter-attack failed and the division retreated again to St Valéry, from where General Victor Fortune planned an evacuation. Unfortunately, by the time boats were ready, Rommel's 7th Panzer tanks were shelling the harbour. Plans were made for a last stand but these were undone at 8.00am on 12 June when St Valéry's French garrison capitulated. With ammunition low, Fortune thought sur-render the only option, and the white flag was lifted shortly after 10.00am, marking the effective end of Allied resistance in France. Ian Campbell, later Duke of Argyll, was Fortune's intelligence officer. Of the capture of 10,000 men, he said: 'No division has ever been more uselessly sacrificed. It could have got away a good week before but the powers that be – owing I think to faulty information – had come to the conclusion that there was a capacity for resistance in France which was not actually there.'

In the Latzel works, Jim Nixon worked alongside Fred Collins, another Cockney. Each day, Jim and Fred would place 'dog ends' in a tin on a windowsill, aiming to collect sufficient leftovers to roll fresh cigarettes. Soon the butts began disappearing, and a surreptitious examination of 'Dr Syn's' pipe, a long-stemmed Turkish *chibouk*, revealed it contained Virginia tobacco. This was normally unavailable because of the Allied blockade, giving it a high black market value – something POWs would exploit when trading with the enemy. Revenge was sweet. Through illicit bartering, they acquired a speck of explosive from the quarry and inserted it into the *chibouk* during their lunch break. Soon after returning from lunch, 'Dr Syn' picked up his pipe, remarked on his '*prima tabak*' ('fine tobacco'), lit it and walked to the kiln. After a dozen paces, the *chibouk* exploded, taking with it an eyebrow, a lock of hair and half his moustache. The pair's 'dog ends' were safe from then on.

Frank Alcock, a lugubrious Australian farmer, was another goon-baiter. Nicknamed 'Speed' because he had only two work speeds, dead slow and stop, Alcock had been posted in 1941 to Greece, where the Australians came up against the Leibstandarte SS Adolf Hitler Brigade, perpetrators of the Worm-houdt POW massacre the previous year, the killing of many more unarmed POWs in Russia and the Malmédy massacre of Americans during Hitler's Ardennes offensive. Alcock, meanwhile, ended the war a free man sheltered by Czech partisans, having escaped in January 1945 by hacking through a barred window in his billet, dropping twelve feet onto the ground below and clambering over an eight-foot fence.

At Setzdorf, 'Speed' worked so slowly that Latzel dispatched him to the works kitchen, where occasionally he would adulterate the guards' lunches, as John 'Laurie' Lawrence, a Royal Sussex Regiment private captured at Haze-brouck, discovered one day after he had taken them some sauerkraut, bacon and dumplings. 'Did they eat it all?' Speed asked Laurie on his return. When he nodded, Speed grinned, an unusual event, and said, 'Well, you know, Laurie, I had a good piss in the sauerkraut.' Things only got better when a guard nicknamed 'Twinkle' told Speed he cooked sauerkraut better than a German *Hausfrau*.

The finest piece of goon-baiting was perpetrated by Les Birch and Hubert 'Bert' Lusted, both from Kent. Les's family farmed at Sellindge, a village near Ashford, Alec's location in the days before Calais. Bert was an electrician from near Canterbury. With his knowledge of farm machinery, Les became Setzdorf's 'spanner boy', maintaining equipment under civilian escort lest he contemplate sabotage. Lusted got involved in anything licit or illicit the POWs might attempt using electricity. Soon after their arrival, Les stole wire from Latzel's workshop and Bert insulated it with paper and leaves and attached it to the electric light, creating an element to heat tea and coffee.

When war broke out, Les joined the Kent Yeomanry. Captured in 1940, he joined the 51st Highlanders' Long March through France but refused to believe his war was over. After a few days he slipped away from the column and asked a milkmaid for help. The girl's family hid him in their pig pen, but a little later guards came looking for fugitive soldiers. Having narrowly avoided being shot, Les rejoined the column to continue the march. Eventually, the men reached the Rhine and were put on barges heading east but Les was so ill from dysentery he was taken to a hospital at Emmerich-am-Rhein.

Les received good treatment from an Oxford-educated doctor, who taught him basic German. When deemed fit, he was driven 25km to *Stalag* VIF at Bocholt. The camp had once housed Austrian Nazis fleeing after their abortive 1934 coup and then held workers press-ganged into Hitler's make-work schemes designed to massage Germany's unemployment statistics. It had become a transit camp in 1940, but Les was not placed with British POWs. Instead, he was held in a compound alongside political prisoners and Polish POWs. There he was befriended by a German Jew, who taught him how to recover his Geneva Convention protection. Thus, one morning at roll-call, Les stepped forward and addressed the commandant in German, saying he was a British POW, not a political prisoner. The colonel replied, 'Yes, you are a fine-looking Englishman, blond hair, blue eyes.' Les was then led away to be reunited with other British POWs.

The wheeze concocted by Les and Bert involved creating a Union Jack out of rags, then flying it from a kiln chimney. They could not simply march

ft) Rifleman Alec Jay, teenage 'Terrier' and anti-Fascist demonstrator; his mother, Annie, had
ercome his father's resistance to his volunteering and Annie kept this 1938 photograph close to
r through the five years of Alec's captivity.

ight) A moment of relaxation for Alec at the Queen Victoria's Rifles' 1938 summer camp at
mpne in Kent. During the fortnight, Alec fought mock battles, learned how to dig a trench and
s introduced to the Army's new light machine gun, the Bren gun.

'humps' Whitbread's Queen Vics B Company platoon on exercises at Lympne, 1938; Alec sits, far
ght, at the back of the platoon's 15cwt truck. The brewing family had close connections with the
een Vics and its sister regiment, the 60th Rifles, and Alec spent most of the 'Phoney War' billeted
the family's hop farm at Beltring in Kent. (*Whitbread Chattels Settlement*)

The Queen Vics B Company group photograph at end of the Lympne summer camp, 1938; Alec stands fifth from left, back row; Reg Dowell stands second from left on the same row. Dowell's dea at Calais, which was so violent his body parts were never discovered, haunted Alec for decades.

Recently-promoted Corporal Alec Jay supervises Bren gun cleaning for the men of Whitbread's B Company platoon at the Queen Vics' 19 summer camp at Burley in the New Forest. The following spring at Calais, Alec fought until he had fired his last Bren gun bullet.

The Queen Vics, recast as an experimental motorcycle reconnaissance battalion, on exercises in the summer of 1939 near Beaulieu in the New Forest with their new motorcycle 'chariots'. To their chagrin, the War Office ordered them to abandon their transport before sending them to France on 22 May 1940, meaning that they marched into battle and fought as infantry.

rence Cuneo's *The Defence of lais 1940*, a post-war painting mmissioned by Rifle Brigade icers for their regimental adquarters and based on rvivors' reminiscences of the st stand at Bastion 1 near the re Maritime. A 1941 painting Charles Gere that appeared a Royal Academy exhibition d been a fictionalized rtrayal of the last stand at the lais Citadel.

Luftwaffe bombers and dive bombers and the entire artillery of Guderian's XIX Panzer Corps reduced Calais to rubble and this destruction was later recorded by Luftwaffe aerial photographers.

eft-wing cartoonist Philip Zec, hose Russian Jewish father had ed to Britain after a Tsarist ogrom, was on Hitler's blacklist people to be arrested once he ad conquered Britain. This was ow Zec portrayed the sacrifice of e Calais garrison in the *Daily Mirror* after Churchill described e battle in his 'we shall fight on e beaches' speech in the termath of Dunkirk.

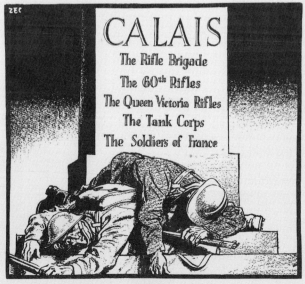

A Wehrmacht propaganda photographer records 30th Infantry Brigade POWs being marched through Calais' ruins, 26 May 1940.

Another Wehrmacht propaganda image showing the Calais captives at the start of their 500km 'Long March' into Germany, 26 May 1940.

On 21 June, Alec arrived at the entrance to the Stalag VIIIB/Stalag 344 prisoner of war camp at Lamsdorf in Silesia. One POW called it 'the Zoo in Silesia'; for another it was 'the home for sacrificed souls'.

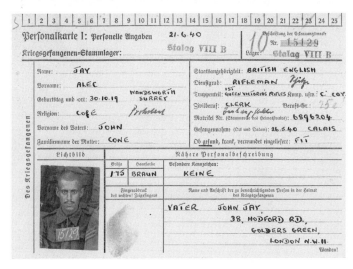

OW no. 15129 fills in his Stalag
rsonalkarte; Alec 'joins' the
*urch of England, downgrades
*mself from stockbroker to clerk
*d recasts his mother, born Annie
*hen, as Annie Cone. Alec had
*ready buried his identity disk
*d Army pay book in the sand at
*lais because both stated he was
*ew.

ft) Lamsdorf, originally built as an artillery firing range during the Franco-Prussian War, became
*OW camp during the Great War. This Wehrmacht plan of the site shows the camp's machine-gun
*atchtowers around its double perimeter fence, the POWs' billets, kitchen, the guards' barracks and
*e night patrol route.

ight) Most of Alec's Queen Vic superiors including C Company commander Major John 'Buster'
*ustin-Brown (left) and battalion commander Lieutenant Colonel John 'Plushy' Ellison-Macartney
*re initially imprisoned in Oflag VIIC in Laufen Castle in Bavaria.

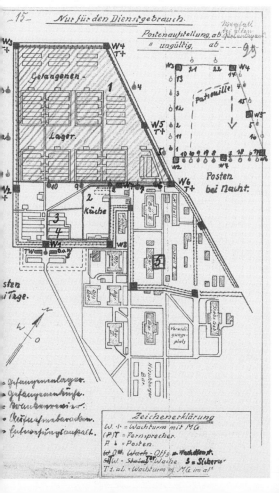

'Clink': Lamsdorf's *Strafe Kompanie*, where Alec attended the escapers' university, and the *Straflage* punishment cells, where he was held on various occasions in solitary confinement, subsisting on a diet of bread and water.

'Greetings from abroad': the official Lamsdorf Christmas card for 1941 given to prisoners of war to send home to their families.

CHRISTMAS Greetings

A little picture to express,
My wishes for your happiness;
A little message from my pen,
To haste the Day we'll meet again;
God grant you every Christmas cheer,
And Joy throughout the Coming
Year.

from Roderick.

STALAG VIII B , Germany . CHRISTMAS 1941

viet Russia did not sign the
neva Convention; the Nazi
sponse was to subject their
ssian 'Untermenschen' POWs
treatment even worse than
at meted out by the Japanese
their Allied prisoners. At
msdorf, they were given no
lets and were thus forced to
e in holes in the ground that
ey themselves had dug.

Some 42,000 corpses of Soviet
POWs were exhumed at
Lamsdorf after the Red Army
liberated the camp in early
1945. Most of the POWs had
been murdered or allowed to
die from starvation or disease;
one of Alec's tasks in the
summer of 1941 had been to
dig mass graves for the Soviet
dead.

teroffizier Joseph Kissel was
e brutal Lamsdorf guard who
rannized prisoners such as
ec who did spells in solitary
nfinement in Lamsdorf's
raflager. Later, 'Ukraine Joe',
the POWs nicknamed him,
ok charge of the RAF
mpound. One of the airmen
atched this photograph of
ssel using a camera hidden in
Red Cross parcel.

The Anton Latzel lime quarry and kilns at Setzdorf in the Sudetenland, where Alec was incarcerate from August 1941until February 1944. This naive painting hangs on the wall in the mayor's office i the town, renamed Vápenná (literally 'Lime') by the Czechs who repopulated the Sudetenland in the wake of the mass flight of Sudeten Germans after the war.

The prisoners of the E173 working party at Setzdorf, pictured in the spring 1942. In this first photograph Alec sent home to his parents, he stands in the middle of the back row behind George Baker, the camp's lead musician; Peter 'Darky' Fish stands on far right; David 'the Demon Barber' Massey sits on far left.

Queen Vics Regimental Sergeant Major George Chapman, a 60th Rifles regular lent to the battalion during the 'Phoney War', pictured at Lamsdorf. During the last stand at Calais, Chapman led a primitive but successful Queen Vics bayonet charge that was the defining moment of Alec's life.

Queen Vics sergeant Bill Brett at a pre-war training camp; Brett was one of Alec's 'muckers' on the Long March from Calais to the German border and was one of the two friends who prevented him from revealing himself as a Jew when he was registered at Lamsdorf as a POW.

Oberst Ludwig von Poschinger, a Bavarian aristocrat and scion of the crystal manufacturing family, had connections to the aristocratic anti-Nazis behind the July 1944 Bomb Plot attempt to kill Hitler. As Lamsdorf commandant, von Poschinger improved British POW conditions, but his liberalism did not extend to Palestinian Jewish POWs, who continued to face brutal treatment from his guards.

Australian sergeant Bill McGuinness was captured in May 1941 during the Battle of Crete. In 1943, he became the 'man of confidence' at E173 at Setzdorf, where he battled alongside Alec to improve POW conditions. In early 1944, the pair led the Setzdorf 'Great Potato Strike', which Alec later claimed, with some excusable exaggeration, as the only successful industrial action ever during Hitler's Third Reich.

The funeral of Nelson Ogg, the Scots POW the Germans allowed to die through neglect yet for whose funeral they provided an honour guard and six-gun salute; Alec stands on far right, his head wrapped in the 'turban' the camp commandant forced him to wear marking him out as *'Alex der Jude'*.

In the spring of 1943, the Setzdorf POWs were photographed formally for a second time; Alec stands in the middle row, third from right; Leslie Birch, one of his 'muckers', who thought Alec 'had no fear' because of his stance against ill-treatment, stands to his right, while a third member of their 'combine', Alex 'Ginger' Hepburn, sits in front of them; this photo, framed, hung on Leslie's study wall until the day he died.

Burgberg mit R.A.D. Lager bei Jägerndorf (Ostsudetenland)

...gerndorf in the Sudetenland, from where Alec escaped with RAF crewman Bob 'Twiggy' ...awthorn in the summer of 1944. The E606 working party billet in the Taschner Gasthof is on the ...r right in the valley; on the hill behind stands the Burgberg, a sixteenth century church visited by ...itler during his triumphant progress through the Sudetenland in October 1938.

... group of Jägerndorf POWs pose in the town's photographic studio for pictures to send home to ...eir families; Alec sits second from the right.

כתיבה וחתימה טובה

Tempelring

A Jewish New Year greetings card showing Jägerndorf's *Rundbogenstil* synagogue on Tempelring (Temple Ring); the townsfolk refused to destroy the synagogue during *Kristallnacht* but stripped out its religious symbols and renamed the street Tuchmacherring (Cloth Make: Ring) – Jägerndorf had variou textile plants including one expropriated from a Jewish family called Bellak.

A second group POW photograph taken in the town photographic studio. Alec stands on the far right, with Les Birch seated in front of him; Bernie Dynes, a New Zealander who had been a Setzdorf striker, stands on the far left. Dynes was later incarcerated within the Theresienstadt concentration camp's *Straflager* after a December 1944 escape attempt

ew members of 103 Squadron Halifax Q-Queenie; standing from left to right: rear gunner Norman
cMaster, who died when the plane crashed on 5 December 1942 in Belgium, Harry Richards, the
d-upper gunner who survived as a POW, pilot Ken Edwards and flight engineer George Green,
ho both also died, front-gunner/bomb aimer Bob 'Twiggy' Hawthorn, who survived to escape from
gerndorf with Alec, and navigator Gordon Mellor, who evaded capture and made a 'home run'.

wiggy' Hawthorn, in infantry khaki, sits second from the right for a group photograph to send
me to his mother. On the back he wrote a cryptic note: 'I'm in the army, now.' 'Laurie' Lawrence,
Setzdorf striker, stands third from the left; Bernie Dynes, another Setzdorf striker, stands far right.

(*Left*) Part Native American Alec Montroy was a Canadian commercial artist who was captured in the Dieppe Raid in 1942. He later became the Lamsdorf Escape Committee's chief document forger. Alec had good reason to thank Montroy for his artistry when his forged papers deceived a Gestapo agent in Vienna during his 1944 escape from Jägerndorf with 'Twiggy' Hawthorn.

(*Centre*) Peter Nagel, alias 'Peter Newman', alias 'Peter Walker', the German-Jewish Special Operations Executive commando who also escaped from the E606 POW working party at Jägerndorf but was recaptured the following day. Nagel was the only commando to take part in both the Bruneval Raid and the Saint-Nazaire Raid, where he was one of 215 troops taken prisoner.

(*Right*) Lance corporal Sidney 'Streaky' Reed of the Middlesex Regiment, one of the 'men of confidence' at E790, the punishment camp at Gurschdorf in the Sudetenland to which Alec was sent in September 1944 for telling the truth about the war to German civilians. Gurschdorf was a mini version of Colditz for other ranks.

William Philo, the merchant mariner stabbed by a Gurschdorf guard for refusing to work. Philo had been captured taking part in Operation Pedestal, the convoy sent to relieve Malta in August 1942. In late 1945, Alec returned to Germany to identify the guard so he could be tried as a war criminal.

The Lamsdorf records office roll call of Setzdorf potato strikers – some of the men who were escorted back to Lamsdorf at bayonet point by a platoon of Landesschützen-bataillon 438 guards; the list shows the POWs' numbers and numbers of the Stalags where they were first registered.

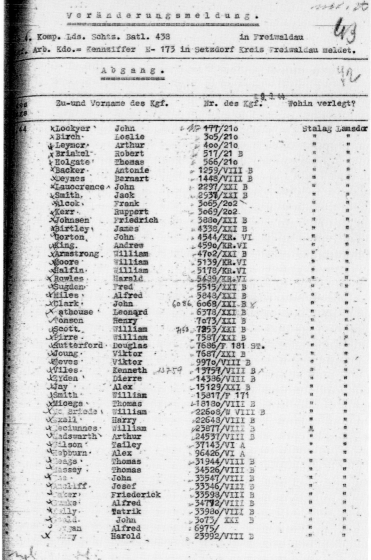

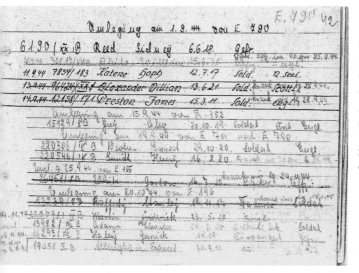

The Lamsdorf records office staff kept a list of POWs whose 'crimes' meant they were sent to the E790 *Strafe Kommando*; Alec's entry shows the date of his arrival, 15 September 1944, and the number of his previous camp, E352 at Freudenthal.

Celebrating the end of the war as an honorary Czech partisan, Alec, kneeling second from right in the front row, poses with his band of fellow British POW escapees for a victory photograph along with Red Army soldiers and Czech freedom fighters.

A final stroll along the banks of the Vltava River before returning home, 10 May 1945: Alec's band of POW escapers line up with Daria Halla, a Czech Red Cross nurse who offered to be their tourist guide around Prague after the Prague Uprising had triumphed. On the back of the photograph she wrote: 'Don't forget Czechoslovakia and its inhabitants, who never lost their hope even in the most critical period of war for the Allies.'

An old soldier returns: Alec on the beachfront at Calais, May 1990, taking part in the 50th anniversary commemoration of the Siege of Calais. Churchill had insisted Alec's regiment 'stand and fight it out to the end' though he knew it 'meant certain death or capture for almost the entire garrison'.

across the yard with their flag. Instead, they volunteered one foggy day to accompany the driver of the miniature train that pulled skips filled with stone, their task being to hook and unhook the skips. With that completed, the two men walked to the nearest chimney and, while Les stood guard, Bert scampered up the ladder and secured his flag on the top. When the fog cleared, the guards were appalled to see the enemy's flag flying over German territory. Unsurprisingly, the prisoners were locked into their barracks on their return from work and denied privileges.

Having a laugh at their guards' expense was a relatively risk-free way of easing the burden. Sabotage was more dangerous, but Les felt it was his duty: 'Wherever we could throw a spanner in the works we did. We had volunteered or been called up to serve King and Country and even though we were prisoners we saw ourselves as fighting for Britain. If we could delay a truck or meddle with some machinery we felt we had achieved something.'

Les's sabotage gang included Private George Bignall, Gunner Harry Excell, Private Percy Eyden and Private Bill Scott. Each had a tale of defeat and surrender.

George Bignall was a Bristol chocolate factory worker who enlisted in the Queen's Royal Regiment, a unit of the 12th (Eastern) Infantry Division charged with defending the Somme. This was a second-line Territorial formation, and some men had not even had rifle training. They proved no match for the 2nd Panzers as they raced towards the Channel in 1940, and Bignall was taken at Abbeville. Bill Scott, a Glasgow warehouseman conscripted into the Argyll & Sutherland Highlanders, was sent to defend another part of the Somme, but the Scots were stretched too thinly and were withdrawn after being mauled by Rommel's 7th Panzers. Bill was captured near Rouen on 9 June.

Percy Eyden was a Dunlop tyre factory worker who joined the Oxford & Buckinghamshire Light Infantry in 1938. In 1940, the Ox & Bucks joined the BEF's 48th Division to defend the Ypres-Commines Canal in Belgium. Outmanned and outgunned, they withdrew on 28 April after heavy casualties, but some troops, including Percy, were overrun. Harry Excell, meanwhile, was taken on Crete in 1941. From Chingford, Essex, he enlisted in 1937 when barely seventeen as an anti-aircraft gunner. Wounded during the German assault, he was captured on 27 April, the day the generals concluded the battle was lost and ordered troops to flee south to be evacuated. After a few weeks in hospital, he reached Lamsdorf in September by way of Dulag 183, Salonika's notorious transit camp.

Such men did not consider themselves out of the war. While breaking rocks in Latzel's quarry, they would 'lose' drills by burying them. In their most spectacular trick, they distracted 'Slim Summerville' so he lost control of his *Bremse*. Thus four skips careered down into the yard and crashed, sending a shower of rocks flying. 'Judge Hardy' dashed from his office screaming 'sabotage', joined by 'Scratch-Arse' and Emil, the engine driver.

Jim Nixon sabotaged equipment in the yard and kilns alongside Durham Light Infantry private Bill Morrell, a coalminer who became a Terrier in April 1939 and an early victim of Hitler's 1940 *Blitzkrieg*. Sent to France without artillery or signals, his battalion was overrun at Arras and Bill was picked up on 20 May at Élincourt, south-east of Cambrai. Wrecking ball-bearings was their particular speciality.

Although sabotage would unite POWs in common purpose against their enemy, it could only partially ameliorate the effects of being held in confinement. The lack of privacy could make even the most mild-mannered, tolerant man irritable, and arguments would erupt over trivia. Nights were worst. Each bunk-bed occupant had the bodies of other men beside him within inches, and another man a yard away above him or below. In such circumstances, men imposed their sounds and smells on each other. Anyone who snored slept within hearing distance of forty colleagues, while a man rising at night to urinate would wake others as he clambered from his bunk. Robert Kee later described how oppressed he felt by not even being able to turn his head without seeing evidence of fellow POWs, 'their clothes or their looks or their photographs'. It was not their fault, but they became hateful. Superficially, Kee was on good terms with his colleagues, yet he ceased seeing them as individuals: 'They were a crowd whose heads you could not see over but not company.' Thus he called his 1947 book *A Crowd is not Company*. It remains the most psychologically insightful POW memoir.

Alec recalled the situation years later when hospitalized after breaking a leg playing rugby against the Metropolitan Police. The NHS 'had thrown all types and all ages together to make the best or worst of their enforced communal life' – his ward included a stockbroker, a docker, a musician, a publican, a bank clerk and an errand boy. The set-up reminded him of Setzdorf, 'all sorts and types trying to help one another but equally ready to utter bitter recriminations if anything went wrong, with that peculiar intolerance that is the legacy of both physical and mental sickness'.

Kee thought POW life 'not quite a state of nature'; but when rations ran low the barrier separating men from barbarism was 'unpleasantly thin'. 'The smooth-faced BBC announcer, the amusing don, the self-confident politician, the jargon-perfect critic, the editor of the literary magazine – all are reducible within a few months to a bewildered defensive creature with hollow cheeks and desperate eyes whose only cares will be to see that he gets his fair share of the potato ration, that nobody steals his bed boards and that he exchanges his cigarette ends for food or vice versa at the best possible price.'

Alec would retreat into verse composition, taking pleasure in the landscape. He explored the contrast between the countryside and breaking stone in a quarry in his first Sudeten poem, Setzdorf:

In all their gloomy grandeur
The pine-clad mountains stand,
And there, beneath their slopes so steep,
The quiet age-old townlets sleep.
Time moves so slow it seems to creep
Like some forgotten fairyland.

Alas, a fable. All is changed.
Only the mountains as before.
Now one beholds a scene so sorry
With all the hustle, bustle, worry,
Pertaining to a limestone quarry
It makes my heart feel sore.

Chapter 15

A Letter from Abroad

For fifteen months Alec hid his survival from his family and Netta. Sunday after Sunday, he watched as prisoners penned postcards and aerogrammes to be sent via Geneva to Britain. The ration was four postcards and two letters per month. Each Sunday, he would also witness their joy as letters arrived from home. After early delays, the flow became regular, with letters typically taking six weeks. Communications from Setzdorf were reviewed by Lamsdorf's censors, whose black lines would obscure complaints and military gossip, leaving POWs with little to say beyond the barest accounts of their lives and feelings. British censors also wielded heavy pencils over letters sent from home. Yet these exchanges did provide contact with loved ones.

Every three months, Alec would also see his muckers smile as they opened their 10lb next-of-kin parcels containing sweaters, pyjamas, underwear and shoes, hairbrushes, razors, soap and up to half a pound of chocolate. Alec had to make do with Red Cross clothing. But had his thinking about the need to protect his family been overtaken by events? And should he now take the chance that correspondence might reveal his ethnicity, a real risk as Julius Green discovered later in Colditz?

The Palestinians' arrival in Lamsdorf showed Alec that if Britain continued to fight – more likely now that Russia had become an ally – Jews in British uniforms would be held broadly according to Geneva Convention rules. They might face discriminatory segregation; they might be sent to the worst *Arbeitskommandos*; but they would not be sent to concentration camps. Alec might be exposed as a Jew, but his survival chances were greater than he previously feared.

It was, therefore, time to write home. Another spur was the arrival in Germany of a British list containing the names of 7,000 men reported 'missing' but not confirmed dead. The German High Command distributed it to *Stalag* commandants in July, and over the next few weeks POWs attempted to enumerate the survivors. Alec had been on the list of Lamsdorf POWs supplied to the Red Cross in 1940 and was also on the new list. It was, therefore, only a matter of time before his parents discovered he was alive, so, he concluded, it was better for him to inform them himself. In deciding to write, he made one assumption – that they had survived the Blitz. He could not be sure – German broadcasts suggested the Luftwaffe had reduced London to cinders. Yet if they were dead his attempt to make contact would cause no harm – it might merely confirm the state of affairs at Hodford Road, however grim.

Their last contact had been on 21 April 1940, when Alec rang from Kent to say he could not come to Gone with the Wind. He could not, however, say why. Only later did the regimental grapevine reveal he had fought at Calais. In the days that followed his departure, the Jays scanned the newspapers for information. Confusion reigned in Whitehall as the Wehrmacht scythed through France, and newspaper reports were often misleading.

On 24 May, the *Daily Mail* published a 'news-map of the fighting fronts' showing the Germans still fifteen miles from Calais. On 27 May, after the surrender, the *Daily Mirror* still reported, 'The battle for Calais is still south of the town. British soldiers fought magnificently with the French to repulse every enemy attack yesterday.' On 28 May, the *Mail* began to wobble, reporting a French spokesman as 'not now in a position to confirm or deny [Berlin's statement that Calais had fallen]'. Yet the following day, the *Mail*'s map showed Calais still in Allied hands, while *The Times*' 30 May headline was 'Calais holding out'.

The *Daily Herald*'s 31 May edition implied the garrison was in trouble, reporting a War Office communiqué that 'a small British force' had been besieged in Calais by 'strong enemy mechanized forces' but quoting the communiqué's conclusion that its refusal to surrender 'will count among the most heroic deeds in the annals of the British Army'. Yet hopes persisted that resistance was being maintained. On 1 June, *The Times* reported a Whitehall statement about RAF squadrons dropping supplies for the garrison – and some Lysanders did fly over on 27 May to re-supply the Citadel. The previous evening at 7.56pm a message was sent from Dover: 'To OC Troops Calais from Secretary of State. Am filled with admiration for your magnificent fight, which is worthy of the highest tradition of the British Army.' It was never received, and the only recipients of the Lysanders' supplies were Calais' newly-installed garrison of Panzer Grenadiers.

Even on 2 June, the French insisted the Allies still held the Citadel. That evening, however, Eden confirmed resistance was over: 'We now know from certain information which we have received that this gallant defence drew off powerful German mechanized forces which must otherwise have been free to attack the flank of the British Expeditionary Force at that time dangerously exposed.' Thus, only on Monday, 3 June, eight days after the surrender, did the newspapers concede Calais had fallen. The *Daily Herald*'s headline was, 'Enemy Pays Tribute to Calais Defenders', beneath which it reported that one Berlin newspaper had referred to the 'proven tenacity of the Anglo-Saxon race' and described the fighting as 'the stiffest resistance of the war'. *The Times* quoted the *Hamburger Fremdenblatt* as saying the British had fought with courage and desperation: 'House by house had to be conquered. The Englishmen had made every house a fortress.'

The following day, with the last British troops lifted from Dunkirk the previous morning, Churchill addressed MPs in a speech best known for 'we shall fight on the beaches'. But before he reached his peroration, with Nicholson's brother, Godfrey, seated behind him, he described the Calais garrison's contribution:

> The Rifle Brigade, the 60th Rifles and the Queen Victoria's Rifles with a battalion of British tanks and 1,000 Frenchmen, in all about four thousand strong, defended Calais to the last ... Their sacrifice, however, was not in vain. At least two armoured divisions, which otherwise would have been turned against the British Expeditionary Force, had to be sent for to overcome them. They have added another page to the glories of the Light Division.

Over subsequent days, the Jays learned more. Shortly after Churchill's speech, a War Office letter arrived informing Annie Jay her son had been posted 'missing' on 22 May 1940. The letter continued:

> The report that he is missing does not necessarily mean that he has been killed, as he may be a prisoner of war or temporarily separated from his regiment. Official reports that men are prisoners of war take some time to reach this country and if he has been captured by the enemy it is probable that unofficial news will reach you first. In that case I am to ask you to forward any postcard or letter received at once to this office and it will be returned to you as soon as possible. Should any further official information be received it will at once be communicated to you.

The Calais garrison's families faced particular problems in trying to discover what had happened. Units rescued at Dunkirk could bring back first-hand information, but only a few dozen Greenjackets were taken off at Calais, so their families had little news. C Company's Larry Lucas revealed what he knew about those killed and those with him on the March before his escape. In the second week of June, *The Times* described how he reached the coast west of Calais, and rowed, despite his wounded arm, across the Channel in a dinghy. Yet he had only limited information. In a letter to one family he wrote, 'There must be of course a period of extreme anxiety until definite news arrives of who was taken prisoner and during that period you have, needless to say, my deepest sympathy.'

The Jays scoured the newspapers for information. Towards the end of June, the papers published War Office-sanctioned narratives. The *Daily Sketch* wrote: 'Heroism never surpassed in the annals of the British Army is revealed in the official story of the defence of Calais.' A 'handful' of men held up two German divisions for four days 'not knowing that they were saving the

BEF' at Dunkirk. Churchill's claim that without Calais the BEF could not have been rescued was taken up by the *Star*:

> Late on Sunday night this battle was finished. Overwhelmed by vastly superior numbers and weight of armament, this gallant force of three Battalions had held out for four days, engaging the two heavy armoured divisions which had been destined to cut off the British Expeditionary Force and thus permitting it to embark ... They were ordered to hold Calais and they did their best, not realising that they were thereby saving the BEF but just all in the day's work.

The *Daily Mirror* cartoonist, Philip Zec, captured the mood. One of eleven children of a Russian Jew who fled a pogrom, he drew with a venom that earned him a place on Hitler's blacklist of people to be arrested once Britain was conquered. Zec drew an English corpse and a French corpse slumped over the steps of a Stone of Remembrance memorial with the word CALAIS chiselled at the top, the names of the four British battalions and 'The Soldiers of France' below, and the caption: 'Their Name Liveth for Evermore!'

A few days after the Zec cartoon, a letter dated 10 July arrived at Hodford Road from Lieutenant Colonel Sir John Maclure, the Rifle Depot commanding officer at Winchester, home of the 60th Rifles. The KRRC's colonel-commandant, wrote Maclure, wished to 'express his sympathy with you and yours during this anxious period of waiting for news of those who were reported "missing" at Calais'. The Winchester records officer, he continued, would notify next-of-kin when information was received and asked the Jays to reciprocate if they heard anything. Finally, he said the Red Cross would transmit parcels from the Jays to Alec once his location was known.

If the Wehrmacht had been overwhelmed by captured soldiers so too had the Red Cross, and it was weeks before a list of more than 40,000 men was sent to London to be cross-referenced against War Office and regimental records. This meant that families of Queen Vics known to be alive had to wait until autumn to receive follow-up letters from Winchester. Each was told a report had 'been received from the War Office to the effect that' their loved one was at a particular camp, and further information received would be passed on.

Around the same time, families began organizing weekly meetings to provide support and exchange information. Edith Haywood, wife of HQ Company Sergeant Archie Haywood, was a leading light in this. Sergeant Edwin Buxton of the Queen Vics veterans association was impressed with her efforts. 'The cheerful encouragement that you gave to them in spite of your own great anxiety is worthy of the best traditions of the QVR,' he wrote. Yet for Annie Jay such meetings yielded nothing about Alec.

'Jumbo' Sampson became a one-man information clearing house, operating from the United University Club off Trafalgar Square and recruiting

George Chapman's wife, Ivy, as helper. For weeks, she camped out in Edith Haywood's home, visiting the Red Cross every day for news. From the scraps she gleaned, she assembled lists of survivors yet to contact their families, and 'Jumbo' passed these to the War Office. The response he received contained good news for most families. 'You will be pleased', wrote an official, 'to see that the majority of the soldiers are prisoners of war; a few are, however, reported as missing, and enquiries are proceeding in respect of a further six.' Thus, most families learned of their loved ones' fates in the autumn, but some remained in limbo. Alec's platoon commander, Bobby Allen, who was wounded in both legs, was still listed as 'missing' in November 1940 as were a few other ranks, including Alec.

In September 1940, the War Office received the first list of confirmed dead. Alec's name was not on it. That meant he was not definitively dead, yet it was not necessarily grounds for hope. The horrific realities of modern war were such that some bodies at Calais were unidentifiable. Thus, some Queen Vics, such as Alec's friend, Reg Dowell, were never given burials, being listed instead on general memorials.

If Alec was dead, John and Annie consoled themselves he had died a hero. After Churchill's description of the Queen Vics' sacrifice and the newspaper articles that followed, the heroism of Calais became a key theme in British propaganda. The day after Churchill spoke, Ironside noted in his diary:

A great effort which I hope we shall never forget. It would have been impossible to have used Dunkirk as a point from which to evacuate the BEF and the 1st French Army without this stand. The most famous regiments in the Army. They fought it out to the end. When I sent them to Calais I was sure they would do their duty and they did. A fitting finish to their history. *Requiescent.* The historic name of Calais should be written once more on British hearts.

The same day, Alexander Hardinge, George VI's private secretary, wrote to Major General Davidson:

The King, as Colonel-in-Chief of The King's Royal Rifle Corps, has learned with pride of the heroic action of the 2nd Battalion and the Queen Victoria's Rifles at Calais, which assisted so materially in the successful evacuation of the British Expeditionary Force. Such self-sacrifice and gallantry are in keeping with the highest traditions of His Majesty's Regiment and mark a glorious page in its history.

After the fall of France, the Army suffered one defeat after another in Greece and North Africa, so the achievements of the 4,000 men at Calais in supposedly holding up two German divisions seemed a beacon of light amid the gloom, a memory to be burnished. There was some myth-making in this. The Calais garrison did hold up the 10th Panzers, but the 1st Panzers bypassed it after a few skirmishes, and eight other Panzer divisions were in the region to encircle the BEF. Dunkirk was as much the result of Hitler's failure to exploit opportunities as it was the product of British heroism. Yet that did not stop the hyperbole, as Roger Nixon and Giles Mills recognized in their *Annals of the King's Royal Rifle Corps* (1971): '[To] create heroic legends, successful and heroic objectives are necessary, and what better one can there be than to sacrifice oneself so that others can escape ... They may not have saved the BEF, but their example certainly did much to save the spirit of England from the despair of defeat.'

A year after the surrender, Calais was still a resonant theme in wartime propaganda as the Jays discovered in the *Illustrated London News'* 3 May 1941 edition, featuring works in that year's Royal Academy exhibition. A Charles Gere painting entitled *The Last Stand at Calais Citadel, May 1940* was on page five. The caption read: 'In a sinister pattern of smoke and flame and flying debris the painter shows a scene in Calais during the last dramatic hours.'

The painting, dedicated to 'the immortal memory of those who stood at Calais and by their sacrifice saved the BEF at Dunkirk', came from Gere's imagination. Resembling a depiction of a medieval siege, it showed Nicholson with his battalion commanders peering through the smoke of battle from the Citadel as the town burned beyond. No such meeting took place, but it did capture the public's imagination and was reproduced many times. For John and Annie, it was a further sign that their son, if dead, had not died in vain. Yet they did not give up hope entirely, and Alec's name remained off Red Cross lists of confirmed dead.

Some months after Calais, a Red Cross friend told Annie Jay that Alec's name was on a POW list. Could he be alive? Decades later, his sister, Phoebe, described the limbo in which the family found itself, hoping against hope yet fearing the news when it did come would be bad: 'For months one just hoped, although it sounded from the Queen Victoria's Rifles reports that Alec was not anything else but dead.' Then, one day in September 1941, a flimsy aerogramme arrived at her parents' home. Phoebe was away and took a phone call from her mother. 'We've just had a letter from Alec,' said Annie. Initially, Phoebe did not understand – her first thought was she did not have any friends called Alec. So who was this Alec person? 'A letter from whom?' she asked. 'From Alec, your brother,' was the reply. At that point Phoebe 'went a bit woozy – it was something of a shock'.

For almost sixteen months, Annie Jay had sat by her drawing room window knitting and crocheting with a photograph of her son in uniform on a bureau nearby, hoping he might be alive but fearing he was dead. Each day, she would recall her support for him when he volunteered, and how she had overcome his father's resistance. Now, for the first time in many months, she could smile and look forward to his return.

After the call to Phoebe, Annie contacted Lieutenant Colonel Maclure to say her son had materialized at a Sudeten *Arbeitskommando*. This was noted on his Army record card, with the stamp 'MISSING' superseded by 'PRISONER OF WAR' on 22 September 1941. She then told A.R. Barton that the stockbroker written off as dead might want his job back and began organizing things to make his incarceration less uncomfortable.

Maclure told her one 11lb 'next-of-kin' parcel could be sent every quarter, although chocolate was the only food permitted. Annie could send her parcel to the Red Cross office in the City or via Winchester's Prisoners of War Parcel Depot. Staffed by volunteers, principally regimental wives living nearby, and funded through charitable appeals and events starting on the first anniversary of the 'never-say-die' Calais siege, the depot was the first of its kind, something appreciated by Calais POWs. 'It was the KRRs and the RBs who were the first in sending parcels and keeping them regular,' wrote one from his *Arbeitskommando*. 'The new clothes, the soap and the toilet gear,' wrote another, 'kept us from being dragged down to the levels of dogs and we were able to walk about as British soldiers, to face the cold of each winter with warm bodies and hearts, knowing we were not forgotten.'

By the war's middle years, 350 Red Cross volunteers were working in St James' Palace. The Picture Gallery housed POW index cards, the Banqueting Room was used for individual files and the Throne Room was open to relatives for meetings. Personal parcels needed special tie-on labels, which would be sent periodically to next-of-kin, otherwise the Post Office would not accept them, while the POWs' names and addresses had to be copied in ink on parcel covers.

Red Cross staff would check, repack and label each box to ensure the contents were acceptable to the Germans, who feared such parcels would contain escape materials. Thus, POWs were given lists of banned items to post home. Pyjamas had to be striped, while civilian suits, trousers, sports jackets and blazers, overcoats and rubber-soled shoes were banned. Tubes or tins that could not be opened for inspection were *verboten*, as were fuel for cooking stoves and matches, as well as binoculars, sextants, compasses, torches and large scissors. Newspapers, medicines and blank paper were off limits, as were playing cards, which might contain coded messages. Conversely, blankets, hairbrushes, underwear, shirts, jumpers and towels were permitted, along with kitbags, knitting needles and wool, pencils, safety razors and blades, tin openers, shoe polish, small musical instruments and soap. This list amused the Queen Vics; one had 'a glorious vision' of his parents receiving it 'while innocently making up a mixed parcel containing a couple of Mills bombs, a revolver and ammunition, a compass, saws and a telephone'.

Maclure's volunteers handled 1,196 parcels during 1941's final quarter, plus quarterly gifts of 250 cigarettes per prisoner, and the following year they processed 3,600 parcels. They also kept records for each man. Thus, Alec's details were recorded on a personal index card that included his name, his Army, POW and Red Cross registration numbers, his *Stalag* address, the number and dispatch date of his personal parcels, his family's address and the date and dispatch of the latest personal parcel. There was also a folder that included records of the contents of Alec's personal parcels plus family correspondence.

Now Alec had made contact, he could also receive his 'First Capture Parcel' from the British Prisoners of War Books and Games Fund, a charity run by Christine Knowles. Her father was Charles Knowles, a Russian Jew born Charles Kino. This was the trading name of his City clothing business, which made enough money for him to become a serious art collector – his pictures form the bulk of the present-day Whistler collection in Cambridge's Fitzwilliam Museum. While her brother Guy, designer of the de Havilland Iris aero-engine, joined the artillery, Christine dedicated her life to caring for POWs. In the 1914–18 conflict, she had donated food and clothes. From early in the Second World War, she sent out First Capture Parcels to each POW 'be he peer or peasant' as soon as his name and *Stalag* address were received. Each contained a bible, a novel, a chess set and approved playing cards.

In January 1941, Knowles asked Sergeant Buxton to supply a Queen Vics POW list. Her team then wrote to the men and their families to discover their tastes in books and their interests and hobbies, so she could send individually-tailored parcels 'they can really enjoy'. For Alec, her parcels helped preserve his sanity. When food was scarce, living conditions overcrowded and cold, when front-line news was poor, Alec always had access to books. One of her gifts was *The Faber Book of Comic Verse*, which Alec received, stamped with a Lamsdorf *geprüft* (checked) stamp, on 12 December 1943. He kept it as he travelled from *Arbeitskommando* to *Arbeitskommando* by way of Lamsdorf's punishment cells, and it was in his haversack along with *The Complete Works of Shakespeare* when he returned to Britain in 1945. Both remained on a bookshelf within reach of his armchair till the day he died.

As autumn turned into winter, Alec waited for a response to his letter home. With most Sudetens keen to pass on 'news' about London's destruction, he did not even know whether his family were alive. For weeks, he waited. Had 38 Hodford Road been hit by a bomb, he asked himself. In reality, his home was still standing but a neighbour's house fifty yards away on the corner of Dunstan Road had been destroyed. And what of Netta?

Chapter 16

'Dear Alec ...'

By early 1941, most prisoners had received letters offering reassurance that life at home continued as normal. They were, thought Richard Pape, 'our greatest joy, the token of reality in an insane and unreal world'. Whenever mail arrived at Setzdorf, 'Dilly' Saunders would shout, 'Mail up! Mail up!' and the men would gather round in anticipatory silence as he distributed missives from relatives and friends. Here were messages from an outside world that, wrote Robert Kee, 'seemed as unattainable as another planet'. Each letter would be read and reread, each word studied for possible hidden meaning.

For the Queen Vics, 'Jumbo' Sampson wrote scores of letters each month from his club in handwriting so small it generated complaints from British censors. One wrote in the margin, 'He may be a member of the University Club but still he has to write clearly – otherwise: waste-basket!' 'Jumbo' acted as a news conduit because prisoners could not write to friends in other camps. Through 'Jumbo', POWs discovered 'Larry' Lucas and Lance Corporal Richard Illingworth had made home runs. Sometimes 'Jumbo's' letters would be censored, but titbits did get through in both directions, helped by POWs addressing him as 'Uncle Sam', implying he was a relation. Men would sign off their letters 'with love from' and describe Queen Vic POWs collectively as 'your Beltring family'.

In an early letter to 'Jumbo', Rifleman Matthew Stafford described Calais and its aftermath: 'We had a rather warm welcome to finish a pleasant boat trip; a remarkable firework display; followed by what would have been a grand hiking tour (under different conditions).' Other messages were plainer. In September 1942, Alec asked Gerry Hathaway of HQ Company, at that point also in Setzdorf, to tell 'Jumbo' he wished to be remembered to him. 'Jumbo' was also tasked with lobbying when parcels were late, following up complaints about pay and contacting relatives whose letters had dried up. Some riflemen even asked him to organize illicit promotions so they might return from *Arbeitskommandos* to Lamsdorf.

Not all correspondence boosted morale. The missive most POWs dreaded was a 'Dear John' or 'Mespot' letter from a wife or girlfriend saying she had found someone new. 'Mespot' derived from the 'it's over' letters airmen received while stationed in Mesopotamia in the 1920s. 'Dear John' had more obscure origins. A love letter might typically begin 'My dearest John' or 'My darling John'. A POW receiving a letter beginning simply 'Dear John' would know it contained bad news.

A 'Dear John' letter might finally cause a man to crack. Some turned '*Stalag*-happy', a condition in which POWs turned in on themselves, abandoning all self-respect. A few '*Stalag*-happy' POWs became 'wire-happy', climbing over the trip wire and inviting sentries to shoot. Others simply committed suicide, such as James Brisk, an anti-tank gunner found hanged at a Sudeten *Arbeitskommando* in 1942.

As growing numbers of Lamsdorf POWs received 'Dear John' letters, a camaraderie of suffering developed. One barrack contained a 'rogues gallery' of unfaithful women, and whenever a new 'Heartbreak Club' member pinned a photo on the wall, he would be invited by the man 'on duty' for a consoling mug of tea. Over the course of the war, papers covering hundreds of divorces travelled between Lamsdorf and Britain via Geneva. Meanwhile, the more callous letters achieved legendary status. One wife said she had had two babies by an Italian POW but would make amends by buying her husband a motorbike on his return. Another explained the recent arrival of a child by saying a stranger had presented her with an abandoned baby during a blackout.

Alec received his 'Mespot' one evening. The envelope's handwriting showed Netta was alive; its contents showed their relationship was dead. Netta had had a tumultuous sixteen months following Alec's departure to Calais. In April 1941, her father, Manny, died. In June, she became engaged to Harold Glassner, the son of a Romanian Jewish immigrant, and in August they married.

The letter was the worst blow of Alec's five-year incarceration and he poured his misery into poetry, making November 1941 the most prolific month of his captivity. The first poem, Sharper than the Axe, echoed the bitterness of King Lear confronted by filial disloyalty ('sharper than a serpent's tooth it is to have a thankless child'):

As the axe bites into the hard white wood,
And scatters the chips apart;
So your letter bit into the depths of my soul,
And ripped into pieces my heart.

As a hawk descends like a bolt from the blue,
Onto the peaceful dove;
So that letter came like a lightning flash,
And struck at my heart and my love.

The breast of the dove is bloody and torn,
The cut in the wood is deep;
And a heart that is wounded as sorely as mine,
Will never know peaceful sleep.

Alec told his muckers what had happened – 51st Highlanders such as Les, Bill Birrell of the Black Watch and Seaforth Highlander Alex 'Ginger' Hepburn. As part of some private joke, Alec called Hepburn 'Duggie'. They came from opposite ends of Britain – Duggie was a Dundee engineer. They were, however, born just two days apart in October 1919, they became Territorials within a month of each other in 1938 and they remained friends long after their confinement ended. Bill Birrell enlisted in 1932 aged twenty, having worked in a Scunthorpe blast furnace. Whatever his muckers might say in consolation, Alec's despair did not dissipate. He called his second poem of November 1941 'Danse Macabre':

As the last red-brown leaves,
Blown by the wild east wind,
Dance, danse macabre
On the hard ground:
As the sharp evening frost
Freezes the ebbing sap,
Ices the puddles and stays their slight motion;
So my heart shivers,
Bared to the stormy blast,
Congealed with sorrow,
Its high hopes torn from it.
Once more in Springtime
Will the sap rise again,
Will the green leaves again
Sprout from the trees.
Puddles will smile again,
Birds once more sing,
But, in the heart
Slain in the autumn,
Rises not hope again,
Burst forth no song.

The autumn leaves were harbingers of his second Eastern European winter, but Danse Macabre (*Totentanz* in German) had a deeper meaning. Alec had absorbed it in musical form through works by Gustav Mahler and Arnold Schoenberg, Jewish composers whose music was banned by Hitler. Mahler built his *Totentanz* into his fourth symphony, featuring a solo violin tuned a tone higher than usual to depict the fiddle-playing skeleton, *Freund Hein*, and lending a ghostly tension to the music. Schoenberg wrote *Totentanz der Prinzipien* (Dance of Death of Principles). Mahler died in 1911 but Schoenberg lived to see Hitler take power and went into exile in America. He was, therefore, an ocean away when the Nazis began purging German culture of 'degenerate music'.

If fallen leaves symbolized the onset of winter, springtime might bring renewal but, with Netta gone, the changing seasons offered Alec little solace. This was the theme of Contrast, his third poem of November 1941:

When the ground has drunk its fill of rain,
Or the heart is over flown with pain,
The wind and the sun will dry ground once more,
But nothing can serve as balm to the heart's core.

Such emotions needed channelling – and Alec found catharsis in translating German poetry, playing intellectual games with Lamsdorf's censors to see whether they might put their *geprüft* stamp on leaves of paper with subtly-subversive intent. His first effort was Goethe's *Wandrers Nachtlied II* (Wanderer's Night Song II), the best-known English translation of which is by Longfellow, one of Alec's favourite poets. For his own free translation, again alluding to Netta, Alec chose the simple title *Evening:*

The peaks of the mountains are silent as death,
And, in the treetops, hardly a breath.
The little birds hush in the wood's deepest dell:
Soon, my beloved one, you'll rest as well.

Why did Alec like this poem? He had been forced to 'wander' at bayonet point from Calais to Aachen in 1940. Now, incarcerated in Setzdorf, 'wandering' was his ambition, yet the Sudeten winter made this perilous to attempt. Goethe lived in an enlightened time before anti-Semitism perverted the course of German history and had friends in the Frankfurt ghetto. In 1930 Sigmund Freud was awarded the fourth annual Goethe Prize, yet Nazis claimed Goethe as a proto-fascist, hence the commentary in the following day's *Völkischer Beobachter*: 'It is well known that renowned scholars have rejected the psychoanalysis of the Jew Sigmund Freud as highly unscientific drivel and nonsense. The anti-Semite Goethe would turn over in his grave if he knew that a Jew had received a prize that carries his name.' Alec knew otherwise.

Alec's second translation was Heinrich Heine's *Die Lorelei*. Once again, Alec chose a free translation, tying the subject matter to his betrayal by Netta:

I really don't know the reason,
Why it will not go out of my head;
This fairy-tale from age-old times,
Which makes my heart heavy as lead.

In the cool of the darkening evening,
When softly flows the Rhine,
The tips of the mountains glitter
In the sun's last lingering shine.

A beautiful girl is sitting
On the peak of the rock up there,
And her golden trinkets sparkle,
As she combs her flaxen hair.

She combs it with a golden comb,
And all the time sings a song.
The music she sings is enchanted,
Bewitching and magically strong.

The fisherman in his little boat
Is filled with the strangest woe.
He can only look at the girl on high,
He sees not the rocks below

At the merciless hands of the waves and rocks
The fisherman meets his doom,
Bewitched by the power of Lorelei's song;
This is the cause of my gloom.

Set to music, *Die Lorelei* was a popular song, presenting the Nazis with a problem because Heine was a Jew. They felt they could not ban it, so they rationalized its use by saying Heine had merely reworked an old folk song. Born in 1797, Heine had become a Lutheran, hoping it would be his 'ticket of admission' into European culture. As he matured, however, he became increasingly fearful of German nationalism, drifting towards socialism and contributing to Karl Marx's newspapers. Peace, he knew, had to be built on tolerance and free speech, and he was appalled when students celebrating the sixth anniversary of Prussia's defeat of Napoleon at the Battle of Leipzig built a bonfire of 'unpatriotic' books – a chilling precursor of the Nazis' book-burning rituals. Two years later, he published *Almansor*, a play in which the hero decries the burning of the Koran following the Christian Reconquista in Spain. His servant, Hassan, responds: 'That was only a prelude; where they burn books, they burn people in the end.' Here was the Holocaust foretold in a sentence.

And so it came to pass: two months after Alec translated *Die Lorelei*, Reinhard Heydrich, Deputy Reich Protector of Bohemia and Moravia, organized the Wannsee Conference to plan 'the Final Solution to the Jewish Question'. Jews would be deported to Eastern Europe to slave away on construction projects; those who did not die during construction would be killed at the end.

Alec, meanwhile, concentrated on his own survival. He had played mind games with Lamsdorf's censors in translating Goethe and Heine, yet his last poem of 1941, Winter, had a Christian message. Here was confirmation for the censors that the author was 'CofE', as stated on his *Personalkarte*. Reading like a carol, Winter echoes Christina Rossetti's In the Bleak Midwinter, which Alec had sung during school carol services.

> The thin white hand of winter,
> Has firmly taken hold
> Of the last lingering leaves on the windswept trees
> And the air bites chill and cold.
>
> The first soft flakes are falling
> Without the slightest sound,
> As winter lays her icy touch
> On the hard barren ground.
>
> And sometimes howls the north east wind,
> Swaying the bare black trees;
> Way up high on the mountain peak,
> And the very sap seems to freeze.
>
> Nearly two thousand years ago,
> When the stars were shining bright,
> A miracle happened in Bethlehem
> On a hard cold winter's night.

Why did Alec's verse shift from gloom to shining stars and miracles? Netta was gone, but his family knew he had survived and he knew they had. As 1941 ended without Germany winning in Russia, he became increasingly convinced victory would come. His motto was '*Illegitimi non carborundum*', a mock-Latin phrase meaning 'Don't let the bastards grind you down'. The metronomic beat of the guards' discourse was '*London kaputt, Coventry kaputt*', while German figures for lost British tonnage implied the merchant fleet had been sunk four times over. Yet Alec had 'this blind unreasoning faith that we would win'.

In their initial eighteen months of captivity, POWs listening on primitive crystal sets constructed from scrounged components noticed that German broadcasts were prompt and accurate as the Wehrmacht advanced through the Balkans, North Africa and Russia. By contrast, BBC broadcasts obfuscated – troops staged 'strategic withdrawals', allowing 'the enemy to extend their lines of communication to breaking point'. During the war's middle years, the situation reversed. The BBC would be first with the news, while new phrases entered the Nazi lexicon: soldiers would 'fight valiantly' in 'heroic stands', showing 'dauntless courage' as they made 'sectional withdrawals'.

Yet sometimes Goebbels' propaganda machine told truths too painful for Alec to believe. On 13 April 1943 Radio Berlin revealed the mass grave of Polish officers killed by the Soviets in the 1940 Katyn massacre. The Germans, keen to show the British how barbarous were their allies, plastered the camps with photographs. POWs responded by tearing down the posters and claiming the Gestapo had committed the massacre, to which guards responded by withdrawing Red Cross parcels.

The alternative to 'blind unreasoning faith', even faith in the goodness of Stalin, was 'to give up and die'. Alec had witnessed men succumbing on *Arbeitskommandos* and at Lamsdorf, where by June 1943 medical staff cared for forty mental patients, most of whom had suffered nervous breakdowns in captivity. Sometimes suicide seemed the only option. John Gambrill, a New Zealand medic, left the *Lazarett* in May 1943 and wandered into no-man's land, where he was shot dead. Bill Holmes, a Royal Sussex private, witnessed another suicide dressed up as an escape attempt. One night he heard shots; the next morning he saw a corpse hanging on the perimeter fence riddled with bullets, and 'they left him there for three days as a warning to us.'

When Alec encountered such cases he would try to help: 'They would lie on their beds; they wouldn't wash and they wouldn't eat. We would get them out and scrub them and sometimes it worked, but many of them weren't mentally equipped to cope with stress for an indefinite period.' He, however, would not give up.

Retaining a sense of humour was critical, and Alec's combine would amuse themselves with catch phrases, codes and riddles. When a guard headed their way, the cry was 'Cinderella's coming to the ball.' Alec became 'Q', to rhyme with Jew, with the result that anyone needing something translated would shout 'Where's Q?' Les gave him a nickname derived from his interest in escaping: 'Alec would say, "I want to be off." He said it so often I would say, "Here comes "I want to be off".' They made an odd quartet – Birch, Birrell and Hepburn with their broad regional accents and Alec with his received pronunciation. Indeed, Alec, the ex-public schoolboy reduced to the rank of rifleman, was the butt of endless jokes. His refrain, repeated so often the guards thought it was code, was 'Come on, boys. Take me as I am'.

All four thought being smartly dressed was important for self-respect, and they would spruce themselves up to trump their guards. Thanks to clothing parcels, each E173 member had two uniforms and two pairs of boots. Their laundry was washed by village women, while two POWs worked as the camp's cobbler and tailor. Hair was the responsibility of 'The Demon Barber', David Massey, a Tyneside Scottish Territorial. Massey's active war was even shorter than Alec's. Leaving school at fourteen, he trained as a photographic engraver on the *Newcastle Evening Chronicle*. At twenty-two, he was called up and shipped to France. On 17 May 1940, the Tyneside Scottish were sent to defend a stretch of the Canal du Nord against Rommel's 7th Panzers. They were overrun after five hours.

As a Queen Vic volunteer, Alec was taught riflemen were a cut above ordinary infantrymen, and such feelings survived incarceration. Mick Walker of the Rifle Brigade, who fought alongside Alec at Calais, would even barter

food for shoe polish, saying, 'I'm a rifleman and will look like one.' At Setzdorf, Les Birch was equally determined to put on a good show despite meagre
materials. Les lost his pistol lanyard after capture but produced a homemade
version at Setzdorf, plaiting grass to create a 'rope', then dyeing it with
powdered lime from Latzel's kilns.

The Setzdorf working day would begin when the men were ordered out
of their billet to line up in fives for *Appell*. POWs would shout, 'We always
stand in threes. What's wrong with you? Can you only count in fives?' Once
counted, they would set off on the quarter-mile march to work. One of Alec's
jobs involved pushing skips loaded with stone across the yard to the kiln. The
weather could be freezing but at least he was in the open air. Another task
involved stacking stones in the kilns and bricking them up to be fired. In the
heat, POWs would become drenched in sweat despite stripping down to their
shorts. The worst task was removing lime from the kilns once it had been
fired and taking it to the mill. The heat was extreme, while the fumes and dust
were noxious; some POWs suffered in later life from lung problems.

Guards would regularly shout, 'Call for Alex', summoning Alec to interpret. Playing intermediary was a balancing act, as he tried to gauge the degree
to which POWs might resist orders. His growing command of idiom enabled
him to crack jokes with Schittenhelm and negotiate over conditions, gaining
ever more leverage as civilian manpower drained into the Wehrmacht. Latzel
would press for more effort, to which Alec's refrain would be, 'No, no, that
can't be done.'

Les thought Alec 'brilliant': 'Even high-ranking officers would take notice
of him when they came into our barrack. He showed us that if you talked to
Germans civilly yet were robust on occasion when answering back you had
them beat.' Les saw Alec's diplomacy at work when a guard mistreated him:
'At one point I lost my temper and went for the guard. If it had not been for
Alec's intervention I would have been bayoneted.' Aware of Alec's ethnicity,
he knew this demanded courage. A growing mastery of idiom was dangerous
because it would enrage guards whose command of their native tongue was
weaker than Alec's. 'The Hun will have you if you keep going on like that,'
Les would say. 'You will get yourself into trouble and one day they will march
you off.'

When Alec ignored him, Les concluded his friend 'had no fear' – and
courage was called for in other ways. Stuck in a remote village, the POWs
were starved of information, but Alec put his German to use in spotting anti-
Nazi civilians. One was a carpenter who had fought in the Great War and
would pass on underground information. Les would warn Alec, 'You'll be
caught and strung up.' But Alec would often creep round to the repair shop to
find the carpenter. Some of the older guards hated the Nazis, and Alec would
winkle news out of more biddable ones, armed with cigarettes, chocolate and
soap as bribes. Within a Third Reich suffering increasingly from shortages,

he learned how much information the phrase, 'Have some chocolate for your children', would yield. Towards the end, soap was an equally powerful 'persuader'.

Alec knew that once a trade had occurred, a guard would be compromised, with the result that bribery could yield items more subversive than news and gossip. If the guard then refused to do a POW's bidding, he faced being betrayed to his superiors, who might send him to the Eastern Front, seen as a virtual death sentence. Caught in the trap, most guards cooperated.

Thanks to his German, Alec was given a peculiar task as Christmas 1941 approached. Schittenhelm pulled him aside one morning, saying the two of them were going to the woods to cut down Christmas trees. Thus they set off, Schittenhelm with his rifle and axe, and Alec at his side. Alec loved the irony. Here was a guard whose brutality was such that Private Jim Nixon reported him to the military authorities for ill-treatment of POWs after liberation in 1945. Yet he wanted to give the POWs Christmas trees. Years later, Alec would recall with a smile, 'What he didn't know was he took a Jew to help him get them down.'

Schittenhelm also distributed Christmas postcards sent from Lamsdorf. They showed an open-top horse-drawn carriage arriving at a cottage with a snow-covered roof and contained six lines of doggerel:

A little picture to express,
My wishes for your happiness;
A little message from my pen,
To haste the Day we'll meet again;
God grant you every Christmas cheer,
And Joy throughout the Coming Year.

The message, leaving space for the POW to insert his name, read: 'Christmas Greetings from *Stalag* VIIIB, Germany. Christmas 1941'.

Schittenhelm's sentimentality even extended to allowing the POWs to stage a Christmas Eve revue and exchanging an accordion and some mouth organs for Red Cross chocolate. George Baker, a 51st Highland lorry driver, was the show's accordionist, while the lead singer was Jimmy McPhee, a Gordon Highlander. 'Laurie' Lawrence thought McPhee had a 'truly remarkable operatic tenor voice' that reminded him of the Austrian Jewish exile, Richard Tauber. McPhee would begin with Gaelic ballads, but the POWs' favourite was Danny Boy. The singing went down so well with Schittenhelm that he supplied the POWs with beer to wash down the contents of their Red Cross Christmas parcels. These contained Christmas pudding, cake, roast pork, steak and tomato pudding, double rations of chocolate, strawberry jam, margarine, sugar, tea, condensed milk and biscuits. A double ration of cigarettes and tobacco was sent separately.

Les described the evening in a letter to his girlfriend, Bernice Funnell. The concert 'was very good, considering there are only 84 men here'. The Christmas feast, 'after so long with just soup ... really did go down good'. Schittenhelm, thought Les, 'did all he could for us'. Les could not, however, disguise his sadness. He had not heard from Bernice for six weeks and he feared the worst:

> I am just waiting now to get a letter from you telling me how you spent Xmas. I am sure that you missed me – I did you. I would give anything for to get back to you again but it looks as though it will be a long time. But Dear, I know you will keep your chin up and wait for me. Must hope for a change in the coming year. Must close with you ever in my thoughts.
> All my love for ever,
> Leslie

Would 1942 bring 'a change'? Alec had grounds for optimism. The Japanese attack on Pearl Harbour had brought America into the war, while Hitler's Russian offensive had halted outside Moscow. In his 1940 speech about the Calais garrison's sacrifice, Churchill had said Britain would carry on fighting until 'the new world, with all its power and might, steps forth to the rescue and the liberation of the old'. That time had come.

Chapter 17

Sehnsucht

In January 1942, with the snow two feet deep, Alec learned how severe a Sudeten winter could be. Poetry provided solace as he retreated in his mind's eye to pre-war Cornish holidays. His first poem, Caerhays, was about a beach near Caerhays Castle, five miles from Mevagissey:

As the north wind loudly whines,
And shakes the tops of gloomy pines,
I think of other trees I've seen,
A lighter and more pleasant green.

An ancient castle, woods around,
Where timid deer in herds abound;
The plashing of a gentle rill.
I see it still.

Then, far beyond, the silver beach,
The waves roar and the corm'rant's screech.
Oh give me back those summer days
I've spent in idling at Caerhays.

The German compound noun for such emotions, *Sehnsucht*, could be translated as painfully-intense nostalgia. C.S. Lewis described *Sehnsucht* as an 'inconsolable longing' for 'we know not what', a feeling like being pierced by a rapier, sparked by such things as 'the sound of wild ducks flying overhead ... or the noise of falling waves'. Alec's longing, however, had a clear object: Netta had abandoned him, yet he could not let her go. His second poem began with a reworking of Cole Porter's Night and Day: 'Like the beat beat beat of the tom-tom / When the jungle shadows fall ...' Porter's lyric has an upbeat ending; Alec's did not.

Like the beat of a native tom-tom,
In the depths of the jungle's gloom;
Like the unceasing race of a shuttle,
As it crosses the weaver's loom;
Like the hour long chatter of prim old maids,
As they sip their cups of tea;
So the longing to be with you once again,
Forever continues in me.

I think of the night I met you;
I acted like one in a trance,
And I think of two cigarettes smoked in the dark
Sitting out a sixth form dance.
The Sundays we walked together.
I think of them once again,
When every day we drank café au lait,
And prayed that it would not rain.
How sharply I feel yet your cheek's touch,
And your hair rustling on my face.
A sharp sweet thrill is with me still.
Your fingers with mine interlace.
The concrete things that divide us
Are your marriage, half Europe, the war
But you are still mine in the abstract,
Locked in my heart's deep core.

Alec would lie awake fantasizing about reversing his journey as 'an involuntary guest of the Third Reich', but reality continued to obtrude – prisoners fighting for food on the March, and the loss of Netta. The conflict was encapsulated in another *Sehnsucht* poem, again addressed to Netta, called Mind's Journey:

In the horrible silences,
So intense, that they deafen,
Almost shattering the ear drums;
When the soul and the mind
Should be at peace and in harmony,
I find myself thinking,
Across vast stretches of country,
Pine forested mountain,
And the patchwork quilt pattern of farms,
Stretched mile upon mile in never ending succession;
Through Rhineland towns with their wonders
Of ecclesiastical architecture;
Past war stricken Belgium,
Where the white cottages,
Sleep in the glance of the noonday sun;
Where once I fought with the dust for breath,
And for food with my fellow-men;
Across the grey wastes of the North Sea,
Where the fish swam and where now float the dead;
Through the Home Counties to England's heart's core,
To London where you are,
And my soul knows no rest.

Other poems looked back to summers in Cornwall. In Mevagissey, Alec wrote of his favourite village, mixing half with full rhymes:

Picture Mevagissey, ancient town.
Slate boarded houses, brown and grey,
And on the sea worn granite quay,
Blue-jerseyed men who sit for hours,
And talk. They smoke their pipes,
As they watch the ships.
They speak their thoughts
In the soft smooth hum
Of the Cornish tongue,
Music that clings, and grips.
The gulls wheel, crying, on the morning breeze,
Or rest on ships' masts, rocks, or on the quays.
The slow and even rhythm of a boat
Just starting, or returning, sets a note
Insistent, yet subdued and hardly heard.
The sun throws sharp relief, no detail blurred,
And yet, amazingly,
The scene is one of lazy harmony.
The old men talk,
Lost in a happy world of yesterday.
The children at their feet, unworried, play,
And look towards the houses on the point,
Where, if I pass Portmellon,
And climb across the rocks,
Then wade through bracken frond,
I see the Gwineas in the sea beyond.
Below the cliffs precipitous, and steep,
A little strip of sand – Bodrugan's Leap.
A host of memories rush through my mind,
Trenarren, and the ever-narrowing wind
Of leafy lane, which leads to Towan Well.
The very place names seem to weave a spell,
Which makes all present misery seem unreal.
He who knows Cornwall, knows the way I feel.

In A Call, Cornish sounds melded into a siren song:

Sometimes, in the long quiet nights,
I lie unsleeping in my bed,
And thoughts, like dancing will o'wisps,
Go racing through my aching head.

I think of happy summer days
I've spent in Caerhays, Hemmick, or Polstreath,
The sun hot on my face and hands.

The surge and ebb of little waves,
The music is still in my ears.
It calls me like a siren's song
Across the intervening years.

The sighing wind is in the trees.
The gulls are crying in the bay.
They call me with magnetic charm.
Come back. Come back some day.

With *Sehnsucht* came survivor guilt. Why had he survived when others died? Did he deserve to live? On the March he had been herded past rows of white headstones in Great War cemeteries. Why was his body not decomposing in some foreign field? Consumed by feelings of unworthiness, he struggled to find a reason for being – perhaps he was simply a vessel for remembering the dead? This was the subject of two poems in early 1942. He called the first For the Fallen:

What of the dead, who died for an ideal?
Something intangible, abstract, scarcely real.
They gave their lives, that we might carry on;
We the unworthy ones, all the best are gone.

They died unthinking of their sacrifice.
They paid their lives and counted that no price.
They lie there cold, that we may bask in sin;
We the unworthy ones, all the best are gone.

Their memory lives, nor will it ever die.
It needs no monument, nor empty pageantry.
It lives and shines as we have never shone;
We the unworthy ones, all the best are gone.

The second he entitled For Those Who Died:

Beneath the white new fallen snow,
Which lies in Belgium, and in France,
Where every careless, casual glance
Recalls the war two years ago:
The fields, where wheat will no more grow,
The rides, where horses no more prance,
The ballrooms, where no couples dance,
Bomb-stricken hearths, where no fires glow;

There lie the men, who gave their all,
Who fought, and then for England died.
Their corpses moulder, stink and rot.
Our recognition is too small,
And if, till we were old, we tried,
Equal their glory we could not.

Alec's third poem from early 1942 was a sonnet, a form he had studied at school. For the first eight lines, or octave, of Sonnet, he used Francesco Petrarch's rhyming scheme, ABBAABBA. For the sestet, he used CDECDE, following Rupert Brooke in The Soldier. Yet Alec avoided both Brooke's romantic patriotism and Petrarch's pursuit of unattainable love. Instead, the octave alluded to German propaganda, while the sestet declared his bitterness at being left to rot in a prison camp.

All you who talk of England's fame,
And idolize her hard-won glory;
If you investigate her story,
And carefully analyse the same,
You'll find that certain people claim
With diplomatic oratory,
That many deeds both dark and gory,
Are England's everlasting shame.

This may be true, but think of those,
Themselves unthinking, simple men,
Who shed their blood, that we may live
In liberty and quiet repose.
Compare our lives with others. Then
Realize how much it is they give.

While Alec felt bitter and unworthy, there was growing recognition at home of the Greenjackets' achievement at Calais. Eric Linklater was selected to write the official account of the action. In his autobiography, *Fanfare for a Tin Hat*, Linklater described being recruited by the War Office's publicity director, Walter Elliot, a former minister whom Churchill sacked in 1940 allegedly because his jokes in Cabinet were too cruel. Elliot instructed Linklater to record 'the courage and military virtues' of the Calais garrison, who 'had done so much to make possible the evacuation of our defeated army from Dunkirk', and to 'make the story as authentic, as close to the truth as was possible'.

For Alec's family, the critical sentence in Linklater's *The Defence of Calais* was:

Between Calais and Dunkirk the French were given time to flood and hold the Gravelines water-lines, and this was a decisive operation in the successful rearguard action that permitted the evacuation of more than three hundred thousand French and British soldiers. The scythe-like sweep of the German divisions stopped, with a jerk, at Calais. The tip of the scythe had met a stone.

Linklater commissioned a poem for the back cover:

Soldiers on a foreign shore
In sight of home we fought, we died.
The flames of Calais flashed our last
Message across the sundering tide –
'Tell them at home their English lads
Fought well, sleep well, side by side.'

Its author was identified merely as 'C.D.L.'; although the verse is not in his *Complete Poems*, the initials probably stood for Cecil Day-Lewis. Linklater's narrative would have passed across his desk at the Ministry of Information, and the two men were friends.

Linklater admitted *The Defence of Calais*, at 56 pages, was 'no more than an interim report' yet said the heroism was such that 'even a fragment of the story was worth the telling'. He was right. The press devoured it, under headlines such as 'With No Hope of Victory They Fought On' and 'Fury of Death-Struggle That Baulked Germans'. The first edition, published in October 1941 and costing 4d, quickly sold out and copies became collectors' items. In 1970, Linklater said they were changing hands at 25s apiece, adding, 'None, alas, of my larger works has appreciated to that extent.' When Nicholson died twenty months later in *Oflag* IX A/Z in Rotenburg, his obituary was headlined 'The Man who Saved an Army'.

People outside Britain were also keen to read about Calais. Even before Linklater's booklet was published, and months before the US entered the war, the story attracted Americans intrigued by the participation of a unit they called the 60th Royal Americans. Major General Davidson decided to harness this interest in his unit's colonial origins in a US recruiting drive, keen that the Army should emulate the RAF's success in recruiting American volunteer pilots after Dunkirk. The first man to respond was Robert Cox, brother of Archibald Cox, later the Watergate prosecutor. Six decades later, Rachel Cox, Archibald's daughter, described how the Greenjackets' performance at Calais was 'a source of pride' to her uncle because 'it was an event well publicized here and viewed as moving and inspiring proof of British valour'. Cox co-opted Charles Bolte, a Dartmouth College student campaigner for US participation in the war, who wanted 'to join the fight the quickest way possible' and said if America 'was going to stay reluctant' he would join 'an army that was fighting'.

Eventually, twelve American volunteers joined the 60th Rifles. The war was not kind to Bolte and his friends: Cox died in Tunisia, Bolte lost a leg at El Alamein and Ted Ellsworth, another Dartmouth student, was captured and imprisoned in Oflag 64 at Schubin, Poland. Yet the survivors remained proud they had volunteered early in the fight against tyranny. Returning to civilian life, Bolte founded the American Veterans Committee, the most liberal of America's post-war veterans' organizations.

In Setzdorf, Alec knew nothing of Linklater's booklet or the new recruits to 'the Royal Americans'. If anyone had tried to smuggle the booklet into the camps it would have been intercepted. The Calais veterans, therefore, remained ignorant of the full significance of their sacrifice, made, in Airey Neave's words, 'in full view of the Kent coast … while the British Expeditionary Force was within thirty miles of them and ships of the Royal Navy stood off Calais'.

Yet a few phrases in letters from home did make it past the censors. The garrison had, according to their families, been 'saviours of the BEF' and had 'made Dunkirk possible'; the defence would 'become part of our history'. One POW received a letter from his brother saying, 'I have just read an account of the action that you were involved in and would like to say I'm proud of you.' In a poem of February 1942, Celer et Audax, Alec set the Calais siege within the context of the 60th Rifles' history:

In former days in time of war,
Wherever they were needed most,
With fearless tread there went one corps
Whose motto was no empty boast.
Wherever there was ground to hold
Celer et audax. Swift and bold.

They followed Wellington in Spain.
They played their part in India's heat
And in the Boer war once again
They never knew the word defeat.
Each man was worth his weight in gold.
Celer et audax. Swift and bold.

This war there seemed to be no hope,
Of making a last desperate rally
Just three battalions had to cope
With sixty, at a place called Calais.
For ever will the tale be told.
Celer et audax. Swift and bold.

Censorship meant POWs' correspondence was mostly confined to trivia, and Alec would wait three more years before he could tell his story to his family.

Help was, however, at hand in January 1942 for the Jays in their hunger for information about *Stalag* life. It came in *Prisoner of War*, a Red Cross booklet containing photographs of POWs engaged in sports and entertainment and describing itself as the 'first authentic account of the lives of British prisoners of war in enemy hands'. Then, in May, the British Red Cross launched a monthly magazine, *The Prisoner of War*.

The first edition carried extracts from Churchill's *My Early Life* about his Boer War incarceration. Churchill wanted to counter the idea that imprisonment resembled an extended holiday camp. Such misconceptions were apparent in letters sent to POWs early in the war asking them about German girls and the quality of German beer. Of POW life, Churchill wrote:

> You are in the power of your enemy. You owe your life to his humanity, and your daily bread to his compassion. You must obey his orders, go where he tells you, stay where you are bid, await his pleasure, possess your soul in patience ... If you have never been under restraint before, and never known what it is to be a captive, you feel a constant humiliation, being confined to a narrow space, fenced in by wire, watched by armed men, and webbed about with a tangle of regulations and restrictions ... I certainly hated every minute of my captivity – more than I have hated any period of my whole life. Looking back on those days, I have always felt the keenest pity for prisoners and captives.

The magazine provided information and advice. One edition included maps, so the Jays could see Alec's location. Another included advice from A.A. Milne on books to send. Then there were knitting patterns for pullovers and advice on personal parcels. A 'perfect first parcel', said the magazine, should contain a vest, a shirt, a pullover, a blanket, a muffler, two pairs of socks and pants, a kitbag or treasure bag, a towel, household and toilet soap, a razor and blades, a shaving stick, a sewing kit, two handkerchiefs and a patch for underwear, some chewing gum and chocolate, a toothbrush and toothpaste.

The Prisoner of War gave the Jays some genuine insights into Alec's life. The first edition showed a photograph captioned, 'Searching the kit of British prisoners of war at *Stalag* VIIIB before they leave camp to join a working party whose job takes them some miles away'. Generally, however, the magazine painted a rosy picture. Whitehall wanted home morale kept high, while German censors would intercept letters in which POWs revealed their privations, stamping them '*Beschlagnahmt*'('seized'). That was the fate of a letter sent by Royal Army Service Corps corporal Frank Hatton to his aunt and uncle in Barnsley. Hatton was suffering from lumbago yet when he refused to work he was made to stand in the sun from 6.30am to 9.00pm without food. He went on to say *The Prisoner of War* reports about prisoners 'being well treated by Jerry' were propaganda and his guards were 'the most lousy square-headed bastards that ever walked'. The work was 'very hard' yet food was insufficient.

Red Cross and Swiss Protecting Power reports were anodyne, while Red Cross prisoner-of-war exhibitions staged in 1943 and 1944 were intended to convey a message of comfort to families such as the Jays, who joined queues so long that the 1944 exhibition at St James' Palace had to be extended. Yet reality would seep through.When some POWs were repatriated in late 1943, a *Times* correspondent interviewed former Lamsdorf inmates and described it as 'among the worst of the camps'.

Once he had contacted his family, Alec wrote home regularly, typically ending his letters with a plea for cigarettes, the *Stalag* currency. Thus, family members would travel to Rothmans in Piccadilly to organize cartons labelled with Alec's POW number and camp details, to be sent via Geneva. An early letter, written in March 1942, was to Phoebe ('Phipp' to her friends). As a teenager, Alec would write verses for 'Phipp's' birthday, 5 April. Phoebe had no birthday greetings in 1941 but she did not miss out in 1942. Alec was determined to be positive:

This year, as your birthday approaches,
I've leisure enough to spend time
In removing my mental cockroaches,
And setting my thoughts into rhyme.

My brain has been getting quite musty,
So that's why I'm taking this chance
Of sweeping away cobwebs dusty,
And making my cerebra dance.

If I were at home in the city,
I might let my memory slip,
And that would of course be a pity.
No verse on her birthday for Phipp!

And though this won't reach you in time dear,
It will do in July or June,
I'll be there next April in person.
In fact, I'll be seeing you soon.

In return, Phoebe wrote often. She was restricted to one piece of paper per letter but would bend the rules by writing on long sheets torn from teleprinter rolls. One involved composing twenty-six limericks, each starting with a different letter, poking fun at family and friends. The first concerned their father, a volunteer fire warden. John Jay was a fastidious character; each night he would stack his loose change in neat piles on his bedside table. This neatness, to the amusement of fellow volunteers, extended to his warden's hut on playing fields near home:

At Warden Post 684
They say there is space there galore
For Post Warden John
Keeps egging them on
To use up the walls, not the floor.

Photographs were also important in maintaining POWs' spirits. From late 1941, the Setzdorf men, Alec not included because of the break-up with Netta, received photos of their sweethearts. Often, these showed them in uniform as members of the ATS and the WAAF. In a letter to Bernice on Sunday, 8 March 1942, Les Birch wrote: 'Darling, every night when I get in bed I always look at the latest photos of you and read your letters, thinking of the good times we have had knowing we have better ones to come. Looking forward to that happy day.'

Alec repeatedly pestered Schittenhelm for a group photo so the POWs could send pictures home in return, yet the only response for months was, 'We will see.' Then, finally, Schittenhelm produced a photographer in April 1942. For this first group photograph, the E173 prisoners were determined to make good impressions. George Baker, accordion on his lap and his boots shining as if on parade, sat in the front row for each photograph. For Alec's group photograph, David Massey, the 'demon barber', sat on George's far right, while Alec, his hair parted and smoothed down, stood behind him. On the far left was Peter 'Darky' Fish of the Royal Norfolks, who was lucky to be alive because ninety-seven of his colleagues had been killed in the SS's Le Paradis massacre. Les Birch was not pleased with his picture, fearing he looked so gaunt Bernice would not recognize him: 'At last I am able to send you a photo but, darling, I was disappointed with it. It is not as good as I thought it would be. I am not smiling. Still never mind, it's a photo.'

Still considering escape, Alec thought Setzdorf too difficult a place from which to break out. He might be able to slip away, yet travelling by foot during the Sudeten winter would have been treacherous, even if the territory had not been full of Sudeten Nazis. Nor did E173 include draughtsmen who might furnish escapers with forged papers. That did not, however, stop Alec joining E173's escape committee and helping others more optimistic about their chances, such as the five men who broke out within a week of his arrival. Alec and Les pledged they 'would help one another whichever way it went. We thought we were probably going to get killed so we might as well try to do something.'

Meetings were held in the billet, with one man posted at the door to warn of approaching guards. In hushed tones, the men would debate escape options while nursing mugs of tea. Water was heated with Lusted's improvised heating element or a 'blower'. This resembled a forced-air burner in a forge, comprising Klim tins and a fan powered by a wooden wheel connected to it by shoelaces or a leather belt. The fuel might be twigs, coal or used tea leaves. When the handle on the wheel was cranked, the airflow produced sufficient heat from the embers in the Klim tin to boil a pint of water.

The best time for a break-out was at night, because escapers then had more time to get away unnoticed. Yet POWs were shut in behind locked doors and windows and inside barbed wire. What if escapers hid in the Latzel works and staged their break from there? In the billet, the other POWs could attempt to hide their absence by claiming they were sick. They could even, copying a classic boarding-school trick, fill their bunks with clothed dummies.

Les was central to such plans because escapers could hide in his workshop, then, if the iron bars could be removed, get out through a window. Les had access to a hacksaw blade in the toolbox of the civilian working alongside him and used it to saw through the bars when left alone in the workshop. The task took many days but his motto was 'passion, patience and perseverance'. To disguise his work-in-progress, he filled the saw cuts with chewing gum discoloured with wet rust. Finally, the job was complete. Thus, one evening, the escapers hid in the workshop, removed the sawn-through bars, eased themselves through the window and fled.

At *Appell*, the tally came up two POWs short, but the guards were told they were sick in their bunks in the upstairs billet. One guard went upstairs to check, and, when there was no movement from either bunk, gave one of the dummies a prod with his bayonet. At that point, pandemonium broke out. Schittenhelm interrogated Alec and the senior POWs and, when no answers were forthcoming, said they would be shot. In the end, however, the collective punishment involved being locked in the billet for two days without German rations. The following day, the guards were lined up beyond the perimeter wire to be interrogated by SS officers. 'We were all locked up inside but we could see through the bars,' recalled Les. 'Funny isn't it? We were not hungry that night. We just stood there laughing.'

Eventually, the Latzel managers discovered a hacksaw blade was missing, but Les denied any knowledge and no further action was taken. There were, however, longer-term consequences. One measure was to prevent the hoarding of Red Cross supplies in preparation for a break-out by puncturing tins of food, so the contents would be ruined if not eaten quickly. Alec said this contravened the Geneva Convention, but Schittenhelm was implacable.

Chapter 18

Alex der Jude

In 1940, the 'good German' at Bathorn had warned Alec not to speak German because it might expose his ethnicity. He ignored the advice. To function effectively as an interpreter he had to develop a rapport with the enemy, and his apparent friendliness meant some POWs distrusted him, thinking he might be a 'plant' tasked with discovering escape plans. At various camps, Germans in British uniforms were inserted into POW ranks. One was executed by the Lamsdorf escape committee – his body, its throat cut, was discovered on 17 July 1944 in Lamsdorf's reservoir.

The bigger danger for Alec, however, came from a different direction – an anti-Semitic POW threatening to expose him as Jewish. The Nazis recruited a few renegade Britons from among Mosley's Fascists, and even during the war anti-Semitism continued to disfigure British life – train travellers would find slogans daubed on their carriages including 'This is a Jewish war', 'Get rid of the Jews' and 'Smash Jews'. Conscription put Fascists in uniform and some were captured in 1940.

Alec was not alone in being targeted by anti-Semitic POWs. Bill Harding saw a Cockney POW betray a Jew after the two fell out over a bartering deal with a Polish civilian; the Jewish soldier was then beaten by the guards. Late in the war, Len Brott of the Queen's Royal Regiment was betrayed by an Afrikaner POW at his *Arbeitskommando*. Len had studied German at school and, like Alec, 'converted' to Christianity after capture, but used his German 'in order not to have my mates pushed around'. When a German officer boasted of the '*Vergeltungsfeuer*' ('retaliation flame') that would destroy London, Brott reminded him of German claims it had been flattened in 1940, 1941 and 1942 and one 'couldn't keep destroying places that were already flattened'. The officer smashed him across the jaw. Then, tipped off by the Afrikaner, he accused him of being Jewish and said he was speaking Yiddish, not German. Fearing he might be shot, Brott conjugated every verb he could think of. 'I must be the only man alive today,' he recalled, 'who owes it all to being a little attentive while in school.'

Some anti-Semitic POWs went further than casual cruelty, including Cyril Hoskins, a Queen Vic from Alec's company, who was imprisoned in *Stalag* XXA at Thorn. In June 1940, William 'Lord Haw-Haw' Joyce arrived to recruit renegades for German radio stations, the aim being to set up

English-language stations masquerading as part of an underground movement in Britain. Joyce offered Hoskins a salary, relocation to Berlin, civilian accommodation and a change of identity. Hoskins took the bait, as did seven others, in the Nazis' most successful exercise in traitor recruitment.

Hoskins was not the only Queen Vics Fascist. Alec trained in B Company in 1939 with Lance Corporal Don Bowler, a medical orderly from Edgware. Bowler and his Irish wife had preached anti-Semitism in London's East End and the Germans thought him ripe for recruiting. Unsurprisingly, fellow POWs thought him a renegade. In a 1944 letter from Lamsdorf, the Queen Vics' quartermaster sergeant, Joe Harbert, made a thinly-disguised request to 'Jumbo' Sampson: 'Will you get in touch with L/Corp Bowler and persuade him to go to work with his old firm, KG&Co Ltd? He is no good in our shop. I have heard so many unfavourable reports about him and can't but believe them.' KG&Co stood for King George and Country.

In fact, Bowler remained loyal to KG&Co, using the cover of his Fascist past to unearth traitors. He asked the senior British officer for orders and was told to appear to cooperate while reporting on renegades, joining the five-man team of renegade hunters led by Oxford-educated brewer and pre-war Fascist, John 'Busty' Brown. Conscripted as a Royal Artillery quartermaster sergeant, Brown was taken outside Dunkirk. He then used his Fascist cover to become a POW spy. He began by writing a sycophantic article for *The Camp* and ingratiating himself with Prinz von Hohenlohe, commandant at Lamsdorf's E3 *Arbeitskommando* at Blechhammer. There, he met Julius Green, the Jewish 51st Highland Division dentist, and both sent home encrypted information that might help the war effort. Brown weaved his messages into letters to his wife and some invented relatives.

His most significant work was done, however, after the Germans selected him in 1943 as senior British officer at *Stalag* IIID/517, a *Sonderkommando* (special camp) at Genshagen, near Berlin. Run by Sonderführer Lange, the Lamsdorf interpreter, this was supposedly a 'holiday camp', where POWs might absorb German civilization through films and sight-seeing tours of Berlin. *Arbeitskommando* commandants provided lists of POWs who showed 'good performance' at work, deserved a holiday and were 'open-minded' towards their captors. The Germans thought Brown a perfect leader. They even allowed him to travel freely in Berlin in civilian clothes, enabling him to send encrypted messages to London about air-raid targets, camouflage and anti-aircraft defences.

Brown's biggest coup came after Lange began recruiting POWs for the British Free Corps. Bowler learned about this from a sick renegade who admitted he had discussed creating a unit 'for blokes like us with anti-British, anti-Bolshevik feelings' with German diplomats. A few months later, MI9 asked Brown to confirm the identity of the Briton behind the BFC. This was John Amery, the son of the industry secretary, Leo Amery, and thus Hitler's highest-profile collaborator, hence his execution for treason in December 1945. Brown organized a meeting in Berlin at which Amery said his BFC target was 5,000 men. The Germans tried to recruit in Lamsdorf's *Arbeitskommandos* in late 1943 and there was a further drive after D-Day. In the event, membership reached 27.

When Brown was later liberated by the Americans, POWs said he was a traitor, but the Americans released him after receiving information from London. Bowler was also labelled a renegade by liberated POWs, but eventually the facts emerged and he joined Brown as a prosecution witness in the post-war treason trials. Brown won the Distinguished Conduct Medal, but there was less recognition for Bowler. Initially, the Queen Vics shunned him, but 'Jumbo' Sampson decided he had 'faithfully carried out' the 'unpleasant and uncongenial role' of a spy. Bowler had told MI9 about traitors such as Thomas Cooper, Edward Jackson of the King's Own Royal Regiment and Edwin Martin, a Canadian captured at Dieppe. At the end of his interview with 'Jumbo', Bowler asked to join the Queen Vics' veterans association, a wish 'Jumbo' granted because Bowler 'had completely vindicated his character'.

Anti-Semitism turned others into traitors. At Setzdorf, Les Birch knew of the traitor before Alec. In 1942, it soon became clear there was a problem in a fresh intake of POWs: 'We had a turncoat or a plant. He was really poisonous. He was so clever. We could not work out why *Unteroffizier* Schittenhelm knew if one of our number was planning an escape.'

The situation clarified itself when a POW revealed his anti-Semitism. Alec was a Jew, the man told Les, so should not be in the camp. 'Alec is a British soldier,' Les replied. 'He is fighting with us.' But from that moment Alec was in danger, as Vick Young, an RASC driver from Renton near Glasgow, discovered. Young, another 51st Highlander, worked on the Latzel limestone ramp and while shovelling stone overheard the traitor telling the foreman, a member of Setzdorf's Hauke clan called Adolf, that Alec was Jewish and should be taken away.

The anti-Semite, however, had picked the wrong man in Hauke, who enjoyed verbal jousts with Alec. As the war turned, Alec would tease him by pointing to the road outside the plant and saying, 'One of these days, Adolf, a big Russian tank will be coming down this street'.

Hauke would gesticulate and exclaim with a chuckle, 'Never, never, never!'

Alec would retort, 'Well, you wait. Maybe tanks will not come down this street but one of these days a tank will come down the main street of Setzdorf with a big bear sitting on top; then watch out, Adolf, because he will be Russian.'

Once again, Hauke would shout, 'Never, never, never!'

In response to the idea of Alec being taken away, Hauke smiled and said, 'Alex, a Jew? He cannot possibly be a Jew – he is such a good fellow.' Young, however, decided the anti-Semitic POW needed punishment; traitors could not be tolerated. 'That evening, when we had been shut up in the billet a terrific fight broke out,' recalled Alec, 'and the bloke who had told the Germans I was Jewish was punched to a jelly.' Young administered the beating, then Les told the traitor he would be drowned in the river if he misbehaved again. Alec knew nothing of the circumstances and asked the other POWs, 'My God, what was all that in aid of?' He later recalled: 'Vick Young, the gentleman who meted out the punishment, was somebody who just did not approve of that sort of thing.'

The beating, however, came too late. Hauke might joke that Alec was 'too good to be Jewish', but others thought differently. A Hitler Youth member who worked alongside Les in the workshop confronted him: 'That Jewish lad you've got in there, we will get him and he will go to a concentration camp.' In the billet after work, Les discussed the situation with a sergeant. 'If ever there were an attempt to take Alec away we must stick together to save him,' said the sergeant. But the Germans would take reprisals, argued a timid POW. 'They couldn't murder us all,' the sergeant replied, 'because the Red Cross would get to know about it and it would become an international incident.'

Such theorizing was tested when Schittenhelm finally decided to have Alec removed. This incident was so troubling that Alec went to his grave without telling his family. For Les Birch, however, it remained fresh in his mind decades later. It was the moment he feared his friend would be killed.

The year had begun well for the Axis Powers as the Japanese advanced. 'The Proud Fortress Shows the White Flag' was the headline in one newspaper marking the surrender on 15 February of Singapore. Events elsewhere, however, showed the Germans were not heading for a speedy victory. In Russia, their advance halted, with Hitler, like Napoleon, blaming the weather, and Georgy Zhukov's counter-attack forcing the Germans into retreat at various points.

Against this background, measures against Jews intensified. Soon after the Wannsee Conference in January, the SS began using Zyklon-B in an improvised gas chamber at Auschwitz for mass killings, having first experimented on Russian POWs from Lamsdorf. Over the spring, the industrialised mass slaughter began further north in Belzec and Sobibor, where guards initially poisoned people with carbon monoxide from engines. During the summer, the Germans deported Jews from France, the Low Countries, Croatia and Poland, while deportations from Germany, Greece and Norway started later in the year. This was the climax of the Holocaust. Almost three quarters of Jews who died during the war were alive in February 1942, but within a year, three quarters were dead.

Some Jews fought back, but the Nazis responded by intensifying their collective reprisals. After Operation Anthropoid, Heydrich's assassination in Prague in May 1942 by two British-trained Czech parachutists, Hitler organized a spectacular funeral for 'the man with the iron heart' and ordered the Gestapo to murder the 152 Jews they knew were still in Berlin. Within Czechoslovakia, the Gestapo killed 1,300 people suspected of involvement in the assassination, the most notorious incident occurring at Lidice. Thinking one assassin was connected to Lidice, Hitler ordered its entire male population killed and the village burned to the ground. Some 199 men and 52 women were executed and the other women were sent to the Ravensbrück concentration camp, where many died. Of the children, a few deemed sufficiently Aryan were adopted by SS families but 82 were gassed at Chełmno. Setzdorf was far from Lidice and even further from the shifting front lines separating the Wehrmacht and the Soviets in 1942, yet the reverberations were felt in a deterioration of the POWs' relations with their 'hosts'.

The first prisoners were aware of the specific threat to Alec came one afternoon when they were playing football. The game was interrupted by Schittenhelm's second-in-command, 'the Sheriff/Sneaky Rat Face', who marched between the players accompanied by a visiting SS officer and ordered the men to line up in fives. 'Where is Alex, the Jew? Where is the hook-nosed bastard?' he shouted. The POWs formed a protective ring around Alec and began booing and hissing; the guards responded by firing shots in the air, and off-duty guards ran from their guardhouse armed with machine guns.

At this point, a British sergeant recently arrived in the camp stepped forward to address the guards, pausing for his words to be translated into German. Decades later, Les remembered his speech:

> You are soldiers of the German Reich; we are soldiers of the British Empire, first-class frontline troops. I don't care whether Alec is a Jew or a Freemason or whatever. He is a British prisoner of war, he is in British uniform and he was captured fighting for his country. He was in the Queen Victoria's Rifles, part of the King's Royal Rifle Corps, and is known by many of his comrades here and he is well respected. He is entitled to Geneva Convention protections and there is no way you are going to take him away from us. The soldiers in this working party are soldiers, they are not riff-raff, and they mean what they say. If you take Alec away, you'll never hold them. They will mutiny and you will have to take us all away by force or shoot us all. And if Alec or anyone else is killed, the world will eventually discover the truth and those people responsible for it will be judged as war criminals.

Alec then stood forward to address the SS officer in German, explaining, in an emollient tone, his work as an interpreter and the role he played in resolving disputes between guards and POWs. This appeared to calm the situation: the

SS officer instructed the guards to lower their weapons. He then ordered Alec and the sergeant to go to the guards' blockhouse for questioning.

'It all started so quickly,' recalled Les. 'It was hair-raising and I was terrified. I stood there praying it would have a good outcome, but we were prepared for the worst and we would have mutinied to save Alec. We hated Nazism, absolutely hated it, and that is what we went to war for.' Once the excitement faded, Alec's muckers felt 'absolutely sour' but triumphant, according to Les: 'In our bunks that evening we felt awful because we did not know what the consequences might be yet we were so pleased Alec was still with us. Alec had been kept – that was the thing.'

Alec remained at Setzdorf until his working party was disbanded in early 1944, but Schittenhelm decided he needed to be humiliated. At a parade shortly after the near-riot, Schittenhelm ordered Alec to stand forward while he subjected the POWs to an anti-Semitic tirade: 'You British, you've got Jews amongst you. Why do you tolerate having Jews? You know where the Jews go.' The POWs' response, recalled Les, was to 'burst out laughing and that made the situation worse but the guards realized we British soldiers were not going to be pushed around. There was mass support for Alec and it was absolutely magic to see the British spirit come out.' But this enraged Schittenhelm, who decided Alec should wear a distinguishing mark – not the yellow star of the Jews of occupied Europe but a long white bandage, which a guard wound round Alec's head until it resembled a turban.

Alec could continue as interpreter, Schittenhelm announced, but he should wear the turban whenever outside the billet. Les thought:

> The aim was to try to turn us into Jew-haters like them. They wanted to shame and humiliate Alec and they wanted to isolate him from the rest of us. White was the colour of surrender while the turban was intended to make Alec look oriental rather than European. They told us Jews were a menace to society and told us what they would do when the war was over. Germany had been cleansed of Jews and they would cleanse England of Jews once they had won the war.

Chapter 19

Gains and Losses

Month after month, Alec endured the tedium of the Setzdorf *Arbeitskommando* – the four-score familiar faces in the billet, the stench of unwashed bodies and the previous night's cooking, the monotonous diet, the interminable debates about 'When will the war end?', the tedious roll-calls, the marches to and from the quarry. The outside world seemed increasingly remote. Robert Kee described how POWs adjusted to captivity: 'Unnatural conditions became natural and as time passed it was more and more difficult to believe that there could be any other life beyond that which went on inside the wire.' Yet the adjustment was 'the only way of making yourself tolerate a condition which you loathed'. For Alec, poetry and the changing seasons continued to give solace, as in Dawn, written in March 1942:

> The day dawns,
> And a soft grey light
> Creeps slowly o'er the mountaintops
> Illumines slight
> The huddled houses,
> In the valley's lap.
> A cock'rel rouses
> Crows and crows again.
> The first pale streaks
> Grow ever larger in the clouded sky.
> Stars disappear, first slow then rapidly.
> The fir-clad mountains
> Pinken, then grow red.
> The worker stretches, yawns,
> Then leaves his bed.
> The idle rich sleep on.
> Up comes the sun in all his morning splendour.
> The pale moon sighs, and knows she must surrender.
> She rules the night, 'tis time,
> But with the dawning,
> She must away, the sun is king.
> It's morning.

Sudeten winters, however, were savage. In November, with the temperature
well below freezing, he wrote Winter:

The hard, white talons of winter's grip
Have taken hold of the world.
With a clasp of steel, the first claws clutch.
The whole world seems congealed.

A few dead leaves on the bare brown trees,
Shiver and shake to the wind's cold blast,
Slowly falling, one by one,
Even down to the last.

Gently sliding through the air,
Responding to every breath,
The snowflakes cover the hard brown earth
With a still white shroud of death.

In the early months at Setzdorf, news came through the distorted prism of
Lord Haw-Haw's broadcasts and *The Camp* magazine, containing glowing
reports of conditions in Germany alongside anti-communist and anti-Semitic
propaganda. Britain's alliance with Russia's Slav *Untermenschen* was also the
subject of *My Ally* by *Winston Churchill*, a propaganda pamphlet. Its 110 pages
featured American and British pre-1941 cartoons lampooning Stalin and anti-
Communist remarks from Churchill's speeches. It was intended to divide
POWs' loyalties and serve as a BFC recruiting manual.

Only a few copies of *The Camp* were distributed at Setzdorf because of the
wartime paper shortage and these were quickly recycled as lavatory paper. But
Alec and his muckers were starved of genuine news and desperate for any scrap
that could suggest when they might be freed. News-hungry POWs would
greet each other with 'What's the gen?', 'What's the dope?' or 'What's the
griff?' During breaks, Alec would bribe guards with a cigarette to look away so
he could engage civilians in conversation. This would, however, only take him
so far, because most gossip was derived from Goebbels-inspired propaganda.
This was known as 'Jerry griff' to distinguish it from 'shithouse griff', 'cook-
house griff', '*Stalag* griff' (information from Lamsdorf) and 'pukka griff' (the
most trustworthy kind).

Possession of a radio receiver could lead to the acquisition of 'BBC griff'.
Radios were 'strictly forbidden', and the ultimate punishment was execution if
its owner had been involved in spying; but Setzdorf's POWs were determined
to acquire one. The Reich's standard radio was the *Volksempfänger* (People's
Receiver), nicknamed 'Goebbels' snout'. This was useless because it only had
a limited range, but the E173 POWs persuaded a teenage worker to bring
components into the works. These were then assembled by Bert Lusted and
hidden in the attic, where Lusted linked the radio up to the electrical supply

for use each evening after the men were locked in. It was a primitive affair, yet Lusted managed to tune into the BBC European Service station, with its faint announcement: 'Here is the news read by Derek Prentice.'

Prentice gained legendary status in occupied Europe, where people used his name as code. Whispered questions such as 'Have you heard from Derek today?' would be an invitation to disclose the contents of BBC broadcasts. At Setzdorf, the main points of each transmission would be scribbled down and distributed, look-out men having been posted to listen for guards on patrol.

The BBC news became a highlight of Alec's life. If the news was good, Alec could convince himself the war might end soon; if Prentice reported the night-time skies full of British bombers, he would conclude that German civilian morale would crack; if winter was severe in Russia it might precipitate the end of a German advance. Some POWs were hyper-optimistic, others, having suffered many disappointments, became super-cynical; yet from summer 1942 Alec could legitimately argue the tide was turning.

The first indicator came in the American naval victory over Japan at the Battle of Midway. Closer to home, however, the tide took longer to turn. The 19 August Dieppe raid was a disaster, abandoned after six hours with more than 3,600 of the raid's 6,000 infantrymen, mostly Canadians, killed or captured, many of the latter imprisoned in Lamsdorf. In North Africa, Rommel recaptured Tobruk, taking 35,000 prisoners, and the Eighth Army retreated to El Alamein, sixty miles west of Alexandria, for a 'final stand'.

Then the tide turned in North Africa. Montgomery had air superiority and knew about Rommel's plans thanks to the breaking of encrypted German communications by Bletchley Park. Within a few weeks, Rommel was back to his original starting lines, and in October 'Monty' went on the offensive, launching the Second Battle of El Alamein. On 1 November, the British breakout began, and on 4 November, the BBC warned listeners to stay tuned lest they miss the best news in years – a communiqué from General Harold Alexander, commander-in-chief of Middle Eastern Command, saying Rommel was in full retreat.

On 10 November, the Eighth Army crossed the Libyan border and its leader was made a full general. The day before, the Setzdorf POWs heard that Churchill had declared, 'Now this is not the end. It is not even the beginning of the end. But it is, perhaps, the end of the beginning.' The men cheered when they learned the Eighth Army had retaken Tobruk on 13 November and entered Benghazi five days later. They also cheered as Operation Pedestal broke the siege of Malta, which the Axis Powers had attempted to bomb and starve into submission.

The most important place name figuring in Prentice's broadcasts was Stalingrad. Hitler's plan to capture Stalingrad and the Caucasus oil fields was conceived in early 1942. The advance began well and at one point Friedrich

Paulus's German Sixth Army controlled nine-tenths of Stalingrad, all but an enclave on the Volga's west bank. Then, in mid-November, the Russians counter-attacked, encircling the Sixth Army inside Stalingrad. On 31 January 1943, Paulus surrendered, and the following day, the POWs heard from the BBC about Russia's 'final liquidation of the encircled German forces at Stalingrad'. It was the end of the war's bloodiest battle – casualties approached 2,000,000. Alec noticed a new phrase creeping into German newspapers – 'planned withdrawal'. From then to the end, the Wehrmacht was never beaten; it always withdrew according to plan.

With the news improving, the E173 inmates addressed their physical and mental fitness as the days shortened. Each night, they instituted an hour of PE, and on some mornings Schittenhelm allowed them outside the wire under guard for exercises. Wednesday nights were reserved for boxing , while on weekend evenings the men would hold dances, some of them sheepishly taking the girls' part. Entertainments including a pantomime were planned for the Christmas holiday period, which Schittenhelm extended to an unprecedented three days. The mother of one POW had been a Lyceum chorus girl and she sent scripts for Cinderella. Arnold Latzel lent some kit, enabling Bert Lusted to improvise stage lighting. Costumes, meanwhile, were created from paper and paint.

As in 1941, each POW was given a Christmas card to send home. The 1942 card showed prisoners at attention delivering a toast, alongside a cartoon of Jimmy Howe's *Stalag* VIIIB Dance Orchestra, which the Germans allowed to tour other camps. Above were four lines of doggerel:

> I'd hoped I might be with you,
> This year on Xmas Day
> But since my thoughts must still suffice,
> I'll greet you in this way.

For New Year's Eve the men held a 'Grand Dance', with those taking the girls' parts clothed in painted paper costumes used in the panto. George Baker's accordion provided the main music, but the POWs also obtained instruments from the Red Cross and the YMCA. Eventually, Setzdorf's band possessed two mandolins, a guitar, a banjo and a clarinet. Once again, conversation turned to when the war might end. As usual, the consensus, supported this time by better news, was they would be 'home by next Christmas'.

The Setzdorf POWs had, however, to confront a loss alongside the gains – the death of Nelson Ogg on Monday, 15 March 1943. The fair-haired, softly-spoken 23-year-old from Dundee was one of E173's most popular men. Nelson, said 'Laurie' Lawrence, 'awoke the admiration of all that knew him, even certain of our guards'. Ogg's death resulted from medical neglect – Les Birch thought it was a war crime. He had been sick for days, yet Schittenhelm insisted he work. On 13 March he threw up but was forced to stand on parade the next morning. Later, he complained of stomach pains and was sick again. After lunch he went to bed complaining of cold. Vic Young called in the guards' *Sanitäter* (medical orderly), who gave Ogg bicarbonate of soda. This achieved nothing, and at 6.00pm Alec asked the *Feldwebel* to call the local doctor. He refused, although the doctor did send some medicine that appeared to ease the pain. Alec called for the doctor at 9.00pm but again he refused to come.

Ogg's condition deteriorated further the following morning. For a third time, Alec asked for the doctor, who finally arrived at 11.30am. He quickly saw the gravity of the situation, prescribing opium and sending for an ambulance to take Ogg to Freiwaldau's hospital 12km away. It arrived too late. At 2.00pm, Ogg stopped breathing, but was revived. At 2.30pm, he complained he could not recognize his friends and asked them to open his eyes. At 2.40pm, he stopped breathing a second time; once again, artificial respiration was used to revive him. At 2.50pm, he stopped breathing a third time. Five minutes later, as a POW was pumping his chest, the ambulance, containing another *Sanitäter* and two nurses, arrived. When the *Sanitäter* saw Ogg's condition, he said the patient should not be moved, and Ogg died as his pulse was being taken.

Ogg died of peritonitis, which is fatal if untreated. In the early 1940s, the only cure was surgery to remove infected tissue, but survival depended on quick diagnosis and treatment. The Germans, however, clearly did not think him a priority. That afternoon, Ogg's friends dressed him in uniform and laid him on his bunk, and the other POWs returned from work to pay their respects, saluting him one by one. 'Laurie' Lawrence recalled the POWs filing by 'in sorrow and respect for this lovely young man, dying in the flush of youth, so far from the Scotland he loved so much, a captive in an alien land'.

The Germans neglected Ogg when he needed treatment but gave his corpse a full military funeral. Alec and Les took charge of preparations, and the following day a guard escorted them to meet the undertaker at Setzdorf's church and inspect the plot in which Nelson would be buried. Twenty-five prisoners were allowed to attend the funeral on 18 March – the rest had to work. The pall-bearers included Les, George Bignall, John Lockyer, Bert Lusted and Percy Eyden. Lockyer, a dairyman, was a Royal Sussex Regiment lance corporal who had been taken outside Dunkirk and spent months in transit camps recovering from leg wounds so severe the doctors initially wanted to amputate.

The mourners, wearing gloves to protect themselves from the cold, included Alec, Vic Young, 'Duggie' Hepburn, Bill Morrell and Bill Scott. 'Dilly' Saunders was there as *Vertrauensmann*. Others included John Birtley, Albert Jessiman, Harry Thomson, and Charlie Whitehouse, as well as three Calais veterans, Norman Goodchild, Fred Johnson and Ralph Wilkinson. Birtley, a County Durham labourer, joined the Durham Light Infantry in

January 1940. Like other second-line Territorial units, it suffered heavy casualties trying to halt the Germans at Arras on 20 May 1940. Jessiman, Thomson
and Whitehouse were 51st Highlanders. Jessiman was a Gordon Highlander,
Thomson was in the Lothians and Border Horse while Whitehouse was an
Essex bus driver who became an anti-aircraft gunner. Whitehouse was one of
the oldest E173 prisoners, having been born in 1903. Alec thought he 'should
never have been in the army at all; his feet were as flat as pancakes'.

Of the Calais men, Wilkinson was a 60th Rifleman who had been with Alec
on the March. Norman Goodchild of the Rifle Brigade was badly wounded at
Calais and spent six months in a Lille hospital before being sent to Lamsdorf.
After a spell down a Silesian coalmine he joined Alec at Setzdorf, where he
was also reunited with Fred Johnson, a Sunderland-born Searchlights gunner.

Some village women turned up to pay their respects, while an officer and six
soldiers from Freiwaldau's *Landesschützen* (Home Guard) provided an honour
guard. Normally on formal occasions the POWs were limited to singing
Land of Hope and Glory but this time Schittenhelm let them sing the
National Anthem. The German soldiers then presented arms and fired three
volleys as the coffin was lowered into the ground. Schittenhelm provided a
photographer so a photo could be sent to Ogg's mother, Margaret Duncan,
along with a message of condolence from RSM Sherriff. Some women wept as
the POWs paid their respects. They were probably thinking of relatives who
had died on the Eastern Front or were perhaps at that moment taking part in
the Germans' counter-attack outside Kharkov in the Ukraine.

Les described Ogg's death in a letter to Bernice the following Sunday:
'Well, Darling, this week I don't feel much like writing as last Monday my pal
Nelson passed over into God's keeping ... The funeral was carried out
without one detail missing, with all honour due to a British Tommy.'

Alec stood at the rear as the German soldiers fired their salute, his eyes
lowered, his battledress tunic buttoned up against the cold, his gloved hands
at his sides and his head still covered by the turban marking him out as *Alex
der Jude*.

Chapter 20

The Great Potato Strike

The E173 POWs spent the next fortnight in mourning. The sing-songs were put on hold and Les and Alec were taken under escort to inspect Nelson Ogg's grave, still covered in snow in April. 'It certainly is looking nice,' Les wrote to Bernice, 'but I would rather it not to have been that way.'

Over the spring, conditions improved. Shortly after Ogg's death, 'the Sheriff', Schittenhelm's second-in-command, was replaced by a tall, slim, grey-haired *Obergefreiter* (senior lance corporal) called Adamshi. He was, 'Laurie' Lawrence thought, 'a different kettle of fish entirely'. A Great War veteran, Adamshi was 'an intelligent man who treated us like soldiers, not just as English rabble'. As usual, the POWs gave him a nickname, 'Bollocks', because 'that appeared to be his favourite, perhaps his only, English expression'. For Alec, in particular, Adamshi's arrival was an improvement: soon afterwards, the order to wear the white turban on parade to mark him out as *ein Jude* was withdrawn.

Other Jewish POWs were not so lucky. After evidence reached Berlin that German POWs in Palestine had been mistreated by Polish guards, Hitler ordered reprisals, and 203 POWs, including 133 Palestinian NCOs from Lamsdorf, were transported in August 1942 to *Stalag* 319, a penal camp in Chełm, Poland, where they were subjected to harsh treatment for nine months. Even the overly-compliant Swiss inspectors agreed that 'Camp 319 is a camp which was built as a retaliation.'

In early 1945, American Jews taken in the Ardennes and sent to *Stalag* IXB at Bad Orb were ordered to identify themselves on parade by taking one step forward. Their gentile comrades told them not to move and said they would stand by them. The commandant responded by giving them a day to identify themselves. If they refused, Jews exposed subsequently would be shot, alongside gentiles who protected them. About 130 men stepped forward and a few days later were transported to a concentration camp, where they worked alongside Buchenwald slave-labourers. Some died from malnutrition or disease, others when they were force-marched west to prevent them falling into Russian hands. In total, seventy-three men were killed, or 6 per cent of all Americans who died in captivity.

At Setzdorf, with the onset of spring, Adamshi organized Sunday walks under escort and football matches. For Easter, the men had an extra day off work for a concert and on Sunday, 6 June Adamshi summoned a photographer to take fresh photos for sending home. It rained most of the day, but there was time between the showers to photograph the *Arbeitskommando* in various groups. Alec selected a shot of E173's choir and band – ten singers and six musicians. His parents cherished it; there was Alec, standing on a bench in the back of three rows, smiling faintly, his face shorn of the moustache he had worn since 1939.

Les picked out a bigger group of twenty men, which he sent to Bernice in hope 'that you get it OK and that it brings happiness to you'. For this photograph, Les and Alec stood side by side in the middle row, with 'Duggie' seated in front. Les chose the photo partly because of the preponderance of 51st Highlanders as well as other men befriended at Setzdorf.

For Alec, sending a photo home produced mixed feelings. Les could send photos to Bernice – and in exchange would receive ones of her in her Women's Land Army uniform or casually seated amongst friends and family. Like other POWs, he would leaf through his steadily-growing photo collection before lights out. For Alec, there was no collection of sweetheart snaps – just the loss of Netta. The pain, still raw after two years, was apparent in Three Questions, a poem written around this time:

> Wound, will you never heal?
> Or must I always feel,
> At every thought of you,
> My senses numb, my very blood congeal?
>
> Brain, must you always think?
> And leave me shuddering on the brink.
> I thirst for not forgotten, former ecstasy.
> I thirst, and may not drink.
>
> Love, will you never die?
> Or am I slave as formerly
> To this unsated passion,
> Which leaves me in such hopeless misery?

Alec lived cocooned from the global conflagration, yet his mind was always focused on distant events, in Africa then Italy, in Russia and in the Pacific. Not all went well in early 1943. Following Allied landings in Vichy-controlled North Africa, the Axis powers poured troops into Tunisia and Rommel defeated the US Army's inexperienced II Corps. In early March, however, Monty's Eighth Army reached the Tunisian border. Thus, Rommel faced a pincer movement by two armies superior in men and weapons; by mid-April, they had pushed him back into a bridgehead around Tunis. The final assault began on 6 May. The next day British tanks entered Tunis and American infantry captured Bizerte to the north. On 10 May, to the south-east, Monty took the port of Hammamet, home to Rommel's headquarters. Two days later, Axis resistance ended with the surrender of 250,000 troops.

Victory was particularly sweet for Alec because Calais regiments figured prominently in Rommel's defeat. The Rifle Brigade's 2nd Battalion were the oldest Desert Rats, having driven into the desert in June 1940, one month after Calais, while the reconstituted 60th Rifles and 1st battalion of the Rifle Brigade had also advanced from El Alamein as Eighth Army units. Moreover, the surrendering Germans included the 10th Panzers, victors at Calais – they had inflicted heavy losses on the Americans at Kasserine Pass but were encircled when the German lines crumbled south of Tunis. In a final humiliation, Lieutenant Colonel Tom Pearson of the Rifle Brigade appeared on 12 May at their headquarters to take the surrender of Lieutenant General Friedrich Freiherr von Broich, their new commander. Broich was dispatched to Trent Park, a London mansion sequestered to house the Wehrmacht elite. The Rifle Brigade officers, meanwhile, held a champagne dinner in Tunis on 16 May to celebrate the victory, fitting revenge for the humiliations three years previously.

With the *Afrika Korps* extinct, the Allies' next objective was the invasion of Sicily, the first Allied landing in Western Europe and strategically important because it happened during the Battle of Kursk on the Eastern Front. Hitler hoped that if he won the war's biggest tank battle Stalin would seek peace. Yet his nerve broke following the Sicilian landings and he switched two SS divisions from Kursk to Italy. Not long afterwards, the Germans retreated from Kursk, leaving the newly-promoted Marshal Zhukov as victor. Even before victory in Sicily was declared, momentous events were taking place. On 25 July, the Italian king removed Mussolini, marking the beginning of the end of Fascism in Italy. Alec described the Eighth Army's achievements in *Monty's Men*:

> Sing to Britain's heroes, to Montgomery's gallant army,
> Who overcame an enemy who had seldom known defeat,
> Who beat the burning sun glare, and the sandstorms of the desert,
> Where a half a pint of water's worth a ton of bread and meat.
>
> They started from El Alamein, where Rommel's troops had pushed them;
> With ambitious resolution to break through the serried ranks
> Of Italians and Germans, boasting how they'd capture Cairo
> With their overwhelming air force and their huge supply of tanks.
>
> At first, a fierce resistance, from a sound defence position,
> Met our armoured columns trying to force that much hoped for
>   "breakthrough"
> But with grim determination they returned to their attack,
> And forced the Germans to retreat to Marsa el Matruk.

From there, the advance quickened, and they drove the fleeing German,
Who fought his rearguard actions, with bravery and skill,
Past Sollum and Fort Capuzzo, on through Tobruk and Benghazi,
And they faced the burning desert with unconquerable will.

From Benghazi to Misrata is a long and weary distance,
Where the water holes are few and far between,
But they battled bravely onward with their faces to the westward,
Till the setting sun's shine on the spires of Tripoli was seen.

When Tripoli was conquered, they pushed onward into Tunis.
They broke through the Mareth Line, and took Sfax and Hammamet,
And they didn't stop advancing when they took the town of Tunis.
For all I know Montgomery's men are pushing onward yet.

The water couldn't hold them, when their blood was really up,
For they wiped up Pantellaria, then they went to Sicily,
And before this war is finished Montgomery's eighth army
Will be marching on to take the town of Berlin on the Spree.

A second poem from late 1943, written in the wake of the Warsaw Ghetto
Uprising, the largest act of Jewish resistance during the Holocaust, was more
sombre. The Nazis had 'concentrated' Poland's 3 million Jews into ghettos,
and by 1942, Warsaw's contained 400,000 people living in squalor and dying
of disease and starvation. The SS deported 300,000 of them to the Treblinka
death camp, and those left in the ghetto rose in revolt, so Heinrich Himmler
sent in Jürgen Stroop, an SS counter-insurgency expert, to destroy the ghetto
building by building. After 13,000 Jews had been killed, most of the 57,000
survivors were transported to death camps, although a few escaped through
the sewers to continue their resistance.

Alec learned of the Treblinka deportations and the uprising via Prentice's
broadcasts. In December 1942, the BBC broadcast an interview with Szmul
Zygielbojm, a Jewish member of the Polish government-in-exile, in which he
outlined the horrors facing Polish Jews. Yet Allied politicians, meeting in
Bermuda in April 1943, concluded no resources should be diverted from
winning the war. A few days later, Zygielbojm committed suicide after discovering his wife and son had died in the uprising.

Alec dared not mention the Warsaw Uprising in his poem. Instead, he
chose, on 1 September, the fourth anniversary of the war's outbreak, to com-
memorate another terrible day in Warsaw's history, the start of the Luftwaffe's air-raids in 1939. By the time the Wehrmacht entered the city, 40,000
civilians were dead and half the buildings damaged or destroyed. Alec called
his poem simply Warsaw:

The Stukas danced their dance of death
Above a stricken town.
Below a gallant army fought,
While myriad bombs hailed down.

As thick as locusts on the wing,
And whining their unearthly song,
They detonate, and scatter death
Among the helpless throng.

Death from the air, death from the guns
A man can face both these
But can a stricken city
Face the ravage of disease?

So Warsaw fell, but from its ruins
A new town will arise,
A town which will not need to face
Destruction from the skies.

In Setzdorf, conditions deteriorated in late 1943 as Red Cross parcels dried up. 'Winter of 1943 came,' recalled 'Laurie' Lawrence, 'the usual Silesian mixture of heavy snow, bitter cold and shortages of everything.' During such times, Alec, as interpreter, would argue the POWs' case for extra food and resist Latzel's demands to work harder. The POWs' resistance was strengthened by the arrival of some stroppy Australians. One was Bill McBride, a New South Wales labourer who transported ammunition for the Royal Australian Army Service Corps and had been captured in Greece in 1941. The second was Sergeant Bill McGuinness, with whom Alec quickly developed a rapport; the two of them – Bill as the new *Vertrauensmann* and Alec as interpreter – forged a double-act in negotiations with the Germans.

In the evenings after work, Bill told Alec his story. Originally a Sydney bank clerk, he volunteered for the Australian Imperial Force in January 1940. After seeing action in Libya, his battalion was dispatched to Greece but were no match for the Wehrmacht, and Bill spent most of late April retreating south. Eventually, the battalion was shipped to Crete to defend the Rethymno airfield against an invasion the British knew was imminent, having broken Enigma, the German military code.

At Rethymno, Bill ordered his men to take up defensive positions in vineyards south of the airstrip. They saw their first German paratroopers in the skies at 4.30pm on 20 May and for the next ten days they fought the invaders in an action that sounded to Alec like a rerun of Calais. Initially, Allied soldiers killed so many paratroopers that Hitler forbade their continued use in large-scale invasions, but infantry reinforcements landed later by boat and plane in sufficient numbers to overwhelm their opponents.

Bill's battalion attacked one German unit with such ferocity that the few unwounded survivors fled towards Heraklion, the capital. By 28 May, however, the lightly-armed Australians had lost contact with other Allied units. Two days later, the sound of engines heralded the arrival of German tanks, and Bill's commanding officer ordered his men to throw down their weapons, convinced further resistance would cause unnecessary deaths. Bill chose not to surrender and fled to the hills, but two days later he was picked up by a German patrol to join 3,000 other Antipodeans in captivity.

The Australians were transported to Salonika, where they were held for weeks before being packed into cattle-trucks for the journey to Annahof. It began auspiciously – the Germans organized a brass band to play Roll out the Barrel – but the 'Hell Train' journey, as it became known, was every bit as awful as Alec's ride in June 1940. Food and water ran out the second day. When the train finally pulled into Annahof in early September, snow was falling as the men dropped from the trucks and lined up to be counted. Bill watched a *Stalag* officer light a cigarette, take a couple of drags then drop it on the ground. Perhaps he was waiting for the POWs to dash forward and fight each other for a puff. Instead, one stepped forward, stubbed the cigarette out with his boot and stepped back into the ranks without even glancing at the German. 'It was beautifully done,' recalled a New Zealand airman, 'and it made us all feel more like men again.'

In Setzdorf the Bill-Alec double act was soon on show. Latzel believed the POWs were slacking and used food as a weapon to lift productivity. Typically, six men shared a two-kilo loaf each day, but this would be reduced or increased as punishment or reward. The bread ration cut did not, however, produce the result Latzel wanted, and he responded by calling in an officer from Freiwaldau to impose discipline.

Now Alec found himself involved in 'by far and away the most remarkable' piece of interpreting during his captivity. 'What's all this about?' the officer began. Tamme, the foreman, outlined the POWs' failings 'at breakneck speed', recalled Alec, 'in the execrable Sudeten dialect that was the only thing he spoke, until he finally ran out of breath'. The officer, who only spoke High German, did not understand a word and turned to Alec in confusion, asking, 'What did he say?' Alec, by then comfortable with Sudeten dialect, found himself in the strange position of interpreting between two enemies. With pride, he would later say, 'We came out best from that dispute.' The POWs would work fewer hours but more productively.

For a while, tempers calmed, with POW morale buoyed by more 'BBC griff'. Allied forces landed in mainland Italy on 3 September and the new Italian regime switched sides on 13 October. The Germans rescued Mussolini and established him as head of a puppet government, but could not stop the Allies' continued advance. The Allies' strategic bombing of Germany intensified, as Alec saw from Nazi propaganda posters, one showing Churchill holding a machine gun against a background of bombers and a caption that read, 'Gangster child murderer'. After the Luftwaffe's raids on London, Alec was unmoved – the Germans invented 'total war'; now they were experiencing the consequences. On the Eastern Front, the Russians recaptured Smolensk in September and Kiev in November. In the Pacific, meanwhile, Allied forces were retaking the Solomons island by island and advancing through Papua New Guinea.

After two years of disputes and delays, 5,096 sick and wounded POWs were repatriated in a prisoner exchange in October 1943. The British played by Geneva Convention rules; the Nazis did not – former *Afrika Korps* POWs were fighting on the Eastern Front within weeks. 'Jumbo' Sampson organized a 'welcome home' party for the repatriated Queen Vics: Stephen Houthakker, the intelligence sergeant, Bill Langley of B Company, John Tonge of D Company and Edward Gartside, the battalion medical officer.

That Christmas, each POW's parcel came with a gift from Arnold Latzel, a bottle of Sudeten beer. On Christmas Eve, the men held a carol service in the lower barrack room, which had been decorated with fir branches. They were a varied bunch – English, Scots, Welsh and Irish, two Cypriots, seven Antipodeans and one South African. At one end, near the tortoise stove, stood George Baker with his accordion, and two guitarists. The singing was led by Jimmy McPhee. 'Maybe it was the occasion,' recalled 'Laurie' Lawrence, 'maybe the one bottle of *Dunkelbier* we had been allowed or maybe it was the magic of that most loved carol, *Stille Nacht, Heilige Nacht*, sung in English, by that Scots lad that night, but I know I had tears in my eyes and I was not the only one.' A week later, the POWs held a New Year's Eve concert and dance that continued until four in the morning. 'I hope you spent a good time at New Year,' Les wrote three days later to Bernice, 'I spent the best this time as a POW.'

The good times did not last long. The war in the east was going against Hitler, reducing German control of territory that could be pillaged for food, while round-the-clock air-raids were affecting domestic distribution. As a result, rationing intensified. In Lamsdorf, supplies of meat, fat, cheese, flour and sugar were cut. On 23 February 1944, the new regime arrived in Setzdorf when Schittenhelm marched through the snow to the billet to declare that from the following day the potato ration would be halved; 'and with an evil grin on his face' Alec recalled, 'he slammed the door and walked out'.

Alec thought potatoes 'were probably the best thing we got to eat from the Germans and the halving of the ration at this time was absolutely devastating news'. For a while, the POWs sat in silence, 'faces long as treadles, corners of mouths all turned down'. Finally, Charlie Whitehouse, the bus conductor, looked at the glum faces around him and, with a wink, said, 'Well, you can't help laughing, can you?' After the laughter subsided, someone suggested the

POWs down tools, and thus began what Alec described, with some exaggeration, as 'probably the only successful strike during the twelve years of Nazi rule in Germany'.

Arbeitskommandos were governed by military law, so striking was mutiny, yet POWs saw strikes, like sabotage and escaping, as a way to continue their struggle. What Alec called 'The Great Potato Strike' was not, therefore, the first time tools were downed. Stephen Houthakker had led fifty men in his *Arbeitskommando* at Rothaus out on strike in 1941 in pursuit of increased rations. The guards called in a *Kontrolle Offizier*, who said the POWs would be shot five at a time until work resumed. Stephen Houthakker 'was in a predicament', but when he saw the men lining up in rows of fives he knew they 'would call the thing a bluff'. The situation descended into farce when a private asked if the men could have extra bread before they were shot. Houthakker translated this, hoping the *Kontrolle Offizier* might have a sense of humour. Fortunately, he did. 'He threw his arms in the air, laughed and stormed out of the room. We had won. A permit doubling the ration was given and a half day's holiday into the bargain.'

Mostly, however, guards responded brusquely. If the threat of a court martial failed, guards could force strikers to work at gunpoint, and bayonet those showing resistance. Often, guards would withdraw food and make strikers stand to attention until they gave in or collapsed, though this breached the Geneva Convention's Article 5. Lamsdorf's chief strike-breaker was a tall thickset *Abwehr* intelligence officer in his forties called Major Birkhoff. In July 1941, Birkhoff was called in to discipline POWs striking against ill-treatment in a coalmine. Speaking in hesitant English, he ordered the strikers to line up in the sunshine without hats facing a wall. There they stood from morning until night. The men were allowed to visit the urinal at noon, but other attempts to fall out resulted in beatings from the guards. Sometimes guards would shoot strikers dead. This was the fate of John 'Sandy' Saunders, a Black Watch lance corporal, and Harry Thomson, one of Alec's E173 'muckers', in July 1944.

At Setzdorf, Schittenhelm moved rapidly to quell the strike. 'The Goons threatened,' recalled Lawrence, 'they shouted, they yelled, they called us everything except legitimate. They said, "No work, no food!" so naturally we replied by reversing the saying to "No food, no work!" They again tried everything short of violence.' Eventually, Schittenhelm locked the POWs in their billet and summoned a *Kontrolle Offizier* from Freiwaldau. 'By the time he arrived,' recalled Alec, 'we were getting quite cocky having won the first round and we said we were not going to work until an officer from the main camp at Lamsdorf was summoned to resolve the dispute.' The *Kontrolle Offizier* was having none of this. 'If you are going on strike,' he declared, 'it might as well be a hunger strike.' He ordered the guards to remove all food from the billet and bolt the doors.

Bill McGuinness was determined, however, to keep going. 'I want you to lie on your beds, not move unless you have to and just take it easy,' he said. 'We have just got to sit it out.' For three days nothing happened, but finally a Lamsdorf officer turned up to haul the POWs back to Lamsdorf. 'He called us all sorts of things such as saboteurs and communists and Lord knows what,' recalled Alec. 'We were highly incorrigible and we would go back to the main camp and from there we should all be sent back down the mines.'

Beneath the bluster, however, Lamsdorf's new commandant, Lieutenant Colonel Josef Messner, had conceded defeat. Messner had run brutal *Stalag*s in Lithuania and he continued to ill-treat Russian POWs at Lamsdorf, yet his attitude to British POWs was different. On 27 February, the day after the Lamsdorf officer's visit, a platoon of *Landesschützen-Bataillon* 438 4th Company guards from Freiwaldau marched into Setzdorf with bayonets fixed to escort the mutinous POWs to Lamsdorf. Alec felt proud: 'There were sixty-seven of us and though we were unarmed we rated a complete platoon of thirty armed German guards to take us back to the main camp.' Word got around, and when the Setzdorf strikers were marched along the snow-covered road through the camp 'people were lining up on the other side of the wire, cheering us as we arrived'.

Messner was not amused. 'I cannot say we were very popular when we arrived back,' recalled 'Laurie' Lawrence. 'Here we were, scruffy, hungry and rebellious.' Most strikers were led into Number 26 compound, but Messner and his *Abwehr* intelligence officers, Captain Görlich and Major Birkhoff, had other ideas for the ringleaders and dispatched Bill and Alec to the new *Straflager* in the camp's north-west corner. Bill, as *Vertrauensmann*, was sentenced to ten days' solitary confinement, while Alec, as number two, got a week. They were, however, happy to do their time. 'We had,' declared Alec, 'won our strike.' The Germans, meanwhile, improved conditions at Setzdorf – when Swiss officials visited E173 the following September, the POWs said conditions were 'reasonably good' and made no complaints about food. The strikers had triumphed.

Chapter 21

'I Want to Be Off'

In some ways, the Lamsdorf to which Alec returned in 1944 was grimly similar to the *Stalag* he left in 1941. Soon after their return, some E173 men were standing near the wire when they saw 'walking corpses' in an adjacent compound housing Russian labourers. They were in a state, thought Lawrence, that 'had to be seen to be believed'. As the British peered through the wire, half a dozen Russians emerged from a hut carrying a corpse towards a burial pit. As this pathetic party staggered forward, Whitehouse threw them a cigarette. Lawrence watched as the body was dropped 'while its erstwhile bearers literally tore at each other for the unexpected treasure that came their way'. The British were appalled, but the sentry in the nearest watchtower roared with laughter.

In other ways, the Lamsdorf of 1944 was different. The British camp, re-named Stalag 344, was better organized, its polyglot community attempting to simulate civilian life despite the barbed wire and machine-gun towers. Alongside the Brits there were Sikhs and Gurkhas, Maoris, Canadians, Free French, Spanish Republicans, Belgians, Poles, Czechs, Estonians and Lithuanians, Australasians, Arabs, Palestinian Jews, Rhodesians, Afrikaners and black Africans. There were even a few Russians rescued by South Africans briefly billeted in the Russian camp prior to registration. Stunned by the Russians' suffering, they clothed some in British uniforms, smuggled them into the British camp saying they were monoglot Afrikaners and provided them with an Afrikaans-speaking spokesman. One inmate thought Lamsdorf felt like 'a European seaport city' with 'the spit and polish of the regular British Army superimposed'. The camp had its own lingo, a blend of Cockney and German plus Americanisms and French introduced by Dieppe Canadians.

The camp was less overcrowded: POWs no longer slept on the lowest of the three-tier bunks and each man had two blankets. Quantities of Red Cross parcels and medical supplies were healthy; the POWs cultivated vegetables and flowers; most barracks had sufficient water; showers were available once a fortnight. Lamsdorf's education classes had course materials from London. The theatre's repertoire ranged from Shakespeare to modern comedies. In 1944, the most poignant production was Journey's End, J.C. Sherriff's drama about Great War trench life.

Celebrations were often fuelled by illicit alcohol. The German ration was four litres of beer per prisoner per month, yet POWs would supplement this by making schnapps in home-made stills from a mash of potato-peelings, rotten vegetables and Red Cross raisins, with boot polish added to provide 'some kick'.

On the sports fields, they gathered to compete in quasi-international soccer and rugby, boxing, wrestling, American football and baseball. For the big games, virtually the entire POW population and off-duty guards would gather to watch from stadium-style seating improvised from benches and tables. During the cricket season, Lamsdorf played host to 'test matches' lasting from 9.00am to 9.00pm. The Aussies were captained by 'Pat' Ferrero, a first-class batsman from Melbourne, while the South Africans' wicket-keeper, 'Billy' Wade, was a real-life international. The pitch, however, was so small that a boundary earned only two runs, while a conventional 'six' scored four. The wicket consisted of mats woven from Red Cross parcel string.

There was even a weekly four-page camp newspaper, the *Stimmt* ('official, accurate or timely'), typed up and exhibited on compound notice boards. Ian Sabey, in later life an airline publicist, was the first editor. Sabey filled his front page with exhortations to prisoners to behave better, thus boring camp censors into giving approval without reading the rest, leaving him free to produce inside material openly critical of the Germans.

POWs now listened to 'BBC griff' on valve sets, the first of which was brought into Lamsdorf by a guard bribed with cigarettes. It seemed to Alec that Messner was less interested in the radios themselves than in the British habit of passing news to the guards. Messner's concern was justified. In one compound, a guard kept a radio hidden in his room so he could obtain reliable information about Russian advances.

Alec was less interested in entertainment than in escape, for which he would need civilian clothes, a cover story, ID papers, German currency and information about escape routes. Released from 'clink', he sought out Lamsdorf's escape organization through Jack Myers, an old school friend captured in North Africa and one of Lamsdorf's 'cigarette barons'. Once Red Cross and personal parcels began to flow, cigarettes became the *Stalag* currency. Alec had traded in cigarettes on *Arbeitskommandos*, but the size of Lamsdorf's population created a deeper, more efficient market – and Jack Myers was a leading trader. When cigarettes were plentiful, 'prices' would inflate; when flows reduced, they would deflate. Jack ran his barony from his 'swap-shop' in Block 9, home to POWs with camp jobs such as cooks, tailors, cobblers and clerks. 'Swap-shops' were micro-businesses through which POWs traded anything from clothing to razor blades. Non-smokers would trade cigarettes for food, Sikhs would barter beef for vegetables, Palestinian Jews would exchange pork for beef, French Canadians would swap tea for coffee.

To Alec, Block 9 resembled Petticoat Lane. Stalls made from barrack tables were often covered with blankets to hide the illicit goods below such as

German bayonets, knives, cut-throat razors and radios. One Lamsdorf trader thought 'anything except freedom could be bought' with enough cigarettes. A Cockney wearing red jacket and tartan trousers, the London Scottish dress uniform, was the most picturesque trader. His speciality involved enabling POWs to repay gambling debts 'denominated' in cigarettes by diverting their army pay to his wife, who organized the UK paperwork and banked the proceeds. This trade became so popular the War Office intervened.

Myers was happy to help Alec: 'For old time's sake, he staked me to some cigarettes and some Red Cross food until such time as the next Red Cross issue came.' Myers also invited him to join a Craps game. Alec, however, said he wanted more than food, a smoke and a gamble, saying he could be useful in an escape because he spoke German. Myers said he knew an RAF sergeant who 'might be able to put something' his way. This was Alec's entrée to Lamsdorf's escape committee, which included some of the most effective break-out organizers in the *Stalag* system. First, Alec had to be vetted – his German was an asset yet it also caused suspicion. Escape committee security had been breached in 1943 and members had to be sure he was not a plant. Through Jack's contact, a flight sergeant, he met 'Mac' MacLean, a Les Fusiliers Mont-Royal sergeant major taken at Dieppe and front man for Lamsdorf's escape organization. After vetting by 'Mac', Alec was 'shunted around from pillar to post, probably through seventeen or eighteen different pairs of hands, all of whom asked little questions'.

The committee members included Sergeant Major Harry Beasley, Sergeant William Lee and Sapper Jimmy Maitland of the Royal Canadian Engineers and Essex Scottish Sergeant Major John Garswood. Like 'Mac', they were taken at Dieppe. It also included airmen such as No. 12 Squadron Warrant Officer Alister Currie, an Australian from Melbourne, Charles Bonter, a Canadian member of 16 Operational Training Unit, based at Upper Heyford, Oxfordshire, and Sergeant Glafkos Clerides, a public school-educated Cypriot rear gunner/wireless operator in 115 Squadron, flying from Marham, Norfolk, and, after the war, Cyprus's fourth president.

Currie, who was captured after his Lancaster was shot down in March 1942 during a raid on St Nazaire, was responsible for selecting the leader of the RAF's escape efforts. Bonter had ditched his damaged Wellington in the North Sea on the night 10/11 September 1942 and had been picked up after five days in a dinghy. Soon after arriving at Lamsdorf, he escaped from an *Arbeitskommando*; recaptured, he took charge of RAF escape efforts. Glafkos Clerides parachuted from his stricken Wellington over Hamburg on 26 July 1942 and was saved by some Luftwaffe ground crew from a lynch mob who thought he was Jewish. At Lamsdorf, he escaped three times, securing some Balkan passports on one of his abortive break-outs. Back in Lamsdorf, he gave them to escape committee forgers to facilitate later escapes.

One by one, Alec's interrogators pressed him on his language skills, his background and his three escape attempts. Finally, he was escorted to the Canadian compound and introduced to a tall, angular man with a guttural accent codenamed 'Big X'. This was Sergeant Larry Pals, a 42-year-old Dutch-Canadian. Though 'Big X' was junior to Lamsdorf's senior NCOs, it was clear he would make the final decision on Alec's suitability. Before he did so, he interrogated Alec one last time. How many times had he escaped and where and how? How good was his German? How good was his French? What route would he take? What would be his cover story?

Pals, who had arrived in Canada in 1928, volunteered on the outbreak of war, but superiors suspicious of his background confined him to cooking duties. When the Canadians arrived in Britain in May 1940, however, the British decided his fluency in German and French and knowledge of Europe suited him for intelligence work. On the Dieppe raid, his task was to blow the post office safe and retrieve documents showing German troop movements; but in the ensuing debacle he never made it off the beach. After their surrender, the Canadians were transported in cattle-trucks to Lamsdorf, and from the moment they marched parade-style through the camp gates singing The Yanks Are Coming, they administered a shot of adrenalin to the camp. Unlike some of the more supine British, they were eager to continue the fight and within days they were Lamsdorf's 'bad boys'.

Pals initially worked alongside Sidney Sherriff's Camp Police Force to restore discipline, ending a Scots razor gang's reign of terror over Indian and Arab POWs in their segregated compound. Working from an office in Lamsdorf's Theatre Compound, the imperturbable Sherriff led a double life. As *Hauptvertrauensmann*, he acted as a shock absorber and the principal liaison point with the Germans, signing his letters to the commandant, 'I am, Sir, yours obediently'. But he was also in overall charge of escaping. His team included his intelligence and security officer, Royal Sussex sergeant major Eric Franks, his secretary, Sergeant Peter Taylor of the Army Educational Corps, and his interpreter, Royal West Kents corporal John Broadway. These men kept tabs on escape efforts and were in charge of clandestine communications with MI9, an intelligence unit established in London by Major Norman Crockatt. Members included Airey Neave and the comedian Michael Bentine.

Sherriff began receiving coded messages from MI9 in November 1940, three months after the first sacks of POW mail arrived in London. Crockatt's messages used codes developed by MI9y, a unit led by Leslie Winterbottom, Gordon Selfridge's personal assistant, and including two Great War POWs, 'Johnny' Evans and Philip Rhodes. Evans was a Royal Flying Corps pilot who wrote *The Escaping Club*; Rhodes, a naval officer captured during the Battle of Jutland in 1916, commanded the RAF Highgate Intelligence School. This trio created 'HK', a simple yet hard-to-break code, then trained soldiers and airmen, who, if captured, could pass it on. Outgoing MI9 messages would rebut German propaganda and list partisans and escape routes, while POWs would send news about troop movements, anti-aircraft sites and traitors.

Sherriff also oversaw the receipt of illicit MI9 escape materials hidden in anything from record sleeves and chess boards to cricket bats and skittles sets. The most ingenious scheme involved Monopoly sets in which maps, compasses, metal files and currency were hidden. MI9 created fake charities to distribute the games, distinguished by a red dot on 'Free Parking', via Switzerland. Playing cards also doubled up as maps, as prisoners discovered when coded letters told them to drop them in water. Once soaked, the front of each card would separate to reveal part of an escape map underneath.

MI9's code was introduced into Lamsdorf by a travelling medic. Franks became the 'cipher man', splitting outgoing messages into sections to be sent by different POWs and, like puzzle pieces, to be reassembled by MI9 staff. POWs' letters were censored by women sent from Berlin; but they were handicapped by the fact that most had only schoolgirl English so would deluge their *Abwehr* superiors with completely innocent correspondence. Perhaps as a result, MI9's communications continued unimpeded.

Sherriff introduced Pals to his escape committee colleagues. At the time, members included Edwin Lawrence, a Londoner downed near Malta in 1941, and Flight Sergeant John Taylor-Gill, the RAF compound's senior officer. Pals was not impressed. As a result of inter-service rivalry, Lamsdorf's escape efforts were fragmented. The committee showed Pals an escape map and a forged *Ausweis* (ID card). Yet the map was inaccurate while the eagle stamp on the *Ausweis* looked, Pals declared, 'like a chicken'. For his insubordination, Pals was ordered before a court of inquiry but he armed himself with supporting evidence from a Viennese-born Palestinian POW. As a result, he was exonerated and put in charge.

Pals began by dividing the POWs' efforts by activity, not service. One group worked on getting POWs out of Lamsdorf. For this, Pals needed a tunnel, so digging commenced in Barrack 19B in the Canadian compound. The tunnel began beneath bunks pushed against the wall facing the perimeter fence and came up in bushes six metres beyond the fence, its exit covered by a trap door. POWs contributed bed boards as props, electric light was installed and ventilation provided by a pipe made from Klim tins and fixed to bellows at the entrance. The excavated earth was placed in Red Cross parcels and dumped in the nearest 'forty-holer'.

The twenty-odd tunnellers were mostly Ontario quarry workers and French Canadians from Quebec's rugged Gaspé Peninsula, but 'Ruby' Rubenstein was also involved. Unlike Alec, 'Ruby' did not hide his identity. His surname was a give-away, so unless he falsified it – a dangerous, possibly life-threatening route – he had little choice. Identified as a Jew, he had 'had more than the average British soldier to worry about' but he continued his 'war against Hitler'. He escaped from the March in 1940, but was recaptured and threatened with execution. At Lamsdorf, he became an *Arbeitskommando* escape committee head, an 'underground news service' operator and a tunneller. He 'made a pact with' himself that he would 'make the Germans' lives as unpleasant as possible' every day of his captivity. The war became a 'personal grudge fight'. Cyril Rofé, the Wellington bomb aimer/navigator, was another Jew unable to disguise his ethnicity. Born in Cairo in 1916, and educated at Bristol's Clifton College, he had worked at Vienna's Bristol Hotel but fled ten days after the *Anschluss*. Wounded when his Wellington was hit, he was identified as Jewish at a German military hospital but, like Alec, became a serial escaper. Unlike Alec, Rofé achieved a home run, reaching Britain via Russia in December 1944.

Pals' second group helped escapers stay out. As the Reich expanded and its armies became stretched, it imported millions of foreign workers. To keep track of this vast floating population, Hitler's security services introduced an array of personal documents. Thus, in addition to civilian clothes and personal papers, an escaper posing as a foreign worker needed an *Ausweis*, an *Arbeitskarte* (work permit), a *Fahrschein* (travel permit) and a ration card.

To source the necessary material, Pals instructed men such as Royal Sussex Regiment corporal Stanley Mills to volunteer for factory *Arbeitskommandos*, of which the best was E3 at Blechhammer. There, Mills and his colleagues would borrow or steal documents from foreign workers and barter Red Cross luxuries with guards and civilians in exchange for escape materials. The priorities were currency, a typewriter, a Leica camera, film and developing chemicals, paper and ink, dyes for clothing and radios. With these tasks accomplished, they would ask for transfers back to Lamsdorf. The items that made it through Lamsdorf's *Vorlager* search were then hidden in suitcases in a barrack used to store spare POW gear.

Once in Lamsdorf, the documents were copied by men more skilled than the amateurs Pals encountered on his arrival. One was Leading Seaman Gerry Holden, an Irish architecture student. Another was Essex Scottish private Alec Montroy. Part Native American, Montroy survived the war to work in advertising before moving into Manhattan's bohemian Chelsea Hotel and devoting himself to painting. In Lamsdorf his raw material consisted of two YMCA logbooks containing 130 high-quality blank pages. One became a visual diary of his captivity. The other was used to create forged passports, work permits and travel permits. He recalled:

> I never understood but certain personnel in *Stalag* VIIIB knew I was coming in and met me as our train pulled in. They knew I was an artist and I was immediately apprenticed to a Palestinian Jew, Schlomo Loewenstein, who proceeded to tutor me in the fine art of forgery – *Stalag*

style. Using indelible pencils I was soon able to make drawings of stamps, in reverse, which [with] one paper dampened by sputum, made excellent reproductions. Making identification cards and permits required great skill and time – to duplicate type – but they worked and our escape committee sent many of our comrades back to Allied lines.

After Montroy created his forged documents, German Jews from the Palestinian compound filled in the handwritten parts. The *Ausweis* needed special care. Handwriting in a police-issued *Vorläufiger Ausweis* had to be traditional, because the war had denuded police stations of young men. For a labour exchange *Arbeitsamt Ausweis*, the handwriting had to be modern, because exchanges were staffed by young women. Jews such as Loewenstein and Herbert Fellner would also compose fictitious letters from an escaper's supposed family or employer and tutor escapers in how to maintain their cover stories. Meanwhile, Judd Lawson, a New Zealand medic captured on Crete, would carve fake *Polizeiamt* and *Arbeitsamt* stamps from rubber boots, including a removable panel so the issuing town's name could be changed.

Lastly, Pals enlisted photographers to take passport-style photos. One was Bill Lawrence, a Yorkshire airman who purloined film and photographic chemicals from the *Lazarett*. He would also hide his camera in a Red Cross box to photograph guards for use in later war crimes trials. The second photographer was Ken 'Tex' Hyde, a Canadian navigator shot down in 1942. Soon after arriving at Lamsdorf, 'Tex' escaped through a hole cut in the perimeter fence during a night-time storm, but was recaptured with his partner, a Polish airman called Piotr Bakalarski, near Gogolin. The third was Stanley Mills, the fourth, Royal East Kents sergeant major Herbert Osborne. Soon, Pals' men were generating plausible documents purportedly issued by Gleiwitz's police and labour exchange, 100km south-east of Lamsdorf.

The team acquired clothing through barter with Polish workers, and civilian-style clothes were also crafted from shirts and blankets sent from home. Meanwhile, guards were bribed to provide train timetables, information about railway security and warnings of impending searches. Three proved particularly corruptible: Lamsdorf's clothing stores guard, a letters censor called Gatis and an *Abwehr* interpreter, Sonderführer Jansen. Working through an intermediary, 'Tex' Hyde 'purchased' from this trio 15 rolls of film, 10 radio valves and 300 sheets of photographic paper during 1944.

Each evening, committee members would toil away creating documents, copying maps and turning uniforms into civilian suits, constantly on alert for the arrival of a guard or a 'ferret', a guard trained to spot illicit activity. At this point, the lookout man, or 'stooge', would shout 'Careful! Bandits!' or 'Goons in the block!' Everything would then be hidden and the guard's arrival greeted by jeers and catcalls. Once he had moved to the next barrack, the escape materials would reappear and work would resume.

Pals' work impressed colleagues. 'Sergeant Pals *was* the committee in *Stalag* VIIIB,' thought Lance Corporal Daniel Green, a commando held at Lamsdorf from 1942. 'Before his arrival there was almost nothing.' An early Pals-sponsored escape occurred on Sunday, 26 September 1943, when Colonel Charles Howie, a South African posing as a Dutch engineer, climbed from the tunnel exit with Tibor Weinstein, a Palestinian Jew. For the next few weeks a stream of POWs followed them, with Pals insisting that one in each pair be an 'important' POW such as a pilot, navigator, officer or technician, while the other had to speak German.

Fearing the tunnel would be discovered, Pals rationed its use, but he did help a parallel escape group sponsoring men considered of less value. This was led by Ted Evans, a Royal Army Ordnance Corps quartermaster sergeant from Stratford-on-Avon, and included Royal Scots sergeant John Hamilton, Staff Sergeant Francis Freller, Sergeant John Hill, Sergeant Phil Burridge and Specialist Royal Engineer Alexander Macdonald, the lead tunneller. Freller was a Palestinian captured on Crete in 1941, Hill was a Layforce commando and Burridge was an airman downed during a raid on Essen during 25/26 February 1942.

Pals' pessimism was justified when prisoners were ordered on to the sports fields one day while guards searched every barrack. He had feared the Germans would plant informants to foil escape attempts. That they succeeded became clear when guards searching Barrack 19B headed straight for the bunks over the tunnel entrance, shifted them aside and lifted the lid. Other losses Pals blamed on the 'stoolpigeon' included a camera, a typewriter and a radio.

The commandant now doubled the number of guards, increasing night-time patrols and equipping watchtowers with stronger searchlights. Pals, meanwhile, decided to make his own escape attempt, accompanying Ian Thompson, a Queen's Royal captain captured in North Africa and serial escaper.

Their first break-out failed when they were heard trying to cut through the perimeter fence, but soon after New Year 1944, they made another attempt using a second tunnel. Starting beneath a toilet bucket, this ran to an exit in the fields beyond the fence. Lacking supports, it was simply a hole through which escapers would crawl, but Pals decided he and Thompson would use it alongside ten others. At 11.00pm on Wednesday, 17 May, Pals wriggled through the tunnel and at a pre-arranged signal – accordion music – pushed out the mud plug blocking the exit and ran towards the woods beyond, followed by Thompson. Two men followed, but a guard spotted the fifth man and fired at him, causing the remaining seven to abandon the attempt.

Pals and Thompson headed 6km south to Nieder Hermsdorf, from where they travelled by local train to Liegnitz, then by express to Metz in Lorraine. Pals had been told by War Office intelligence staff in 1942 about a partisan there codenamed 'Joseph', supposedly the son of a Metz café proprietor but in reality an Italian called Lorenzini. Unfortunately, Lorenzini said he was being watched so could no longer help escapers. This was bad news, because other Lamsdorf escapers were relying on 'Joseph'. Reluctantly, Pals sacrificed his escape attempt so Thompson might continue; if the Italian agreed to help Thompson, he, Pals, would surrender and return to Lamsdorf to warn colleagues.

With the deal agreed, Pals boarded a train and waited for the inevitable request for papers. He was duly arrested, held in the *Stalag* XIIF *Straflager* at Forbach, tortured and returned, after D-Day, to Lamsdorf, where the commandant sentenced him to four weeks' solitary confinement in the *Straflager*, back under Ukraine Joe's harsh regime. Pals said he had already served time at Forbach, to which the commandant replied, 'Yes, but you are no ordinary prisoner of war, Mr Pals.' Meanwhile, Lorenzini introduced Thompson to the Resistance, and for a few weeks he trained partisans before making contact with Allied soldiers as they advanced through France.

Once Pals was comfortable Alec was a suitable escape candidate, he was sent for one last meeting with a senior airman. This was Bill Harrison, an Australian member of 16 OTU. Like Charles Bonter, his active war ended during the 10/11 September 1942 raid on Düsseldorf. He led the RAF Escape Committee from late 1943 after a recaptured escaper revealed the organization had a camera and Bonter was a member. Bonter was told he would not be punished if he surrendered the camera. He gave nothing away but was put under surveillance, so Harrison took over.

Harrison told Alec he would receive documents and money if he took an airman with him – on one condition. 'Our man,' said Harrison, 'will have first pick of everything. If you are walking through a door and that means walking to safety, he goes first and you go after him. If walking through a door means walking into danger, then you will go first.' Why, Alec asked himself, should he play 'second fiddle' when his German would be critical in the escape. To an extent, he was suffering from the inter-service rivalry that bedevilled Army-RAF relations at Lamsdorf. Infantrymen would belittle the RAF's grammar-school types as 'Brylcreem boys' or 'mummy's little darlings'. Although class was not an issue for Alec, he resented the lack of air cover at Calais; he had suffered the privations of the March while captured airmen travelled to Lamsdorf by lorry and passenger trains; and as a mere rifleman he had to work while airmen idled away their time because all aircrew were NCOs exempted from work under the Geneva Convention.

Yet Alec warmed to the men of Block 5, Lamsdorf's RAF compound. As an ex-public schoolboy Territorial, he felt at ease with the volunteer 'boys in blue' whose activities featured frequently in BBC reports as, night after night, Wellingtons, Halifaxes and, latterly, Lancasters degraded German industry, creating shortages and undermining civilian morale. A high note was Operation Chastise, the 617 Squadron attack on German dams on 16 and 17 May 1943. Using bouncing bombs, the 'Dambusters' breached the Möhne and Edersee dams, causing the Ruhr Valley to flood and putting vital power stations, industrial water supplies and communications out of action.

Critically, Lamsdorf's airmen were full of ideas for escapes. If Alec went out alone, he would face 'the ever present feeling of being a hunted animal', in the words of Aidan Crawley, an airman who became a politician and broadcaster after the war. As one of a pair, he would have a partner to keep his spirits up.

Chapter 22

'Twiggy MacDonald'

Shortly after his escape committee vetting, Alec was introduced to his intended partner, a Scotsman with dark hair and a moustache who resembled the actor Ronald Colman. To the guards, this was Private John Alexander MacDonald of the Seaforth Highlanders. But, as Alec discovered when the pair were left alone, the man in Army khaki was really Flight Sergeant Bob 'Twiggy' Hawthorn, a 23-year-old 103 Squadron front gunner/bomb aimer, who had bailed out of his Halifax over the Belgian/Dutch border on Monday, 5 October 1942.

The Germans said they segregated airmen because the Geneva Convention excused them from work. The real reason was that they wanted to reduce their chances of escape. An Army private could only achieve so much after reaching home; but a liberated airman could return to the night skies over Germany and do further damage. Consequently, airmen were banned from *Arbeitskommandos*; but an identity swap offered an airman a potential passage to freedom, while an infantryman gained a rest from work. Swapping with a 'Winger' was risky, however: if he committed a crime during an escape, this would be listed on the infantryman's *Personalkarte*. Yet this did not deter MacDonald. Before the switch, 'Twiggy' spent hours learning MacDonald's life story. Having exchanged details, the two men undertook to correspond with each other's families. Finally, they swapped identity tags, clothing, correspondence from home and other documents, and 'Twiggy' became John Alexander MacDonald, service number 2822277, POW number 10721, taking MacDonald's bunk. MacDonald, meanwhile, went to the RAF compound as Bob Hawthorn. The same day, a POW working in the *Vorlager* switched the photographs on their registration cards.

As they rehearsed their plans, Bob told Alec his story. Bob's childhood home was a schoolhouse on the Galloway coast, where he dreamed of being an aviator. He joined up just after his sixteenth birthday, and RAF Elsham Wolds became his home in 1942. His squadron comprised about 140 airmen and 1,400 ground support staff. Initially, 103 Squadron flew single-engine Fairey Battles, then twin-engine Wellingtons, but it was re-equipped with four-engine Halifax Mark II bombers in 1942. This meant the five-man Wellington crews were reformed as sevens – pilot, navigator, flight engineer, wireless operator and three gunners, front, mid and rear.

Bob's machine took its maiden 103 Squadron flight on 4 August. Its identity was W1216 PM-Q – 'Q-Queenie' to its crew. Halifaxes were larger and more deadly than Wellingtons. With four Rolls Royce Merlin engines spread along its 99-foot wingspan, Queenie had a 265mph top speed and a 1,100-mile range. Halifaxes did, however, have handling problems, as Queenie's crew discovered during the three weeks of practice flights in which they got to know their new machine. Training complete, the crew joined raids on the Ruhr – 'Happy Valley' in airman lingo – under Wing Commander Robert Carter, who had led a daylight raid on the German battleship *Gneisenau* and continued to lead from the front, flying frequently on missions.

The 5 October operation was a modest run and not all planes were involved. Take-off was late, and Queenie's crew were looking forward to completing the short trip and being back in time for an early breakfast. Ahead of raids, the crews would assemble wearing white sweaters beneath their blue uniforms, on the collar of which was a whistle to attract attention should they ditch at sea. First, an intelligence officer would explain the plan, then a meteorologist would discuss weather conditions. A record would be playing on the mess gramophone, often Tristesse, a 1939 song set to Chopin's Étude No. 3 in E major. The lyrics seemed fitting:

So deep is the night.
No moon tonight,
No friendly star
To guide me with its light
Be still my heart,
Silent lest my love should be returning
From the world, far apart.

Most men took off full of fear; in 1942, a fifth of RAF bomber crews would not return, and the war's ultimate death rate reached 44 per cent (55,000 men), while 9,000 were captured. These casualty rates approximated to the losses during the Battle of the Somme, yet the crews would hide their fear beneath a mask of nonchalance as they contemplated those who had gone before but not returned.

In 1942, airmen received evade-and-escape lectures more sophisticated than the minimal advice Alec received in 1940, based on information from home-runners such as Royal Artilleryman William Dothie, a Calais veteran, and Basil Embry. The airmen were also kitted out with MI9 escape packs containing concentrated food, chocolate, silk maps disguised as scarves, miniature compasses disguised as buttons or cufflinks or hidden in pipes or pens, hacksaw blades, 'wakey-wakey' pills and foreign currency. Great War pilot Christopher Clayton-Hutton, a real-life version of Ian Fleming's Q, invented aids such as left-hand threads for button compasses (if a German tried to unscrew them they would tighten) and boots that became shoes when their leggings were removed.

Queenie, Bob told Alec, carried eight men on 5 October. The captain was Ken Edwards, George Green was flight engineer, Bob as front gunner operated two Browning machine guns, Doug Giddens, a New Zealander, was radio operator and Gordon Mellor was navigator. Harry Richards was mid-upper gunner, also with two Brownings, while Norman McMaster was rear-gunner with four Brownings – the 'Tail-end Charlie' charged with watching out for German night-fighters. The eighth man was Mark Mead, a recently qualified pilot. Mead's plane, 'R-Robert', was surplus to requirements that night but Carter suggested he join Edwards for 'a bit more experience'.

At 5.00pm, Edwards lifted Queenie off the runway in driving rain and flew south to the Channel then east towards Aachen. Once over land, Edwards ran into flak and went into a corkscrew manoeuvre, diving to port then climbing to starboard, to evade searchlights. When the plane reached Germany, Bob could see the raid was running into trouble. For best results, bombing had to be concentrated, yet the planes ahead were dropping bombs across a wide area, possibly confused by decoy fires below. Edwards flew over what he thought was the target area twice, releasing his bombs on the second run, then turning Queenie for home. The flak decreased, but with the moon bright the crew sat nervously in silence. Then, Bob heard four dreaded words over the intercom from McMaster: 'Fighter! Fighter! Below port!' Before he finished speaking, shells from a Messerschmitt Bf 110 tore into Queenie's fabric. The Messerschmitt pilot, Hans Autenrieth, belonged to *Nachtjagdgeschwader 1*, Germany's most successful night-fighter squadron.

McMaster opened fire the moment he saw the Messerschmitt, but it was an unequal contest. A skilled Messerschmitt pilot had advantages of speed and manoeuvrability, and neither Edwards' weaving and diving nor McMaster's gunfire could shake Autenrieth off. One burst of cannon fire wounded McMaster, a second set the port engines on fire, a third damaged a starboard engine. Edwards realized Queenie would not make it home. With the plane at only 1,500 feet and with the Messerschmitt still following, he gave the order, 'Parachute! Parachute! Jump! Jump!'

The crew scrambled to bail out. Mellor was nearest the escape hatch and was thus first out. Bob was next, followed by Green and Mead, who left the cockpit after clipping on Edwards' parachute. In the rear, McMaster could not extricate himself. Although wounded, Giddens tried to help McMaster, but the turret was jammed so he returned to the main escape hatch and dropped out, followed by Richards.

At this point, Queenie was still 900 feet from the ground so Edwards could have climbed through his escape hatch, leaving McMaster to die. He chose, instead, to try to save his colleague, but it was too late, and both were killed as the plane crashed. The noise awakened people in farmhouses nearby as

Queenie's ammunition exploded. The impact was such that farmers press-ganged into retrieving components the next day had to dig down two metres to discover anything of interest to the Germans. They wanted to examine the engines; the civilians were more interested in souvenirs. One found McMaster's watch, with his initials, NMcM, and the date of his 21st birthday, 1.10.31, on the back. It had stopped at 10.47pm, the moment the plane hit the ground.

Of the crew who bailed out, Green died crashing into a house but the others survived. As Bob descended, he could see Queenie plunging towards the ground and a curve in the Albert Canal, silver in the moonlight to the east and north. He was supposed to count to ten before opening his parachute but was so close to the ground he pulled his ripcord the moment he was clear of Queenie's tail.

Mellor's descent took him into some trees and his landing was sufficiently noisy to set dogs barking in a nearby house, but he found a road and headed south. At one point he heard movement and froze, thinking it was a German soldier. In reality, it was Bob. 'I dropped to my knees so my sounds stopped,' he recalled. 'Then his sound stopped. We did this two or three times but eventually Bob moved away. Then I got up and started walking south. We had been close enough to be in hearing distance of each other but each of us thought the other one was the "oppo".'

Mellor was rescued by Belgian resistance members who took him to Brussels, the first leg of his journey to freedom. The others were not so lucky. Having failed to make contact with Mellor, Bob decided to take a risk when he next heard sounds in the darkness. This time he let out a whistle. Initially, there was no response so he whistled again and elicited in reply a few notes from Hitler Has Only Got One Ball. This had to be an Englishman – and so it was: Mark Mead.

At dawn, the pair snacked on chocolate and Horlicks tablets then headed south through some woods. After a few miles, they saw an isolated house and decided to approach the inhabitants. Speaking schoolboy French, Mead explained they were RAF airmen and asked for help. 'No,' was the answer in broken English, 'but I can take you to someone who can.' This conjured up visions of the Resistance. Such hopes were dashed, however, when the family escorted them to the local mayor. He appeared friendly, serving coffee and reminiscing about 1940, but the airmen became increasingly anxious and Mead said they were leaving. 'Leave? You can't leave,' the mayor replied, moving to the door and locking it. 'If I let you escape the Germans will shoot me. The whole village knows you are here. I would risk my life.'

Shortly afterwards, the increasingly acrimonious discussion was ended when two lorries and two motorcycles with sidecars pulled up outside, disgorging a dozen soldiers. They had, it emerged, been summoned by the mayor from the Sint-Truiden airbase. The two airmen were marched out, seated on motorcycle pillion seats and driven to the base. The next morning, they were ordered into a tarpaulin-covered lorry and told to sit. There were no seats, but in the gloom they made out three coffins and moved forward to sit on them. At this point, one soldier pointed at the coffins and said with a smirk, '*Kamerad, dein Kamerad.*' Thus, they knew three of the crew were dead.

Of the other survivors, Giddens was captured on 10 October and taken to Sint-Truiden, while Richards was taken to a military hospital in Maastricht, having broken both legs on landing. As for Mellor, Bob received news at Lamsdorf that he had got back to England, although only later did he learn the details of Mellor's passage along 'Dédée' de Jongh's *Réseau Comète* (Comet Line) by way of safe houses in Paris, Tours, Bordeaux and Bayonne, 20km short of the Spanish border. One of his last hiding places was in Anglet outside Bayonne, home of 'Tante Go', a Belgian whose real name was Elvire de Greef-Berlemont. While her husband and father interpreted for the Germans, 'Tante Go' and her daughter would shepherd escapers over the border. De Jongh's father was betrayed and executed, while de Jongh herself was arrested and sent to Ravensbrück. She told the Germans she had created the Comet Line yet she survived, perhaps because the Gestapo thought she was too young at twenty-six to be its mastermind.

Mellor was 'missing in action' for so long that his friends were shocked when he reappeared in November at Elsham Wolds. He had been considered dead and for some time 'had only been mentioned in a regretful sort of way'. His laconic humour was, however, unchanged. This 'shade' of Mellor glanced around the mess, then addressed his colleagues: 'Has anyone seen my great-coat? I left it hanging here the night we went missing.'

While Mellor was being shepherded down the Comet Line, Bob and Mead were taken by lorry to Liège, put on a train to Frankfurt-am-Main, then driven to a transit camp near Oberursel and reunited with Giddens. This was *Durchgangslager der Luftwaffe* (*Dulag Luft* for short), a camp established to extract secrets from captured airmen. Its cell blocks contained hidden microphones and had insulated walls to prevent inmates communicating – although that did not stop airmen banging out Morse code on the pipes. Lieutenant Colonel Erich Killinger was commandant, while Major Heinz Junge and Lieutenant Heinrich Eberhardt led interrogations. All three later were convicted of torturing prisoners.

On arrival at 'the Hotel', as *Dulag Luft*'s permanent RAF staff described it, Bob was strip-searched and supplied with pyjamas and a dressing gown, a Red Cross parcel, a razor, toothbrush, soap and towel. He was then placed in a cell six feet by twelve containing a bed, table, chair, bell to call for a guard and barred window overlooking a central yard. An orderly, he was told, would escort him to the lavatory. In the evening he was served a meagre meal with wooden cutlery. The following morning, he was taken to the interrogation block and introduced to a man in civilian clothes claiming to be from the Red Cross. He gave Bob a postcard to fill in so his family would know he was alive; but Bob's suspicions were aroused when the man asked about his background. In the lectures at Elsham Wolds, the rubric had been: disclose only name, rank and service number.

Over two days, Luftwaffe interrogators probed Bob about his career, his squadron, his crew, the target on 5 October and his plane's bomb-load. Then he was driven with Mead and Giddens to Frankfurt, where they boarded a train heading east. The windows were boarded up, but through a slit Bob peered at trains going past, their locomotives bearing the recently-introduced slogan, 'Wheels must roll for victory' – indicating Germany's growing logistics problems. Each morning, the men were given sausage and bread, and the train would stop twice a day so they could relieve themselves beside the tracks. Finally, on Thursday, 15 October, the train pulled into Annahof and the trio were marched to Lamsdorf.

After a night in a grim barrack for temporary inmates, Bob was inducted into Lamsdorf life. It was a less malign place than when Alec arrived two years previously, partly as a result of changes made by Colonel Ludwig von Poschinger, a Great War artilleryman and commandant for part of 1942. Poschinger, aged 52, was no Nazi thug. His family were Bavarian aristocrats who owned a fine glassware manufacturer, and their friends included Adolf Victor von Koerber, an anti-Nazi journalist who was sent to the Sachsenhausen concentration camp after the 20 July 1944 Hitler bomb plot. The bespectacled Poschinger was no liberal, and he backed his guards when they beat Palestinian Jews. But he did relax the *Straflager* regime. During Alec's periods in 'clink' in 1941, he was totally isolated, but Poschinger allowed the inmates books, letter-forms and postcards. He also cracked down on ill-treatment on *Arbeitskommandos* and allowed each Lamsdorf inmate a hot shower every ten days.

After being deloused, Mead was registered as POW 27209, Giddens as 27225 and Bob as 27226. Then the Queenie trio were issued with cutlery, two blankets, a straw-filled mattress and bed boards and led to the RAF compound, located far from the perimeter fence to deter tunnelling. At the entrance, they were welcomed by smiling faces in blue uniforms asking for news from home.

A hut with tin sheets, cardboard and sacking substituting for glass in most windows was to be Bob's home for the next eighteen months. The inside was a shock, the air polluted by tobacco and wood smoke and sweaty flesh. The dim light from the few weak bulbs not removed by the Germans revealed, in Richard Pape's words, 'a seething mass of humanity' as hut inhabitants jostled, shouted and swore. Drying clothes were strung overhead, while twigs, Red Cross boxes, tins and other rubbish lay against the walls. Each bunk had begun with ten boards but these were reduced to four as the rest were plundered for firewood. This left just enough support to prevent the men above from crashing on to those below but did not prevent dust and dirt drifting down through the three tiers. The barrack was 'bedlam in a dustbin'.

The old-timers had a grim surprise for Bob – their hands were tied with twine. This was part of a German collective punishment of non-working prisoners. Hitler had been planning a showdown over POW treatment, thinking this would weaken Churchill's hold on power. The Dieppe Raid gave him his chance because the raiders had tied prisoners' hands to prevent them escaping, on the grounds that the Geneva Convention allowed such temporary measures. Some prisoners had been shot as they tried to raise the alarm, while others had died in the cross-fire. None had been executed, but this did not stop Hitler, at that point gassing millions of Jews a year, from claiming the Allies had broken the Convention.

On 2 September, Berlin said troops taken at Dieppe would be bound unless Britain apologized, a demand repeated following a British commando raid on Sark on 3 October in which four bound prisoners were shot trying to escape. Churchill's reply was that an equal number of Germans would be bound if Allied POWs were. Hitler then said three Allied POWs would be bound for every German, taking the number of manacled Allied POWs to 4,128, including Alec's company commander, Major Austin-Brown, and his platoon commander, Bobby Allen.

Lamsdorf POWs were first aware of something unusual at morning *Appell* on Thursday, 8 October. The day began with the usual barrack-room ribaldry – 'Hands off cocks! Put on socks!' was one wake-up call. Yet having been woken by their guards, the men found themselves staring at fresh troops carrying hand-grenades and submachine guns, while armoured cars lined the road through the middle of the camp. These were not garrison soldiers. With the death's head insignia on their collars, they were Waffen-SS troops withdrawn from Russia.

The *Appell* began normally, with the POWs falling in and being counted. Then, the new commandant, Captain Rudolf Gylek, portly in his gold-braided uniform, with a cigar between his fingers, marched into the compound with his adjutant and 'American Joe', the interpreter, and summoned John Taylor-Gill as compound senior officer and a Jewish interpreter from the Palestinian compound. With SS soldiers standing behind, Gylek read a declaration, after which the Jewish interpreter translated. Atrocities had been committed at Dieppe, so Canadians, Jews and airmen would be punished by having their hands tied from morning to night. To Goebbels, conveniently ignoring the Luftwaffe crews that blitzed British cities, the RAF bomber crew were *Terrorflieger* (terrorist airmen) or *Luftgangsters* (air gangsters). At first there was silence, then one airman giggled, setting off waves of laughter across the compound. But as the laughter subsided, 'Ukraine Joe' ordered the POWs to line up and cross their wrists in front, while SS troops tied their hands with twine. The guards returned to untie the men so they could eat their midday soup and visit the 'forty-holer'. They were then tied up again until 9.00pm.

For weeks, this daily ritual was repeated for 2,300 Lamsdorf inmates. Each day, guards would patrol the huts to check the ties remained in place and prevent men from lying on their bunks. There was, however, insufficient room for them to sit, so some had to stand or walk around outside in the cold. Any man caught loosening his bindings would be forced to stand outside the guardroom for an hour or two with his nose and toes touching the wall. If he collapsed he would be beaten and made to begin his punishment again.

In addition, Gylek restricted Red Cross parcels, cigarettes and mail and banned sport, entertainment and education classes. For a while, Bob subsisted on meagre German rations, and, with blankets and fuel in short supply, his conditions that winter were as severe as Alec experienced in 1940.

Soon after New Year 1943, the twine was replaced with metal handcuffs, but their chains, at about 16ins, were so short most normal activities remained impossible. There was, however, some amelioration in spring 1943 when Gylek introduced handcuffs with 2ft chains and reinstated entertainment activities. The new handcuffs allowed Bob sufficient room to put his hands in his pockets and keep them warm. Then he discovered the locks were so primitive they could be prised open with the keys that opened Klim milk tins. Thus, immediately after morning *Appell*, airmen would release each other; but should a guard appear, they could thrust their hands into their pockets and still appear to be shackled.

Some turned the collective punishment into 'goon-baiting' opportunities. In the early weeks, POWs would remove the twine once they had been bound, then rejoin the back of the line, lengthening the tying process by hours. New tricks were developed with the handcuffs. One involved two prisoners entangling their chains as if in a conjuring trick; another was to hide handcuffs before evening *Appell*. This would result in tirades from the guards, who would run around waving their revolvers and whacking POWs with the flats of their bayonets until the 'missing' handcuffs were found.

After a few months, however, chains became a formality. As long as they were distributed each morning and returned each evening, Gylek appeared comfortable. In March, he cut the number of chained men to 1,800, freeing 500 airmen and 87 infantrymen, and in November, following concessions by Churchill, the punishment was dropped as part of a broader relaxation of regulations. Previously, airmen might only attend specially-arranged church services and plays, but now they were permitted to wander freely through the camp, take part in entertainment and sport and attend education classes.

Lamsdorf had, however, become 'shockingly overcrowded' according to a Swiss inspector. Following the Allies' invasion of Italy, the Wehrmacht transferred POWs from Italian camps, with 5,000 arriving in Lamsdorf over the autumn, an influx that lifted its population to 13,000, more than double the capacity the Swiss deemed reasonable. Wounded and diseased POWs over-whelmed the *Lazarett*; rations were cut; some men slept on bare concrete without blankets; showers were cut to one per month, and drinking water had to be brought from outside the camp. As a result, Swiss diplomats protested to Berlin, while Dr Paul Ruggli, a member of the Swiss delegation in Germany, reported to London: 'In comparison with the usual average standard of camps for British prisoners, this *Stalag* must be classified as a bad one.'

Apart from manacling, squalor and hunger, the Queenie trio's biggest enemy was boredom. Harry Levy, a Jewish airman who had previously been held in solitary confinement, said of Lamsdorf in his book, *The Dark Side of the Sky*:

> It was almost as if the recent past had been blotted out. All that had become an irrelevant memory. That life is now as if it had never been and in its place other preoccupations: the next parcel, the next letter, dirt, hunger, discomfort and over all above all the endless tedium; each day the same with no sight of the end, the same faces, the same conversations, the same squalid routine.

Distractions included endless bridge games and labyrinthine story-telling, each man trying to outdo his neighbour with tales of burning and crashing planes. At worst, boredom led to insanity – Lamsdorf's airmen were more at risk of becoming '*Stalag*-happy' than working POWs. Some would weep at night; others would wake from nightmares, screaming 'Jump, jump, jump!' One undergraduate airman refused to leave his bed and ended up lying in his own excrement. Another attempted suicide after being caught stealing food. In response, a kindly officer presented him with a guitar, sheet music and instructions on how to play. At first, he appeared trapped in a fantasy world, giggling as he strummed away. Eventually, however, he recovered and even formed his own little band.

Many airmen got involved in theatre, and Lamsdorf's star actor was Denholm Elliott, who had studied drama before becoming a Halifax wireless operator/gunner. Hit by flak during a raid on U-boat pens on the Baltic coast in September 1942, his plane ditched at sea and only three men survived. At Lamsdorf, Elliott put on Shakespeare plays, lending a professional gloss to the efforts of those around him. Initially, everything was improvised, with actors fashioning costumes from paper. But the Germans, claiming Shake-speare was a proto-Nazi, lent Elliott Breslau opera house costumes for his 1943 production of Twelfth Night and provided transport so the production could tour other camps.

Airmen knew their chances of a break would be greater from an *Arbeitskom-mando*, where security was weaker. Their inspiration was Douglas Bader, who was held at Lamsdorf – without his artificial legs – after an escape from *Stalag Luft* III. In Lamsdorf, he wanted to cause maximum difficulties for the guards, goon-baiting and organizing escapes. Two months before Bob's arrival, Bader was sent to Colditz, but his influence lived on. 'Escape, escape, escape,' he would say. 'Never mind hunger pains, discomfort or any other agony. Let escape become your passion, your one and only obsession until you finally reach home.' To one acquiescent airman, Bader shouted, 'Blast you and your kind! You're getting paid while you're in captivity. Earn that money. If you get recaptured twenty times you're helping the war effort by making the Germans spend time, money and manpower in organizing manhunts.'

Spring and summer were the escape seasons, so the activity became known as 'The Airmen's Spring Handicap'. Rofé described the atmosphere as infantrymen replaced airmen via identity swaps:

> With the approach of spring, escape fever got a real hold on the compound. Hundreds of enthusiasts were doing their daily circuits and in every barrack there were men copying maps, planning routes and laying in all necessary stores. Every day there were new faces in the compound. Enquiry always elicited the same answer. 'Oh, I'm so-and-so now. He's doing a bunk.'

The 1943 'Spring Handicap' was constrained by post-Dieppe chaining and other restrictions, but Bob decided to enter in 1944. His escape with Alec involved the pair persuading Reg Charters to send them to the same *Arbeitskommando*. Thus, they were both sent to E606 at Jägerndorf, a Sudeten town with good railway connections. Bob spoke little German and had no idea of life beyond Lamsdorf, so Alec made the critical decisions in planning their escape. Pals opposed Switzerland because successful escapers would be 'put under the protection of the International Red Cross' to live 'the life of Riley', which 'wouldn't be good to anybody', preferring the southern route to Yugoslavia. But Alec decided he and Bob would travel by train to southern Austria posing as Czech workers, then cross into Italy on foot. This route was taken by numerous escapers following the Italian armistice.

In 1944, foreign workers were a commonplace sight; 7,000,000 – including 250,000 Czechs – were propping up Germany's economy, making weapons, building forts, repairing railways and roads and bringing in the harvest. Posing as Czech had benefits. While many Czechs spoke German, few Germans spoke Czech, an *Untermenschen* language, and Alec could use local knowledge gained at Setzdorf. Travelling by passenger train required him to be convincing in German, but it was the quickest way to distance themselves from Jägerndorf, and German trains were full of *Fremdarbeiter* (foreign workers). Once in Italy, he hoped to find partisans to guide them towards the Allies, who by this time had reached Ortona on the east coast. Alec would say he and Bob were employed by *Organisation Todt*, the Nazi construction monolith headed by Albert Speer, Hitler's armaments minister, and were heading for the Adriatic port of Trieste to work on fortifications designed to prevent an Allied landing. This was a reasonable cover story, for in 1944 *Organisation Todt* employed 1,400,000 foreigners.

First, they needed forged papers, and this meant visiting the secret studios of Bill Lawrence or 'Tex' Hyde for passport-style photos. 'Tex', who had been a photographer in Calgary, would clothe escapers in a jacket and tie hidden beneath his bunk before photographing them. Then Fellner's draughtsmen would fill in each man's travel permit and ID cards. The police *Ausweis* contained surname, first name, date and place of birth, nationality, occupation, hair colour, eye colour, address, place of issue – Gleiwitz – and date. Then they would forge the signature of Gleiwitz's police chief on both documents and the photo would be glued into the *Ausweis*. Finally, the *Ausweis* would be stamped with the forged image of an eagle astride a swastika.

Chapter 23

A New Place ... and New Faces

On Monday, 6 March 1944, a clerk typed out a schedule of POWs to be sent to *Arbeitskommando* E606 in Jägerndorf. Alongside Alec, the list included Les Birch and 'Duggie' Hepburn, other Setzdorf veterans such as 'Laurie' Lawrence and John Lockyer, two Australians, 'Speed' Alcock and Bill McBride, Fred Johnson, the Calais artilleryman, and Ken Viles and Harry Excell, also artillerymen. It did not include Bill McGuinness, whom the Germans segregated from his fellow strikers and put to work in Oppeln's rail yard, where he continued to make mischief, at one point being threatened with being shot.

On the morning of his departure, Alec was escorted into the *Vorlager* for his exit search, with his forged documents well hidden. Typically, would-be escapers would secrete contraband in underwear deep in their kitbags, while placing cigarettes and soap on top to tempt the guards. The search went smoothly, and Alec marched towards Annahof for the train journey to Jägerndorf, which he discovered was an impressive town: its station had a classical facade, while its central square was dominated by a salmon pink-and-white neo-classical town hall topped by a clock tower. Here, Hitler had spoken to cheering crowds during his October 1938 tour of his new Sudeten territories. It was home to a number of wealthy manufacturers, and the townspeople were mostly Sudeten Germans, but Jägerndorf had had a thriving Jewish community, including the Bellaks, owners of a textile factory, and the Gesslers, distillers of Altvater, a popular herbal liqueur.

The billet was in Weisskirch on Jägerndorf's outskirts in a *Gasthof* (inn) run by the Taschner family, one of whose members, Gerhard, was a celebrated musician. Through the barred windows of the first-floor dormitory, the inn's former dance hall, Alec could see meadows running down to the Gold Oppa river. To the south, stood the Burgberg, a sixteenth century church with twin onion-dome towers built for pilgrims to benefit from the supposed healing powers of a painting of the Virgin Mary. A cylindrical sawdust-burning stove stood in the middle of the room. This kept the billet warm, and the men heated water on its flat top. There was also room for a crude still in which Alec and his muckers made spirits from Red Cross fruit and sugar.

Some aspects of the billet were less impressive. Half the garden was sectioned off and surrounded by an electrified wire fence three metres high, but this was insufficient for decent exercise. According to a Swiss inspection report, the kitchen comprised merely a table, bench and copper pan for soup. Insufficient fuel was given for cooking, the washing bowls leaked and POWs were denied a midday meal.

The work was, however, less onerous than in Setzdorf. The employer was Jägerndorf's town council, which had been stripped of workers by conscription so needed POWs to harvest timber, clear snow, dig air-raid shelters, unload goods trains and maintain its grain stores. Jägerndorf was also a better place from which to escape, as Alec discovered when he accompanied E606's cook each week to collect rations in a hand-barrow and take washing to the laundry. Though banned from the pavement, he would dress smartly, displaying the superior quality of British military cloth and boot leather 'so as completely to shame' his shabbily-dressed escort.

On such trips he would 'suss out the lay of the land', pick up copies of the *Völkischer Beobachter* and talk to civilians, including a baker who was one of Jägerndorf's few anti-Nazis. The baker would say to the guard, 'My wife has just baked some cakes upstairs. Why don't you go and have some coffee and cakes? Give me your rifle and I will look after these two.' The guard would disappear upstairs and the baker would tell Alec the latest BBC news. He would even slip extra loaves into Alec's sack beyond the mandated ration of one loaf between six during the week and one between seven on Sundays. At the end of one visit the baker's wife, a motherly type, gave Alec some cherries before admonishing him, 'And don't spit the stones out on the street.'

For Alec, one of the strangest sights was a *Rundbogenstil* synagogue with Schönbrunn Yellow walls, twin towers and round-arched windows. Built in 1871 by Ernest Latzel of the Setzdorf quarry family, it was one of the few synagogues in Hitler's Reich to survive *Kristallnacht*. In fact, the town councillors had hoodwinked the Nazis despite having played host to Hitler a month previously: they destroyed a Jewish funeral hall but left the synagogue intact, merely removing its religious symbols and changing the name of the road on which it stood from *Tempelring* to *Tuchmacherring*.

If the synagogue sat strangely amidst Swastika-clad buildings, an even stranger sight was an old man wearing a yellow star. Alec would toss him cigarettes when the guard was not looking. 'Why he was still at large at that stage of the war I don't know, but he was, and I just hope he survived,' Alec recalled. 'Having caught his cigarettes he used to give us a very surreptitious "V for Victory" sign.' The presence of the old Jew was even stranger because cattle-trucks taking Jews to death camps, typically travelling at night to avoid contact with civilians, were still passing through. On one occasion, Alec saw a long line of cattle-trucks standing in the station guarded by Ukrainian SS men. He heard women and children screaming inside the train, yet could do nothing.

The E606 POWs' least unpleasant activity was forestry work in woods twenty-five minutes' march from the *Gasthof*. After breakfasting on bread, the men would start their working day at 8.00am. The march – ten minutes along the road and fifteen minutes on a path through cornfields – was a treat, according to John Elwyn, a Welsh Guardsman taken at Boulogne: 'On a warm summer morning, with larks soaring and singing as they climbed, butterflies winging their way from flower to flower and a gentle breeze swaying the ears of ripening corn, it was a joy to experience – even in Nazi Germany in 1944.'

The POWs worked in groups of six, producing six cubic metres of wood per day to be fed into gasifiers to create fuel gas or for sawmills and paper factories. This work rate was decided by Jägerndorf's military commander and the local Nazi leader. Of the six men, one pair would fell the trees with a two-man saw, two would hack off the branches with axes and strip the bark; the two sawyers would then cut the trunks into metre lengths, the fifth man would stack the lengths at the roadside and the sixth would clear up and burn the branches. This was not a punishing regime. In poor weather, POWs would finish by 3.00pm; if it was good, they would dawdle, enjoying the fresh air.

Other tasks involved shovelling grain and street cleaning, which on one particular street provided opportunities for mischief, as Les Birch recalled:

> While we were cleaning the street, we would distract the guards by staging a mock fight. While the guards were trying to restore calm, some of us would run into the photographic studio and bribe the owner with chocolate and cigarettes to take photographs. The owner would then develop the photos and leave them outside in a milk bottle for us to grab the next time we were marched down the street.

The guards would turn a blind eye to such shenanigans and allowed the POWs to send the photos home with letters. The Jägerndorf studio backdrop, with its painted screen suggesting antique furniture and elegant curtains, implied POWs conditions were comfortable, an illusion the Wehrmacht liked to promulgate. For his first group photo, taken in late March, Alec, with moustache restored, stood in the back row, with Birch seated in front. To Alec's right stood a more recent friend, New Zealand private Bernie Dynes, a power company linesman captured on Crete in 1941.

By early 1944, *Arbeitskommando* security had eased. With the Russian front absorbing most able-bodied German soldiers, the E606 guards, led by a 438th *Landesschützen* Battalion *Feldwebel* called Parsch, were mostly elderly or wounded. The POWs nicknamed one veteran with a Hitler-style brush moustache 'Mousie' because he resembled a dormouse. 'Mousie' and his colleagues would allow a certain amount of bad behaviour as long as POWs did not try to escape. 'If you want to go home, it is a long way to go,' Parsch would say. 'Well, we are not taking you with us,' Alec would reply.

Occasionally, the POWs' insubordination would be punished – once by being marched through Jägerndorf with hands above their heads. Yet their guards became increasingly disenchanted as Germany's prospects darkened and sometimes they even shielded POWs from the uglier aspects of Nazi rule. One evening, Parsch appeared in the billet to warn that Gestapo officers were coming to search for contraband and the POWs should destroy their home-made darts lest the Gestapo think they were weapons. The dartboard went into the stove – it was easily replaceable. The darts had, however, been lovingly crafted, and no one wanted to lose them. As the POWs were debating what to do, three Gestapo officers in trilby hats and leather coats arrived outside. 'Quick as a flash,' wrote 'Laurie' Lawrence, 'Harry 'Tex' Excell threw all six [darts] point first into the ceiling right above the door through which they entered a few minutes later.' The Gestapo officers conducted what they thought was a thorough search, tearing up photographs, treading on Red Cross biscuits and emptying tea and coffee on to the floor. They did not, however, look up at the ceiling, and the POWs kept their darts.

On Saturday afternoons, the POWs would clean their billet, wash and have their hair cut. In the evenings, they would sing, accompanied by 'Tex' Excell on guitar. Occasionally, townsfolk would hold meetings in the *Gasthof*, pro-viding bartering opportunities. 'They would give us a wink as a signal that we could trade,' said Les Birch. 'The men would trade sugar or Klim milk for cigarettes and we would trade chocolate with the girls.'

Once the snow was gone, the men would be escorted on Sundays to the river meadows to play football. Wearing clean clothes, polished boots and side hats or caps, they would march in step, singing marching songs, using the occasion to show locals the superiority of their morale to that of their guards. Sometimes, they would play amongst themselves. Sometimes, locals would field a side and their womenfolk would watch. Normally, such games were good-tempered but not always. On one occasion, they were challenged to a game by Hitler Youth teenagers. 'We took the piss out of them,' recalled Les, 'but we got it back. There was lots of foul play – they would kick us in the shins knowing we could not kick back and would, instead, have to suffer in silence.'

Nor were conflicts between Jägerndorf's Hitler Youth and the POWs confined to the pitch. One Sunday, the POWs arrived at the meadow to find teenagers swimming in the river. With the game finished, George Rogers, a former Bondi Beach lifeguard, suggested the players join the teenagers for a post-match dip. The guard forbade this but Rogers ignored him, yelling 'Follow me, lads!' 'The ensuing uproar and goings on had to be seen to be believed,' wrote 'Laurie' Lawrence 'The guards were dashing up and down threatening to shoot us, the prisoners were whooping with laughter, and the Hitler maids were trying to get out while their male counterparts tried to "protect" them. As the girls were not being molested, this seemed rather

pointless, but one or two of the Hitler lads, did get ducked – just a little.'
Eventually, order was restored and the POWs were marched back to camp
'sopping wet, laughing like schoolboys and singing all the rather bawdy, anti-
Nazi songs we could remember'. The punishment was a two-week ban on
Sunday soccer.

Most footballers were veterans of Setzdorf's Great Potato Strike, but there
were some new faces. One was Royal West Kent private Harry Archer. For
Alec, his story was a familiar one. From 21 May 1940 until capture on 29 May,
the West Kents fought defensive actions as they retreated towards Dunkirk.
Some were evacuated, but not Archer. Like Alec, he became a serial escaper.
Other new faces had had less familiar experiences: one was Private Frank
Embury; the other was a diminutive man with brown hair, blue eyes and a
strange accent. He said he was Royal Northumberland Fusilier Peter Walker,
but 'Laurie' Lawrence thought him 'a bit of a mystery', suspecting he was a
German plant. Then there was another rumour: 'Walker' was 'some kind of
scientist' who had joined E606 so he might escape and be 'taken back home
for some important project'.

'Walker' did escape; the rest was untrue. In reality, both men had taken part
in Lord Mountbatten's Combined Operations raids on Occupied France
during the dark days of early 1942. With a Second Front years away,
Churchill wanted combined units of soldiers, sailors and airmen to harass the
enemy, refine tactics, test equipment and offer the British people some hope
amidst the gloom. This was a new kind of warfare fought by a new elite force,
who would blend tough military training with the spirit of the guerrilla. Frank
Embury and 'Peter Walker' both took part in Operation Biting, the first
Mountbatten raid, aimed at capturing components from a Würzburg radar
station near Bruneval on the Normandy coast.

Spitfire pilots identified the Würzburg parabolic dishes in 1941 and scientists concluded they were contributing to the heavy losses of bombers by
warning anti-aircraft gunners and night-fighters of their arrival. The commandos began training at Tilshead on Salisbury Plain in January 1942 under
the leadership of 'Johnny' Frost, later a hero at Arnhem. To aid their planning, the raid's organizers built a scale model of the Würzburg and the nearby
chateau, using intelligence provided by French Resistance agents. In
February, the commandos, many of them Scottish, shifted to Loch Fyne to
rehearse night embarkations on landing craft, before returning south to prac-
tise parachute drops from specially-adapted Whitley bombers. Finally, after
delays for bad weather, the men took off from RAF Thruxton, Hampshire, on
27 February, piped aboard by a Scottish piper.

The Whitleys encountered flak as they reached the French coast, yet the
parachutists' descent went mostly to plan. Landing in snow 600m from the
Würzburg, the main group advanced through the frosty night towards their
target. After a brief skirmish, they overwhelmed the defenders and captured a

technician, while fighting off an attack from Germans stationed at a nearby farm. Once the Würzburg's electrical components had been dismantled and the rest of the installation destroyed to make the raid look like a 'search and destroy' mission, Frost's team headed for the beach.

Unfortunately, a detachment under Lieutenant Euan Charteris, nicknamed 'Junior' because he was only twenty, was dropped 2.5km south of the drop point so arrived late for the task of clearing the beach of defenders. In the nick of time, however, as the Germans advanced towards him, Frost heard the Seaforth Highlanders' battle cry, '*Cabar Feidh*' (Stag's Antlers): Charteris' men were engaging the enemy, preventing them impeding the raiders' departure on landing craft dispatched from HMS *Prins Albert*. From the landing craft, the commandos transferred into motor gun boats for the journey home and at dawn four destroyers and some Spitfires appeared to escort the flotilla into Portsmouth. There, with the destroyers playing *Rule Britannia* over loudspeakers, they received a hero's welcome.

Of the 120 raiders, two died, six were wounded and six captured. Meanwhile, the kit brought home gave Britain an advantage in the 'Battle of the Beams' as the two sides developed radio navigation and counter-measures aimed at jamming and distortion. From their examination of the kit and from interrogating the captured technician, the scientists saw the Würzburg could not be jammed by conventional means. This brought forward the deployment of 'Window', used first during the devastating Hamburg air-raid on 24/25 July 1943, when its defenders were 'blinded', leaving the RAF to bomb almost unhindered.

An added bonus came from Hitler's reaction. The Führer was shocked at the ease with which the raiders defeated the garrison and demanded the Luftwaffe strengthen the barbed-wire defences around radar stations. This meant the grass within grew ungrazed by cows or sheep, making the installations easily visible on aerial reconnaissance photos. They were, therefore, subject to intense, accurate bombing before D-Day in 1944, depriving the Germans of precise warnings of Operation Overlord.

Embury was among the six captured commandos. A butcher from Stoke-on-Trent, he joined the Army at eighteen in 1934 and became a parachutist in 1941. He was in the last Whitley bomber and was dropped on the wrong side of the Bruneval valley after the pilot changed course to avoid flak. Thus, Embury, George Cornell, a Bren gunner, and Alan Scott, a radio operator, sat out the fire-fights as spectators. Scott listened in vain for a radio signal but then crawled towards the cliff edge, lost his footing and crashed to his death on the beach. Embury and Cornell were pinned down by enemy fire and when they finally reached the beach the last landing craft was pulling away under heavy gunfire.

The pair crept away in the dark in search of locals who might shepherd them into Vichy France. They were introduced to Maurice de la Joie and his girlfriend, subsequently his wife, who provided food, civilian clothing and forged papers describing them as travelling salesmen and escorted them to Bléré, a village 20km east of Tours, where they hoped to cross the River Cher into Vichy France. Unfortunately, they stumbled over their explanations to a customs officer on the bridge and were arrested. The Germans suspected they were Bruneval raiders so they were taken to Paris for interrogation before being transported to Lamsdorf by way of *Dulag Luft*. De la Joie and his girlfriend were also rounded up and questioned. When they gave their address as near Bruneval, they were arrested and condemned to death, but the sentences were not carried out. Instead, de la Joie was imprisoned in Dachau while his fiancée was sent to Ravensbrück.

'Peter Walker's' tale was even more intriguing. Unlike Embury, he got home from Bruneval, but was captured at St Nazaire. His real name was Peter Nagel; his mother was a German Catholic, his father an Austrian Jew. He was, therefore, one of 8,000 German refugees who fought for Britain, styling themselves the 'King's Own Loyal Enemy Aliens' or 'Koleas'.

Nagel's childhood illustrated the integration of Jews into German society before Hitler. He was circumcised at birth but baptised as a Lutheran so he could enter Berlin's Friedrichs-Werdersches Gymnasium, where Bismarck was educated. After Hitler took power, Nagel went with his mother to Paris, where he learned French, while his father used a bogus business deal to send his savings to Britain then claimed he had to visit Leicester for a meeting. He never returned and brought his son over soon after his arrival.

Jewish refugees rushed to volunteer in 1939, but the authorities were nervous about allowing 'aliens' to fight so put them in the Pioneer Corps, the Army's manual labour force, which was led by the 2nd Marquess of Reading, himself a Jew. Thus 'Koleas' became 'coolies'. Nagel impressed Reading, however, and within a few months he had joined the Special Operations Executive, Churchill's espionage and sabotage unit, calling himself Peter Walker and becoming an 'Anglican'. For Operation Biting, he was recast again as 'Peter Newman', a pre-war deserter, and tasked with interrogating captured Germans and confusing the enemy by shouting contradictory orders. Only Frost, his second-in-command and his sergeant major knew Nagel's real identity. Frost initially felt uneasy about having 'a Hun' in his team, as he told Mountbatten during training. Mountbatten responded by submitting Nagel to interrogation in German in front of Frost. He then shook his hand and dismissed him before turning to Frost and saying: 'Take him along; you won't regret it for he is bound to be very useful. I judge him to be brave and intelligent. After all, he risks far more than you do and of course he would never have been attached to you if he had not passed security on every count.'

Nagel did, indeed, show his uses, as General Sir Frederick 'Boy' Browning confirmed in a secret report. After the initial radar-pit attack, Nagel interrogated the German captured there, securing information about his regiment and his success in tracking the Whitleys as they came in for the drop. As the fighting continued, Nagel saw another radar operator dash towards the cliff. The commandos hauled him back and Nagel tore the swastika from his uniform 'for my personal satisfaction' as a souvenir. Then, he recalled:

> I started to interrogate him about the number of German troops and their positions – we only had some information till then – and I thought he was lying. So I shook him by his lapels and said so, and my comrade said we should kill him. But I said no as we had to have prisoners and he was very young and started to cry and was shaking with fear, so I said we should take him along and we did.

Unsurprisingly, Mountbatten sponsored Nagel when he volunteered for another Combined Opps venture, one that yielded five Victoria Crosses and became known as 'the greatest raid of all'. The target was St Nazaire's Normandie dry dock on the Loire estuary, where HMT *Lancastria* was sent after Dunkirk to evacuate troops from Western France – only to be sunk in an air-raid with 4,000 men on board, the worst single loss of life in British maritime history. For the Germans, St Nazaire was strategically important because the dry dock was large enough to service *Bismarck*-class battleships, enabling them to prowl the Atlantic in pursuit of British shipping. Although the *Bismarck* herself had been sunk in May 1941, the *Tirpitz* was still a potential threat.

The Germans thought the dock impregnable: its location five miles up the estuary rendered it safe from naval gunfire, while the volume of explosives needed was too great for land-based sabotage. Something more ingenious was required. This was Operation Chariot, a scheme that would succeed, thought Lieutenant Colonel Charles Newman, its joint head, because the Germans would think it impossible. It involved sending an obsolete destroyer, HMS *Campbeltown*, disguised to look German and packed with hidden delayed-action explosives, to St Nazaire, accompanied by four destroyers, a submarine and seventeen smaller boats, some of which would be armed with delayed-action torpedoes. The *Campbeltown* would be rammed into the Normandie gates, primed to explode the next morning. The commandos would disembark and destroy harbour equipment, while the torpedo boats would target lock-gates leading to the Bassin de St Nazaire. After this orgy of destruction, the commandos would return to their boats and flee. This was derring-do on a grand scale. 'If we succeed ... we will have struck a great blow for the cause of freedom,' wrote Major Bill Copland, Newman's second-in-command, in a 'last letter' to his wife, Ethel. 'Remember too that if I do get blotted out I shall probably die in good company – for never did a finer crowd set out on a doughtier task. I shall always believe that Commandos are the real spirit of Britain at her best.'

Nagel was Newman's interpreter. As the boat glided in, he thought the estuary 'calm as a lake', the tension 'unbearable'. Eventually, however, the garrison realized they faced a raid. Within seconds, tracer bullets formed a 'giant firework display' as defenders fired on the boats and raiders trained machine guns on searchlights sweeping the water. Several launches exploded but then Nagel saw the *Campbeltown* steam past the wrecked *Lancastria* and crash into the Normandie gates, rising 'like a horse leaping over a hedge'.

Ten hours after the *Campbeltown* mounted the Normandie gates, the mission's main aim was accomplished when she exploded, putting the dock out of service for the duration. Two days later, the Germans were again thrown into confusion when the delayed-action torpedoes fired into the Bassin de St Nazaire entrance erupted, destroying the lock-gates.

Yet the price was high for the raiders. Nagel was wounded soon after Newman's team disembarked at the Bassin de St Nazaire and was sent back to their boat. As he ran, he came under fire but fought off his attackers, arriving at the jetty to see some boats burning in the water below and others withdrawing to safety. He returned to Newman to say re-embarkation was impossible. Newman agreed and, gathering survivors together, said they should try to get home and if that was not possible only surrender once their ammunition was exhausted. The code-words to identify each other in the dark were 'war weapons week', a phrase few Germans could have pronounced.

Newman then led his men from the port into the new town across a bridge raked by machine-gun fire, hoping to fight through to the countryside and head for Spain. 'Get on, lads, get on! Keep going, lads', he yelled as the commandos charged 'like a pack of rugger forwards' according to Corran Purdon, a Royal Ulster Rifleman who ended up in Colditz, laughing and cursing as Germans fired on them from windows and street corners. In what became known as 'the St Nazaire Obstacle Race', men clambered over garden walls and through houses. Even if their freedom dash failed, they wanted to get away from the *Campbeltown* lest she go up early.

Eventually, with ammunition running low, the commandos sought shelter in cellars and other hiding places. Nagel hid between cement sacks in a warehouse, hoping the warehousemen arriving for work the following morning would give him civilian clothes, enabling him to slip away unnoticed. As he contemplated being sent to a concentration camp, a wave of depression swept over him: 'I knew *Campbeltown* should have exploded three hours after the beginning of the raid and nothing had happened. There I was crouching in my hole, counting the minutes, cursing that so much sweat and blood had been spilt to achieve nothing.' Eventually, a German patrol entered the warehouse and sprayed it with bullets. Nagel raised his hands in defeat.

Only five raiders made it out of town and evaded capture during the 500km journey to the Pyrenees and freedom. Some 169 were killed and 215 were captured, mostly during the Germans' house-to-house searches at dawn, while

228 got home by boat. Yet the raiders had triumphed. As German medics dressed Nagel's wounds, the *Campbeltown* exploded, sending the lock gates vaulting into the air. Suddenly, he and fellow survivors were transformed from wretched captives into victors who had caused havoc the Germans would never reverse.

When the commandos cheered, their guards threatened to shoot them; but calm prevailed and Nagel and the other wounded were given medical attention. Nagel's first camp was at *Marlag und Milag Nord*, the naval *Stalag* at Westertimke, Lower Saxony, where he feared he would be exposed as a German Jew and sent to a concentration camp or killed. One German interpreter thought he had a strange accent. He was told 'Walker' came from Leicester and 'they all talk a bit like that up there', yet the Germans remained suspicious and gave Nagel a written arithmetic test, thinking he might cross his sevens, Continental-style. He succeeded in maintaining his cover, but this confused the British authorities when the German POW list reached London via Geneva. His father received a War Office letter saying he was 'missing presumed dead in action', a mistake that resulted in Norman Bentwich listing him in a roll of honour of dead heroes in *I Understand the Risks*, a 1950 book on German Jews who fought for Britain. Yet Nagel was alive and determined to keep fighting. At *Marlag*, he was thrown into 'clink' after an escape bid, then sent to Lamsdorf, and thence to several *Arbeitskommandos*. Returned to Lamsdorf after a strike attempt, he, like Alec, contacted the escape committee and was partnered with an airman to make a break from Jägerndorf posing as a French worker.

Chapter 24

So Near Yet So Far

As Alec waited for 'Twiggy MacDonald' to arrive from Lamsdorf, he resumed poetry writing. When sleep proved elusive, he would listen to the snoring men around him and the distant sounds of trains transporting Jews to death camps and recall Cornish nights before the war. This was the theme of a poem written on 21 March, Wakeful Dream:

> The night is black as pitch, and quiet outside.
> Within, the steady breathing of the sleeping men
> Is like the ebb and flow of little waves,
> Which press their watery bosoms on the shore.
> I sit here listening, and the sighing sound
> Removes me from the confines of the room,
> Transports me over miles, and back through years,
> And puts me on a starlit Cornish beach,
> Where waves caress the moon swept shining sand.
> They are the only sound, which breaks the soft
> And fragrant beauty of a summer's night.
> The night is drawn around me like a net,
> Star-punctured in a million glittering points.
> Lost in a world of deep imagining.
> The beauty of that starlit summer's night
> Drew forth my soul and laid it shivering bare.
> I could have wept to listen to the waves.
> Like hungry infants sucking at the breast
> They came and went upon the shifting sand,
> And I was filled with sorrow. Why was I
> Unhappy on a night which stole my soul
> And let it drink of beauty, till I was
> Intoxicated? Some day I shall know.
> A distant train howled in the quiet night.
> A man stirred, coughed and sighed aloud.
> The spell was broken, and once more I sat
> And listened, while my sleeping comrades breathed.

As Alec toiled, the war was coming closer. In the east, the Russians liberated Odessa and Sevastopol. In Italy, the Allies triumphed in the Battle of Monte

Cassino, broke out of their Anzio bridgehead and finally entered Rome. Then came the news Alec had waited years for – the Normandy landings on D-Day, Tuesday, 6 June. One POW thought this 'the greatest day' of his prison life.

The POWs were ahead of their guards. Nazi radio announced the invasion to international listeners before the BBC, but the news was not initially transmitted in Germany. Only the following day did Jägerndorf's townsfolk learn what had happened. The *Völkischer Beobachter* carried huge red headlines saying 'The Battle in the West Has Started' and declared that Germans were entering a struggle 'passionately determined not to terminate it until victory is ours, and life, honour and freedom are assured for our people for generations to come'. The nation was closing 'ranks round the Führer in the firm belief in the triumph of its just cause'.

Alec's emotions 'see-sawed' as setbacks followed advances. The BBC was over-optimistic in early broadcasts, saying Monty's men had reached Caen on D-Day; yet Caen only fell on 18 July. The Jägerndorf POWs charted the moving front line on home-made maps, and Germans would respond by describing the havoc caused by their 'retaliation' weapons. The first *Vergeltungswaffe 1* flying-bomb attack came on 13 June, featuring in the *Völkischer Beobachter*. Hitler claimed these *Sprengkörper* (explosive devices) would lead to victory, and attacks by V-1s, nicknamed 'doodlebugs' or 'buzz bombs', caused carnage in London.

If the front lines remained hundreds of miles away, American air-raids brought the war to Jägerndorf itself. Daylight raids in Alec's part of the sky started in July. He had not seen a friendly plane in four years, yet there above were hundreds of four-engine 15th Air Force heavy bombers with fighters in support, flying north-east apparently untroubled by opposition. He enjoyed watching Sudeten civilians counting them then fleeing into their shelters. Baiting guards who had previously regaled him with English bomb damage reports was piquant. One taunt was to point to the sky and say, 'This must be propaganda. You told us England and America had no planes.'

Alec did not know where the planes came from, or where they were headed, but he knew they marked a further step towards victory. Gordon Woodroofe, who swapped identities to join the neighbouring *Arbeitskommando* E585, wrote in his 7 July diary entry, 'The sun was glinting on the silver bodies. Fighters with them were mere flecks moving across.' Having flown over Jägerndorf, the planes turned east. This was the first move in a 'box attack' in which the thirty-six bombers in each 'box' opened their bomb doors as part of a drill. On this occasion, bombs came adrift and 'came whistling down to explode within half a mile' of the POWs.

Only after the war did Jägerndorf veterans learn where the bombers were flying that Friday: Blechhammer's synthetic oil plants, a vital resource after the Russians overran Rumania's oilfields three months previously. More than 560 planes took off from Bari that morning, mostly B-17 Flying Fortresses, rugged machines able to survive significant damage, and faster, longer-range but more vulnerable B-24 Liberators. Fighter support was provided by Lockheed P-38 Lightnings, which the Luftwaffe nicknamed 'fork-tailed devils', P-47 Thunderbolts, the heaviest of America's single-engine machines, and low-cost P-40 Warhawks and P51 Mustangs. On the way, they were attacked by 300 German fighters, and 18 US aircraft were 'definitely destroyed', with many reported 'missing'; German losses were put at more than 50.

A month later, an even larger fleet, comprising 353 bombers and 300 fighters, passed over Jägerndorf on a second mission to Blechhammer. 'Wave upon wave of them glistening in the sun as they weaved,' noted Woodroofe. 'Two shot down near here. Heavy bombs easily heard. Horrible to see the smoke trail.' Other targets included Auschwitz's Monowitz chemical complex, where IG Farben used Jewish slave labour to make artificial rubber.

Between the first and second raids, Germany was convulsed by two events. On 17 July, the *Völkischer Beobachter* reported Rommel had been injured in an air attack. Three days later came 'Operation Valkyrie', a failed coup attempt by senior officers including Rommel. This was intended to follow the assassination of Hitler at his 'Wolf's Lair' field headquarters in East Prussia by Claus von Stauffenberg. Rommel chose suicide to protect his family, while Stauffenberg's failure meant organized German resistance was crushed for the duration.

With the plot extinguished, Hitler moved to embed the Wehrmacht more deeply in the Nazi system. This was clear when camp guards replaced their traditional salutes with the Nazi raised right arm followed by 'Heil Hitler!' Yet the mere fact that an assassination had been attempted implied the end was near, and Alec thought the moment as electrifying as Hitler's 1941 invasion of Russia. Should he still try to escape? If he stayed, he would be safe from civilian retribution. Airmen in Lamsdorf had told him about *Lynchjustiz*, the officially-inspired violence meted out by civilians and sometimes ending in death. Behind a barbed wire fence and wearing uniform, Alec was safe from the Gestapo. If he were caught escaping in civilian clothes he might be shot as a spy.

Most POWs accepted that for them the war was over and toiled away as forced labourers awaiting the end; some used their time to improve themselves for eventual peacetime employment. In the early years, defeatists thought heroics unnecessary because the enemy were winning. Later, as the tide turned, the arguments against escaping seemed equally strong. Only a minority, probably fewer than 5 per cent, fell outside this group – typically those with a low boredom threshold and sufficient mental and physical toughness to overcome repeated failure. Aidan Crawley wrote:

> A few rare people, who live for action, are never in any doubt what they should do. For them capture is always unbearable and escape their only

interest from the start; but for the great majority the immediate difficulties often seem insuperable and arguments for postponing the attempt
overwhelming.

A big man who snored 'like a buffalo', Crawley knew his subject. Downed
over Italy in 1941, he was imprisoned at Schubin, where he took part in a mass
break-out through a tunnel, accompanied by Tony Barber, the future Tory
chancellor, and Robert Kee. The others included Peter Stevens, a German
Jew born Georg Franz Hein, who crash-landed his plane in 1941 after a raid
on Berlin. Of the thirty-five escapers, thirty-three were recaptured, while two
died as they tried to row a canoe to Sweden.

Serial escapers were not always popular, because their actions showed up the
majority's quietism and exposed them to collective punishments. Canadian
airman Andy Carswell swapped identities with an infantryman intending to
escape from a brewery *Arbeitskommando*. Yet the *Vertrauensmann* protested
that his 'fucking Air Force swap-over' would 'screw up the cushiest set-up
we've ever had'. Carswell's response was equally colourful:

> There is a fucking war going on. We are all British. The Jerries are the
> fucking enemy, not us. It is our duty to try to escape and it is your fuck-
> ing duty to try to help us. And remember one thing, this fucking war will
> be over some day and we are going to fucking well win it. After that
> there'll be a fucking reckoning.

Officers and NCOs, wrote Crawley, were the most active escapers because
'the qualities of enterprise and initiative that helped to make a man a successful escaper or evader were just those qualities that were likely to have
raised anyone who had them to the rank of corporal, at least'. Rifleman Jay
was, therefore, an unusual serial escaper.

As Alec contemplated his break-out, one event weighted the scales heavily
against joining the 1944 'Spring Handicap'. This was 'the Great Escape'
through a tunnel beneath *Stalag Luft* III on 24 March and the subsequent
mass murder of recaptured men. POWs recaptured after previous mass break-
outs had, typically, faced a spell in a *Straflager*, with the worst 'bad apples' sent
to Colditz. Many thought break-outs 'a game' until the Great Escape. Afterwards, the rules changed.

The British public became aware of the massacre on 19 May when Anthony
Eden informed the Commons. On 24 June, a Wehrmacht notice headlined
'To all Prisoners of War!' was distributed. The message was that escaping was
'no longer a sport'. To protect its industries and military centres, Germany
had created 'strictly forbidden zones' in which trespassers would be 'immediately shot on sight'. Escapers entering such 'death zones' would die because
they would be taken for spies or saboteurs. The conclusion was an 'Urgent
Warning': 'In plain English, stay in the camp where you will be safe! Breaking

out of it is now a damned dangerous act. The chances of preserving your life are almost nil! All police and military guards have been given the strictest orders to shoot on sight all suspected persons.'

Following the Great Escape, Hitler put Himmler's SS in charge of POW camps and intensified POW persecution. In September 1944, forty-seven recaptured Allied airmen were sent to the Mauthausen concentration camp. There they were made to carry stones from the camp quarry up steps then forced to run down again. POWs who stumbled and fell were kicked, beaten and stoned by guards, then dispatched with machine guns. Twenty-one died the first day; the other twenty-six the next morning. A month later, Lieutenant Jack Taylor, a captured US commando, was beaten by the Gestapo then taken to Mauthausen. There he witnessed SS men killing POWs in various ways, including making them stand naked in the snow for forty-eight hours while having cold water poured on them, and pushing them over a 100ft cliff. MI9 knew nothing of such atrocities but knew enough about the Great Escape massacre to send coded instructions to Lamsdorf's escape committee: the 'increasing German ruthlessness and lack of regard to Geneva Convention' meant POWs no longer had a duty to escape.

Despite the dangers and the good news from the front, Alec remained one of Crawley's 'few rare people', wanting to 'balance the books' for surrendering in 1940. His German helped his chances; he might be an asset to Britain if he could fight again; he could contribute to morale, showing capture did not necessarily involve endless incarceration. On an *Arbeitskommando*, one German guarded ten POWs; at the front, the fighting ratio was nearer one to one. Even if an escape failed, it diverted resources – each escaper tied up ten Germans trying to recapture him – and showed civilians that Allied spirits were unbroken. The mere act of plotting a break-out lifted morale. In digging a tunnel, making clothes, forging papers or preparing maps, POWs shared in a common effort, regaining a feeling of serving a community, thought Crawley: 'Instead of being thrown in upon themselves they began to rely upon and judge each other by qualities more positive than unobtrusiveness.'

A few weeks after Alec's arrival, the waiting for his escape partner ended when 'Twiggy MacDonald' arrived at Jägerndorf. Most men on later transports to Jägerndorf travelled under their own names, including Frank Embury, the Bruneval commando, and Maurice Raw, an East Griqualand farmer. As a Natal Mounted Rifleman, Raw was taken in Libya in June 1942 and held in Italian camps before being transported to Lamsdorf following Italy's capitulation. But not everyone was as they seemed: Nagel travelled as Peter Walker, occupation 'spinner'. He was planning to escape with a second RAF officer in E606 posing as Ronald Macdonald, POW no. 22890. In reality this was Norman Culblaith, POW no. 27127, who had crash-landed his Wellington in September 1942 after it was hit over Egypt. Nagel and Culblaith escaped from E606 on 10 July but were recaptured the next day by railway police at Klagenfurt in southern Austria, 20km from the Slovenian border.

Ahead of their break-out, Alec and Bob traded Red Cross food with locals in exchange for civilian clothes. Before setting off for work each day, Alec would secrete food and cigarettes in his uniform – armpits were best because then one's uniform did not bulge too much – in preparation for trading. Czechs would show their sympathies by surreptitiously flashing an English cigarette packet in their windows as he marched past.

A few days before the break, the men made a second trip to the photographic studio for portraits to send home. Alec, shorn of his moustache, sat in the front row of one group photo while Bob, in his newly-assumed khaki uniform, took part in another. On the back, he scribbled a cryptic message that confused his family: 'I'm in the army, now.'

On the morning of the break, Alec and Bob put their civilian clothes on beneath their uniforms, stowed food in their haversacks and joined the line for *Appell*. Alec had studied the guards' behaviour on the journey to work. He knew when it was best to slip away unnoticed, his departure masked by his muckers distracting the guards: 'We made our initial break without any real hitches,' he recalled. 'On the way to work,' said Les Birch, 'we got together and staged a bit of a riot. The guards were not intelligent. They fixed their bayonets and rushed to see what was going on rather than looking to see if anyone had disappeared.'

Having slipped away, Alec and Bob doubled back into town. At the station, Alec asked the ticket office clerk in his best German for two tickets for Troppau, 24km south-east, from where express trains could be caught. Local trains were dangerous because anybody unusual would attract attention, and the pair had a nervous half hour avoiding eye contact as the train passed along the Opava river, marking the old Czech border. From Troppau, they planned to take express trains on a zigzag route through central Europe towards the Italian border. The first leg took them 340km west to Prague. The journey was uneventful – a railway official and a military policeman looking for deserters asked for papers but both appeared satisfied. Prague's main station was full of migrant workers and the pair slipped through the crowds.

The second leg took them to Vienna, a journey of a similar distance south-east. As the train pulled into town, Alec could see the air-raid damage. In Vienna, Alec's language skills were put seriously to the test as the pair were about to start the third leg of their zigzag trip – the 480km journey south-west to Innsbruck. The moment of truth came when a platform policeman asked for their ID cards. Alec presented his papers, but the policeman, clearly unsatisfied, said: 'You, wait here. I'm going to fetch my superior.' Alec feared the worst: 'This is it,' he thought. 'However good our forged papers are, they don't stand up to really expert scrutiny.'

His fears were justified. Each day, Berlin's police headquarters would distribute alerts to stations across Germany. Mostly, these covered standard crimes, but as the war progressed they were increasingly taken up with information about deserters, saboteurs and escapers – in March 1944, the Great Escape merited a special edition. The problem for Alec was the newsletters contained examples of poorly-forged documents, with photos showing the forgers' mistakes.

At that moment, Alec saw a man hovering nearby: 'In any country in the world you would have written him down for a plain-clothes policeman.' Alec felt he had nothing to lose. Either the policeman would declare the papers genuine or the pair would be arrested. Thus, Alec walked over to the policeman, shaking inside but acting confident, and said, 'The railway policeman doesn't think our papers are in order. Would you care to take a look at them?' '*Ja, Ja*,' he replied and, after taking a quick look, declared, 'I don't see anything wrong with these.' Then, the man did his bit for Czech-German relations and 'took us and put us on the train, so that was brilliant'.

As the train left Vienna, Alec felt full of admiration for the Lamsdorf forgers' work, and his spirits were high as it steamed into Innsbruck a few hours later, its rhythm seeming to say 'Clickity-clack, I'm taking you home, Clickity-clack, I'm taking you home'. As in Vienna, he marvelled at the damage left by air-raids on the town, which had suffered a particularly heavy raid in June 1944.

Alec and Bob hoped Innsbruck would be the last checkpoint before the Italian border. They aimed to walk the final stretch, crossing over via the Brenner Pass, 70km to the south. Yet Innsbruck was where their luck ran out. Their plan's weakness was that Alec spoke little Czech, and 'by some terrible misfortune' the man who examined their papers was a Sudeten German 'who prided himself on his knowledge of Czech'.

'Oh, you're Czechs, are you?' said the policeman, reeling out 'a great sort of yard and a half of Czech'. Alec's jaw dropped as he stared uncomprehendingly, trying to decide his next move as the policeman reached for his revolver. This was the greatest moment of danger for escapers. If they fled, the policeman would shoot. If they tried to bluff, there were other dangers – in their civilian clothes they could be shot as spies. The sensible course was to admit defeat, which Alec did by pulling out his Lamsdorf ID tag from beneath his shirt.

'Come with me!' barked the policemen and led the pair away to be taken to Innsbruck's Gestapo headquarters on Herrengasse, where they were put in separate cells. Under the Geneva Convention, Alec and Bob should have been held until a Wehrmacht guard arrived to escort them to Lamsdorf for punishment. But Innsbruck's Gestapo wanted first to discover who had forged their papers. Alec knew torture was possible and his ability to take punishment was limited. Typically, torture victims held out for a couple of days. Sometimes

POWs did not last that long; the mere threat of torture proved sufficient – and some men returned from the war plagued by guilt about civilian helpers to whose violent deaths they had contributed. If Alec and Bob were to avoid divulging anything, they needed a stratagem – something to 'reveal' under duress. 'We needed something we could use as a get-out that would eventually stop whatever was happening,' recalled Alec. 'It would be an apparent breakdown.'

The solution came from 'griff' about an airman shot while gathering wood the wrong side of Lamsdorf's trip-wire. POWs knew they would be shot at if they entered the 'death strip', and the airman was wounded in the leg. What happened next was unusual, because guards then killed him in cold blood. The incident yielded Alec and Bob their 'get-out': 'We agreed that if we were caught and interrogated we would take as much punishment as we could and would then break down and give the name of this dead airman and we would say he supplied us with our forged papers, our civilian clothes, our money and travel permits and all the various paraphernalia that go to make an organized escape.'

Alec was thrust into his cell and told to 'await further developments'. When three men carrying rubber truncheons stepped in and demanded he reveal everything about his escape he knew those 'developments' would be 'very unpleasant indeed': 'I got chucked around that blessed cell like a ping-pong ball. I took as much as I could and then I said, "Oh, alright, I'll tell you" because it wasn't exactly a pleasurable experience. I then gave them the name of this bloke, whereupon they, as it were, put up their truncheons, marched out of the cell and locked the door.' Bob received a similar beating.

The pair were left in solitary confinement for two days pondering whether they would be 'shot while trying to escape'. Then, they were brought before a Gestapo officer, who said the Lamsdorf airman had been executed thanks to their treachery. Alec felt relieved: the Germans were lying to make him feel bad. But the relief was fleeting. What happened next was the most frightening episode of his captivity. The officer signalled to his colleagues, who marched Alec and Bob into a yard near the cells and handed them two spades. 'Dig!' shouted one guard. 'Dig a hole two metres long, a metre wide, a metre and a half deep.' Alec and Bob dug until one of the half dozen guards standing around them said, 'Right, that's enough. Each of you stand at one end of the hole that you have dug.'

Alec was 'in a state of very, very blue funk' as he contemplated being shot and buried in an unmarked grave having survived four years' captivity, but Bob saw the fear in his eyes and whispered: 'This is it. You might just as well put a bloody good face on it. Let's show them that Britons don't care.'

The Germans formed a half circle as the pair stood at the ends of their 'graves' and waited for the sounds of rifles being raised. But no shots came. Instead, they were thumped with rifle butts and sent tumbling into the holes they had just dug. As they lay floundering in the mud, a voice from above said, 'Think yourself lucky because that is what has happened to your comrade, who you so blatantly and rottenly betrayed, and let that be a warning to you.'

Alec's mind surged with relief. He had survived, he had not divulged any secrets and would soon be returned to the comparative safety and familiarity of the Lamsdorf *Straflager*. His hopes were fulfilled the next day when he was taken from his cell and presented to a soldier in field-grey uniform. He was a beautiful sight. There were 'two Germanies', thought Robert Kee, 'the Wehrmacht Germany', which 'saluted when it passed you in the camp and allowed you to write home three times a month', and 'the SS Germany', which 'beat you in the stomach with lengths of hose pipe and shot you in the early morning'. The soldier's arrival meant Alec was returning from 'SS Germany' to 'Wehrmacht Germany'.

Other Lamsdorf inmates who broke out in late 1944 were not so lucky. Bernie Dynes, the New Zealander Alec met at Jägerndorf, escaped in December 1944 but was recaptured and taken to the Gestapo's Prague prison, where 1,079 people were guillotined between 1943 and 1945, and then to Theresienstadt, a camp Adolf Eichmann, the Holocaust's logistics head, had created in a Habsburg-era barracks on the river Ohře 60km to the north. To outsiders, Theresienstadt was a 'model' community for prominent Jews. The reality was the camp was overcrowded, had little water and no electricity. Some 33,000 people died there from ill-treatment, starvation or disease, Theresienstadt's main purpose being to serve as a transit camp for Jews heading for Auschwitz and Treblinka.

Dynes was held in Theresienstadt's 'Small Fortress', a *Straflager* for Jews, political prisoners and, during the war's closing months, almost a hundred recaptured POWs. It was run by a group of SS and Gestapo torturers and murderers led by Heinrich Jöckel and including Anton Malloth, an Innsbruck Nazi nicknamed '*Der schöne Toni*' (beautiful Toni). During his six-week incarceration, Dynes dug tank traps alongside Jews. As the prisoners toiled, SS guards would mingle while others stood guard with machine guns. 'Two or three times a day on the Jewish section the guards would disperse and the guns would fire into their ranks,' he wrote. Any Jew too slow to hit the ground was killed or wounded.

Dynes survived Theresienstadt to tell his story. Other escapers were not so lucky. Six months before the Great Escape massacre, two aristocratic Grenadier Guards officers, Lord Brabourne and Arnold Vivian, were captured by SS men in a German-speaking Alpine village and killed.

Chapter 25

Reading the News ...
and Paying the Price

Commandant Messner was impressed that Alec and Bob had reached Innsbruck, but their punishment was twenty-eight days' solitary confinement.
Familiar with the routine, Alec knew how to cope. For Bob, it was tougher –
his only previous experience of solitary had been five days in 1942. After
their sentences, they were sent to *Arbeitskommandos*, giving them little opportunity to experience Messner's improvements to Lamsdorf: an enhanced
water supply, refurbished toilets – raw sewage no longer overflowed on to the
ground around – and extra fresh vegetables.

Bob returned to E606, while Alec joined *Arbeitskommando* E352 in a textile
plant in Freudenthal, 24km south-west of Jägerndorf. The Macholds, owners
of the factory, were a prominent local family. Wilhelm Machold sat on the
Deutsche Bank's Sudeten advisory council, and Alec saw the family name
emblazoned on wagons and railway station posters as his train pulled in on
Tuesday, 5 September 1944. The POWs' billet was a stable-block near the
factory entrance, comprising a dormitory accommodating twenty men in
double bunks, a recreation room, a washroom and toilets.

Swiss inspectors reported that the stoves and lights were 'good' and
prisoners had one bath per fortnight. The food was cooked by a POW in 'a
small well-equipped kitchen' and rations were 'satisfactory'. Dirty clothes were
taken to a laundry, and the cook could visit local shops to buy small items. The
Vertrauensmann, Thomas Moonie, a Cameron Highlander, was 'supplied with
the necessary drugs', while seriously sick prisoners attended the town *Lazarett*.
Mail was regular, although some personal parcels went missing – possibly
stolen by postal workers. Overall, E352 was 'fairly satisfactory', although pro-
vision for leisure time was primitive and Moonie asked the YMCA to provide
items such as a football, quoits, playing cards, a Monopoly set and a gramophone. Alec was told he would work eight hours a day, six days a week.

The SS had constructed 'a mini-concentration camp' behind the mill
where 300 Jewesses, some as young as twelve, were used as slave labour for
Machold's textile lines and for an SS business that made mineral-enriched
fruit drinks for German troops. These slave workers were guarded by a 21-
strong SS detachment led by Paul Ulbort. Most had been among the 437,000
Jews deported from Hungary during early 1944. The Nazis' slaughter came

late to Hungary, yet Hungarians accounted for a third of the deaths at Auschwitz-Birkenau by the war's end. The Germans occupied Hungary on 19 March and the following day, Eichmann's SS team arrived to make it *judenfrei* (free of Jews). On 21 May, Ungvár's ghetto inhabitants were transported to Auschwitz-Birkenau, among them a teenage girl who was shaved and clothed in a ragged dress. For some time, she lived off 'some green, infinitely disgusting liquid in where there were pieces of wood and coal and pebbles', suffered regular beatings and slept in a bunk with thirteen others. Then she fell sick and was transferred to Dr Josef Mengele's 'infirmary'. Mengele 'had a double mind', she said of her encounter with Auschwitz's 'Angel of Death'. He would cure the sick then send them to the gas chamber. Sometimes he would play with new-born babies then send them with their mothers to be gassed the next morning.

One day, Mengele saw the young Hungarian laughing with another inmate, who was dictating a song to her. 'When he saw I was writing in German, he asked me how I came to know German so well,' she recalled. 'I told him I had studied it at school. Generally, I did not panic and responded to him bravely. The following day, he brought me a piece of chocolate and told me that I got it because I knew German so well.' Her German saved her life. When she recovered, Mengele said she could join a slave labour transport. Thus she was thrust one night into a cattle-truck and given half a kilo of bread and two salami slices for the journey to Freudenthal, arriving at noon the next day.

A few Poles and Czechs worked alongside the Hungarians in the Machold plant. Ella was a teenager from Cracow. Of the fifty-five members of her extended family, only five survived. When Cracow's ghetto was liquidated, Ella was taken to Płaszów's concentration camp, commanded by Amon Göth, a Viennese who would shoot one inmate before breakfast each day. One morning, Göth selected Ella but then changed his mind and decided to conduct an experiment in pain. Thus Ella was 'placed on a table and beaten into unconsciousness' by Ukrainian guards. After two years, an emaciated and enfeebled Ella was transported to Auschwitz, where she was sent to Mengele's clinic and stripped naked to stand in line for his selection process. She was, however, warned by a woman nearby of what might happen, so when Mengele momentarily left the room she jumped out of a window and blended in with women being assembled for working parties, thus joining a transport to Freudenthal.

The accommodation at Freudenthal was less primitive than Auschwitz-Birkenau's stable-block wooden billets. The buildings were of stone, the bathrooms were tiled and prisoners were allowed to heat water for washing. Each slave had a bunk with a straw mattress and blanket. Emmerich Machold, son of the company's founder, was a relatively enlightened exploiter of slave labour. Turning fifty in 1944 and 'quite a handsome man' with a French wife, Machold provided some comforts, according to Judith Angell, who came from Romania. He let his slaves have a little library and a radio and gave them waste wool to knit pullovers. Angell knitted socks, mittens and a hat for Machold's daughter, who lived with her parents in a grand house near the factory. Another Rumanian, 28-year-old Ileana, later described the factory as 'heaven' after Auschwitz.

Machold needed his slaves to be fit enough to operate machines churning out uniforms and gas masks. He thought they should eat in the civilian canteen, but the SS insisted on a tougher regime – two slices of bread per day, soup and ersatz coffee. Yet sometimes civilians on the day shift would leave apples near their machines, having seen the Jewesses' emaciated state as they arrived for the night shift. They would even benefit from small acts of kindness by the factory chef. The Germans banned POWs from bringing Red Cross food into factories, but Alec also did what he could for the Jewesses in their striped Auschwitz uniforms.

There were occasional opportunities to slip them food and cigarettes at the start and end of their shifts, although it was hard to get past their whip-wielding guards, including three *Aufseherinnen* (female overseers). The cruellest *Aufseherin* was Erna Bodem, a 24-year-old Sudeten farm labourer later prosecuted for war crimes. 'We helped as much as we could but that wasn't very much,' said Alec. 'It was very difficult to get near enough even to throw them a few cigarettes.'

Over the summer of 1944, the Allies achieved victories that mirrored Hitler's 1939–41 *Blitzkriegs*. The Soviets reached Majdanek outside Lublin in July, seeing the Holocaust's full extent for the first time; by the autumn, they had liberated much of eastern Poland and Rumania and advanced into East Prussia. In August, the Western Allies defeated retreating Germans in the 'Falaise Pocket', one of the war's hardest-fought engagements, while the Operation Dragoon landings on the Riviera led to German surrenders on the coast and inland. On 25 August, the German garrison in Paris surrendered and de Gaulle's Free French paraded down the Champs-Élysées the following day. Canadian troops entered Dieppe, scene of their 1942 rout, in early September, while the British liberated Brussels and Antwerp. In Italy, British troops reached the Gothic Line across the Apennines in August, while in Asia the Americans took Tinian, the island from which their atomic bombers later departed for Hiroshima and Nagasaki.

Alec's German now came in handy again. 'In the middle of the morning, we used to have a half-hour break, which the Germans called a *Frühstückspause*, in other words a breakfast break,' he said. 'I used the time we had during that break to explain the news to the other Kriegies.'

They were a classic POW blend. Many were 51st Highlanders taken at St Valéry, including farmer Alex Anderson and labourer Thomas Hill of the Gordon Highlanders, construction worker David Baguley of the Duke of Wellington's Regiment, baker William Carlin and lorry driver Patrick

McGregor of the Royal Army Service Corps, shoemaker Cyril Jefford of the Border Regiment, decorator William McGowan of the Glasgow Highlanders, painter Albert Stockwell of the Royal Northumberland Fusiliers and dairyman James Thain of the Gordon Highlanders. The other 1940 veterans had been taken outside Dunkirk, such as machinist John Jackson of the Border Regiment, Royal Artillery gunner Edward Liptrott, Ox & Bucks Light Infantryman William Miller, a warehouse clerk, Black Watch private Allan Petrie and Welsh Guardsman David Stanford, a steelworker. More recent captives included Royal Artillery lance sergeant Michael Baker, a motor mechanic taken in Egypt in 1942 as the British retreated towards El Alamein, and Green Howards lance corporal Chris Barry, taken in Libya a few days previously. George Foster, an Essex Regiment private, and brickmaker James Millis of the Royal East Kents were taken the previous year.

Soon after Alec's *Frühstückspause* lectures began, Sudeten civilians joined the POW circle. He said, 'I decided to explain the situation first in English then translate into German what the news really meant as far as I was concerned.' This was dangerous behaviour. 'Spreading alarm and despondency' was worse than escaping because it undermined Goebbels' edifice of lies. In 1939, Hitler had introduced the death penalty for listening to foreign radio and, as the Allies advanced after Stalingrad, Nazi officials would listen outside homes to catch people listening to the BBC. Then expressing defeatist sentiments became a capital offence. Civilians were also banned from talking to POWs and foreign labourers unless communication was necessary and were told only to give orders.

Alec's lectures inevitably became known to the factory Gestapo, and one day officers marched up to him as he was 'busily explaining what a right royal thumping the Germans were getting on all fronts and how day and night bombing was gradually reducing Germany to an ash-heap'. They were not impressed, 'and in the vernacular I got my collar felt'. He was again taken to a Gestapo jail, this time at Troppau, for a further period in solitary confinement.

When his term ended, Alec expected to be sent to a conventional *Arbeitskommando*. Instead, his reward for 'spreading alarm and despondency' was incarceration in a *Strafkommando* (punishment camp) at Gurschdorf, a hamlet near Setzdorf. The train taking him to the camp, E790, halted at Friedeberg in the valley below Gurschdorf on 15 September 1944. He was then marched to the *Sonderlager* (special camp), a barbed wire-enclosed stable on a hill near a quarry to which it provided labour. There he met the *Vertrauensmänner*, Albert Brand and Sidney 'Streaky' Reed. A Bedford & Hertfordshire Regiment private, Brand was captured in Greece and sent to Gurschdorf having made a nuisance of himself at Setzdorf. 'Streaky', so called because he was a fine sprinter, was a Middlesex Regiment lance corporal taken at St Valéry.

Brand and Reed explained the regime administered by the commandant, Captain Globish of the 438th *Landesschützen* Battalion's No. 4 Company. Each morning at 5.30am, a guard pushed open the billet door, yelled '*Aufstehen!*' and used his rifle butt to prod the POWs awake. They were then marched to a quarry operated by a company called Granit where two-man POW teams lifted broken rocks into skips for processing. After each skip was unloaded the POWs received a disc; work stopped after all discs were distributed. Typically, Monday-to-Friday shifts lasted eleven hours; Saturday was a half day; Sunday was a rest day but behind locked doors.

E790 was a mini-equivalent for other ranks of Oflag IV-C in Colditz. The Germans thought Colditz's fortifications made it escape-proof. At Gurschdorf, they thought E790's remoteness would discourage escapes, although it did not prevent six men breaking out within days of the camp's creation. 'Gurschdorf was a "bad boys" working party. There was not a single man there who hadn't made themselves a nuisance to the Germans,' said Alec. 'So by working us eleven hours a day in a granite quarry I suppose they thought that was their way of paying us out for not being as cooperative as they would have liked.'

Some, like Alec, had been taken in 1940. Rifle Brigade rifleman Norman Goodchild had fought at Calais and was a Setzdorf striker. Dunkirk veterans included Highland Light Infantry privates William Alexander, a barman, and Patrick Tominey, a glass worker, Royal West Kents private Cyril Barwell, an aircraft fitter, Royal Sussex lance corporal James Brown, West Surreys private James Holland, a clerk who used his knowledge of German to bait his captors, Ox & Bucks Light Infantryman Cyril Hymas, an electrician, Royal Engineers sapper Edward Lynch, a textile worker, Suffolk Regiment private William Smith, a lorry driver, King's Own Royal Regiment private David Vaughan, a gardener, and Royal Army Service Corps lorry driver Charles Wooding. Royal Horse Artillery gunner James Preston and Gordon Highlanders private James Wilkinson were 51st Highlanders.

The Crete captives included Thomas Craven, a paint sprayer, and Arthur Thorpe, a shop assistant, both RAF radar specialists, Royal Signals lance corporal Gilbert Mason, a Layforce commando, and anti-aircraft gunner Victor Valpy, an insurance clerk. The Africa contingent comprised Joseph Black, a tank crewman captured at Tobruk, 65th Anti-tank Regiment driver William Forsyth, taken at Gazala, Royal Artillery gunner William Lancaster, East Surrey private Frederick Martin and Royal Northumberland Fusilier Fred Smith. Alongside the British were an American airman who had swapped identities with an infantryman, Gordon White, an Essex Scottish private taken at Dieppe, and two Maoris. One, Private Hopa Katene, was a 27-year-old lumberjack taken on Crete. Katene was wounded during battles involving Great War-style bayonet charges. When he realized he was holding colleagues back during the retreat he told his commander to abandon him to the Germans.

Occasionally, the monotony of breaking stone was broken, as when POWs were ordered to lift potatoes. This was also back-breaking work, as Alec described in Potato Harvest, one of two poems he wrote at Gurschdorf:

Heads bowed, backs bent, we search the muddy ground,
The grey cloud sky envelopes like a pall;
Our baskets fill, are emptied, fill again.
Rising, I see the distant pine trees tall,
Like candle shadows thrown on the grey wall.

The teamster shouts to urge the straining pair
Of horses, as they pull the stubborn plough.
We move behind them like a native crew
In rhythm, as they tow their puny pram.
The sweat drops slowly from my steaming brow.

The day wanes and the night comes dropping down,
Clutching the earth with fingers cold and damp.
With aching backs we slowly stagger home
Along the road which leads us to our camp.
The darkness grips me like an iron clamp.

Sidney Sherriff was concerned by reports about Gurschdorf so he asked Swiss inspectors to visit. As a *Straflager*, it 'very much' deserved inspection, he thought. This was confirmed when Albert Kadler, the inspector, issued his report following a visit on 27 September 1944.

The E790 POWs, Kadler wrote, were billeted 'in a former stable with little or no alterations'. One half was 'an overcrowded sleeping room with bad ventilation and concrete floor, bugs and rats'; the men had double bunks but no cupboards, no stools, no stove and no electric light. The rest was a 'day room with two long tables and some benches' plus a small stove on which men could heat Red Cross food but deliveries were 'very bad'. The men had no musical instruments or board games, with playing cards the only means of entertainment. Although the walls were whitewashed, E790 made 'a dark and gloomy impression'. The yard was 'too small for any sporting exercise', the outside toilet was in 'a bad state' and infrequently emptied, leaving a powerful stench, and the outside water pump for cooking and washing was 'most of the time ... out of order'. No hot water was provided, although the quarry provided baths. The local cook's food was 'very monotonous'. Each man had two uniforms but their boots were in such a bad state that Kadler said a cobbler should be excused quarrying once a week to do repairs. No laundry facilities or military doctors were provided although the stable had a first-aid kit. Gurschdorf had a doctor but Friedeberg's dentist only did extractions. Kadler said conditions were so bad E790 should be 'removed or dissolved', but Lamsdorf's commandant gave him 'no definite assurance' so he told the German High Command that the camp was 'not a suitable place for men to live in'.

When the British Embassy in Berne received Kadler's report they passed it on to the Foreign Office. Yet, with Germany imploding, nothing was done. That Kadler thought Gurschdorf sufficiently poor for it to be closed was a telling indictment, because the Nazis were experts in disguising camp conditions. Four months before Kadler's visit to Gurschdorf, two Red Cross colleagues, Dr Maurice Rossel, the Berlin representative, and Dr Otto Lehner, visited Lamsdorf, declaring it 'made a good impression'. Shortly afterwards, Rossel inspected Theresienstadt after the Germans had turned it into a Potemkin village; sick patients were hidden, a defunct park was reopened and healthier-looking prisoners were ordered to sit playing chess. Completely hoodwinked, Rossel duly described Theresienstadt in glowing terms, encouraging the SS to revive an earlier plan to make a film about it. Once the footage for The Führer Gives the Jews a City had been shot, most participants were killed at Auschwitz.

For Alec, Gurschdorf life was not all bad. Hauptmann Globish, a short fair-haired man with a small moustache, behaved decently. Before winter set in, he allowed POWs to swim in quarry pools and even organized shopping trips. In the evenings, with only playing cards for entertainment, Alec played bridge 'to saturation point': 'When the doors were locked at night, we used to have six tables of bridge going.' Everyone would take part except the man tasked with making tea and keeping the stove burning. This was fuelled by wood gathered in the quarry and hidden from the guards, a vital resource as temperatures dropped to −20° centigrade.

When not playing bridge or working, the POWs indulged in 'goon-baiting'. 'Streaky' Reed would sharpen his canteen knife on sandstone, telling the guards, 'This is for you later on.' Even marching between the stable and the quarry provided entertainment as American bombers passed overhead. Between Saturday 23 September and New Year, twenty-five 15th Air Force daylight missions flew over. 'We didn't half cheer,' said Streaky. 'It did our nerves no end of good and it upset the Jerries.'

Globish ensured his 'bad boys' were fed enough to keep them working at a time when Red Cross parcel supplies were diminishing. Once France became a warzone in June, Red Cross shipments only resumed after a route through Sweden was negotiated. Even then, distributing parcels to POWs was not a Wehrmacht priority. The Red Cross organized truck convoys painted white with red crosses to criss-cross the shrinking Reich, but these 'White Angels' were insufficient to bridge the gap.

For non-working prisoners in Lamsdorf, this resulted in a return to 1940 conditions. By comparison, the Gurschdorf inmates were relatively well fed;

yet the guards could be brutal, as Alec soon discovered. The older ones, too infirm for frontline service, were quiescent; the younger ones were dangerous. Globish's number two was an Austrian called Strauss – the POWs nicknamed him 'Johann'. In his late twenties, the broadly-built Strauss had been excused front-line service because of a weak heart, but would compensate by bullying POWs. 'I have never fired a bullet in anger at an Englishman,' he would say, 'but I hope you will give me a chance.'

Strauss got his chance to kill an Englishman on Monday, 2 October 1944. The incident involved William Philo, a merchant seaman, whose ship, the SS *Clan Ferguson*, had been sunk during the relief of Malta. At twenty-four he was 'a hard, tough, violent and angry man' not shy of confrontation. While others submitted to E790's regime, Philo insisted his rank and merchant mariner status rendered him exempt. Alec thought him 'a lead-swinger' who 'generally didn't pull his weight in any respect'. Strauss insisted he must work, but Philo feigned sickness and asked for a doctor. Strauss then arrived, shouting 'You are not sick, get up and go to work!' Philo asked again for a doctor. In response, Strauss seized a rifle with fixed bayonet from another guard and lunged towards Philo on his bunk, aiming at his stomach. Philo, however, twisted over and the bayonet sank into his thigh.

After calm was restored, Reed, the *Vertrauensmann*, said Philo needed hospital treatment, but Strauss refused and Gilbert Mason dressed the wound. Even then, Strauss insisted Philo work, but the next day Globish dispatched him to a detention cell at Freiwaldau. Alec, meanwhile, began gathering evidence to have Strauss prosecuted as a war criminal, because his bayoneting of an unarmed prisoner was a 'breach of the laws and usages of war'. The priority was to obtain information – Strauss's full name, where he lived, his pre-war job and the names of family members. Alec, therefore, spent the next few days being 'very friendly' and gained enough information 'to be able to work my trap when I got home'.

With Philo gone, life at E790 settled into a rhythm – long shifts breaking granite followed by evenings locked in the stable. Alec was hungry for news and bribed a weak-willed German to provide a radio – his third in captivity. The news was not all good. Stalin refused to support the Second Warsaw Uprising, enabling the Germans to regain control of the Polish capital. Of the captured partisans, 6,000 went to Lamsdorf, including Witold Pilecki, a cavalryman who had escaped from Auschwitz in 1943 and written the first report convincing the Allies the Holocaust was real. He survived Lamsdorf only to be executed by Polish Communists in 1948 as a spy. The tally also included child soldiers such as 10-year-old Jerzy Szulc, thought to be the war's youngest participant. Not until 17 January 1945 did the Red Army liberate the rubble that had been Warsaw.

In the west, Operation Market Garden was a debacle. 'Monty' wanted to seize a Rhine bridge at Arnhem with airborne troops, then pour tanks over it to turn the German left flank and beat Stalin to Berlin. News of the Arnhem landings raised Alec's hopes, yet Market Garden was Monty's worst failure, with 6,000 paratroopers becoming late entrants into Hitler's prison camps. Meanwhile, from the Home Front, Alec learned about V-2 rockets, Hitler's latest *Vergeltungswaffen*, of which more than 1,100 landed on London and the South East before attacks petered out in March 1945. Elsewhere, there was better news. Allied troops entered Germany on 10 September, heading towards Aachen, an event that gave Alec a wry smile after his 1940 experiences. German garrisons surrendered at Brest, Boulogne and Calais; once again, Alec had particular cause to cheer.

The year ended with Hitler's 'Battle of the Bulge' Ardennes offensive featuring SS brutality towards POWs as bestial as the behaviour in France in 1940 and in Russia from 1941. At Malmédy, SS troops executed eighty-six Americans, and they picked out Jews from among surrendering Americans and killed them. The Americans, it must be said, also committed war crimes, if not on the same scale. The liberation of France was not 'a gentleman's war' according to Ted Ellsworth, one of the Americans who joined the 60th Rifles in 1941: 'Sending the prisoners back in those days meant giving direct orders to the guards not to shoot.' Ellsworth himself was captured, but not before seeing the bodies of sixteen Germans executed after surrender.

Defeat in the Battle of the Bulge cost Hitler men and matériel that could have been deployed in the East, which was where the best news was as 1944 drew to a close – and POWs did not need a radio to know this. At Lamsdorf, Russian planes would fly overhead seeking targets, while Stukas flew in the opposite direction. By estimating their speed and monitoring the time it took them to return, POWs could calculate where the front was. In November it was 200 miles away, by December only 100. Then confirmation that liberation was close came with the sound of artillery fire. On New Year's Eve, the POWs thought they could hear the occasional rumble, but by mid-January it was quite distinct. On Sunday, 27 January, the Red Army's 332nd Rifle Division arrived at Auschwitz. Almost all the 60,000 inmates had been herded west, but 7,500 of the weakest had been left behind.

As the fighting drew nearer, there were other comforts for Gurschdorf's POWs. In a village stripped of men, the *Engländer* were befriended by local women, and some contact was more than platonic despite the law that guards read out every week:

> Prisoners of War are forbidden to have any intercourse with a German Woman. This not only pertains to sexual intercourse. But Prisoners have to Abstain from approaching them to start a conversation or touching them. Conversation is only permitted where Working Conditions make it necessary. Offenders of this rule may be punishable by death or long periods of sentence in – The House of Correction.

Women working in the quarry would gather round giggling when the *Engländer* went skinny-dipping and would flirt with them during the potato harvest. Alec had particular opportunities to meet girls because he would interpret on shopping trips, while 'Streaky' Reed confessed in his nineties to two liaisons:

> Many of the women were war widows or wives whose husbands were away at the front. We did our best to console them and I think we did OK. We could not care less about the law. [Reed was put to work in a barn, where he was given a pitchfork and told to toss hay bales up to the farmer's daughter.] One fell back on me and I asked her if she had done it on purpose and said that if she had I would come up and sort her out. She just laughed and threw another down on me. Well, I did go up and sort her out and soon we were rolling around on the floor together.

Alec never mentioned his dalliance but he did leave behind a poem written on 26 September 1944 entitled Sonnet:

> I was a homeless stranger in the land,
> Enchanted by the smile upon her face.
> Although we met in an unpleasant place,
> My cares took wings, when first I clasped her hand.
> I found it very hard to understand
> How she was filled with such exquisite grace.
> And then, my admiration grew apace,
> Until I was her servant to command.
>
> She went and I was desolate with grief.
> I knew not where to lay my aching head;
> And while the howling wind moaned through the trees
> Stripping them bare of every shivering leaf
> I mourned that she was gone. My world seemed dead
> And I myself unable to find peace.

Chapter 26

Escape and Back in Action – as a Partisan

Alec spent early 1945 waiting for the Russians to arrive. Food was short – his Red Cross Christmas parcel was delayed until late January and then he only received half. On 30 January, the BBC said the Russians were 'well over the German frontier north-east of Berlin'. On 18 February, Marshal Ivan Konyev's troops were encircling Breslau. In the west, the 'Colmar Pocket', the last German foothold west of the Rhine, was eliminated on 9 February, and on 7 March American troops poured over the Rhine at Remagen. Meanwhile, air-raids intensified, climaxing on the 13 and 14 February, when Allied bombers attacked Dresden, a city swollen by tens of thousands of refugees, producing a firestorm that killed 25,000 people.

Then, on Sunday 17 March, a guard burst into the Gurschdorf billet at dawn shouting, 'Everybody out; get your things together; we are leaving.' Thus, *Sonderlager* E790's twenty-five 'bad boys' assembled Red Cross food, clothes, books and cigarettes in preparation for their part in an evacuation that became known as the Death March. Alec's hopes of travelling by train were quickly disabused – the Germans planned to force-march him west as they had force-marched him east in 1940.

Alec had already heard BBC reports about POW marches from camps further east. Lamsdorf's new commandant, Colonel Georg Braxator, had emptied Lamsdorf of all POWs other than the sick, starting on 22 January. Their destination was *Stalag* VIIIA in Görlitz, Lower Silesia, 240km to the north-west. Each man received a Red Cross parcel and a loaf of bread for the journey, and Braxator equipped the twenty-five *Landesschützen* guards allotted to police each 1,000-strong group with hand-grenades, rifles and two guard dogs. According to a Swiss inspector, the men marched out 'in very high spirits, all expecting to be captured by the advancing Russian Army before they would reach Görlitz'.

Harry Levy described a 'sea of men' standing in ten inches of snow, with kitbags, rucksacks and bundles at their feet, stretching from Lamsdorf's gates to the far perimeter fence, their disparate uniforms reflecting their diversity. Those in khaki included infantrymen taken at Dunkirk, Calais and St Valéry, Canadians captured at Dieppe, Desert Rats plucked from Italian camps following the 1943 armistice and Lamsdorf's most recent involuntary guests, paratroopers taken at Arnhem. Then there were 1,000 'boys in blue', airmen incarcerated at Lamsdorf after parachuting out of burning planes during Bomber Command's four-year campaign of destruction. 'Balaclavas were the favoured headgear, often surmounted by a khaki or coloured forage cap, a beret or knitted bonnet,' he wrote. 'The general effect was of a defeated army, a horde of refugees.'

The Death March earned its name because POWs were subjected to ill-treatment far surpassing what happened after Dunkirk. About 3,000 died, some murdered, some succumbing to disease, some killed by friendly fire. They were part of a vast miserable human tide flowing west. Skeletal concentration camp inmates were their saddest fellow travellers and their death toll was awful, with almost half the 700,000 Jews held by the Nazis in December 1944 dead by May 1945. Then there were Russian POWs, some semi-naked with bayonet gashes in their buttocks, intermingled with German refugees hoping to avoid the atrocities Russian soldiers were perpetrating in the east – industrial-scale rapes and executions. Though better clothed and fed, the refugees were a sorry sight – old men, women and children, carrying possessions on rickety carts. Not that Alec sympathized – he had seen similar sights in 1940 as French civilians fled the advancing Panzers. These people had cheered as Hitler conquered most of Europe. Now it was their turn to suffer.

Even before the marches began, the POWs were weak because Red Cross parcels had dried up. Now they were on the road, German soldiers, Wehrmacht and SS, abandoned all pretence of honouring the Geneva Convention, and POWs were killed for ducking out of their columns to scavenge in fields or being slow to fall in line. Only a few Red Cross parcels got through. On 8 March, Paul de Blonay, a Swiss delegate, escorted Allied POWs from Lübeck to Konstanz on the Swiss border, where trucks were waiting to be driven into Germany to feed the columns. De Blonay had secured agreement from the Germans on the condition that the drivers did not attempt to escape. Not all Germans stuck to de Blonay's deal, with SS men stealing food and petrol despite Waffen-SS *laissez-passer* certificates saying thieves would be court-martialled. They did, however, manage to supply one parcel per man once every five days to 14,000 marchers. They also took 800 Jews to the coast, where Swedish ships carried them to safety. But SS diehards were not the POWs' only concern. As airmen marched along, civilians hurled bricks at them, while some were bombed by Allied Typhoons, suffering 'friendly-fire' deaths whose purposelessness haunted survivors for decades.

Hitler had ordered that slave workers and POWs be marched west in the face of Russian advances. He then placed Germany's Reserve Army, which would organize the evacuations, under Himmler's control. The SS leader put one of his 'Twelve Apostles' in charge. This was Gottlob Berger, co-author with him of *Der Untermensch*, an anti-Semitic/anti-Slav pamphlet published after Operation Barbarossa in 1941. The 'subhuman', they wrote, was 'the greatest enemy of the dominant species on earth, mankind'. The subhuman had 'hands, legs, eyes and mouth, even the semblance of a brain' but was 'only a partial human being' inside of which lurked 'wild and unrestrained passions', 'an incessant need to destroy' and 'the most primitive desires, chaos and cold-hearted villainy'.

As the Russians advanced, POWs began to fear liberation might not be their fate. They were a burden on Germany, yet, if they fell into Russian hands, they could be re-armed, enabling them to turn on their captors. In 1944, the War Office had, indeed, considered re-arming liberated POWs but feared they would be too unfit, demoralised and ill-trained. Despite evidence from repatriated POWs about German cruelty, one officer thought camp life might 'make it more difficult to hate the enemy'. Alec feared he would be marched into the Bavarian mountains. There, SS fanatics would surround themselves with POWs and issue a challenge to the Allies: 'If you want to blast us out of here you have got to blast them out of here first.'

In London, Churchill feared 'a deliberate threat by Hitler and his associates to murder some or all of the prisoners'. After his Ardennes defeat, Hitler had told colleagues, 'We can go down but we'll take a world with us.' Then, in the wake of Dresden, Goebbels wanted thousands of POWs executed. Hitler initially agreed, but eventually his generals and diplomats persuaded him a massacre would be counter-productive. For months, Allied governments agonised over how to react to these threats. Finally, on 23 April, planes dropped 6 million leaflets saying: 'Do not think of taking revenge on Allied prisoners of war. Their safety is the responsibility of every single one of you, and you will – have no doubt – be called to account.'

Eight weeks after Lamsdorf's Death March began, Alec stepped from his billet into the snow for Gurschdorf's last *Appell*, a haversack on his back containing Red Cross food, his poetry, his *Faber Book of Comic Verse* and his *Complete Works of William Shakespeare*. Around him, POWs were wrapped up against the cold in greatcoats, gloves, scarves and balaclavas. His spirits rose during the first hours as he chatted with friends about the coming victory. It was pleasant not to trudge to the quarry but embark instead on a journey that would end – finally – in liberation. The winter landscape and snow-coated trees looked charming as he marched down the valley from the isolated billet.

The servant-master relationship with the guards had changed. Alec and his muckers looked like the refugees streaming towards Calais in 1940, but so too did the guards, with heavy packs on their backs as they pushed bicycles burdened with personal possessions. Some were Sudetens fearing they might never return home. While Alec thought of victory, the end of his five-year torment, they could only contemplate defeat and the start of some grand settling of scores within Eastern Europe's ethnic patchwork. Some modified their language – Alec switched from being *Schweinehund* to *Kamerad*.

As they marched, the guards distributed leaflets calling for volunteers to defend civilization against the Russians. Beneath a double-deck headline, 'Soldiers of the British Commonwealth! Soldiers of the United States of America', the hastily-drafted leaflet riddled with spelling mistakes declared: 'The great Bolshevik offensive has now crossed the frontiers of Germany. The men in the Moscow Kremlin believe the way is open for the conquest of the Western world. This will certainly be the decisive battle for us. But it will also be the decisive battle for England, for the United States and for the maintenance of Western civilisation.' This meant the fate of England was at stake as well as everything that 'makes life livable [*sic*], lovable and honourable'. The Nazis addressed the British and Americans 'as white men to other white men', a phrase that produced an ironic smile among Jewish POWs. In the face of the 'most brutal Asiatic rule', the leaflet continued, 'We think that our fight has also become your fight.' Any British soldier willing to 'join the common fight for the common cause' would 'be freed immediately after the victory of the present offensive and then return to his own country via Switzerland'. 'Are you for the culture of the West or the barbaric Asiatic East?' the leaflet concluded. 'Make your decision now!' This recruiting drive achieved nothing; POWs merely pocketed the leaflets as souvenirs.

When Alec's column reached Setzdorf, they were joined by other POWs and the column swelled to 200 as the men marched down the main street, lined by villagers watching as if it were a parade. Alec spotted Adolf Hauke, Latzel's foreman, looking apprehensive, and could not resist one last tease: 'Watch out, Adolf! Look out for the bear.'

After his initial exhilaration ebbed, Alec began to contemplate the future. For four days, the column marched up to 30km a day, subsisting on potatoes and soup, drinking from roadside ditches and scooping up snow when water was scarce. Each evening, they would be herded into a barn or warehouse and locked in until dawn. The nights were so cold Alec slept in his boots for fear they would freeze. Keeping clean was difficult without soap or water; lice and diarrhoea were the inevitable consequences. By the fourth day, Alec had had enough: 'I had been marched all the way from Calais into Germany in 1940 and I didn't fancy another long-distance hike. Furthermore, I had a nasty feeling that if the Russians got too close, we would be massacred before we were liberated.'

Alec debated escaping with those nearby. Most thought escape futile. The Allies were advancing towards them and the guards had said anyone attempting to escape would be shot. This was no idle threat; on 13 January, Doug Carnie, one of Alec's Setzdorf muckers, was killed outside his *Arbeitskommando* fence during an escape attempt. Unsurprisingly, the War Office wanted POWs to stick with their columns until they could be liberated. An escape attempt might end in no-man's-land, with the POW caught between retreating Germans and advancing Russians.

Yet Alec thought the chances of linking up with friendly locals were reasonable if he could reach areas populated by Czechs. The guards were mostly from the recently-assembled *Volkssturm* (People's Assault):

We had been marched all day through the snow and so had our guards and we reasoned that they would be just as tired as everybody else, probably more so. By that time in the war, any German who was at all fit was fighting and our guards were elderly and unfit, a load of weary Willies and tired Tims who had either been wounded or were too old for front line service even by German standards.

As night fell on 20 March, the guards herded the POWs into a barn and locked the doors. The skies were clear, the moon shining, the temperature below freezing, hardly the best conditions for an escape, but Alec wanted 'to be off'. 'Right,' he told the other POWs, 'it's now or never. We know that through the other side of these wooded mountains only about fifteen miles due south is Czechoslovakia proper. Let's take our chances with the Czechs.' When he asked if anyone would join him, seven said 'yes'.

At 1.00am, when they thought their guards in the farmhouse were asleep Alec produced 'that standby of all would-be escapers', a hacksaw blade, which he had secreted in a seam in his uniform. For the next hour, the men took it in shifts to saw away at the barn wall until they had created a hole through which they could squeeze one by one.

Alec steeled himself. Had the guards been woken by the sawing? Were they waiting outside to pick the escapers off 'like sitting ducks'? 'I was to go first and in a state of absolute funk I crawled through the opening into the glare of the moon on the snow-covered farmyard,' he recalled. Neither man nor beast had woken. 'So far so good,' he thought. Anxious to get out of the moonlight, he crept round the barn into the shadows and after looking around and listening for a moment, tapped on the wall to give the all-clear.

It seemed 'an eternity' until the other seven were out. The next few minutes were vital because they had to tiptoe clear of the farmyard and reach the woods. Yet the only shadow was provided by the farmhouse, where the guards were sleeping. Alec gingerly crossed the yard to the farmhouse and the others followed. Working their way along one wall, they got to within five steps of the farm gate. Alec paused, whispered, 'Right' and led the charge. With nerves 'strained to breaking point', he thought they sounded 'as loud as a Cup Final crowd' as they dashed the first fifty yards, yet the guards remained asleep. After a few seconds they reached a wood, where they halted momentarily, gasping for breath and almost sobbing with nervous relief. They were free, but as Alec tramped through the night, he asked himself, 'Is it worth it? Is any escape worth the risk?' Four times in five years he had 'gone through the wire' without success. He did not regret those failures, even though he had been tortured and told to dig his own grave. What about this time?

Suddenly, the answer came to him: 'Any escape from an evil one cannot fight must be worthwhile.'

As the sky lightened in the east, practical matters trumped philosophical speculation. Alec needed to reach Hitler's Protectorate of Bohemia and Moravia, where he hoped to find 'a more sympathetic population than we would in the Sudetenland'. For some hours, he led his band through wood-covered hills, navigating by his watch and the position of the sun. Then came the moment when he thought his freedom had come to a premature end. Without warning, gunfire erupted from the undergrowth. 'We immediately froze with our hands up because at this stage of the game we didn't want to throw our lives away needlessly. Yet the people who arrived, one of whom had done the shooting, were not Germans but Czech partisans.'

Keeping his hands above his head, Alec asked if they spoke German. When one nodded, he said his little band were escaped POWs and asked for help. The answer 'was in the affirmative' with one condition: the Brits should fight alongside the Czechs until their occupiers were defeated. This would involve them surrendering their Geneva Convention protection, but the POWs, after a brief debate, accepted the condition. Thus, for the war's remaining seven weeks, Alec became an honorary Czech partisan, a period that was, for him, 'possibly the most bizarre part of the war'.

The partisans took the POWs to their base, a rudimentary affair – wood choppers' huts and makeshift lean-to shelters surrounded by what Alec thought a 'primitive' defence ring manned by sentries. It was, however, located far from the nearest garrison town. The living was rough – water came from a stream, deer and birds were snared for food and cooked on open fires. The partisans did, however, have access to a radio, on which they received BBC broadcasts and messages from their leaders. Thus, Alec discovered that Monty had crossed the Rhine on 24 March and, a month later, American and Russian troops had celebrated together on reaching the Elbe at Torgau.

Round the camp fire, Alec learned about the partisan struggle. The main unit styled itself the 1st Czechoslovak Partisan Brigade of Jana Žižka in honour of a leader in Bohemia's fifteenth century religious wars. In spring 1945, their ranks swelled to 7,500 fighters, including escaped Russian, French and English POWs, who would bomb stations, tracks, troop trains and bridges and attack barracks and police stations. They were not equipped for full-scale confrontation, but picked off isolated Germans, stealing weapons, ammunition and food.

Their scouts would comb the foothills in search of Germans. 'I never knew exactly how it happened although it was something like the old British grapevine in the POW camps,' recalled Alec. Then they would attack. 'Sooner or later word would come to us there was a village in which there were just a few Germans and off we would go marching through the mountains down snow-covered tracks towards this village.' On arrival, the partisans would take up positions on roads leading into the village and at a given signal, typically an owl-like hoot or a dog-like bark, they would attack: 'We would go in shooting at every German in sight, grabbing what food, arms and ammunition we could and then at a pre-arranged signal we would melt back into the woods and return to one of our hide-outs deep in the forests.'

Finally, on 5 May, Alec's partisans tuned into their radio to hear the words, '*Volame vsechny Cechy*' (Calling all Czechs), the signal to attack the occupiers simultaneously in three towns. The Prague Uprising began at 11.00am when Czech flags were unfurled and weapons secreted in cellars and attics were hauled out. This marked the start of four days of street-fighting in which 30,000 Czechs confronted the Germans before Russian tanks arrived on 9 May, one day after the official VE Day. The insurgents quickly gained control of half the city, and the Wehrmacht garrison were surrounded in their bases, with electricity, water supplies and telephones cut off.

The commander, General Rudolf Toussaint, wanted to surrender, but Field Marshal Ferdinand Schörner, the newly-promoted Wehrmacht commander-in-chief, thought otherwise and sent in SS troops. By this stage in the war, the standard SS tactic to stiffen resolve was to shoot retreating soldiers and prop up their arms so their corpses gave a permanent Nazi salute once rigor mortis set in. Even after the official surrender, their cry as they roamed Prague was 'We continue to fight alone.' Aided by air-raids, the SS reversed the tide of battle and on 7 May it appeared the insurgents would be overwhelmed. At this point, however, help came in the form of the anti-Bolshevik Russian Liberation Army created by General Andrei Vlasov, a Soviet traitor. Some of Vlasov's army of renegade POWs thought that, if they switched sides again, the Western Allies might prove friendly. They held off the SS for a day, but Czech Communists refused to embrace them as allies and they were later killed or captured by the Soviets.

When Alec arrived, the fighting was in full flow, and he soon discovered his little band were not the only ex-POWs in Prague. One was a Scot called William Greig, who was asked by the Czechs to broadcast appeals to the Americans of General George S. Patton's Third Army, less than 100km from Prague, to come to their aid. Patton wanted to help, but Dwight Eisenhower insisted as Supreme Allied Commander that Prague was out of bounds, so its liberation was left to the Czechs and to the Russians, who reached the city's eastern outskirts on 8 May.

The Prague Uprising was on a different scale to the street-fighting Alec experienced in 1940. The SS used women as human shields, and the Czechs were similarly barbaric. In a 5 April broadcast, Edvard Beneš, head of the government-in-exile, declared, 'Woe, woe, woe, thrice to the Germans, we will liquidate you', before issuing decrees categorizing all Germans as 'politically unreliable' and expropriating them. 'When you chop wood, the splinters fly,' declared Antonin Zapotocky, Czech Communist Party co-founder and Sachsenhausen concentration camp inmate from 1940.

Alec witnessed this score-settling when his partisans took some prisoners. One fighter, so Alec thought, was ordered to take the Germans to a safe location, and he told a fellow POW to accompany them. Seconds later, Alec heard machine-gun fire, and the POW returned 'looking as white as a sheet'. 'What happened?' Alec asked. The reply was grim: 'When we got round a couple of corners, he just shot the lot of them.' There were similar incidents throughout Prague as Czechs shot unarmed soldiers and civilians. Other vengeance-seekers did not waste bullets – instead they strung up their captives, including children, by their feet from lampposts, doused them in petrol and set fire to them as 'living torches'.

Bob Hawthorn witnessed one such lynching. His Death March had taken him to Mährisch-Weisswasser, where 1,000 Jewesses were incarcerated, having previously been slave labourers making aircraft parts in Mittelsteine, Silesia. When Bob arrived the inmates were enjoying their first fruits of freedom and gave him 'a great welcome'. From there, Bob hitch-hiked to Prague, arriving as the uprising ended. 'What a sight! The place had been bombed and machine-gunned the previous day,' he recalled. 'The streets were lined with dead three or four deep and the gutters were flowing with blood.' He witnessed the 'living torch' shortly afterwards. It was 'the most horrible scene one could imagine'. An SS man had been masquerading as an ordinary soldier, but the removal of his lightning-flash insignia had left a tell-tale mark on his collar. Now, he was to pay – and the Czechs thought their British guest a suitable audience: 'He was tied by his legs to a lamp standard and a can of petrol was thrown over him. Someone then ran forward and threw a lighted match and off he went. He gave one death-like yell, a shudder and that was the end.'

Across Prague, SS women were beaten and forced to roll naked in puddles. At the Strahov Stadium, built in 1926 as a monument to the new republic's optimism, Germans were made to run around the field and used for target practice. In Wenceslas Square, a dead German dangled from every lamppost. In the Sudetenland, Latzel family members incarcerated in the former E250 *Arbeitskommando* at Adelsdorf witnessed Hitler Youth members being shot. Meanwhile, over the border in Poland, *Stalag* 344 at Lamsdorf, renamed Łambinowice, became a death camp for German Silesians. Queen Vics rifleman Edward Watson witnessed the wrath of newly-liberated Polish slave workers when he walked down the main street of Wittingen, Lower Saxony. There he saw dozens of dead policemen and soldiers tied to roadside trees. Their jackets and trousers were undone but neatly folded back to reveal they had been castrated, while at their feet the Poles had placed their penises.

Alec struggled to make sense of the carnage. It 'was unjustifiable by the rules of war' yet could be understood as a reaction to the atrocities inflicted on the Czechs. 'We must never forget,' he told his children, 'the Czechs were six years under the German heel, which was longer than any other of the free peoples.' Bob had similar feelings: 'This may be a hard-hearted thing to say but I can honestly say I was pleased.'

At midday on 8 May, the Czech National Council declared a truce and allowed the Germans to flee. That afternoon, most German troops moved west towards Patton's Army. The next day, the Russians set about killing or capturing the few snipers still firing from rooftops. It was Alec's first glimpse of the Soviets' primitive but effective tactics: 'The Russians made very short shrift of what remaining German resistance there was. If there were Germans in a building they just surrounded it with tanks and blew the hell out of it.'

During the first days of peace, Alec's band camped out in a partisan flat, listening to tales of insurgency. Few Czechs spoke English, so German was the means of communication, with Alec as interpreter. One couple, surnamed Pollack, were particularly kind, supplying them with soap and towels. He was a Jewish doctor, his wife, Istenka, a Christian. She took a particular liking to Alec, presenting him with a lace handkerchief embroidered with her initials. Pollack was one of seven brothers who all married gentiles. Six wives divorced their husbands to avoid discrimination, but not Istenka. As the anti-Semitic crackdown intensified in 1941, Dr Pollack went underground. Before he left, Istenka gave him her jewellery as 'currency'. For years, she heard nothing. Then, as the war drew to a close, she returned home to find her jewellery on the kitchen table. 'That was,' said Alec, 'the first inkling she had that her husband was still alive.'

By this time, hundreds of POWs were in Prague – Brits, Australasians, South Africans, Cypriots, Serbs and Sikhs. Among this heterodox group was a Gordon Highlander still wearing his kilt after five years' captivity. Some, like Alec, had fought with the partisans; others had simply gone into hiding. Now, with the war over, Prague's citizens showered them with food and champagne and placed garlands round their necks. Some threw open their homes to POWs; others stayed in hotels for free.

On Thursday, 10 May, the Russians announced that they wanted POWs to register at the Hotel Bristol prior to being sent home. But Alec's host had other ideas, promising to put him on a train to Beroun, where the Americans were. Thus, Alec travelled on the first train going west from Prague in post-war Czechoslovakia, arriving home earlier than he might have had he obeyed the Russian instruction. The Russians sent some liberated POWs east to Odessa to be evacuated by boat, and it was weeks before they were reunited with their families.

Knowing he was finally going home, Alec spent his last day in Prague sight-seeing with Daria Halla, an English-speaking Red Cross nurse. It was the first real day of peace and a time to relax and pose for souvenir photographs on the fourteenth century Charles IV Bridge and on the Vltava riverbank. Before

Alec left Prague, however, he had one last reminder he was not yet out of harm's way. After supper, his host came into the POWs' room accompanied by a soldier in British battledress. 'Here's a colleague of yours to spend the night with you,' he said, 'and I'll put him on the train with you tomorrow.'

Alec engaged the man in conversation, asking standard questions: 'Where were you captured? How long have you been a prisoner of war? What lot were you in? Where do you live?' His English was fluent enough but the accent was strange. Then, when he said he was in 'the 152nd Infantry Regiment' and came from 'the little village of Greenwich near London', Alec knew he had a problem. The 152nd was an American unit, while the expression 'little village of Greenwich near London' was odd. No Englishman would have used it – but Greenwich did figure prominently on German military maps of Britain. After a few minutes' conversation, Alec made an excuse to go downstairs and told his host, 'Look, there is something wrong here. You've worked a German in with us.'

'Don't worry,' his host replied. 'Go back to the room; don't make a fuss. I'll sort it out.' A few minutes later, the door burst open and his host marched in followed by two policemen. Alec spoke first, saying, in German, 'I'm glad you are here.' This confused the policemen and one made as if to arrest Alec, shouting, 'You're a German!' His host intervened to put the policeman right. The man was then ordered to raise his hands while his pockets were searched. These yielded nothing more than shaving soap. The policeman then said, 'Drop your trousers!' At this point, the POWs discovered the danger they had been in. Beneath the man's khaki trousers were German field greys, and when he dropped these they could see a loaded Beretta semi-automatic pistol hanging from a tape around his waist. Having allowed him to pull up his trousers, the policemen took the German downstairs. Alec heard the front door slam and then a bang. 'And I guess,' he recalled, 'that was the end of the gentleman that came from "the little village of Greenwich".'

Chapter 27

Going Home, 'Half in Love with Easeful Death'

Decades later, Alec would recall every hour of his journey home. The afternoon after the brush with 'the gentleman from Greenwich', he boarded the train to Pilsen. The passengers were a strange mix – POWs and civilians sitting beside Jews still in concentration-camp uniforms.

The train moved slowly and just before nightfall it halted. Had they been held up by diehard SS men, Alec asked himself, or were the Soviets interfering to stop people reaching the American lines? Peering into the half-light, however, Alec could see Americans patrolling the track. Opening the carriage window, he asked what was happening. 'This train is not going to move until daylight,' was the reply, 'because we want to have a good look through it to see who is on it.' He understood their caution and was pleased when the Americans distributed food and cigarettes. The following morning, the Americans, looking to Alec almost impossibly fit and well-padded, questioned each passenger. They were hunting for war criminals and other soldiers – the deal with Stalin was that Germans surrendering west of the VE Day halt line would be Allied prisoners; those to the east would belong to the Soviets.

On arriving at Pilsen, Alec was directed to a transit camp in woods outside the town. Before he left the station, however, he was called on to interpret one last time. A tall American military police sergeant was struggling to deal with an elderly man with a goatee beard talking rapidly in German in an authoritative tone.

'Say, do any of you guys speak German?' the sergeant yelled towards the crowd on the platform.

Alec volunteered, and the American asked, 'What's this damn Kraut saying?'

'So I listened,' recalled Alec, 'and he said he was a retired Wehrmacht colonel who wanted to go home and didn't see why he should be kept waiting at the station.'

When Alec explained this to the military policeman, he smiled and said, 'Say, buddy, you can spread it on thick and I guess you will enjoy it.'

Alec then took great pleasure in tearing 'this retired colonel off the most enormous strip', telling him he would stay on the station for a week if the American so desired.

So much for Hitler's master race, thought Alec as he ambled through Pilsen. The town was packed with American military hardware of a sophistication that made the weapons at Calais look like Great War relics. At the transit camp entrance, intelligence clerks were registering arrivals, aiming to root out any Germans. Having persuaded the clerks of his bona fides, Alec spent a day and a half gorging on American K Rations, dried produce issued when fresh food was not available. 'The American troops wouldn't look at it because they considered stuff used by combat forces in the front line was beneath them,' recalled Alec, 'but we tucked in and we thoroughly enjoyed ourselves.' After five years of prison-camp food, K Rations were a luxury – though Alec subsequently suffered intense stomach pains because his digestive system struggled with such unaccustomed quantities.

Alec was told he would travel in a convoy of American troop carriers to Regensburg the following morning, Monday, 14 May. The open-backed GMC 2½ton trucks, each with an African-American driver, pulled into the transit camp at 7.15. Fifteen minutes later, the convoy of 'Jimmy-Deuce-and-a-Half' vehicles, as they were nicknamed, began a seven-hour journey into the heart of the Reich through towns reduced to rubble by air-raids – 'a grand sight', thought Hawthorn.

The trip 'was very, very hairy indeed' as the drivers tested their trucks to the limit on twisting roads. 'Anyone with more than two wheels on the ground is a sissy,' was their motto, thought Alec. Finally, the convoy entered Regensburg. During his summer 1944 escape journey, Alec had seen the 15th Air Force's handiwork in Vienna and Innsbruck but it was insignificant compared to what happened to Regensburg, home to a Messerschmitt plant. The city had been 'comprehensively flattened'. The sight of hundreds of American tanks, with ladies' knickers flying from their radio aerials, was equally impressive. Above them, white 'surrender' sheets billowed from the windows of houses still standing.

That night, the ex-POWs were billeted at the Messerschmitt aerodrome and given fresh American uniforms. The next morning, they breakfasted on porridge sweetened with sugar, real coffee and white bread, the first Alec had eaten in five years. Then, they were taken to a runway pock-marked with bomb craters and told to wait in groups of twenty-seven for Douglas Dakotas to carry them to Reims in France. It was Alec's first flight. Before he climbed aboard, a Red Cross truck pulled on to the runway and a woman inside with a loud-hailer called out, 'Are there any British amongst you?' She was one of twenty British Red Cross staff flown out to welcome returning POWs. Alec waved and was presented with a 'Dorothy' bag containing a flannel, soap, shaving brush, chocolate, cigarettes and a card that read: 'Best wishes for a Happy Return Home from the British Red Cross. We Salute you and wish you the very Best of Luck.'

The twin-engine Dakotas then flew in and taxied around the bomb craters and German POWs labouring to repair them. Take-off was delayed because the planes contained ration crates and the aircrews said 'nobody goes home' until they were unloaded. This provoked protests, but Alec's little band 'wanted home'. While the Americans were arguing such things were beneath them, 'the eight of us piled in, unloaded our plane and were sitting inside it waiting for take-off before some of the other planes had even started to be unloaded'.

This was hardly luxury travel, although the pilots, in their sunglasses, peaked caps, flying jackets, razor-sharp creased trousers and polished boots, had an air of studied nonchalance as they chomped on their cigars. The men in Alec's plane were given boiled sweets to combat air sickness and told to sit on the fuselage floor in two rows facing each other and hang on to straps dangling from the roof. There was a bucket at the back for anyone who felt sick. Yet, this cold, draughty workhorse of the US Air Force was 'the most beautiful thing in the whole world', thought one ex-POW, 'a vital link between the normalities of civilized life and the exceedingly low state' to which he had been reduced.

After a bumpy take off from the hastily-repaired runway, the Dakota pilots flew at 10,000ft, so Alec could see enemy terrain passing beneath like a map. Not since being force-marched through Calais' ruins had he seen such devastation. After a while, he picked out Hitler's *Westwall* fortifications; then, Reims's fourteenth century cathedral came into view.

After touchdown, the Dakota taxied between bomb craters and halted near a line of six-wheel troop carriers, in which the ex-prisoners were driven to 'Tent City 1', a transit camp in a park near the cathedral. The truck journey was an eye-opener. George Moreton, an airman-turned-medic at Lamsdorf, watched Germans marching through the town guarded by Americans on scout cars armed with machine guns. The SS appeared as 'arrogant and defiant as they had been before capitulation', but the older Wehrmacht men and boy soldiers looked 'dishevelled, beaten and tired'. Sitting on their trucks, the British shouted insults, but their demands that the Americans 'kill a few of the bastards' went unheeded.

On arrival, Alec was registered again and received a War Office booklet that began: 'We want you to know how glad we are that you are at last on your way home. We are sure you can now look forward to receiving every care and attention to make up in some way for all you have undergone.' A clerk explained the repatriation process and provided information about back pay and leave. There was also advice about the difficulties of re-entering civilian life, some prophetic:

> Changes have taken place in Civvy Street. Your friends have been engaged in war work. Many are on jobs that did not exist before. There

are ration cards and wartime regulations. Your wives, mothers and sisters have carried the burden of war work as well as the extra difficulties of wartime housekeeping. It is a different world in many ways from the one you have left. [Returning POWs were more experienced, with a new and] quite possibly a better [outlook on life but they would need time to adjust]. Going back after all these changes will not be easy. You may feel confused until you have got used to civil life again. [Resettlement units had been created to help] bridge this gap between the Army and civil life.

After registration, Alec was deloused by orderlies wielding DDT powder guns, allocated a place in a tent with six-foot walls and electric light and told supper would be an American-style chicken dinner. He never got to savour it, or Tent City 1's other treats – a bath, medical inspection and a German POW to cut his hair and polish his boots. This was because, a short while after he sat down on a camp bed that seemed, with its sheets and pillow, luxurious after years of POW bunks, a soldier poked his head round the tent flap and said, 'There are eight places left on a plane flying back to England this afternoon. Any of you guys want to go now?' Before anyone else could stir, Alec's group had leapt from their cots. Thus they boarded trucks for the 30km journey to Juvincourt, a Luftwaffe base near Berry-au-Bac.

On arrival, Alec saw some 7 Squadron Lancasters lined up beside the run-way, each bomb bay removed to make way for twenty-four men for the flight to England. This was part of an exercise that eventually involved 3,000 round trips, carrying home 74,000 ex-POWs. On boarding his Lancaster, Alec was given more boiled sweets, an air sickness bag, a 'Mae West' life-jacket, a cushion and a blanket. There were no windows, so French towns scarred by air-raids during the liberation passed by beneath unseen. But when the plane reached the Channel, the pilot announced 'English coast ahead', an invitation for passengers to visit the cockpit one by one for a glimpse of Dover's white cliffs. Alec had last seen them glinting in the afternoon sunshine on 26 May 1940, tantalisingly near yet beyond reach as the Calais garrison made its last stand. Then, the fields of Kent, where he had trained as a rifleman, rolled out below, followed by London, scarred by V-1s and V-2s, and more fields as the plane headed towards RAF Wing near Leighton Buzzard, Bedfordshire.

Finally, late in the afternoon of Tuesday, 15 May, the Lancaster landed, and Alec, weighing just seven stone, walked gingerly down the steps and stood on the tarmac. It was four years and 354 days since he had set foot on English soil. For everyone, this was a highly charged experience – some men bent down and kissed the ground.

From the moment the ex-POWs stepped from the plane, the station staff smothered them in kindness. The reception committee consisted of WAAF volunteers, who ran across the apron from a brightly lit hangar, greeting the men and relieving them of their meagre possessions. Then orderlies with delousing guns administered fresh blasts of insecticide down their necks, up their sleeves and down their trousers.

With this ritual cleansing over, the WAAFs took the arms of the returning warriors and escorted them to the hangar. A 'welcome home' banner was over the entrance. Inside, trestle tables were groaning with sandwiches, cakes and tea urns. Music played from a loudspeaker, as each man sat with a WAAF on either side. One ex-POW described his companion, clad in a uniform that 'fitted like a glove', as 'a vision, a goddess'. The white-bread sandwiches were equally intoxicating. Finally, having gorged himself on 'the feast for the eyes' beside him and the food in front, and having listened to a mercifully short welcome speech from the base commander, Alec collected his free newspaper and some cigarettes.

The next step was a 15-mile truck ride to Army barracks in Berkhamsted. The countryside looked comfortingly familiar, although there were no signposts, a legacy of the invasion threat. At Berkhamsted, Alec experienced 'the storybook welcome back to England'. A Cockney sergeant was waiting as the convoy pulled into the yard. 'All right, you blokes,' he said, 'you're back in the Army now; get off them trucks and get fell in.' Then, as an afterthought, he added, 'You'll be allowed to send a telegram home.'

Alec had waited for this moment. In the Lancaster he had composed the telegram he would send his parents, who had not received letters for months. In early January the BBC had said POWs were being herded west; then a German propaganda broadcast said *Stalag Luft* III airmen had begged to be taken west to avoid being liberated by the Soviets. Supposedly, thirty officers and numerous other ranks had volunteered for the British Free Corps, while those POWs who fell into Soviet hands were being shot or arrested if they failed to join the Red Army.

The Prisoner of War's February edition said POW marchers had little food; then, on 21 February, American Red Cross officials revealed that POWs were being force-marched west in temperatures of thirty degrees below zero 'without proper clothing'. *The Prisoner of War*'s March edition said German transport was 'in almost complete disorganization'. On 8 April, *The Sunday Times* contained an interview with three ex-POWs who said seven of the 170 men on their march were dead, while a dozen had been abandoned as sick. Five days later, the *Daily Telegraph* contained an interview with survivors who had taken part 'in one of the worst forced marches of the war'. They had come from Lamsdorf. 'No one knows how many died en route,' wrote the reporter, 'but I have the word of one British soldier . . . that he had seen four men die a week ago.' Finally, John and Annie Jay learned from *The Prisoner of War*'s May edition that 850 POWs on the Lamsdorf march had escaped to the Russian lines and were being repatriated from Odessa.

Alec, innocent of what was known back home, had pondered the matter for days, casting around for suitable quotations, rejecting 'quite a few answers'.

Finally, he decided the telegram would be biblical: 'Fatted calf for one – the prodigal son is returning.' This was not, however, to be; he was 'back in the Army now' and such lyricism was not allowed. Instead, his pre-printed telegram simply read: 'I'm back in England, will be home on leave shortly.'

The ex-POWs were then shown to their billets, where they bathed, received a medical examination and were given new uniforms. The next morning, Alec was asked to fill in an MI9 form describing his experiences. Unsurprisingly, he wanted to get home to his family as fast as possible and filled in only the barest of details, making no mention of his escapes or his time with the Czech partisans. He did, however, write that an *Unteroffizier* had thrust a rifle butt in his jaw at his first working party, knocking out thirteen teeth, 'to find out if I was a Jew'. He also made sure Bill McGuinness achieved recognition for leading the Setzdorf strike, writing: 'I wish to bring the conduct of Sgt W. McGuinness AIF to notice. He was responsible in the main for breaking up a bad working party in Feb '44 by organizing a strike with myself. At all times he stood out for correct treatment of POW and never in any circumstances let himself be dictated to by the Germans.' Alec was not alone. John Lockyer wrote, 'I wish to recommend Sgt McGuinness AIF from Sydney on the way he handled working party E173 during a four-day strike against the Germans at Setzdorf', and Bill Morrell's form concluded McGuinness was 'A FINE CHAP'.

The MI9 form instructed POWs to ask for a 'Form Q' if they had witnessed war crimes, so Alec described the Philo assault at Gurschdorf and when he showed it to an intelligence officer he was asked further questions, after which he was sent on his way with the words, 'We'll be in touch.'

Later, he received an identity card, leave pass, ration card, pay advance and rail warrant to travel to Marylebone Station the following morning. This was his real re-entry into civilian life, with its pleasures and irritations, as he discovered when he arrived at the station taxi rank. He asked to be taken to Golders Green, only to be told, 'Oh no! That's too far.' At that moment, some cleaning ladies from the Great Central Hotel gave the cabbie 'a mouthful'. 'They were going on at him so hard and so loud,' Alec recalled, 'he was only too pleased to bundle me in the cab and take me up to Golders Green.' Only later did he realize why the cleaners were so vehement. The hotel was the 'London Transit Camp' for successful escapers, and the cleaners had been among the first women to greet home-runners, so there was no way they were going to allow a cabbie to mistreat a soldier returning home.

The 38 Hodford Road reunion was a grand affair – too grand for Alec's jangled nerves. He was so emaciated his parents barely recognized him, yet, within hours of his arrival, the extended Jay family and friends had turned up to reacquaint themselves with the returning hero.

Then, a few weeks later, Alec suffered one last blow: his father's death at just sixty. On the evening of Monday, 9 July, John complained of chest pain but no one suspected anything seriously wrong. During the night, however, he succumbed to a coronary thrombosis and Annie awoke to find him dead beside her. Alec did not have the mental resources to cope and 'went to pieces', according to Phoebe, blaming himself. Phoebe was a WAAF, providing weather forecasts for aircrews operating from Boscombe Down, Wiltshire. Her mother was so fearful of her reaction that she initially said John was sick. Only after Phoebe obtained compassionate leave did she learn the truth. With Alec so disturbed he was incapable of activity, Phoebe took charge of the funeral and caring for her mother.

This was not the homecoming of which Alec had dreamt. His father's death deepened the emotional chasm between him and his family. It was as if they lived in different worlds. They did not understand the stress of combat or the privations of imprisonment. He felt isolated, detached from his past, adrift in the present. He had left home as a teenager, returning six years later as a man changed in ways his family could not comprehend. He felt he was a curiosity to visitors to Hodford Road and was impatient of their well-intentioned but intrusive questions. His overwhelming need was for calm. Simple behaviours had to be relearned. He needed to moderate his language and relearn his table manners, using cutlery and not licking his plate for the last crumb or drop of gravy. Alec was not alone. One officer lecturing ex-POWs would say, 'When you go home, don't say "pass the fucking butter!" Say "pass the fucking butter – please!"'

The War Office had concerns about ex-POWs' mental health – officials reckoned 70,000 longer-term POWs would need counselling. Military psychiatrists surveyed repatriated POWs to develop 'dos' and 'don'ts'. They thought returning POWs needed to be left free to relearn how to make decisions, even which radio station to listen to or whether to go to the pub. They might swing wildly from being cheerful and sociable to becoming depressed and introverted. They might also display temper tantrums. If they wanted to talk, their families should listen; if they wished to remain silent, they should be left alone. A leaflet was compiled but not distributed. Thus, the War Office left families such as the Jays to 'muddle through' in ignorance, although Christine Knowles did try to help with her booklet, *The House not Built with Hands - a Guide to the Future for Next of Kin of Returned British Prisoners of War*.

Knowles understood the emotional gulf between ex-POWs and their families. In her advice to POWs' families, she posed rhetorical questions:

> What do you feel will be necessary? What do you think you personally will want to do? How do you feel about it all? Do you think you are going to find the same man that you said goodbye to? Do you think you are going to find somebody immeasurably better or do you feel that you are worried? Are you thinking how you are going to readjust yourself and how are you going on into the new world that is coming?

Such questions needed answers because families needed 'to think seriously not only about the big planning but the small planning too'. From her conversations with repatriated POWs, Knowles knew their home life and their families' behaviour mattered 'more than anything that any public body or private body or anybody can do'.

For Alec, escape once again seemed the answer – this time to Mevagissey to revisit teenage haunts, the subject matter of many of his POW poems. Fortunately, returning POWs were sent on extended leave, so he had no obligations to fulfil as he tried to nurse his bruised mind back to health. One early letter gave him particular pleasure; it was from Knowles, whose books had helped preserve his sanity as a POW:

Dear Mr Jay,
Welcome home after your many adventures! We salute your bravery in action, courage and patience in captivity; we wish you all good fortune in the future. God bless you and yours is the wish of your faithful friend. P.S. I shall be glad to advise you and help you if you so desire and hope to be seeing you soon but please ring up and make an appointment, as I should not want to miss you. I hope you will find the enclosed booklet helpful and of interest.

Having returned weighing seven stone, Alec gained weight rapidly and was almost back to his natural twelve stone by the time of his Army medical in late August. The doctor thought his physique, general condition and state of nutrition 'good' but reported that since the closing weeks of imprisonment he had been plagued by headaches lasting up to two days. His teeth were in a shocking state. At about the same time, he was summoned by Colonel Sir Henry MacGeagh, Judge Advocate-General, to York to swear an affidavit about the Philo stabbing. He was told Strauss had been located among Germans captured by the Western Allies and was asked to identify him. Thus, a few days later, Alec flew to *Stalag* 357 at Fallingbostel on the edge of Lüneburger Heide, a vast heath north of Hanover. In early 1945, 17,000 POWs had been crammed into Fallingbostel. It then became a German POW camp after VE Day.

Soon after Alec arrived, the Germans were called out on parade. 'There were all these square heads on parade, standing laughing and chatting – the war was over for them too,' Alec recalled. The commandant took him aside and said, 'I want you to walk along these ranks and if you see this fellow I want you to point him out.' In the event, 'I got within twenty yards of him and he just broke out of the ranks and ran for the wire.' Alec never learned of Strauss' punishment because he gave his evidence by affidavit but he knew he was now even with one of the brutal guards who terrorized him from 1940 to 1945.

Back home, Alec attempted to reassemble his pre-war life. His teeth needed fixing and he went to Shaftesbury Military Hospital on 27 November for multiple extractions and to be fitted with false teeth. His gums took three weeks to heal, after which he was assigned to the Rangers, the Queen Vics' Territorial sister unit. On 25 February 1946, he received his 'Notification of impending release' papers, complete with a statement saying his military conduct had been 'exemplary'. Below, Lieutenant Colonel Sir William Heathcoat-Amory, the Rifle Depot Infantry Training Centre commanding officer, added a testimonial, quintessentially English in its brevity. Alec's time in the Army had 'shown him to be a reliable and trustworthy man, an efficient soldier and a good rugger player'.

Alec returned to A.R. Barton in the City two weeks later. To his colleagues, he was no longer the boy who made the tea, but rather the returning hero, fit to be a partner alongside Albert Barton. In May, he applied for Stock Exchange membership and was registered as owner of one Stock Exchange share on 19 June, two days before his release from army duties.

Five years of his youth had gone, but there were benefits. Thanks to Knowles, he returned better read than he might otherwise have been. He also thought he was wiser: 'I learnt how to get on with people on equal terms,' he told his children. He did, however, lose his faith: 'I learnt that you can survive most things but you can't survive death. I don't believe in the life hereafter.' Gris Davies-Scourfield, with whom Alec would reminisce during reunions, thought his POW years 'were for the most part wasted years, years "eaten by the locust" and gone forever with the wind'. Yet, on the credit side he 'had at least survived and learnt such things as patience, fortitude, some measure of resourcefulness and an ability to improvise and look after myself. I and others like me had perhaps suffered something like Isaiah's "furnace of affliction" and been to some extent refined.'

The torment experienced by ex-POWs was analyzed by Lieutenant Colonel 'Tommy' Wilson, founder of the Tavistock Clinic. Wilson coined the term '*Stalag* mentality'. This was 'essential in the prison camp' but increased 'the difficulties of re-adaptation on return'. The POWs' main burden was bitterness stemming from 'the sterility, deprivations and enforced passivity of *Stalag* life' and regret that a large chunk of their lives had been wasted.

According to a post-war study, POWs became embarrassed in company, found children irritating, felt they were being watched and were suspicious of neighbours. Some struggled to make decisions and, after the excitement of repatriation, found life flat. A fifth showed symptoms 'that would be worrying if they were to continue for any length of time'. These were 'restlessness and excitability, lethargy and loss of confidence'. For some, *Stalag* life was 'a broadening experience' in which they 'read, developed new hobbies and learned to understand and feel a deeper affection for their comrades'. For most, incarceration was 'a period of regression, a return to a more egocentric pattern of life and a more emotionally determined type of life'.

Some Calais veterans became prominent public figures such as Airey Neave, Margaret Thatcher's confidant before an INLA bomb cut short his life. Sam Kydd returned to the stage and 'Pooh' Heard and Tim Munby headed for Cambridge to become, respectively, dean of Peterhouse and librarian of King's. Terence Prittie became a journalist, Martin Gilliat served as the Queen Mother's Private Secretary, Gris Davies-Scourfield became a brigadier and Philip Pardoe a colonel, while Andy Vincent became a children's magazine editor.

Among Alec's muckers, Les Birch returned to the family farm and married Bernice. Unlike many girlfriends, Bernice stayed loyal during his locust years in response to anguished letters from Les asking her to wait for his return or put him out of his misery. Bob Hawthorn became an executive with Philips, while David Massey, Setzdorf's 'demon barber', returned to the *Newcastle Evening Chronicle and News*.

Robert Kee thought POW life 'drab and demoralising' causing men to lose their 'dignity'. It was both 'humdrum and fear-filled'. Some, he observed, 'sailed blithely through prison-camp life and returned home unaffected'; others 'were tormented for the rest of their lives'. Alec, oscillating between melancholia and fury, was in the latter group. He could not enjoy life as he had done before 1940. In 1950, after some short relationships, he fell in love with a woman with whom he thought he could settle down. This was my mother, June Bromberg, a 21-year-old Jewess brought south from Aberdeen by her father to find 'a suitable husband'. After a brief courtship, Alec took his future bride for a drink in a Hampstead pub and asked her to be 'the mother of my children'. Theirs was the rockiest of marriages, even though, like some impossibly elongated war of attrition, it lasted the rest of his life, producing three children along the way.

Playing the City gent, with bowler hat and starched collar, no longer satisfied Alec. He 'had been quite happy as a stockbroker before the war – geared to make a fortune – and suddenly it didn't seem important anymore'. He had 'a different set of values'. Unquenchable anger was his biggest demon. Hatred of 'the Huns' kept him going during his captivity. He had seen Hitler's Germany from the inside, seen the atrocities visited on Poles and Czechs and witnessed the Holocaust first-hand. Yet while hatred was a useful wartime emotion, it served little purpose in peacetime, poisoning his relationships with family, friends and colleagues.

Life had lost its meaning. 'Life is not life,' Alec would say. 'It is merely existence.' He loved to quote from Keats's Ode to a Nightingale, written in Hampstead in 1819, 100 years before his birth. He had a love-hate relationship with Keats. He loved To Autumn ('Season of mists and mellow fruitfulness/Close bosom-friend of the maturing sun') yet peppered the margins of his schoolboy edition with criticisms. One phrase from Nightingale was, however, often on his lips: he was 'half in love with easeful Death'.

Night-times were worst, as he recorded in Homecoming, a poem written in July 1945:

How can I explain this experience,
This waking dream, this snatch back
From a living death to life itself,
This nightmare journey from the blunt Sudeten mountains,
From existence primitive in a straw-covered, dung-smelling barn.
Through the kaleidoscope of bomb-scarred war-suffering Europe:
Prague, shell-battered, but proud of its strange new dress,
To England, the dreamed-of, the "Ultima Thule"
Unchanged, spits her wounds.
Did I not touch the telephone twice, once tentative, once reassuring?
Did I not walk down the garden path feeling "I have done all this before"?
Am I not home, back in the England that bred me?
Then why do I wake at night, sweating and wishing to scream?
Victim of nightmare, doubly invented,
Believing it all a dream, from which I awake to the sound of a guttural
   "*Aufstehen*"
And trudge through the snow, up the hill to the quarry,
Which awaits me remorseless, and crushes my very being.

Epilogue

In recent years I have often puzzled over why my father began yet abandoned his memoir. Perhaps he began because he felt he could finally confront his demons; perhaps he stopped because he felt no one would be interested; perhaps it was too painful. Yet the experience defined his life; it was the reference point against which everything was measured and to which he returned time and time again. His post-war experiences – falling in love, marriage and three children – seemed merely an epilogue. His life's big event was over, and those who had not suffered with him could not understand.

In 1978 he wrote a poem before taking my mother to Eastern Europe on a journey of return and remembrance, a sequel to When I Go Back on page 124:

> My children do not understand
> My coming back.
> They don't know what it is to strive
> To keep a spark of hope alive.
> They think I should forget, forgive
> Now that I'm back.

I choke back the tears as I transcribe these lines. Should we, his children, have tried harder to empathize? Should he have tried harder to talk? Instead, he built a fortress around his feelings. How could others understand when they had not experienced the sufferings of war?

This is a common question among old soldiers. At the end of the film of Joan Littlewood's Great War satire, *Oh! What a Lovely War*, a grandmother, her daughters and granddaughter sit having a picnic. The child picks poppies as her father's ghost passes behind to join fallen comrades in the Elysian Fields, then she asks her grandmother, 'What did Daddy do in the war?' The camera returns to the fallen as they are transformed into white crosses. It then pulls back to reveal crosses too numerous to count. Through them, the women wander, the child skipping as she leads the way, with the voices of the dead singing We'll Never Tell Them to the tune of Jerome Kern's They Didn't Believe Me. The lyrics contain an old soldier's response to the girl's question – and the answer to our questions as Alec Jay's children:

> And when they ask us, how dangerous it was,
> Oh, we'll never tell them, no, we'll never tell them:

We spent our pay in some cafe,
And fought wild women night and day,
'Twas the cushiest job we ever had.
And when they ask us, and they're certainly going to ask us,
The reason why we didn't win the Croix de Guerre,
Oh, we'll never tell them, oh, we'll never tell them
There was a front, but damned if we knew where.

My father did not talk much about his experiences but they cast a shadow over our childhood. As Jewish children born into a slightly precarious middle-class environment in post-war North London – my father struggled to put bread on the family table – we absorbed the war and the Holocaust, or so it seemed, through our mother's milk. The taste was bitter. Once, he reluctantly agreed to see a psychiatrist to address the multi-decade war of attrition that was his marriage – the Somme meets Passchendaele. Unsurprisingly, the psychiatrist quickly spotted the canker beneath the surface, but his approach lacked subtlety. 'Alec,' he said, 'I need to break you down.'

'Well, you won't,' my father replied. 'The Germans spent five years trying to break me down. They failed and there's no way I am going to let you.' With that, he marched from the consulting room. Thus ended my mother's attempt to fix their fragmented relationship through counselling.

That day on the psychiatrist's couch, my father returned in his mind to 30 April 1940, when his company commander told him a POW should reveal only his name, rank and service number. He would often appear transported back to the war. To him it was still so close. It seemed he never stopped fighting the Germans. He was like the Japanese soldier who was sent to a remote island in 1944, never learned the war was over, hid in the jungle living off wild fruit waiting for orders and only emerged in 1972, twenty-seven years after Hiroshima. My father was still at war the day he died, 15 October 1993, fifteen days short of his seventy-fourth birthday and fifty-five years after joining the Territorial Army.

He would be back in the war when waking up screaming after some nightmare. He would be back in the war when we burned the toast. The smell, he said, was like the smell of burned bodies – and he had been 'within smelling distance of Auschwitz'. He would be back in the war when driving behind a Mercedes driver who displayed less than perfect highway manners – and that happened, he declared, a lot. He would be back in the war if he overheard someone speaking German. He would be back in the war when we went shopping – no German goods, he determined, would enter his home.

He would be back in the war in virtually any situation at the slightest provocation – and in verbal combat he took no prisoners. Once, while holidaying in Croatia, he came down to breakfast by the pool in his trunks. An elderly German couple were behind him in the buffet queue. Unimpressed by his bare torso, they began muttering about English bad manners, confident few English people had sufficient German to pick up their whispers. Their confidence was misplaced. Quick as a flash, my father turned round and tore into them in perfect German: 'You did not care how Jews dressed when you herded women and children naked into the gas chambers. But here is one Jew you did not kill and he is going to dress as he pleases.' My father had a way with words.

Towards the end of my father's life, however, his fortress began to decay. Perhaps the passage of time caused the mortar to crumble. Perhaps he gained succour from reading Primo Levi's memoirs of Auschwitz. Whatever the cause, we sensed the previously insuperable walls were being dismantled. Curiously, the first bricks fell out during a rare post-war visit to Germany with some acceptance that not all Hitler's soldiers were necessarily evil – they suffered too. He was buying food from a market stall, impressing the stall-holder and those around with his command of German, when a silver-haired man asked him: 'How do you speak such good German?' My father replied, 'I was in a prisoner-of-war camp for five years.' The man said he had fought at Stalingrad, where the German casualty toll was 850,000 killed, maimed or captured. Though he struggled to explain his motivation afterwards, my father responded by shaking his hand.

My brother David, a film-maker, achieved the next breach when he persuaded my father his experiences might make a documentary. David tapped into our father's pride that he volunteered rather than being conscripted. It was a point of honour. 'There was always a difference,' he said, 'between volunteers and conscripts.' The project proved abortive, but not before he had sat with a tape-recorder and described a few incidents. He began:

> Calais is still a confused memory to me. I can remember snatching some sleep on the sand dunes, waking up with an unexploded incendiary bomb between my legs and I can remember clearing a warehouse of infiltrated Fifth Columnists. I can remember being bombed by a squadron of Blenheims, fortunately without too many casualties, and I can remember being Stuka'ed on the Friday [24 May 1940] and the Saturday and the Sunday, unfortunately with lots of casualties.

The final breach came in May 1990, fifty years after the Dunkirk rescue of 229,000 British troops. At the time, I was the *Sunday Telegraph*'s City editor and conscious that most coverage ignored the 45,000 British soldiers who 'missed the boat' and were marched off into captivity. I had read the transcript of David's tapes and felt the *Sunday Telegraph* should avoid merely repeating one more anecdote about 'the miracle of the little ships' and present instead a tale as resonant though more bitter. Perhaps, I suggested to the editor, Trevor Grove, we should do something about the men left behind. Trevor was intrigued, so I told him my father had been in a brigade sent to hold Calais. Unlike the men at Dunkirk, they were abandoned, I said, and virtually all survivors were captured, spending the rest of the war 'in the bag'.

Trevor liked the idea and asked Maureen Cleave to interview my father. Some twenty-four years previously, Maureen achieved a scoop when she quoted John Lennon as saying the Beatles were 'more popular than Jesus' – she knew how to get the best out of her subjects. She visited my father at home and they talked for four hours. He had just returned from a Calais beachfront memorial service and the interview was an important experience for him – he had never before talked in such depth about his war. It was good for Maureen, too. The following Sunday, 27 May 1990, fifty years and one day after the Calais garrison surrendered, the *Telegraph* ran Maureen's article on its Review section front page beneath the headline, 'The Men Who Stayed Behind'. It produced a big postbag – many veterans were *Telegraph* readers. My father received letters from old comrades not seen for decades, and old friendships were renewed.

My father talked to Maureen about his guilt, not for surrendering but for surviving. This phenomenon is alien to we who have not had to 'survive' anything more than the normal strains of everyday life. We find it strange that victims of disasters, man-made and natural, should think they have sinned by surviving. This cannot be so, yet the syndrome's symptoms are clear – and several were suffered by my father: anxiety, depression, social withdrawal, sleep disturbance, nightmares, emotional incontinence and loss of drive. We children wanted a 'normal' father, yet few POWs returned home entirely normal – the inner demons were too powerful. Calais was the hinge in his life, and the years of captivity afterwards shattered the values he took to war. Before the war he was a City stockbroker; he returned uninterested in the typical middle-class preoccupations of career advancement, social status and material comfort. He found small talk impossible. What was the point? Yet some trivial incident or throwaway remark would be blown up out of all proportion in his mind.

Today we categorize such behaviour as post-traumatic stress disorder and train therapists to address it. Such counselling did not exist when my father returned from the war. By the 1960s, when the condition was identified among Holocaust survivors, he was probably past helping. Primo Levi thought survivor guilt came from being defenceless when facing evil, witnessing terrible things yet recognizing one could not prevent them. During his captivity, my father was forced to dig pits in which were buried thousands of mistreated Russian POWs, and he worked alongside Jewish slave workers in a Sudeten textile factory yet felt powerless to intervene as they were beaten by SS guards. He could have risked his life in their defence yet concluded his duty was to survive and continue the fight. But the survivor guilt remained, and he would make pilgrimages of regret to Calais, to Lamsdorf and to the Sudeten towns in which he was forced to labour for Hitler's benefit.

He wept as he reminisced with Maureen that spring afternoon:

> I left an awful lot of good friends in Calais, you know. For them I have to go back. One is always hoping to find a catharsis but so far I have not. You have to forgive me. I get that tiny bit knotted up. There are still times when one feels one has no right to be alive.

The guilt stayed with him until a ruptured aorta killed him in October 1993, two weeks short of his seventy-fourth birthday. A few days later, his funeral took place at Golders Green Crematorium and his ashes were dug into the garden of remembrance alongside his father's. It was an old soldier's occasion. For the ceremony, his side hat and rifleman's 'sword' were placed on his coffin and at the end a Greenjacket bugler blew *The Last Post*. When we retrieved his side hat after the ceremony we found a 1943 POW group photograph hidden inside it; his 'muckers', the men with whom he shared his locust years, had been with him at the very end.

Glossary of Place Names

German name	Polish/Czech/Lithuanian name
Adelsdorf	Adolfovice
Annahof	Sowin
Auschwitz	Oświęcim
Barzdorf	Bernartice
Beuthen	Bytom
Blechhammer	Blachownia Slaska
Breslau	Wrocław
Freiwaldau	Jeseník
Freudenthal	Bruntál
Friedeberg	Žulová
Gleiwitz	Gliwice
Groschowitz	Groszowice
Gross Strehlitz	Strzelce Opolskie
Gumpertsdorf	Komprachcice
Gurschdorf	Skorošice
Heuerstein	Szymiszów
Hindenburg	Zabrze
Jägerndorf	Krnov
Kattowitz	Katowice
Lamsdorf	Łambinowice
Neisse	Nysa
Neudorf Polska	Nowa Wieś
Nieder Hermsdorf	Jasienica Dolna
Oppeln	Opole
Pilsen	Plzeň
Posen	Poznań
Ratibor	Racibórz
Saubsdorf	Supíkovice
Setzdorf	Vápenná
Stettin	Szczecin
Teschen	Cieszyn
Theresienstadt	Terezin
Troppau	Opava
Weisskirch	Kostelec

Bibliography

Autobiographies, first-hand accounts, family histories and memoirs

Allan, James, *No Citation*, Angus & Robertson, 1955.

Annetts, Ed, *Campaign without Medals*, Book Guild, 1990.

Ash, William and Foley, Brendan, *Under The Wire*, Bantam Press, 2005.

Beattie, Reg and Beattie, Trevor, *Captive Plans, The POW Diary of Reg Beattie*, LMNOP Books, 2011.

Bolte, Charles G., *The New Veteran*, Penguin, 1945.

Bonney, Anne, *POW to Lancashire Farmer – The Remarkable Life of Alec Barker*, Helm Press, 2005.

Borrie, John, *Despite Captivity: A Doctor's Life as Prisoner of War*, Kimber, 1975.

Brown, John, *In Durance Vile*, Robert Hale, 1981.

Buchanan, Kelpie, *Mektoub – War Memories 1939–1945*, Sue Buchanan, 2007.

Carswell, Andrew, *Over the Wire: A Canadian Pilot's Memoir of War and Survival as a POW*, Wiley, 2011.

Castle, John, *The Password is Courage*, Souvenir Press, 1954.

Charlwood, Don, *No Moon Tonight (Witness to War)*, Goodall, 1984.

Collins, Douglas, *POW: A Soldier's Story of his Ten Escapes from Nazi Prison Camps*, W.W. Norton & Company, 1968.

Coulter, James, *Guests of Hitler's Reich: The Wartime Diary of Devonian Army Chaplain Geoffrey Kestell-Cornish, with Contributions from Fellow Prisoners of War*, James Coulter, 2006.

Coward, Roger V., *Sailors in Cages*, Macdonald, 1967.

Croall, Charles, *"You! Croall?"*, Brian Riggir Computers, 2010.

Davies-Scourfield, *In Presence of My Foes: A Memoir of Calais, Colditz and Wartime Escape Adventures*, Wilton 65, 1991.

Donald, C. and Barker, P.B., 'Louse-borne typhus fever', *British Medical Journal*, September 1942.

Ellsworth, Ted, *Yank: The Memoir of a World War II Soldier (1941–1945)*, Thunder's Mouth Press, 2006.

Elwyn, John, *At the Fifth Attempt: An Escape Story*, Leo Cooper, 1987.

Embry, Sir Basil, *Mission Completed*, Methuen, 1957.

Evans, Arthur, *Sojourn in Silesia 1940–1945*, Ashford Writers, 1995.

Gant, Roland, *How Like a Wilderness*, Gollancz, 1946.

Gayler, Robert, *Private Prisoner – An Astonishing Story of Survival under the Nazis*, Patrick Stephens, 1984.

Greasley, Horace, *Do The Birds Still Sing In Hell?*, Libros International, 2008.

Green, J.M., *From Colditz in Code*, Robert Hale, 1971.

Guderian, Hans and Bance, Alan (translator), *Blitzkrieg: In Their Own Words: First-Hand Accounts from German Soldiers, 1939–1940*, Zenith Press, 2005.

Gurner, Bert and Newman, William, *A Prisoner's Story 1940–45*, Burt Gurner.

Harding, Robert, *Copper Wire*, Chess Mail, 2001.

Harding, William, *A Cockney Soldier: Duty Before Pleasure*, Merlin, 1989.

Howie, Claerwen, *Agent by Accident*, Lindlife Publishers, 1997.

Hoy, Denis, *The Long March*, Edmonton Hundred Historical Society.

Instone, Gordon, *Freedom the Spur*, Burke, 1953.

Ismay, Hastings, *The Memoirs of Lord Ismay*, Heinemann, 1960.

James, David, *Escaper's Progress – The Remarkable POW Experiences of a Royal Naval Officer*, Blackwoods, 1947.

Kee, Robert, *A Crowd is not Company*, Eyre & Spottiswoode, 1947.

Kindersley, Philip, *For You the War is Over*, Midas Books, 1983.

Kydd, Sam, *For YOU the War is Over …*, Bachman & Turner, 1973.

Lawrence, John, *2297 – a POW's Story*, Woodfield Publishing, 1991.

Levy, Harry *The Dark Side of the Sky – The Story of a Young Jewish Airman in Nazi Germany*, Pen & Sword Books, 1995.

Linklater, Eric, *Fanfare for a Tin Hat*, Macmillan, 1970.

Littledale, R.B., *Escape to Freedom*, The King's Royal Rifle Corps Association, 2004.

Lyme, Edward, *A Soldier in the Circus*, Book Guild, 1997.

Matthewson, Gillian and Matthewson, John, *14056 – The World War II diaries, recollections and collections of Bertram Matthewson of the Queen Victoria's Rifles*, Gillian Matthewson.

McCallum, John, *The Long Way Home – The Other Great Escape*, ISIS Publishing, 2006.

McEntee-Taylor, Carole, *The Weekend Trippers – A Rifleman's Diary, Calais 1940*, Carole McEntee-Taylor.

Moreton, George, *Doctor in Chains*, Howard Baker, 1970.

Palmer, Graham, *Prisoner of Death – Gripping Memoir of Courage and Survival under the Third Reich*, Patrick Stephens, 1990.

Pape, Richard, *Boldness Be My Friend*, Elek Books, 1953.

Poolton, Jack A. and Poolton-Turvey, Jane, *Destined to Survive: A Dieppe Veteran's Story*, Jack Poolton, 1998.

Pringle, Jack, *Colditz Last Stop: Four Countries, Eleven Prisons, Six Escapes*, William Kimber, 1988.

Prittie, T.C.F. and Edwards, W.E., *Escape to Freedom*, Hutchinson, 1946.

Radford, R.A., *The Economic Organization of a P.O.W. Camp*, The London School of Economics and Political Science, 1945.

Roberts, J., *A Terrier Goes To War*, Minerva Press, 1998.

Rofé, Cyril, *Against the Wind*, Hodder & Stoughton, 1956.

Rubenstein, Norman, *The Invisibly Wounded*, Hyperion Books, 1989.

Rushton, Colin, *Spectator in Hell – A British Soldier's Story of Imprisonment at Auschwitz*, Pharoah Press, 1998.

Sabey, Ian, *Stalag Scrapbook*, F.W. Cheshire, 1947.

Taylor, Frank, *Barbed Wire and Footlights*, Merlin Books, 1988.

Vaughan, Geoffrey D., *Prisoner of War during World War II Recounts the Way it Really Was*, The Granary Press, 1985.

Vincent, Adrian, *The Long Road Home*, Howard Baker, 1970.

Woodroofe, Gordon T., *GeTaWay*, Riverside Publications, 1998.

Woolley, H.E. and Woolley, Ted, *No Time Off for Good Behaviour*, General Store Publishing House, 1990.

General histories, reference works, fiction and other secondary sources
Andrew, Christopher, *The Defence of the Realm: The Authorized History of MI5*, Allen Lane, 2009.

Beevor, Anthony, *Crete, the Battle and the Resistance*, John Murray, 1991.

Bentwich, Norman, *I Understand the Risks*, Gollancz, 1950.

Briggs, Asa, *The War of Words: The History of Broadcasting in the United Kingdom*, Volume III, Oxford University Press, 1970.

Burleigh, Michael, *Moral Combat: A History of World War II*, Harper Press, 2010.

Connelly, Mark and Miller, Walter, *The BEF and the Issue of Surrender on the Western Front in 1940*, War in History, 2004.

Cooksey, Jon, *Calais – Fight to the Finish, May 1940*, Pen and Sword, 2000.

Cooper, Wyllis, *A Ribbon of Lincoln Green*, broadcast 31.08.47.

Crawley, Aidan, *Escape from Germany 1939–1945: A History of RAF Escapes during the War*, Simon and Schuster, 1956.

Crow, David M., *Oskar Schindler*, Westview Press, 2004.

Day-Lewis, Sean, *C. Day-Lewis – An English Literary Life*, Weidenfeld & Nicholson, 1980.

Dieckmann, Christoph, *Murders of Prisoners of War*, The International Commission for the Nazi and Soviet Occupation Regimes in Lithuania.

Dixon, Norman F., *On the Psychology of Military Incompetence*, Basic Books, 1976.

Doherty, M.A., *Nazi Wireless Propaganda – Lord Haw-Haw and British Public Opinion in the Second World War*, Edinburgh University Press, 2000.

Doyle, Peter, *Prisoner of War in Germany*, Shire Publications, 2008.

Edgerton, David, *Britain's War Machine: Weapons, Resources, and Experts in the Second World War*, Oxford University Press, 2011.

Elliot, S.R., *Scarlet to Green: A History of Intelligence in the Canadian Army 1903–1963*, Canadian Intelligence and Security Assn., 1981.

Evans, Richard J., *The Third Reich at War*, Allen Lane, 2008.

Foot, M.R.D. and Langley, J.M., *MI9 Escape and Evasion*, The Bodley Head, 1979.

Ford, Ken, *St Nazaire 1942: The Great Commando Raid*, Osprey, 2001.

Ford, Ken, *The Bruneval Raid, Operation Biting 1942*, Osprey 2010.

Forsyth, Frederick, *The Fourth Protocol*, Century, 1984.

Fowler, Will, *France, Holland and Belgium, 1940–41*, Ian Allan Publishing, 2002.

Fuller, Robert Paul, *Last Shots for Patton's Third Army*, New England Transportation Research, 2003.

Ganglmair, Siegwald, *Resistance and Persecution in Austria 1938–1945*, Federal Press Service, 1988.

Gelber, Yoav, *Palestinian POWs in German Captivity*, Shoah Resource Center, The International School for Holocaust Studies, 1981.

Gilbert, Adrian, *POW – Allied Prisoners in Europe 1939–1945*, John Murray, 2006.

Glover, Michael, *The Fight for the Channel Ports*, Secker & Warburg, 1985.

Green, Gerald, *The Artists of Terezin*, Hawthorn Books, 1959.

Grosssman, Vasily, *Life and Fate*, Collins Harvill, 1985.

Halliday, Hugh A., *Relief amid Chaos: The Story of Canadian POWs Driving Red Cross*, Canadian Military History, 2012.

Hastings, R.H.W.S., *The Rifle Brigade in the Second World War, 1939–1945*, Gale & Polden, 1950.

Hastings, Max, *All Hell Let Loose: The World at War, 1939–1945*, Harper Press, 2011.

HMSO, *Prisoners of War, British Army 1939–1945*, J.B. Hayward & Son, 1990.

HMSO, *Prisoners of War, Armies and other Land Forces of the British Empire 1939–1945*, J.B. Hayward & Son, 1990.

HMSO, *Prisoners of War, Naval and Air Forces of Great Britain and the Empire 1939–1945*, J.B. Hayward & Son, 1990.

Iveson, Tony and Milton, Brian, *Lancaster, the Biography*, André Deutsch, 2011.

Jakl, Tomas, *May 1945 in the Czech Lands – Ground Operations of the Axis and Allied Forces*, Miroslaw Bily, 2004.

King's Royal Rifle Corps, wartime editions of *The King's Royal Rifle Corps Chronicle*, Warren and Son, 1939–1945.

King's Royal Rifle Corps Association's annual *Journals*.

Kippenberger, Howard and Fairbrother, Monty C., *The Official History of New Zealand in the Second World War 1939–45*, War History Branch of the Department of Internal Affairs, 1949–1986.

Lehmann, David, *The Allied Troops Encircled in the North*.

Linklater, Eric, *The Defence of Calais*, HMSO, 1941.

Longden, Sean, *Hitler's British Slaves – Allied POWs in Germany 1939–1945*, Arris Books, 2005.

Longden, Sean, *Dunkirk: The Men They Left Behind*, Constable, 2008.

Lucas Phillips, C.E., *The Greatest Raid of All*, Little Brown, 1960.

Macdonogh, Giles, *After the Reich: From the Fall of Vienna to the Berlin Airlift*, John Murray, 2007.

Mackenzie, S.P., *The Colditz Myth: The Real Story of POW Life in Nazi Germany*, Oxford University Press, 2004.

Megargee, Geoffrey P., *The United States Holocaust Memorial Museum Encyclopedia of Camps and Ghettos, 1933–1945*, Indiana University Press, 2009.

Millar, George, *The Bruneval Raid – Stealing Hitler's Radar*, Cassell, 1974.

Mills, Giles and Nixon, Roger, *The Annals of the King's Royal Rifle Corps*, Volume VI 1921–1943, Leo Cooper, 1971.

Morris, Henry and Sugarman, Martin, *We Will Remember Them*, Valentine Mitchell, 2011.

Moses, Sam, *At All Costs: How a Crippled Ship and Two American Merchant Mariners Turned the Tide of World War*, Random House, 2006.

Neave, Airey, *The Flames of Calais: A Soldier's Battle, 1940*, Hodder & Stoughton, 1972.

Nichol, John and Rennell, Tony, *Home Run: Escape from Nazi Europe*, Viking, 2007.

Nichol, John and Rennell, Tony, *The Last Escape: The Untold Story of Allied Prisoners of War in Germany 1944–1945*, Viking, 2002.

O'Donnell, Patrick K., *The Brenner Assignment*, Da Capo Press, 2008.

O'Donnell, Patrick K., *They Dared Return*, Da Capo Press, 2009.

Parkyn, H.G., *The Rifle Brigade Chronicle for 1945*, Rifle Brigade Club, 1946.

Parnell, Michael, *Eric Linklater – A Critical Biography*, John Murray, 1984.

Peatling, Robert, *Without Tradition – 2 Para 1941–1945*, Pen & Sword, 1994.

Pecka, Jindrich, *Prisoners of War in the Protectorate of Bohemia and Moravia (1939–45)*, Institute of Contemporary History, Prague, 1996.

Pitchfork, Graham, *Shot Down and on the Run*, The Dundurn Group, 2003.

Queen Victoria's Rifles Association, *News-Circulars*.

Rabinowitz, Louis I., *Soldiers from Judaea; Palestinian Jewish Units in the Middle East, 1941–1943*, Gollancz, 1944.

Rea, Paul, *Voices from the Fortress*, ABC Books, 2001.

The British Red Cross Prisoner of War Department, *The Prisoner of War* magazine, 1940–45.

Restayn, J. and Moller, N., *The 10 Panzer Division – In action in the East, the West and North Africa, 1939–1943*, J.J. Fedorowicz Publishing, 2003.

Rolf, David, *Prisoners of the Reich*, Leo Cooper, 1988.

Rollings, Charles, *Prisoner of War: Voices from behind the Wire in the Second World War*, Ebury Press, 2008.

Sebag-Montefiore, Hugh, *Dunkirk: Fight to the Last Man*, Viking, 2006.

Sugarman, Martin, *Fighting Back: British Jewry's Military Contribution in the Second World War*, Valentine Mitchell, 2010.

Taylor, M.D., *Motorcycle Reconnaissance Battalions*.

Vourkoutiotis, Vasilis, *Prisoners of War and the German High Command*, Palgrave Macmillan, 2003.

Wake, Hereward and Deedes, W.F., *Swift and Bold – The Story of the King's Royal Rifle Corps in the Second World War 1939–1945*, Gale and Polden, 1949.

Wallace, Christopher, *The King's Royal Rifle Corps ... The 60th Rifles: A Brief History: 1755 to 1965*, The Royal Green Jackets Museum Trust, 2005.

Weale, Adrian, *Renegades – Hitler's Englishmen*, Weidenfeld & Nicolson, 1994.
Wyllie, Neville, *Barbed Wire Diplomacy: Britain, Germany and the Politics of Prisoners of War, 1939–1945*, Oxford University Press, 2010.

Websites/online forums
Axis History Forum, forum.axishistory.com
Balmer, Bill, *My Service Life*, billbalmer.angelfire.com
The Memoirs of John Bell, www.freewebs.com/johnbellsmemoirs
Bomb Sight, Mapping the WW2 Bomb Census, bombsight.org
Conscript Heroes, conscript-heroes.com
DEGOB, Recollections on the Holocaust – the world's most extensive testimonial site, degob.org
Donohoe, Thomas F., *Memoir of Battle of Crete and Imprisonment*,
    familytreemaker.genealogy.com/users/r/i/s/Bernadette-W-Risebury-Tyne-and-Wear/
    FILE/0001page.html
Flames of War, flamesofwar.com
Fusniak, Joseph and Fusniak, Richard, *Lamsdorf Death March 1945*,
    buckdenpike.co.uk/lamsdorfmarch.html
Holocaust Education & Archive Research Team, holocaustresearchproject.org
Jewish Virtual Library, jewishvirtuallibrary.org
The King's Royal Rifle Corps Association, krrcassociation.com
Lamsdorf: Stalag VIIIB 344 Prisoner of War Camp 1940–1945, lamsdorf.com
Lamsdorf Remembered, lamsdorfremembered.co.uk
Military History Network, milhist.net
Military History Encyclopedia on the Web, historyofwar.org
Murmelstein, Wolf, *Ten basic facts about Theresienstadt (Terezin)*,
    scrapbookpages.com/Contributions/Murmelstein/Theresienstadt01.html
The National Ex-Prisoner of War Association, prisonerofwar.org.uk/
The Pegasus Archive, pegasusarchive.org
The Personal World War II memoir of, F/O Don Hall (R.C.A.F. Retd.),
    trasksdad.com/Don%20Hall/hallindx.htm
RAF Bomber Command, raf.mod.uk/bombercommand
WW2 Forums, ww2f.com
WW2 People's War, bbc.co.uk/history/ww2peopleswar
WW2 Talk, ww2talk.com

Manuscripts, interviews, lectures, diaries and letters
Banbury, Basil, Calais war diary written in POW camp.
Bartlett, Peter, *Stories of life in prisoner of war camps 1940–1945*.
Birch, Leslie, POW letters and postcards (author's interview).
Austin-Brown, J., war diary written in POW camp and correspondence with his wife.
Davies-Scourfield, Gris, Imperial War Museum oral history interview.
Day, Neil, Imperial War Museum oral history interview.
Doe, Edward, Imperial War Museum oral history interview.
Ellison-Macartney, J.A.M., *The First Battalion Queen Victoria's Rifles, Kings Royal Rifle Corps at Calais May 22nd–26th 1940*.
Hawthorn, Robert, *My Journey to Freedom*.
Hummerstone, Norman, author's interview.
Houthakker, H.S., *The private and confidential report on my life and experiences as a prisoner of war in Germany 1940–1943*.
Hoy, Denis, Imperial War Museum oral history interview.
Jabez-Smith, A.R., Calais war diary written in POW camp.

Lane, R.C., Imperial War Museum oral history interview.
Mathias, Vernon, Calais and POW narrative.
Mead, Mark A., *A Long Walk Home: Life in my 20th Century*.
Monico, Peter, Imperial War Museum oral history interview.
Pardoe, Philip, Imperial War Museum oral history interview.
Phillips, Len, POW memoir.
Sampson, R.H., correspondence with POWs 1940–45.
Saaler, Dennis, author's interview.
Suppan, Arnold, *Between Hitler, Beneš, and Tito. Czechoslovak-German and Yugoslav-German Confrontations in World War II*, University of Stanford, 2008.
Timpson, T.L., *The 1st Bn. Queen Victoria's Rifles, at Calais, May 1940*, war diary written in POW camp.
Walter, F.E., Calais narrative.
Watson, E.W., Imperial War Museum oral history interview.
Wright, Leslie, Battle of Calais lecture, Liddell Hart Centre for Military Archives.
Wynn, Ken, letters and POW diary.

Archives and museums
Army Medical Services Museum.
Auckland War Memorial Museum.
Auschwitz-Birkenau Museum.
BBC Written Archives.
The Museum of the Black Watch.
British Medical Journal Archive.
The British Library.
The British Newspaper Archive.
Central Museum of Prisoners-of-War, Łambinowice-Opole.
Dulwich College Archive.
Enfield Local Studies Centre & Archive.
Highlanders Museum.
Imperial War Museum.
The International Committee of the Red Cross Archives Division.
Liddell Hart Centre for Military Archives, King's College London.
Lincolnshire Archives.
London Metropolitan Archives.
King's Royal Rifle Corps Association archive.
Moscow State Military Archive.
National Archives.
National Army Museum.
Parliamentary Archives, Houses of Parliament.
The Prague Military History Institute Archive.
Queen Mary, University of London Archive.
The Royal Green Jackets (Rifles) Museum.
USC Shoah Foundation Institute for Visual History and Education, University of Southern California.
Soldiers of Oxfordshire Museum.
State Archive of the Russian Federation.
The Suffolk Regiment Archive.
The Wiener Library for the Study of the Holocaust & Genocide.
Whitbread family archive, Southill.

Index

Mons, 96
Cemeteries
Beaumetz-lès-Cambrai, 92
Gommecourt Wood, 91
Louverval, 92
Pozieres, 91
POW escapers, 85, 199
Fischer, Wolfgang von, Oberst, 10th Panzer
Division, 40, 42, 49–50
Fish, Peter 'Darky', Private, Setzdorf POW,
173
Flanagan, Bud, *see* Crazy Gang, the
Forbach, *Stalag* XIIF, *see* Prisoner of war
camps and working parties
Foreign workers, *see Fremdarbeiter*
Forsyth, Frederick, novelist, 102, 275
Forsyth, William, Gunner, Gurschdorf
POW, 240
Fortune, Victor, Major General,
51st Highland Division
commanding officer, 141
Foster, George, Private, Freudenthal POW,
239
Franco, Francisco, 59, 131
Franks, Eric, Sergeant Major, Lamsdorf
escape committee member,
199–200
Freiwaldau, Sudetenland, 138–9, 185–6, 192,
194–5, 243, 272
Freudenthal E352 *Arbeitskommando*, 236–9,
272
Freller, Francis, Staff Sergeant, Palestinian
Jewish POW, 203
Fremdarbeiter (foreign workers), 130, 201,
215
French Riviera landings (Operation
Dragoon), 238
Frost, 'Johnny', Major, Bruneval and
Arnhem commanding officer,
221–3
Frost, Richard, CBE, Hon. Sec., King's
Royal Rifle Corps Association, xiv
Funnell, Bernice, girlfriend, later wife of
Leslie Birch, 163, 173, 186–8, 193,
265

Gabriel, Joseph, Setzdorf villager, 140
Gambrill, John, Private, Lamsdorf POW,
160

Garswood, John, Sergeant Major, Lamsdorf
escape committee member, 198
Gartside, Edward, Lieutenant, Queen
Victoria's Rifles, 3, 46, 122, 193
Gatis, Lamsdorf censor, 202
Gaulle, Charles de, 138, 238
Geneva Convention, 85, 104, 107, 112, 125,
127, 142, 146, 204, 206, 212, 251
German breaches, 51, 79, 84, 91, 105,
108–11, 119–20, 174, 179, 193–4,
212, 231, 233, 247
Genshagen, *Stalag* IIID/517, *see* Prisoner of
War camps and working parties
Gere, Charles, painter, 151
Gerschel, André, mayor of Calais, 31
Giddens, Doug, Flight Sergeant,
103 Squadron POW at Lamsdorf,
208, 210–11
Gilliat, Martin, Captain, 60th Rifles, 85, 265
Gleiwitz, 202, 216, 272
'Gleiwitz incident', 69
Globish, Hauptmann, Gurschdorf
commandant, 240, 242–3
Glover, Michael, military historian, 27, 275
Gneisenau, *see* Naval vessels, German
Goebbels, Joseph, 55, 132, 159, 182, 212,
239, 248
Goethe, Johann Wolfgang von, 157–8
George VI, HM King, 61, 150, 176
Goodchild, Norman, Rifleman, 1st battalion,
Rifle Brigade, 185–6, 240
Goon-baiting, *see* Prisoner of war goon-
baiting
Görlich, Captain, Lamsdorf guard, 195
Göth, Amon, SS-Hauptsturmführer, 237
Gravelines, 10, 17–20, 24, 168
Greece, Battle of, 124, 131, 141, 150, 191,
239
Greef-Berlemont, Elvire 'Tante Go' de,
Belgian Resistance, 210
Green, Daniel, Lance Corporal, Lamsdorf
POW, 203
Green, George, Sergeant, 103 Squadron,
208–9
Green, Julius, Captain, Lamsdorf British
dentist, 108, 146, 176
Greig, William, Private, Prague Uprising
British fighter, 252
Groschowitz E34 Arbeitskommando,
113–16, 118–19, 123, 126, 272